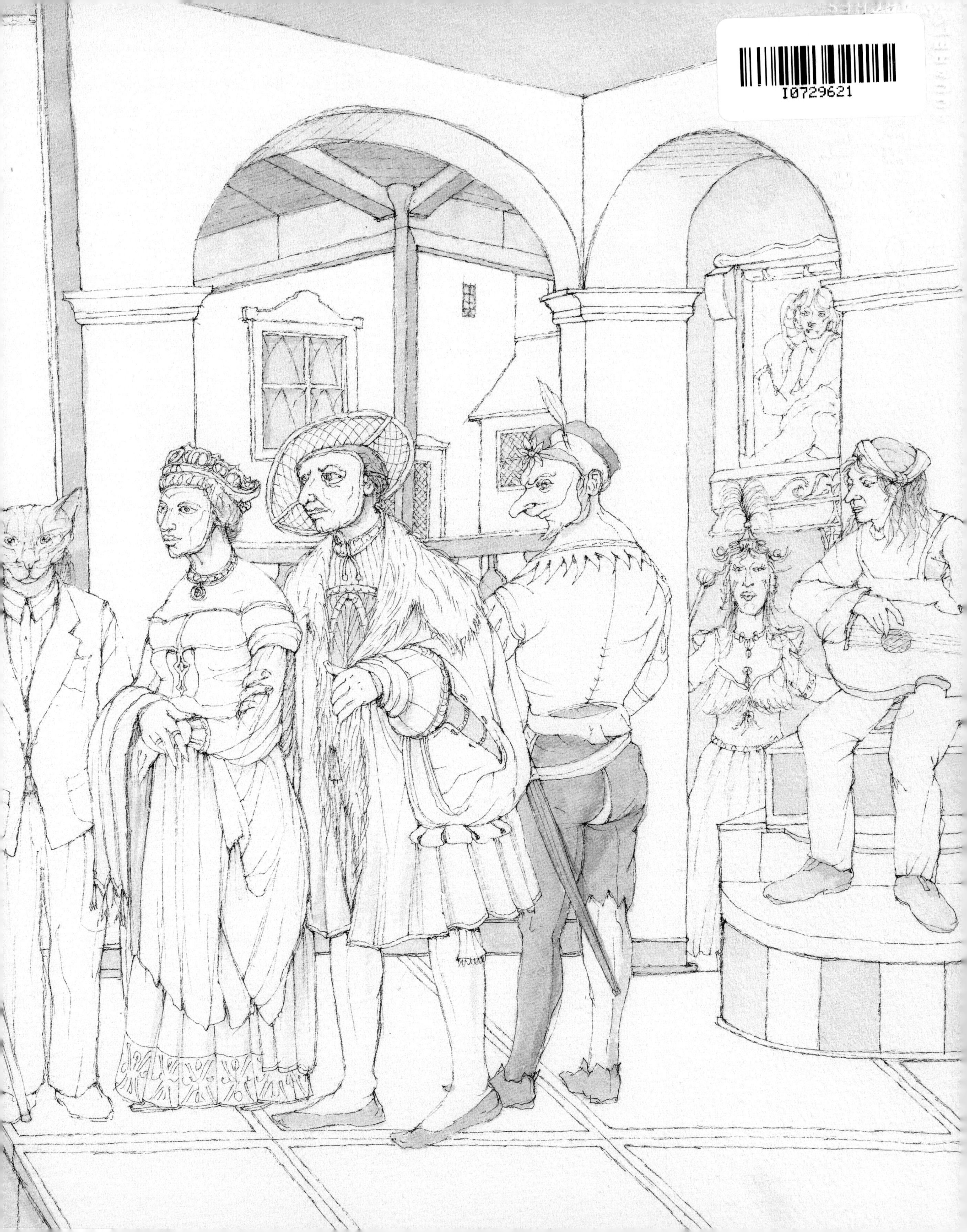

# BODY LANGUAGE

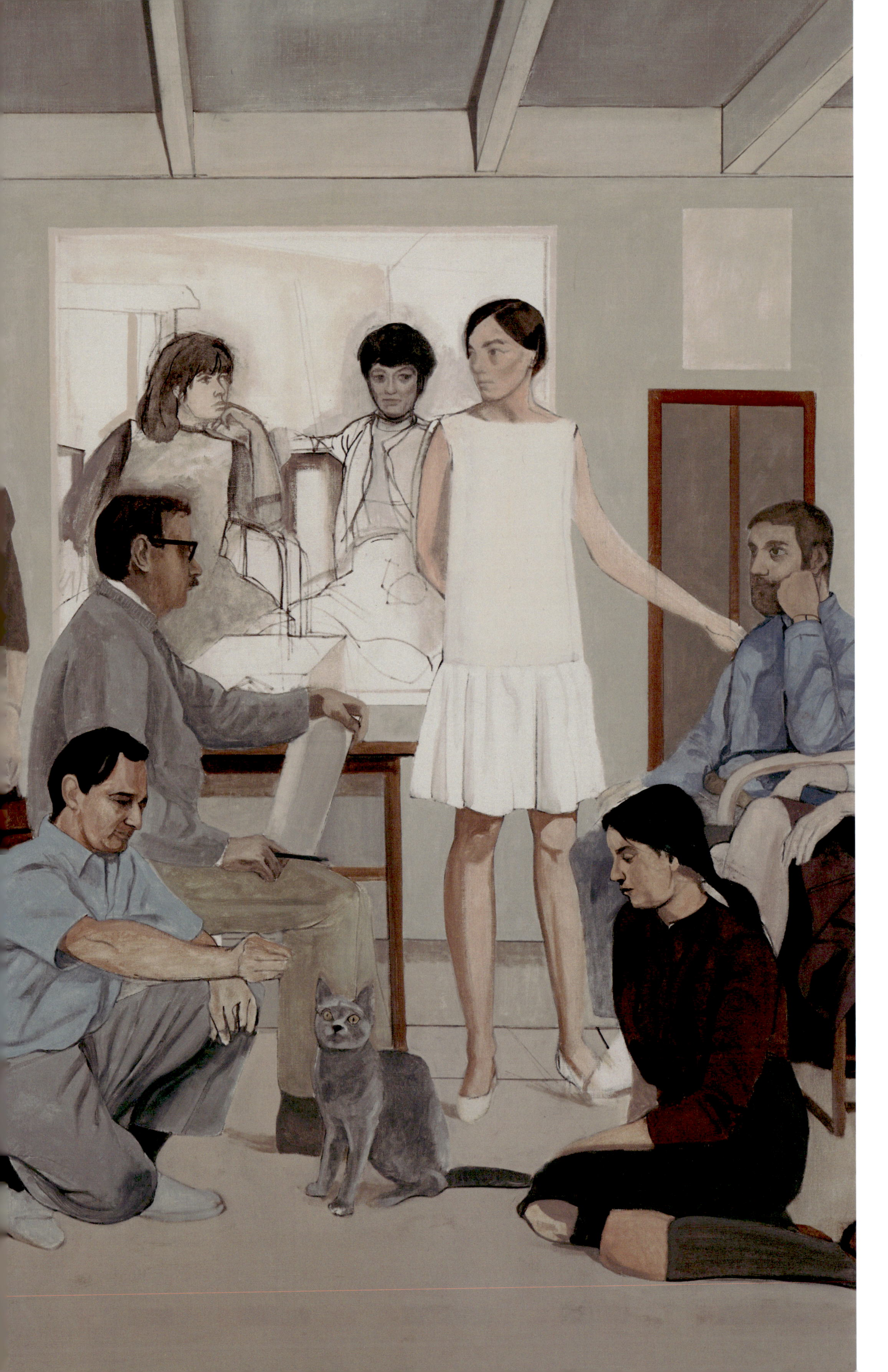

# Body Language

## THE ART OF LARRY DAY

*David Bindman*

With contributions by

*Jonathan Bober*

*Larry Day*

*Ruth Fine*

*John Hollander*

*Eileen Neff*

*Sid Sachs*

Woodmere Art Museum

Distributed by
the University of Pennsylvania Press

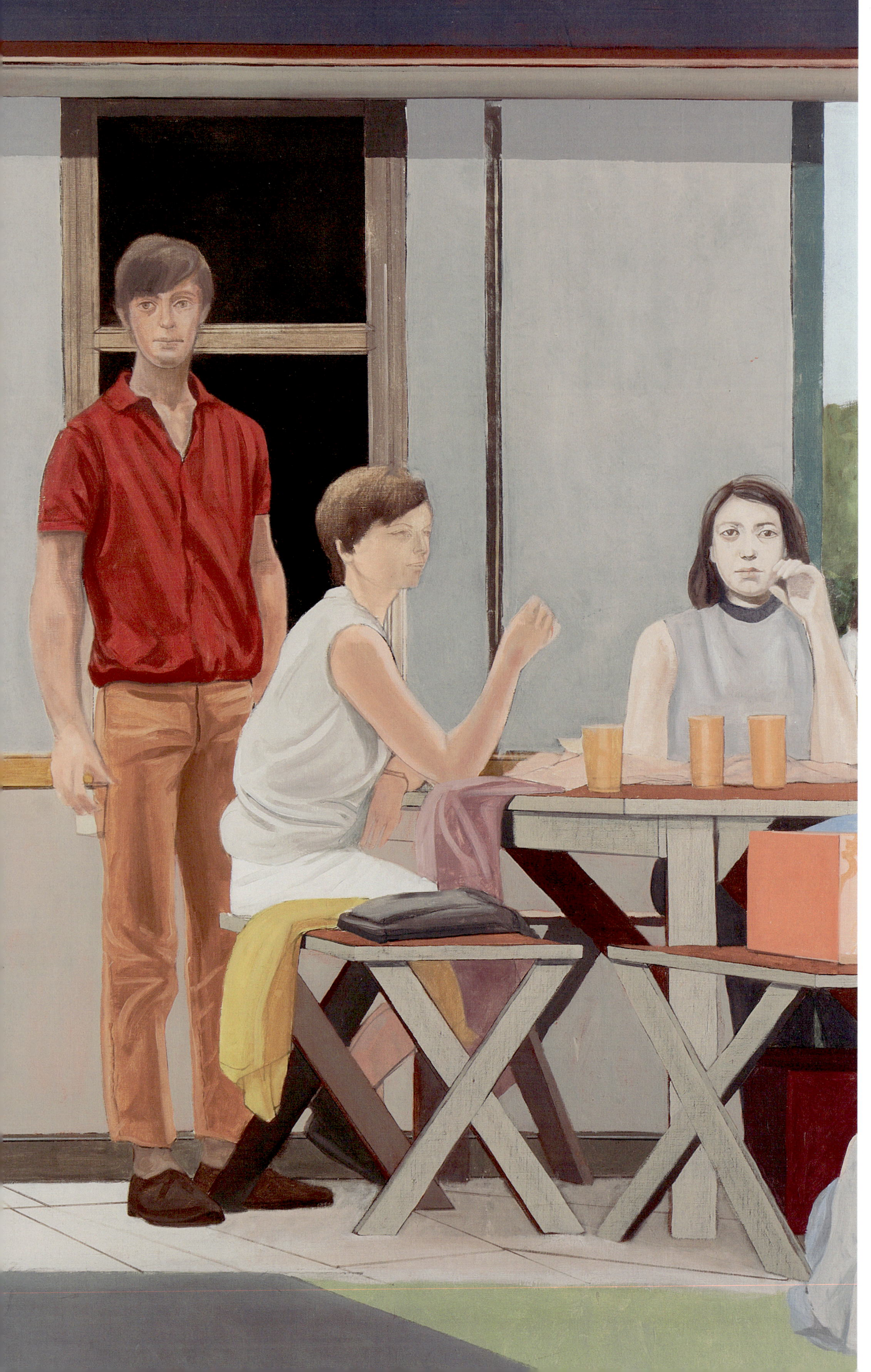

# Contents

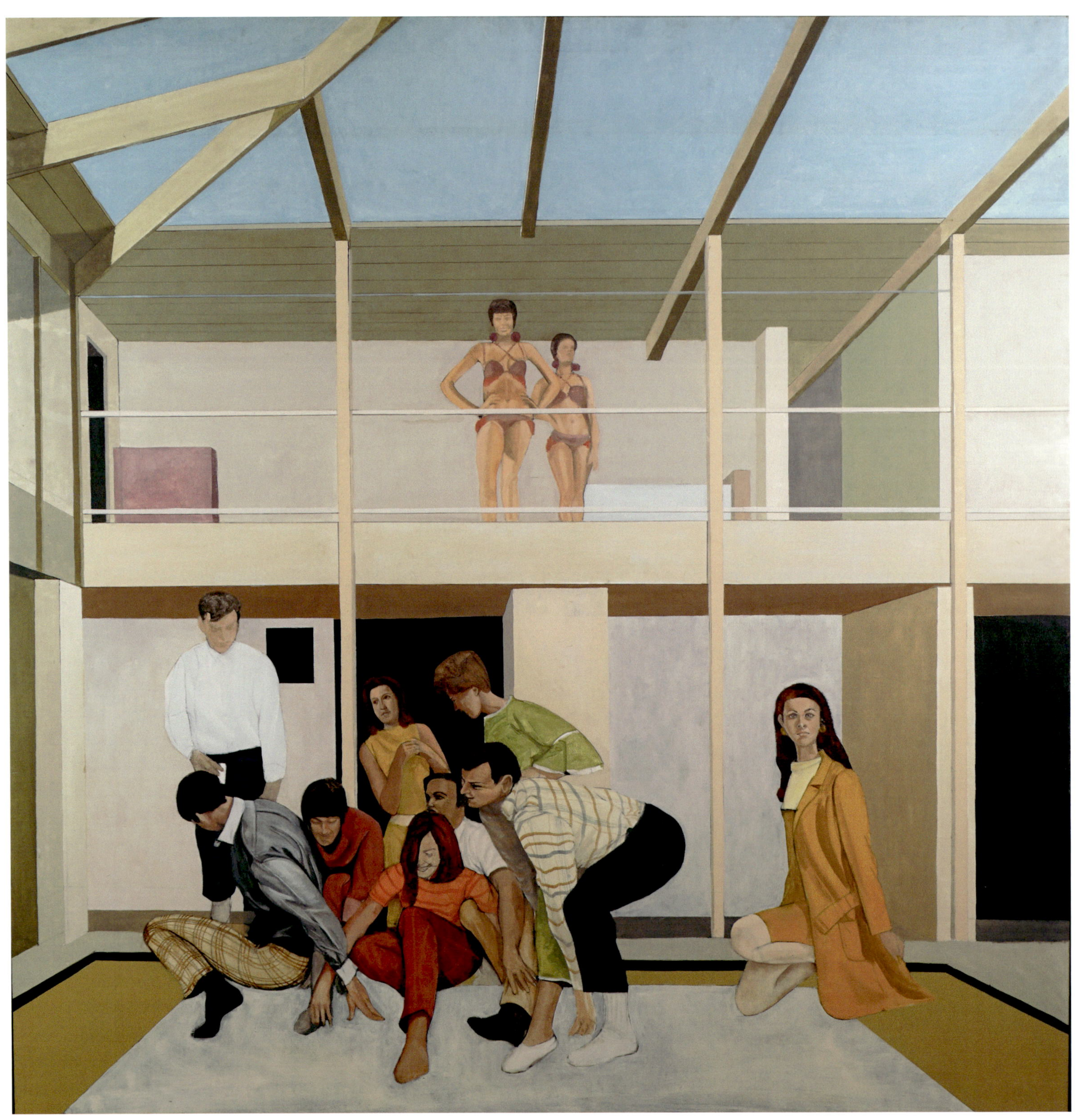

PLATE 1

*Games*, 1967

# Directors' Foreword

Acollaboration between three institutions is generally more complicated than a project undertaken by a single entity. However, the artistic and creative legacy of Larry Day (1921–1998) is of such scale that three of Philadelphia's venerable arts institutions—a museum and two universities—felt the necessity to pool resources and talent to organize *Body Language: The Art of Larry Day,* an exhibition in three parts: *Nature Abstracted, Silent Conversations,* and *Absent Presence.* It was a shared understanding of Day's unique institutional significance to each that drove Arcadia University and University of the Arts to join Woodmere Art Museum in telling Day's story. Almost one hundred and fifty of the artist's paintings, drawings, and prints are assembled across our three venues, a selection of works that makes the case for Day's continuing relevance to the creative intellectual life of Philadelphia and to the expanding international conversations about American art.

The galleries of each institution will show a distinct aspect of Day's output, and it is in the issues revolving around our ability to neatly impose a three-part division of his career into thematic categories that the artist's significance can be discerned. Infrequently, in our view, have the structural decisions in the organization of an exhibition been so worthy of an extended explanation. Day's nature-based abstractions of the 1950s and early 1960s will be shown at UArts with the title *Nature Abstracted.* Alternately earthy with a warm materiality, or light and ethereal like a fresh cloudscape, these paintings established a solid career for Day in both Philadelphia and New York. He could well have continued on this path. However, he would make a decisive break with abstraction, as described in the essay by Sid Sachs in this publication. Starting around 1962, twin fascinations would emerge and run parallel in Day's oeuvre. With the title *Absent Presence,* Day's cityscapes (along with a selection of prints) will be shown at Arcadia. Measured, evocative, and uninhabited, these works assert quixotic geometric relationships between spaces, facades, doors, and windows, combined with trees that are mostly leafless and cutaway views of architecture, some of it recognizable. The artist's multifigure ensembles will be shown at Woodmere with the title *Silent Conversations.* These paintings and drawings document the realms of activity that filled the artist's life: the studio, the classroom, and the homes of friends, with portraits and self-portraits throughout. Games that Day enjoyed, like poker, bridge, charades, and Twister, serve as metaphors for the activities and foibles of human relationships.

How did Day find his voice as a painter of cityscapes and self-referential figuration? The exhibition itself and the essays in this catalogue explore Day's fascination with the art of the old masters as a deeply thoughtful journey that helped him find a consistent, though evolving voice as a representational painter and as an active participant in exhibitions and the public life of the arts until his death in 1998. This was a self-conscious, immersive journey in which Day continuously explored his incessant compulsion as a draftsman. As can been seen at all three venues, Day's drawings stand on their own as fully complete works of art. The artist also possessed a sharp intellect and bottomless curiosity when it came to classical music and jazz, popular culture, and the most esoteric of philosophical writings, as well as a full gamut of Eastern and Western literature, from early Celtic works to Rilke to the poetry of his renowned friend John Hollander (whose previously unpublished essay on Day's cityscapes appears in these pages). Day's identity was also that of an art historian-artist. Philadelphia is a city in which realism in the arts has reigned and been redefined from generation to generation, and Day knew that his undertaking to build a new approach was to engage in conversations that spanned centuries, reaching back to the Peales, Thomas Eakins and his circle, Violet Oakley, and the city's other great illustrators and muralists, as well as to the Ashcan painters and social realists such as Benton Spruance, Jacob Landau, and Albert Gold, artists who taught side by side with Day at UArts. They likely gave inspiration to the pedagogical dimension of his practice. Dedicated to teaching, Day would become known as "the dean of Philadelphia painters," as Spruance, an instructor at Arcadia University (then Beaver College), was the "dean of Philadelphia printmakers." Day, in turn, would inspire younger artists, not only through his position at UArts, but also at the Tyler School of Art, the Pennsylvania Academy of the Fine Arts, and the University of Pennsylvania, and through his visiting lectureships across the country. Teaching, and the ethics associated with it, came naturally to Day, and the confidence of his work and occasional didacticism stems from his comfort in the role of teacher.

Day's work and the drama of his break from abstraction is significant because it is part of a sea change in Western culture. At a surface level, we refer to a revival of realism and representation in American art that came into being in the 1960s, not only in Philadelphia, but also in many other cities. However, and on a deeper level, the new realism must be further understood in relation to the larger intellectual tent that encompassed it: post-structuralist thought and the beginnings of a post-modernist intellectual sensibility. Like many scholars and artists of his time, Day probed the centuries-old patterns of progressivist thought that shaped the proscribed understanding of history itself and every art movement from the Enlightenment to modernism writ large, including the then-current notion that mid-twentieth-century abstraction—like that practiced by Day himself and by the New York School— represented an arrival of the arts at a place that expressed a preordained essence. Day's extensive writings, along with his paintings and drawings, show that he not only understood the falsity of this premise, but also knew that his twin fascinations

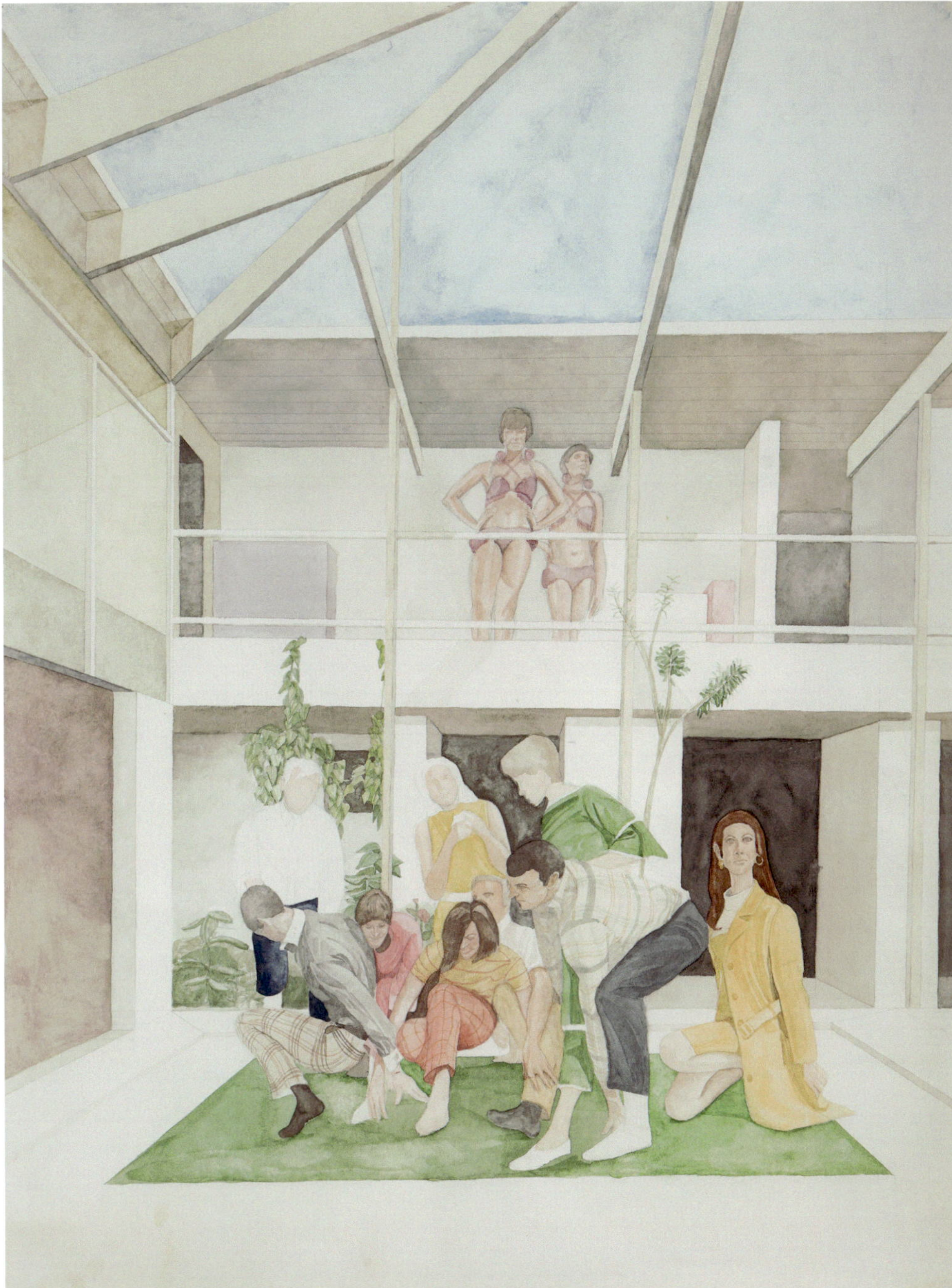

with cityscapes and multifigure tableaus were part of a paradigm shift to new thought patterns that looked to the future.

Another element of self-awareness runs through Day's work and must be described as a part of the forwardness of his thinking. More than once in organizing this exhibition, we came up against the impression that Day seems to represent the archetypal dead white male artist: the heroic guy-artist at his easel, as he depicts himself in a painting titled *Changes* (plate 19) and many others, who privileges the male creator in relation to women as subjects. But everything that is written by our curator David Bindman and by our other catalogue authors reveals Day to be profoundly conscious and meticulously self-critical, an artist who composes works and explores subjects in order to inspire a curiosity about the peculiar questions they pose. The title *Changes*, for example, suggests a daring ability to self-represent as the central figure amidst shifting, changing social relationships, as depicted between artist and model, man and woman, teacher and student, and contemporary artist and old master. As we know from today's vantage point, waves of social change would transpire in

Day's lifetime: the civil rights movement, feminism, gay rights, the disasters of the Vietnam War, the cynicism in politics wrought by Watergate, and much more. All of this influenced Day's thinking and is relevant to the organizing structure of our show. *Nature Abstracted* offers visual poetry and engaging pleasures. The works of art are wonderful in every way, and we don't wish to suggest that the paintings themselves are anything less than completely satisfying on their own terms. However, it was the intellectual foundation that the abstract paintings stood upon that had changed. The amazing fact of Day's reinvention of his art can only be understood in relation to an evolving understanding of life's dynamic, in which the older privileges are not necessarily preserved. *Silent Conversations* and *Absent Presence* represent the invention of a voice, style, and repertoire of subjects that explore the changing structures of thought in the public sphere and in the artist's more intimate human relationships.

As stated above, each of our three institutions approaches the exhibition from the perspective of distinct relationships to Day and his work. At the same time, as universities, UArts and Arcadia must always ask how an exhibition will connect to the lives of the young people who have come to them for intellectual growth and advancement. Museums too, if they hope to engage young visitors, must ask this question. Our exhibition's value to students may be found in the manner in which Day's practice can be described as one propelled by questions of identity, in particular, the persona of the artist in the studio. Many of the examples in the Woodmere exhibition can be read not merely as self-portraits, but as images of Day surrounded by friends, staged in a location serving as an atelier. As "slow" and analog as they may be, these works underscore the role of the artist as both actor and recording observer, a duality that proposes a parallel to social media memes. In terms of traditional art pedagogy, the many works on paper included in the exhibition provide a master class in drawing as an extension of seeing, if not thinking, while also honoring the role of process as an end in it itself. The contemporary pertinence of Day's work extends well beyond the academy, however. In one totally unforeseen interpretation, the unpeopled cityscapes at Arcadia may strike some viewers as evocations of pandemic lockdown. These canvases, as Eileen Neff observes in her essay, "introduce the importance of the spectator," assuring their relevance to viewers in perpetuity.

There is a tangible institutional history at both schools. At UArts, Day was an anchor in the painting department from 1953 to 1988, and as such played a formative role in the development of curriculum and touched the lives of generations of students and colleagues. On Broad Street, Day's effect was sweeping; not only was his teaching well regarded, but he framed the rather catholic and exciting faculty, which included Edna Andrade, Cynthia Carlson, Rafael Ferrer, Eileen Goodman, Sidney Goodman, Jerome Kaplan, Paul Keene, David Kettner, Edith Neff, Jerry Nichols, Jane Piper, and Doris Staffel. It was at UArts that Day's legacy was built. Arcadia was also close-to-home in many respects. Having resided in Cheltenham Township most of his life, Day was no doubt familiar from childhood with the university's distinctive, medieval-inspired facades. His participation in four important drawing shows in the 1960s and 1970s at the Atwood Library gallery helped to establish the *Works on Paper* exhibition series, highlighting drawing as an independent and primary medium, a mainstay of Arcadia's programming for over thirty years.

As a collecting museum dedicated to the arts of Philadelphia, Woodmere exists to care for art that tells the stories embedded in the cultural life of our city: stories of artists' careers and art movements, and narratives of cultural change in the city and region. The Museum has made a deep commitment to stewarding Day's work, acquiring a large number of paintings and drawings in order to become the "go to" place where his legacy is stewarded, to be shown, studied in a complete manner, and enjoyed by visitors for years to come. Day's work contributes incisively to the ongoing sweep of the arts in Philadelphia by illuminating a unique tension between the realist mainstream, on the one hand, and the practitioners of the avant-garde, on the other.

The three of us, as directors of our respective art spaces, are indebted to our friend Ruth Fine for sharing her enthusiasm and passion. We add our thanks to those of David Bindman, our guest curator, whose acknowledgments offer well-deserved accolades to the many individuals involved in this exhibition and catalogue. At Woodmere, our former trustee and partner in so many collecting initiatives, Joe Yohlin, must be singled out for his focus on the importance of Day's work and his long-held view that the Museum needed to carve out the special place in our collection that Day now occupies. Finally, at each institution there have been right-hand people, without whom the exhibition and this catalogue would have been impossible: at Arcadia, Exhibitions Coordinator Matthew Borgen; at UArts, Director of Exhibitions Management and Head Preparator Michael Ciervo; and at Woodmere, the curatorial team of Deputy Director Rick Ortwein, Assistant Curator Rachel Hruszkewycz, and Registrar Laura Heemer. A smaller iteration of our three-part show is traveling to the David Owsley Museum of Art at Ball State University. We thank its staff and director, Robert G. La France. *Body Language: The Art of Larry Day* would not have been possible without the support of the funders who contributed to this project. As the catalogue goes to press, they are The Imperfect Family Foundation, Jordan D. Schnitzer and His Family Foundation, Elizabeth Glassman, Dorothy Lichtenstein, Terra Foundation for American Art, The Lunder Foundation–Peter & Paula Lunder Family, Leslie Samuels & Augusta Gross, Muriel Fine Sherman & Dr. Neil Sherman, Pamela & Joseph Yohlin, Michael Heizer Studio, Gloria Spivak, Norman Fein, Susan Sillins, Judith Brodsky, Ronald Rumford, and several other generous contributors, including those who wish to remain anonymous. Thank you all.

Sid Sachs
Director of Exhibitions and Chief Curator, University of the Arts

Richard Torchia
Director of Arcadia Exhibitions, Arcadia University

William R. Valerio
 The Patricia Van Burgh Allison Director and CEO, Woodmere Art Museum

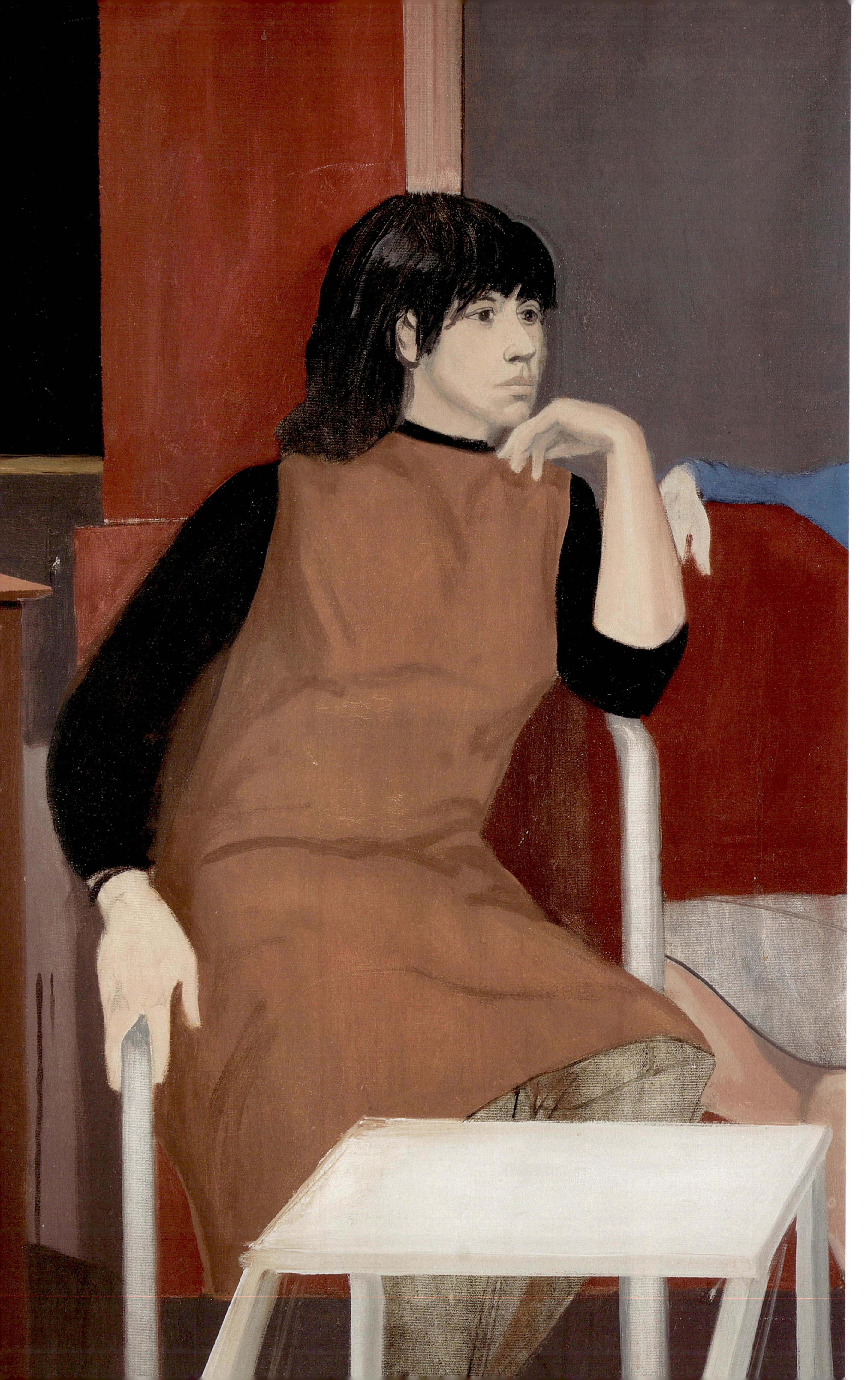

*David Bindman*

# Larry Day:
# A Consummately Reflective Artist

Larry Day was a man of immense learning and intellectual subtlety. He was thoroughly steeped in earlier European art, and seemed to have read every canonical literary and philosophical text from the past, though he wore his erudition modestly. His writings on art demonstrate a real philosophical mind, in their verbal precision and use of syllogistic reasoning, and his mature paintings are constantly in dialogue with early masters. It is essential to an understanding of him to know that he was a hugely admired teacher and a sociable man with many long-standing friendships.

My fondest memories of him are of going together to the National Gallery of Art in Washington, DC, especially looking at the great Bellini-Titian *Feast of the Gods*, which I believe is the one painting above all that haunts his art. At the same time, he could be surprisingly quirky in his tastes. I remember him insisting, against my resistance, that there was great merit in a painting in the gallery by eighteenth-century English provincial artist Arthur Devis. I was eventually persuaded (sort of), but to this day I cannot understand his warmth toward an even more unlikely artist, late nineteenth-century English etcher Hedley Fitton, whose current fate is to pass disregarded through the dingier auction rooms. But, who knows? Fitton may be a rediscovery of future generations.

Day's art is all of a piece with his personality. That is to say it is philosophical, reflective, and perpetually in dialogue with his artistic predecessors, not in an imitative or subordinate way, but in an animated conversation with them that brings out Day's own originality of vision, a certain cussedness and love of irony. He did not want to be understood too quickly. His account of the painter Balthus (Balthasar Klossowski de Rola) could well be applied to himself: "[He] is a consummately reflective artist. Every inch of his paintings appears to have the most scrupulous attention—nothing seems to have crept in unawares and no form seems casual or tentative."[1]

### Abstract Expressionism in the 1950s

Seen as a whole, Day's art can be divided into three types of production that have only indirect connections with each other. Following his student paintings and prints made at Temple University's Tyler School of Art, in Philadelphia, by the mid-1950s Day had settled into a distinctive form of Abstract Expressionism, very much to be understood in terms of the New York painting of his day. Though still based in Philadelphia, he spent much time in New York in the company of such artists as his particular friend Franz Kline, but he was pictorially closer to the great Willem de Kooning. The Abstract Expressionists were as a group much less uniform in practice and purpose than their spokesmen Clement Greenberg and Harold Rosenberg had us believe. Applying an oversimplified version of Kant's idea of the autonomy of the aesthetic, Greenberg argued for non-referentiality to nature and the outside world as a unifying principle of their art. While this might apply more readily to some members of the group than others, it was emphatically not the case with de Kooning, who arguably never lost touch with place and nature.

To be clear, Day's paintings of 1955 to 1960 belong with Abstract Expressionism in their open, gestural handling and their allover painting, but they are only rarely abstract. Despite a lack of horizon in most cases, they make open and explicit reference to vegetation in the form of undergrowth and bushes, and sometimes figurative elements, always holding in balance free, gestural brushwork and representational suggestions that give them a vibrant surface (plates 2 and 3).

## Body Language and Ironic Realism: From the 1960s Onward

Though Day had much success with these paintings, and there is ample evidence in the current exhibition of their mastery and power, in 1962 he dramatically and irrecoverably abandoned this whole way of painting. The change began with a free copy of a painting after Jan Steen of a merry company (plate 7), redolent of human interaction and drama. He then embarked on an explicitly figurative style, in which tightly drawn and thinly colored contemporary figures enact dramas that in varying degrees evoke old master paintings. At roughly the same time, he embarked on a separate group of architectural paintings, producing unpopulated scenes, primarily in Philadelphia, where he spent most of his life, and Washington, DC (when he lived in Maryland in the late 1980s and early 1990s), in a deliberately formal way (plate 10). All the time, as he had done from the beginning, he made copious drawings for the figure paintings, in some cases in series, but—unexpectedly—many fewer for the architectural compositions.

What lay behind this dramatic and far-reaching change in his painterly practice? One answer might be that the assumptions behind his Abstract Expressionist paintings no longer corresponded with his wider interests or, indeed, his personality. The years between 1960 and 1962 were a time of crisis for New York Abstract Expressionism, which had by then long outgrown its modest origins in the city and become what critic Robert Hughes described as "a mandatory world style,"[2] promoted by the US government. It was around this time that there were calls for renewed engagement between art and life rather than with art alone. As Day put it succinctly in a 1991 interview with Marina Pacini for the Archives of American Art: "It's again this *and* that, rather than just this or just that."[3] The feeling that the pure aestheticism that characterized Greenberg's view of the purpose of painting, though not necessarily that of the artists he claimed to speak for, was insufficient had been growing through the 1950s. It burst out in the following decade in its most famous consequence, an

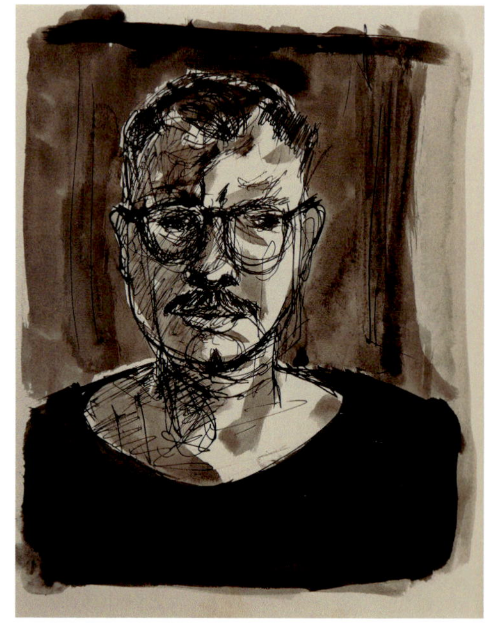

Figure 2.1 *Self-Portrait*, c. 1950, pen and ink and wash on paper, 12 × 9 in. (Woodmere Art Museum: Gift of the Larry Day Art Trust, 2021)

emphatic engagement with the world of advertising and consumerism, seen in its most extreme form in Pop Art and the work of Andy Warhol.

The feeling of discontent with the "just this-ness" of Abstract Expressionism was expressed in 1960 by Day's friend Philip Guston, who had also made a journey from a highly aestheticized form of color-based abstraction to a form of realism: "There is something ridiculous and miserly in the myth we inherit from abstract art—that painting is autonomous, pure and for itself. . . . But painting is 'impure.' We are image-makers and image-ridden."[4]

While Pop Art was the most highly publicized reaction against Abstract Expressionism, there is a whole history to be written about the many artists in different countries who sought in other ways to bring realism back into art from the early 1960s onward, and in some cases much earlier, like the British Independent Group of the 1950s, in whom Day was greatly interested.[5] What is remarkable in retrospect is how quickly and completely Day adopted an entirely new approach and set of ambitions. As he said himself, "It was a cut and dried, overnight thing."[6] He, in effect, became a full-fledged history painter in the traditional sense, making works that were deliberately in dialogue not only with earlier art, but also with the larger Western tradition of literature and philosophy. His extraordinary range of mind at last found full expression in his art. The spontaneity of his previous work became a deliberative and cumulative process, carried out often in series of preparatory drawings.

Above all, the single note that characterized Day's Abstract Expressionist paintings gave way to a profusion of different registers. If we look at what is arguably the artist's masterpiece, *Poker Game*, and its preliminary drawings (plates 12 and 105), we can see the force of his claim for being a painter of "this *and* that."[7] As he said himself:

> I'm not a mess of things, but one thing that incorporates all these things. And so all these experiences—the way one looks at work, the way one looks at one's own work, the way one looks at other work. I've always felt that looking at, say, a painting by somebody, is as creative an act as painting a painting. So it all fits together that way. I would say that is the key to me, if there is such a thing.[8]

We can see now the emphasis on process, the working out of a composition through many stages and painstaking adjustments. There is the openly stated *hommage* to Paul Cézanne's great painting *Card Players* in the Barnes Foundation, a reference obvious to anyone in Philadelphia, and then there is the celebration of sociability and friendship. The players are all fellow artists, highly individualized and self-contained, but also unified in camaraderie and mutual regard. The names of all five players in Day's painting are known—Armand Mednick, Dennis Leon, David Pease, Massimo Pierucci, and Jimmy Lueders—and some of them appear again in other paintings. The poker game was something of a local institution, notable for celebrating its fiftieth anniversary in 2013, though by then hardly any of the original players were still alive. Day himself, though he appears in some of the preparatory drawings, is represented in the final painting by an empty chair, which connects the theme of the canvas to his own life. In a broader sense, it is a meditation on the social life of the teacher-artist; could there also be an implied contrast between the sociability of Philadelphia artists and the notoriously competitive art world of New York?

The evocation of Cézanne is more than just a reference. It is at the heart of the composition, because a key purpose of the painting is to apply to everyday reality what Cézanne described as "solid and lasting like the art in the museums,"[9] the transcendent value of the classical tradition from the ancient world through the Italian Renaissance to Poussin, and to more recent times. It is a matter of imposing a higher order on the inevitable fragmentation of reality. As Day put it:

> I feel very aware of fragmentation as an issue, and it's a way we sort of understand or approach reality. And then, at the same time, there's that sense of unity, and whether a unity is possible. And I think this is one of the things I see in Balthus—is the ability to unify fragmentation to create a sense of wholeness, and still not dissipate, the fragmentation [that] exists within it, so that you have again, this and that, rather than just this or just that.[10]

It is this unity that both incorporates and at the same time transcends the real. Day's figurative paintings are "real" in the sense that they often represent real people, but such reality is always undercut by fictional elements. The artist responded positively to curator Nan Rosenthal's description of his work as "ironic realism":

> I think that was perfect. That's how I think of my work. That's how I thought of it even before she named it. Because irony always seemed a key issue . . . one of the influences on my thinking was Thomas Mann, who has always dealt with irony.[11]

A painting that might seem at first to be a reasonably accurate account of a real scene begins to come apart as one looks into it, a process Day describes in connection with his painting and drawings of Salome (plates 37–39):

> The figure compositions are usually based on multi-sources, from let's say, photographs. Sometimes somebody posing, fragments of different places. For instance, the painting I did of Salome—part of it is this sofa, and this part of it is—the table part of it is from an old nineteenth-century print. Part of it is Jerry Nichols, who posed as Herod. Salome came from a Bloomingdale ad . . . you know, the whole thing is a mixture.[12]

The essentially literary background to such a strategy is made clear when he quotes Irvin Ehrenpreis on T. S. Eliot to give a sense of the visual dislocation he expects the viewer to experience upon entering the process of examining his paintings:

> Disruptions of syntax and meaning that startle the reader into attention
> while forcing him to reconsider the purpose and value of literary experience:
> proper names intruding with no reference to identify them, until we question
> the significance of identity; verb tenses slyly melting into one another, till we
> ponder the reality of time; third persons becoming second and first, till we
> stumble in the relativity of perceptions.[13]

A notable example of this visual dislocation can be found in the painting *Group* (plate 13), which seems to show a gathering of a large group of friends, mainly married couples with children, with Day at the center seated next to a double portrait in progress of artists Natalie Charkow and Mitzi Melnicoff (plate 16). But then among the group of identifiable figures—the repertory company, as it were, of his paintings—is the then-famous Italian actress Monica Vitti. Her presence underscores the fictional nature of the scene, but it also raises the question of Italy in both present and past, and is a reminder of Day's own Italian ancestry (he was born Lorenzo del Giorno). If Vitti represents the modern, fashionable Italy of the great filmmakers, then the formality of the painting makes reference to earlier Italian traditions. As Day noted, "Then [the artists] I feel closest to are people like Piero della Francesca, Morandi—you know, that quiet Italian. That sort of calm balance is the one that I feel is my heritage, you might say. And so I'm sort of drawn to that."[14]

As in *Poker Game,* the participants seem to exist within their own world and do not visibly interact with each other. The effect is very much like a pre-Renaissance painting in which the figures seem slightly awkward in themselves and quite detached from one another, though clearly some are closely connected by friendship, marriage, or parentage. That this was deliberate is made clear from the artist's remark:

> Something slightly stiff and awkward about the figures is something I've
> always been drawn to. As if they're not quite comfortable in there. For
> instance, I've always liked the figures of Dieric Bouts, because there's a kind
> of stiffness about his figures. I think there's that sense of, I guess, a person-
> ality being imbedded in the form, as well as the source image, or something
> like that.[15]

Day talks of the effect of Piero della Francesca on him when he went to the National Gallery in London, when he was based in Paris for several months in 1952, and the Italian artist is as much a presence in *Poker Game* as Cézanne, bringing a certain distance and detachment to the representation. He noted, "We reverence all that is quiet, cold, distinguished, distant and past, whatever does not, as we look at it, make us taut and put us on the defensive, whatever we can converse with without having to shout."[16] There is also a strong tendency in many of his compositions toward the frieze-like, which he attributed to his early Abstract Expressionist work and to the influence of Poussin:

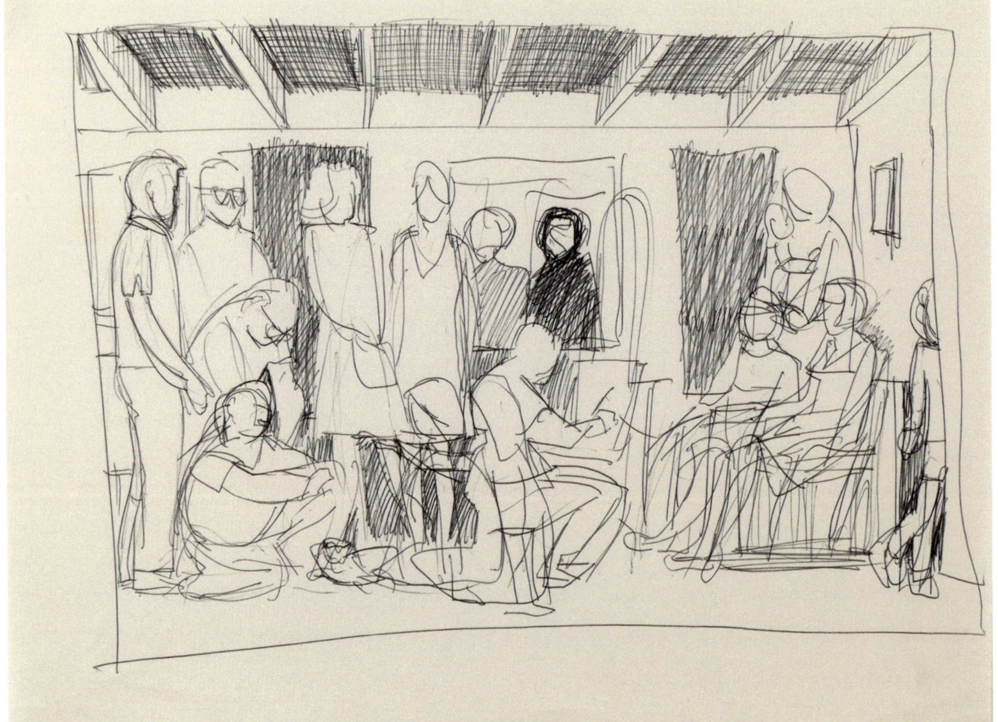

Figure 2.2  *Untitled, study for "Group,"* c. 1967, pen and ink on paper, 8¼ × 10¾ in. (Pennsylvania Academy of the Fine Arts, Philadelphia, Gift of Ruth Fine, 2019.20.2)

And that frieze quality, I think part of that grows out of my nonrepresentational work, which is a close to the surface kind of thing. So that when there are depths, the depths are treated with a kind of limiting. But figures usually—and also, I think, that grows out of another of my great pantheon, Poussin. I guess in drawing, I draw more from Poussin than any other artist. His structures continuously intrigue and enlighten me.[17]

If there are strong affinities with earlier Italian and French art, Day also recognized an affinity with contemporary English artists in their pursuit of allegory. He cites American-born, London-based painter R.B. Kitaj, who specialized in layered, highly literary history paintings that were known—and often challenged—for their density of cultural reference, though they frequently incorporated the tortuous politics of twentieth-century Europe. There are also perhaps analogies in his incisive drawing technique with Slade School painters William Coldstream and Euan Uglow, though their paintings were not at all allegorical. Not surprisingly, Day also admits to a strong taste for the eccentric work of Stanley Spencer:

I'm very fond of that strange, strange painter Stanley Spencer. Guy Davenport . . . he's one of the few people who also likes Stanley Spencer in this country. Another one is my friend, Raoul Middleman . . . he mentions the fact that both Balthus and Spencer like the sense of the canvas being part of the physical property, rather than paint. And I felt the immediate kinship with that.[18]

Taken as a whole, Day's realist paintings from the early 1960s until his death in 1998 represent an oeuvre of extraordinary richness and complexity. They are endlessly inventive and surprising, but certain themes become intensified. In the painting *Poker Game,* Day is, as previously mentioned, present as an empty chair at the table at which the game is being played, but in a self-portrait trilogy, including *Break* (Eleanor D. Wilson Museum), *Changes* (plate 19), and *Limit* (fig. 3.3), as well as *Day by Day* (plate 42), he not only appears in the paintings, but is clearly at the center. The same is true of one of his later works, *Dialogue* (plate 34). In *Changes,* Day is painting or drawing directly on a canvas, evidently from a naked model seated before him. Behind him is a female student, standing against the background of a huge, wall-sized unfinished painting of a bacchanale (referencing Rosso Fiorentino) with numerous naked female figures; there is another, less animated wall painting behind the seated model (referencing Joachim Wtewael).

According to Day's interview with Marina Pacini, the scene is based on a very specific allegory, with each element playing a part. The painting on the left wall is "an Italian mannerist work," and the one on the right wall is "a northern European mannerist work." He goes on to remark:

> One of the things about my figure paintings is they have a lot of symbolism and so on. Conscious symbolism. So this [painting on the left] was representing my father, the Italian. This one [on the right] representing my mother. The model [on the right] representing life, or something outside. This [figure on the left] was a former student of mine, so it represents my teaching. This dark area represents the abyss between the drawing and reality, that the drawing tries to bridge. So these were all conscious things. I like to think as much as I can, knowing that beyond the thinking, there are things you're never going to—that other people discover, and so on.[19]

Despite the seeming reality of the scene, it is a fiction that contrasts the everyday nature of the artist's painterly activity with the imagined world of the classical tradition, with its uninhibited grandeur and sexuality, and there is, as always, a sly humor in the contrast between the mundanity of the real life of the painter and the visions to which he gives form.

What these works provide is an image of the artist not as omniscient creator, but as a social being who inhabits different environments, all of which contribute to his art. His vision is the very opposite of hermetic, drawing together the comradeship of the art school, ordinary social gatherings, the studio as a place of interaction, the role of models and students, and yet paradoxically there is an unavoidable element of the private and the personal imagination, even fantasy, in the making of art. As always, life and art are full of contradictions and it is these that provide his art's animating force.

## Absent Presence: The Site Paintings

Day's architectural paintings are almost—if not quite—a separate genre within the artist's work. Sometimes the elements of the site are strong in his figurative paintings, but the architectural paintings are invariably without figures, though human activity is usually signaled in some way. What they have in common is the urban banality of each setting, though some are not without drama. Their subjects are the most unassuming, undistinguished urban architecture of Philadelphia and elsewhere. The challenge for the artist is to give meaning to scenes that are familiar and essentially featureless, and this he has done by imposing on them a rigidly classical order. There are always archetypes lingering in the background, and I would suggest in this case a particular kind of Italian Renaissance city perspective view that Day would surely have known from *The Ideal City* panel (fig. 2.3) from the 1480s, attributed to Fra Carnevale, in the Walters Art Museum in Baltimore. This is one of three such city views almost certainly commissioned by Federico da Montefeltro for his palace in Urbino. It is a highly intellectual exercise in perspective under the direct influence of Alberti, and it expresses, from a princely viewpoint, an ideal city state, with a colosseum and baptistery flanking a triumphal arch, unified by rigidly mathematical single-point perspective.

There is an obvious irony in applying such elevated values to the architecture-scape of the non-touristic parts of Philadelphia and its suburbs, but there is also value for Day in the seeming detachment from humanity: "Distancing. I guess there is a sense of loneliness or solitariness that I feel emotionally in tune with. That sense of—I guess always being, in some way, slightly isolated, as being part of the human condition from my vantage point. So, I think that comes through in the paintings without figures in them."[21]

Yet they also have meanings for Day that are quite different from the figure paintings:

> It's a totally different activity for me than the figure paintings, which is another kind of thing. In the site paintings, it's like every part of it is in some way directed to the viewer, in terms of creating an entity of some sort that illuminates. In the figure paintings, every part of it is directed within itself, illuminating that which is occurring there. In the figure paintings, I think of myself more as a voyeur or a witness, where in the site paintings, I think of myself as a participant.[22]

Figure 2.3   Attributed to Fra Carnevale, *The Ideal City*, c. 1480–84, oil and tempera on panel, 30½ × 86⅝ in. (The Walters Art Museum, Baltimore)

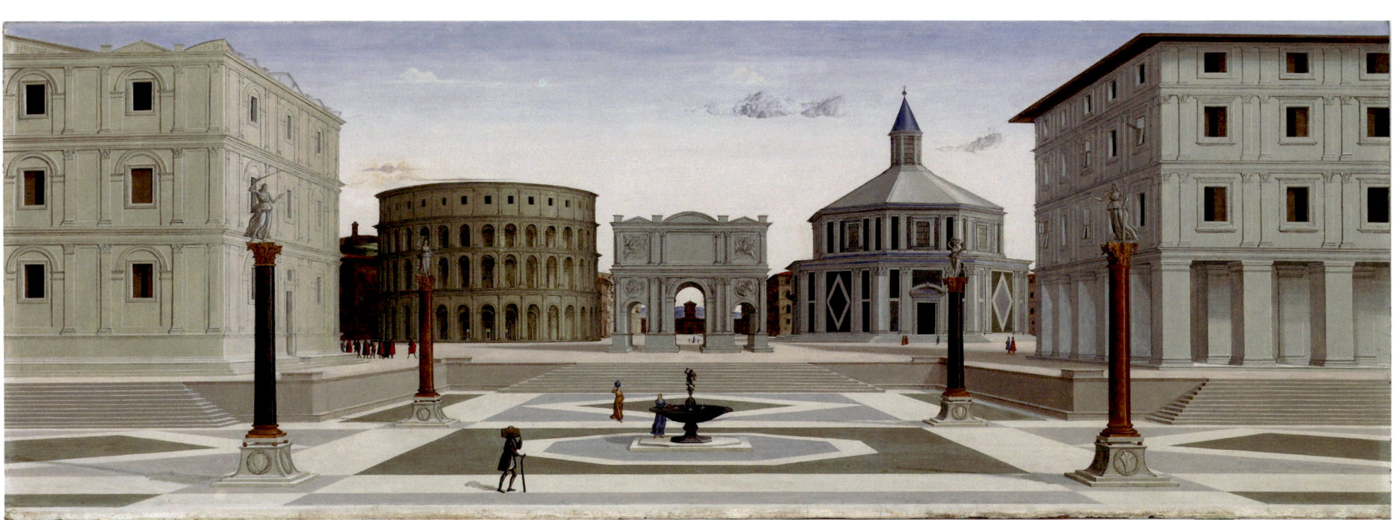

The artist himself is the human presence in what he calls his "site paintings," but human activity is always implied. In perhaps the most dramatic of all his architectural paintings, *Extension*, a huge concrete support for a roadway stands proud against the sky (figs. 2.4 and 2.5). The reductive, simplifying process of the final work is clear from a preparatory photograph, which contains the fussy, random detail of the real scene. Far from emphasizing the texture of the buildings in the site paintings, Day reduces structures to a state of geometric purity that evokes abstract ideas of proportion like the Renaissance Golden Section, recalling ironically the perspectival purity of the Walters' painting of *The Ideal City*.

## Mysterious Narratives: Independent Drawings and Series

Day was an inveterate draftsman from the beginning of his career until the end. He made sketches on any piece of paper around (napkins, notebooks, Post-its, scraps of any sort) to finished works, some entirely from his imagination, some from memory of his own work and that of the masters from every period. In addition, he made several series of drawings, beginning with the eight colored drawings of about 1967 titled *The Venus Society* (plates 24–31), and ending, in the year he died, with the series of ten detailed ink drawings titled *Elegies (Homage to Rilke)* (plates 46–55).

*The Venus Society* is unusual among the drawing series in essential respects. It is one of a few in the 1960s that Day conceived in watercolor with pencil underdrawing, and it has an ostensibly clear narrative, though it would be hard to work it out without the titles, which are unexpectedly deterministic: *The Foundation; The Establishment of Ritual; The Discovery of Another Society; The Other Society's Base; The Struggle for the Uncommitted; The Search, Atonement; The Merger;* and *The Dance.* The scenes are set evidently by the Mediterranean, and the society involves women perhaps even more than men. Though there are implied tensions between two different societies, they are eventually reconciled and merged, celebrating with a dance. As always in Day's work, the scenes mix past and present, and the setting is reminiscent of the backgrounds of paintings and prints by eighteenth-century masters Giovanni Battista and Giovanni Domenico Tiepolo.

Day's later series are entirely conceived in pencil or pen and ink, and they show an intensified engagement with two series of etchings by G. B. Tiepolo. Day was deeply impressed by an exhibition of work by both Tiepolos, curated by H. Diane Russell at the National Gallery of Art in 1972. The exhibition was developed from two extraordinary albums, including proofs as well as final impressions, donated to the gallery by Lessing J. Rosenwald.[23] One album included G. D. Tiepolo's *Via Crucis* (sixteen images) and *Flight into Egypt* (twenty-four images). The other, perhaps of greatest impact on Day, included G. B. Tiepolo's *Vari Capricci* (ten images) and *Scherzi di Fantasia* (twenty-three images). Both *Capricci* and *Scherzi* are remarkable for their evocative and imaginative qualities that seemed the very height of poetic expression to their eighteenth-century admirers. They have no set subjects, but seem to refer to biblical and classical imagery, including fauns and harlequins, without ever allowing specific

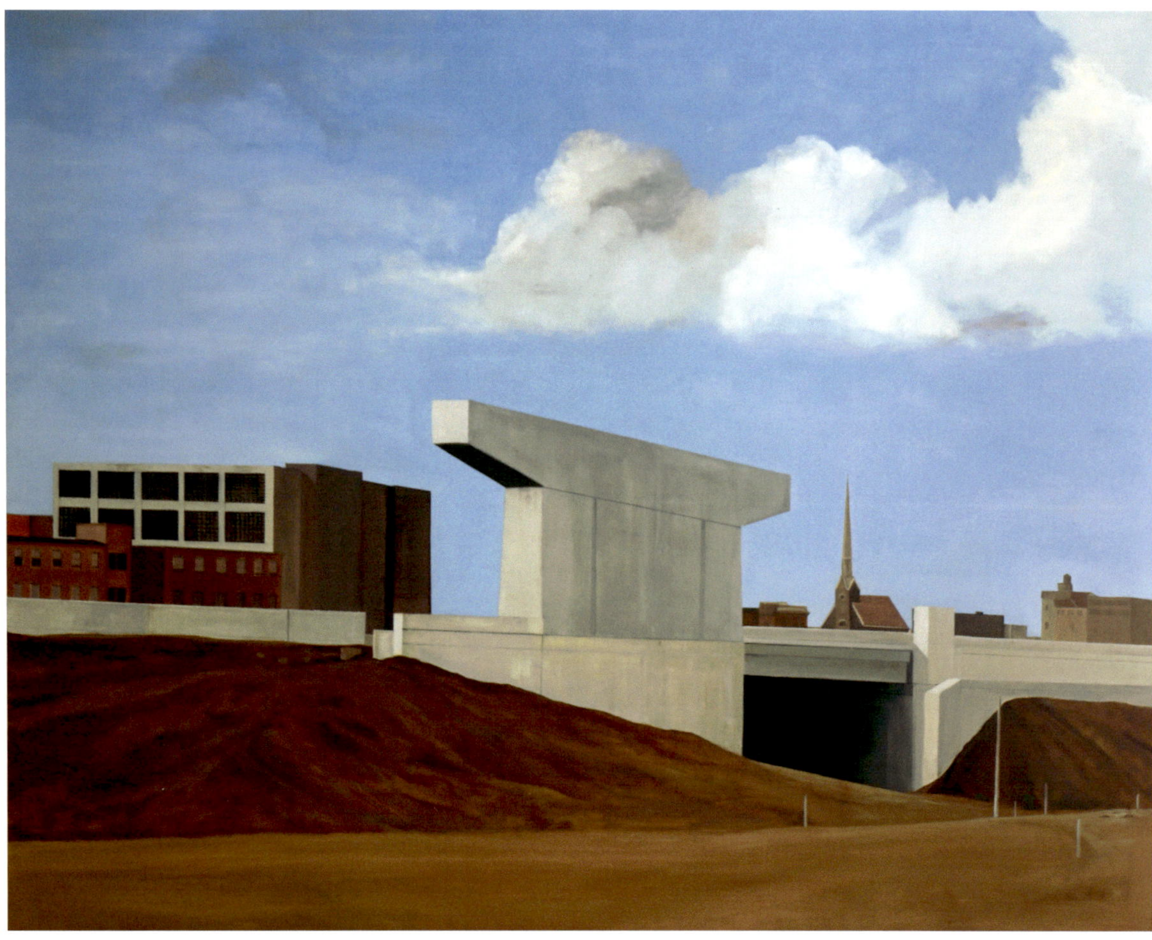

Figure 2.4  *Extension*, 1977, oil on canvas, 54 × 66 in. (Private Collection)

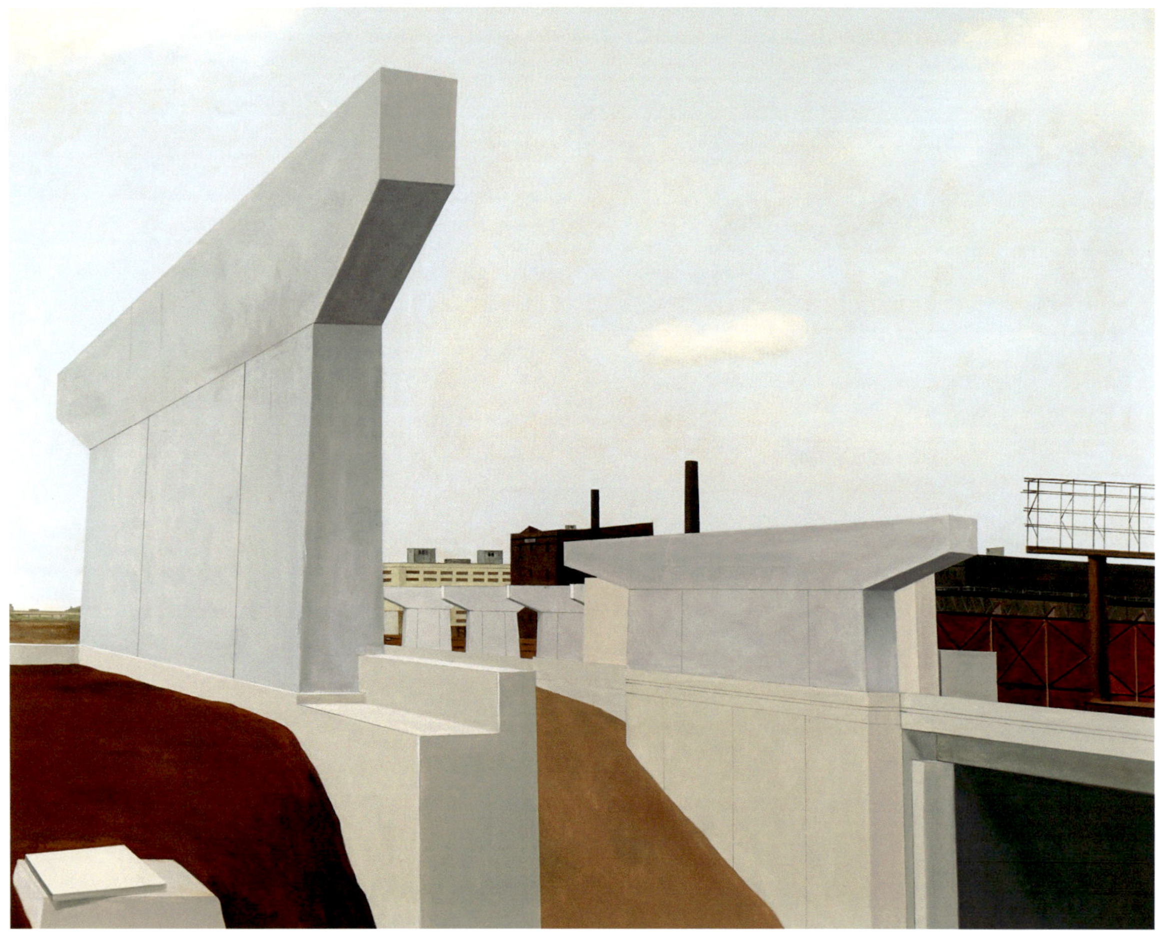

Figure 2.5  *Extension II*, 1978, oil on canvas, 54 × 66 in. (Private Collection)

identification. The general sense is of the vanity of human ambitions; grand, monarchical figures are confronted with fragments of tombs and are seemingly impotent in the face of death. The one unambiguous image is a skeleton representing death reading from a book to a group of disconcerted, noble-looking figures.

The influence of the Tiepolo etchings is evident in Day's series *Tempi del Giorno*, which as the punning title suggests were largely autobiographical, with the artist appearing in every drawing. In his introduction to an exhibition of the series, John Hollander suggests that Day created a kind of alter ego, an Italian sixteenth-century Mannerist artist called Lorenzo del Giorno, which was the artist's given name.[24] The series is a profound meditation on the role of the artist and his relationship to past art, and, indeed, of all our relationships to the past, themes that have been central to Day's painting.

In the tellingly named series of pen and ink drawings, *Caprices* (figs. 4.9 and 4.10), there are similar confrontations between seemingly incompatible types of people, invariably between contemporaries and people who exist only in the past and/or in art.[25] The poetry lies precisely in the uneasy confrontation of difference, which raises questions of the relationship between art and life, and between the present and the past. To take just one example, *Caprice #1* shows a magnificent Ottoman potentate seemingly offering charity to an old man who is either a Greek philosopher or a hermit saint, in a grand interior set against the background of a semi-ruined classical city. Entering the room is a group of youngish males, who appear to be contemporary tourists, coming off an eighteenth-century European street. All of this is highly incongruous, but then it says something about our ambiguous yet sometimes casual attitude toward the past.

His final group, *Elegies* (plates 46–55), drawn in the last year of his life, consists of ten drawings. All of the artist's drawing series have a large element of fantasy, of the conjuring of worlds beyond mundane experience, but *Elegies* takes this tendency to a new poetic level. The drawings are unified by a relatively even touch of the pen and an allover quality that recalls Day's Abstract Expressionist paintings. The emphasis is firmly on architecture, extraordinary in its variety and density, varying between Italian medieval expansiveness, modern cities, and ruins being assessed for rebuilding. There is no obvious narrative, though there are hints of architectural intervention among the groups of figures in each drawing contemplating the urban fabric. Other drawings from the 1990s reflect similar tendencies.

How to sum up Larry Day's achievement as an artist? I want to attempt this by focusing briefly on one of the latest paintings in the exhibition: *Dialogue,* depicting in its final form Day and his friend Mervin Richard, then head of exhibition conservation and, more recently, chief of conservation at the National Gallery of Art.[26] It shows the two men in conversation: Richard is animated, Day is contemplative, even resigned. There are hints of the relationship between Plato pointing to heaven and Aristotle to earth in Raphael's *School of Athens,* which is in turn suggestive of the contrast between the *vita activa* and *vita contemplativa*. (One can be sure that Day would have read *The Human Condition,* Hannah Arendt's 1958 book on the contrast between the two.) There is something humorous in the artist's abjection surrounded by evidence of his host's expertise as a packer of works of art.

The setting is a construction site in Washington, DC, probably inspired by work along 7th Street near the National Gallery. It is connected with buildings that do not resemble the museum, where the two men often met in the 1990s. But then it is also a self-referential space, beautifully complex and rational, referring to Day's site paintings rather than those that normally contain figures. The work is evidence that by the end of his career Day had achieved a wonderful fluency in the interplay between all his different accomplishments: philosophical, literary and artistic, figural and architectural. It was no longer for him as it had been in his early career, a matter of "just this and that," but "and that and that" ad infinitum.

## Notes

1   "Balthus: The Turkish Room," unpublished manuscript, courtesy of Ruth Fine.

2   Robert Hughes, *The Spectacle of Skill: Selected Writings of Robert Hughes* (New York: Vintage Books, 2016), 77.

3   Larry Day, oral history by Marina Pacini, February 21, 1991, Archives of American Art, Smithsonian Institution, 104.

4   Timothy Hyman, *The World New Made: Figurative Painting in the Twentieth Century* (New York: Thames & Hudson, 2016), 197.

5   Alex Potts, *Experiments in Modern Realism* (New Haven, CT: Yale University Press, 2013), 155–96.

6   Day, oral history, 100.

7   See *The Poker Game and Its Circle*, digital exhibition catalogue, Woodmere Art Museum, 2013, https://issuu.com /woodmereartmuseum/docs/poker _game_8.8.2013_final_12.

8   Day, oral history, 58.

9   *Propos rapport par Joachim Gasquet*, Cézanne, 1921 (*Paul Cézanne,* Paroles d'Artiste, n.d., 26), in *Paul Cézanne, Letters,* ed. John Rewald, 1984.

10   Day, oral history, 123–24.

11   Day, oral history, 124.

12   Day, oral history, 110. Nichols, a painter also, was one of Day's colleagues at the University of the Arts, Philadelphia.

13   Larry Day, manuscript notebook, 29–30, courtesy of Ruth Fine.

14   Day, oral history, 119.

15   Day, oral history, 46–47.

16   Day, oral history, 105.

17   Day, oral history, 120.

18   Day, oral history, 128.

19   Day, oral history, 115.

20   Day, oral history, 107.

21   Day, oral history, 113.

22   Day, oral history, 113.

23   H. Diane Russell, *Rare Etchings by Giovanni Battista and Giovanni Domenico Tiepolo* (Washington, DC: National Gallery of Art, 1972). Russell was a friend of Day's and owned an important architectural painting by him titled *Parking Garage*.

24   John Hollander, "Introduction," in *Tempi del Giorno* (Lawrenceville: Rider College Art Gallery and Cullowhee: Belk Art Gallery, Western Carolina University). Day's name was not legally changed to Lawrence Day until 1985, owing to a legal requirement when he moved to Maryland.

25   The series is reproduced in *Larry Day: Ironic Realist* (Roanoke, VA: Eleanor D. Wilson Museum, 2008), https://www.hollins.edu /museum/catalogs/documents/larryday _cat.pdf.

26   In earlier drawings the figure with Richard is not Day but his friend William Bowser, who worked in the design and installation division of the National Gallery of Art, Washington, DC.

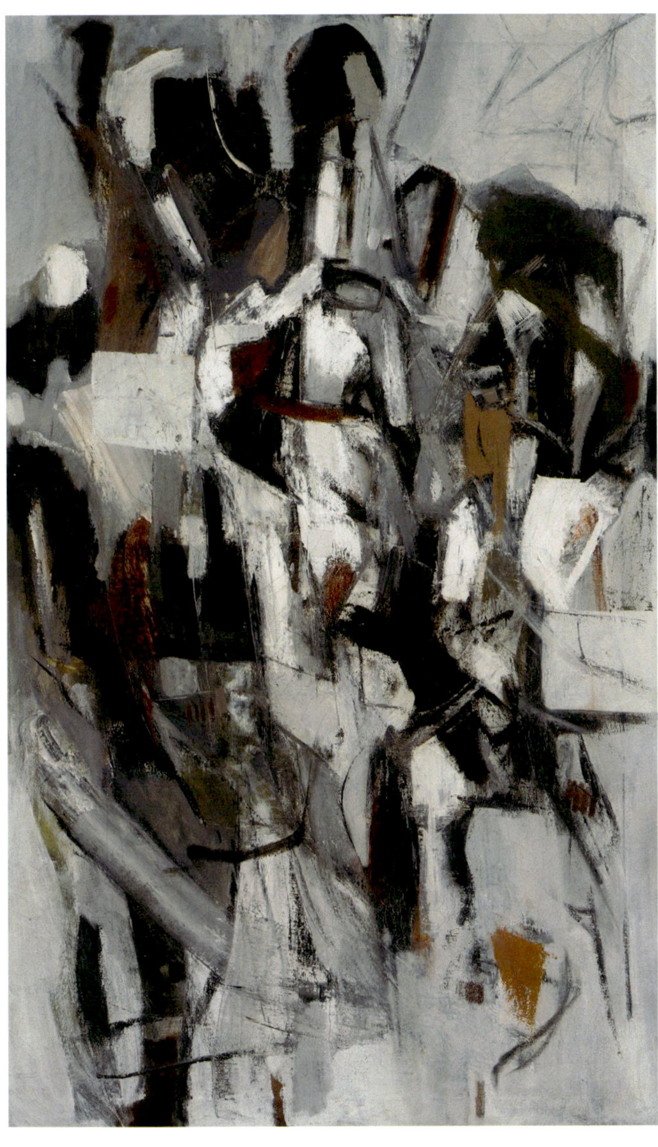



PLATE 2
*(Abstract Figure [Natalie Charkow?])*, c. 1955

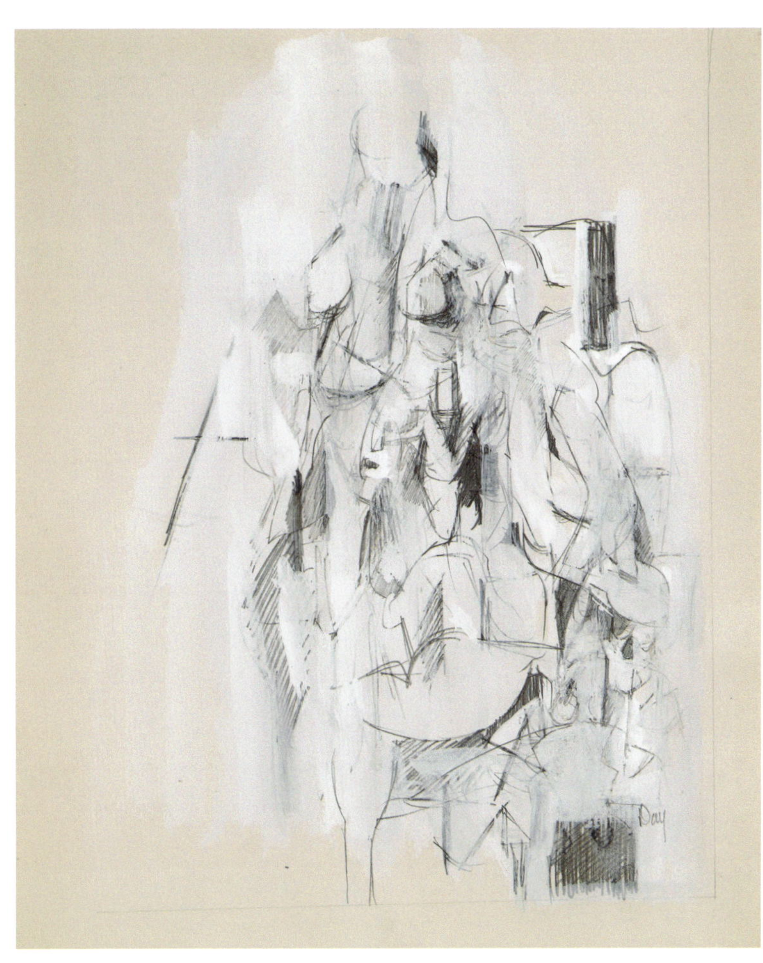

PLATE 3
*(Abstract Figure)*, c. 1955

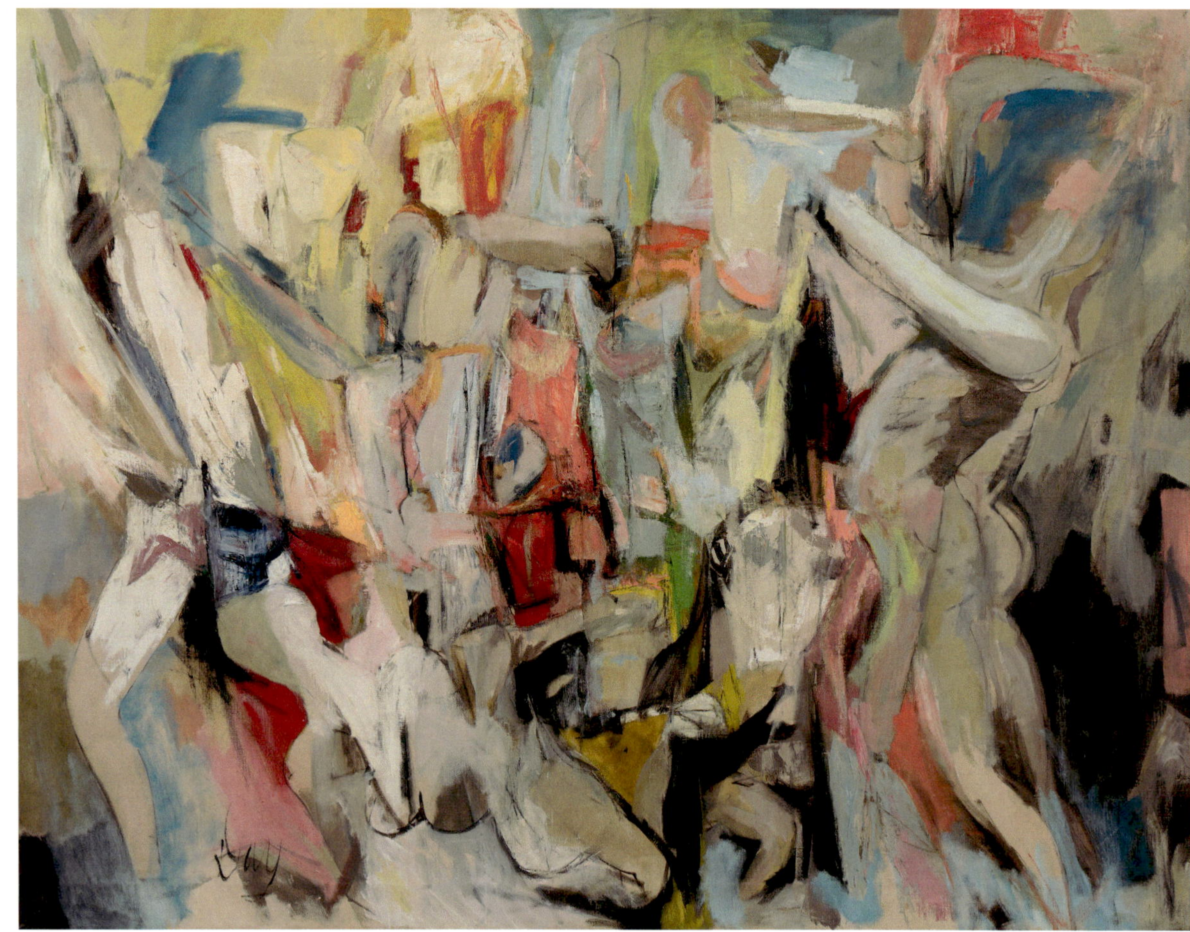

PLATE 4
*To Pergamon*, 1958–59

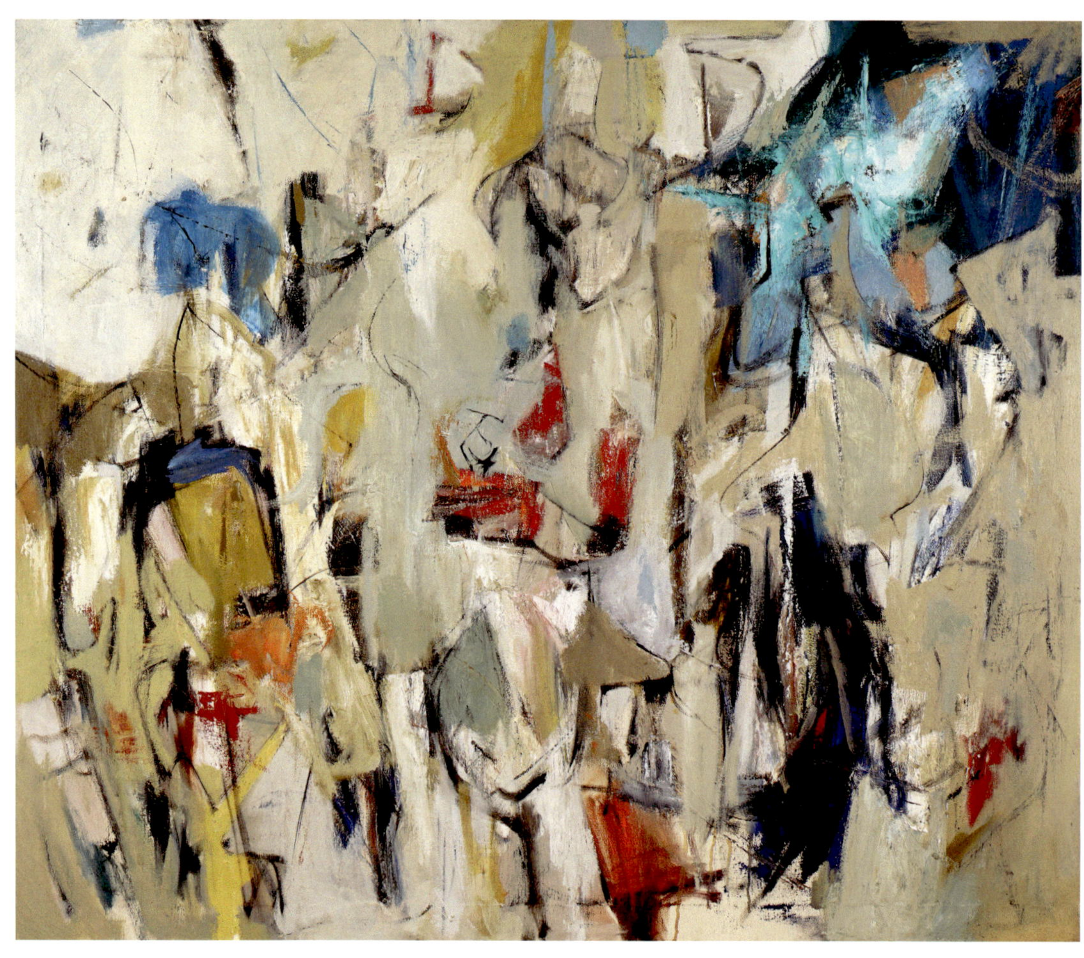

PLATE 5
*Journey*, 1956

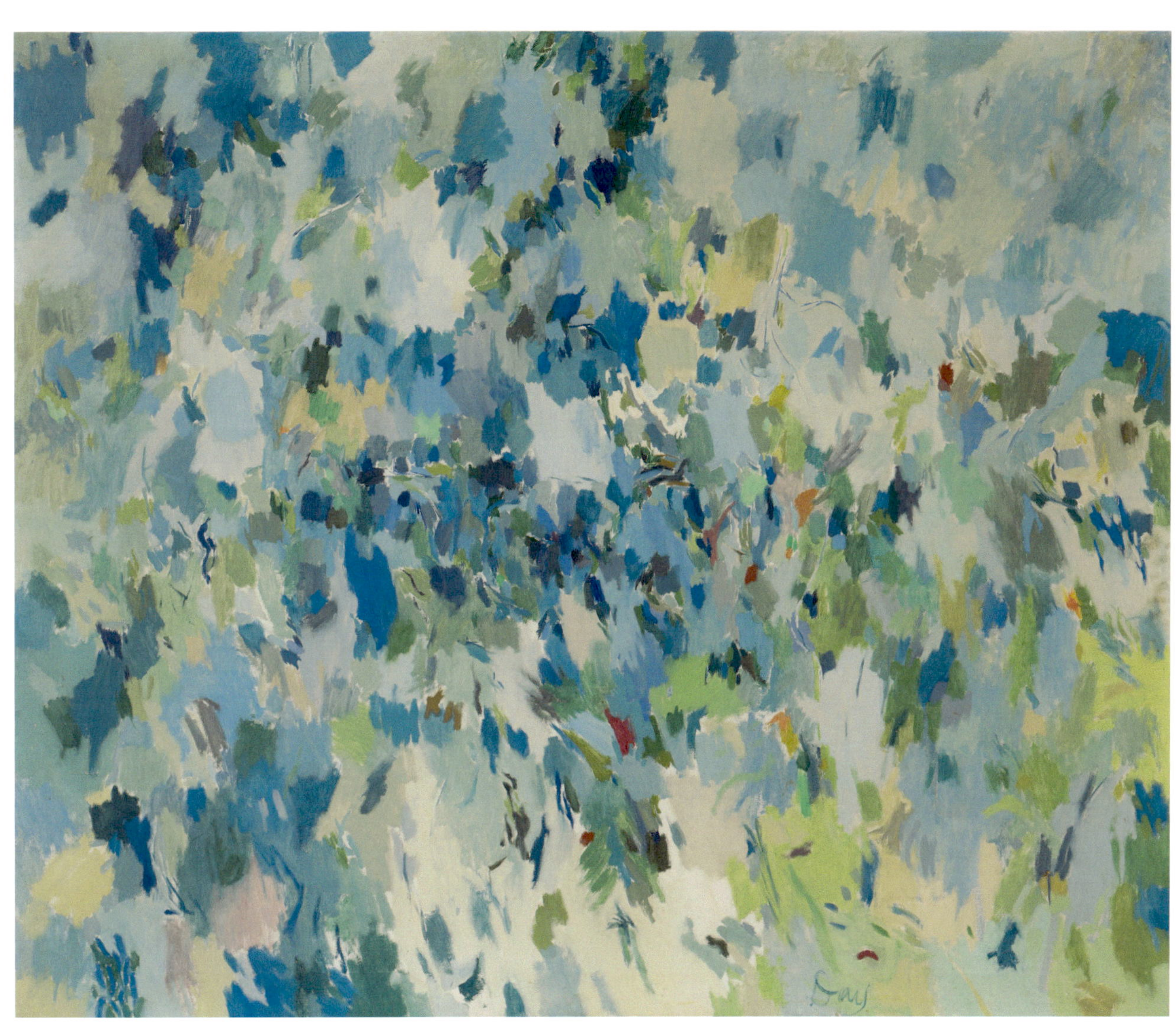



PLATE 6
*Abstraction*, c. 1958

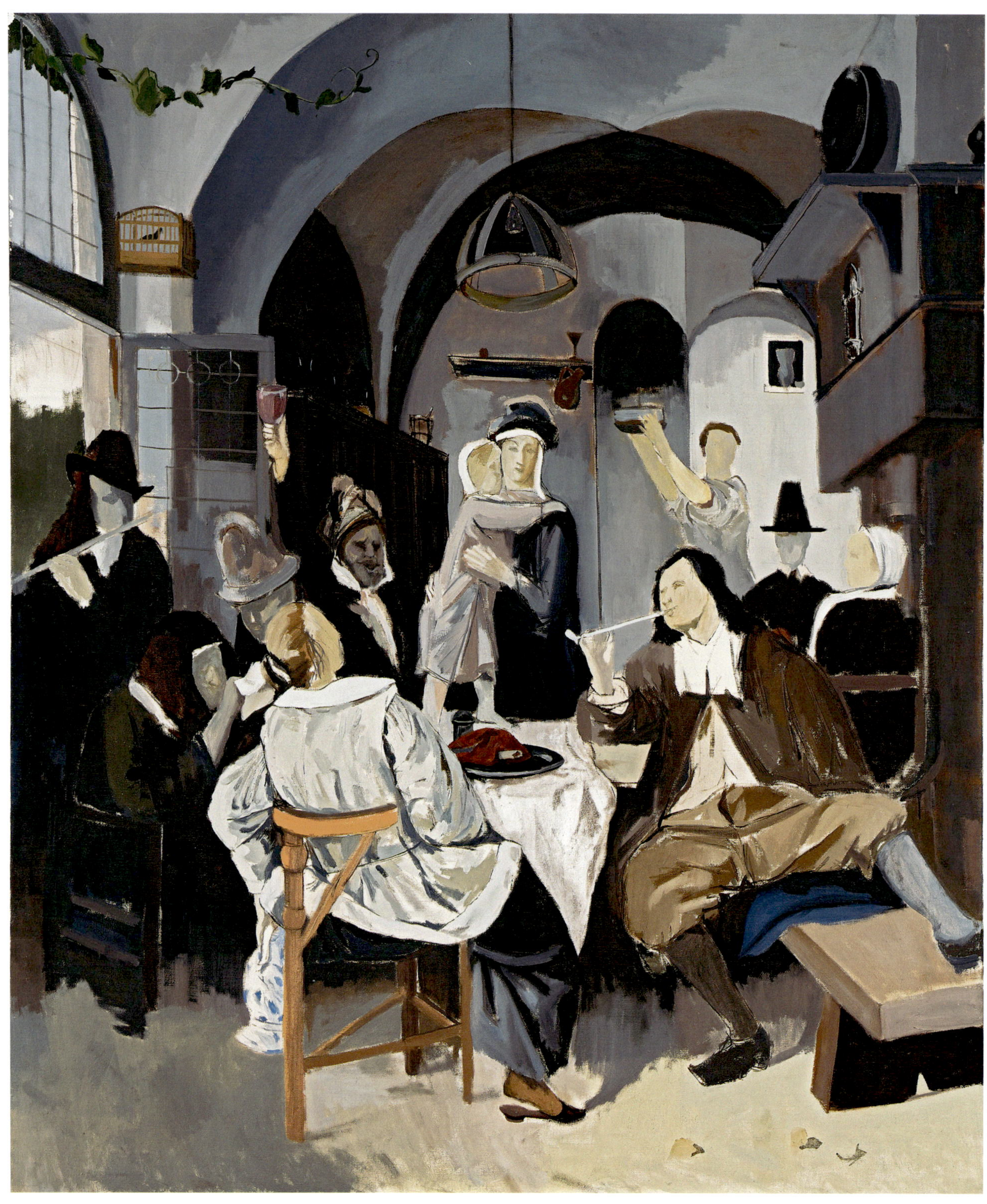

PLATE 7
*After Jan Steen*, 1962

28

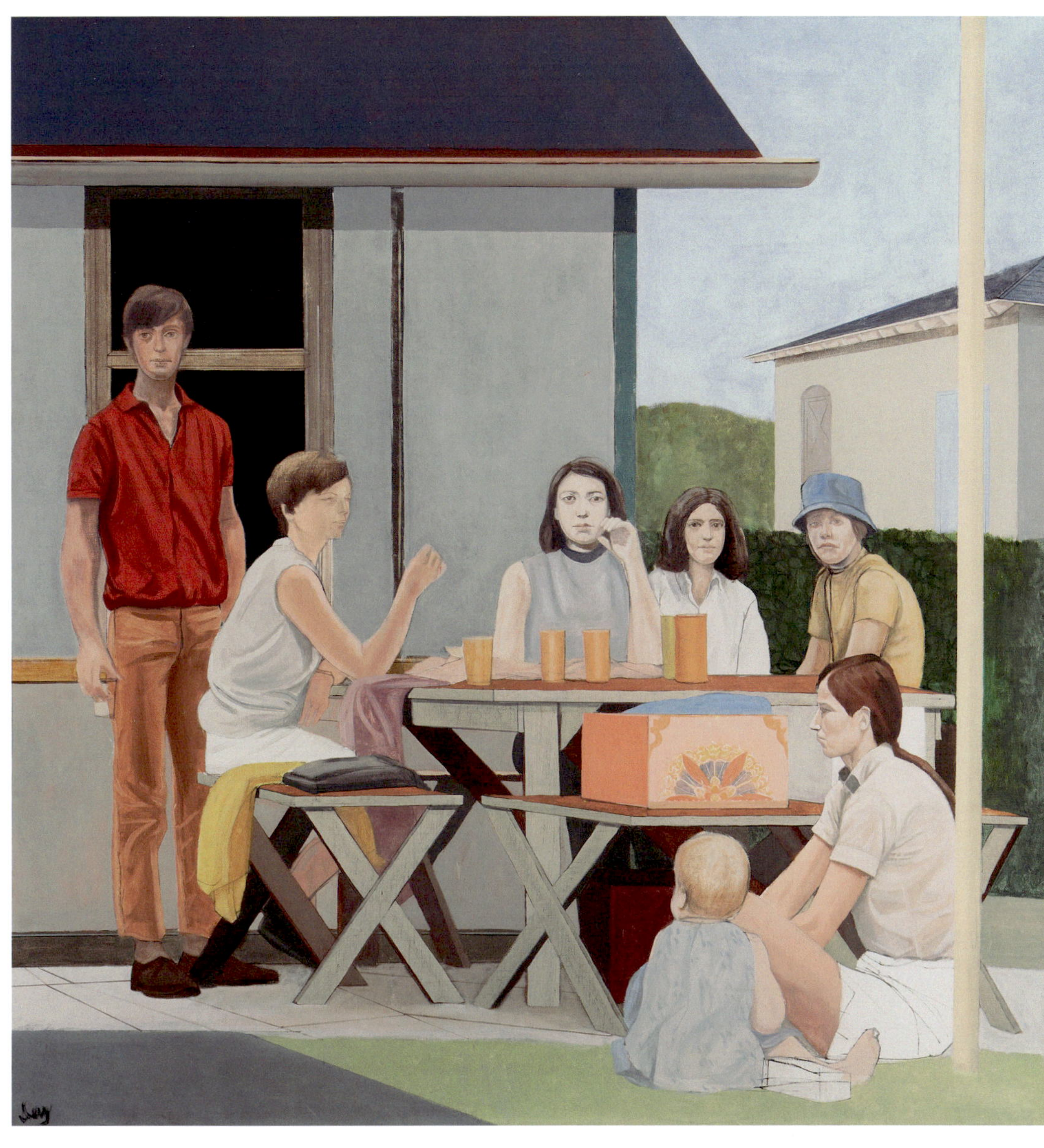


PLATE 8
*Picnic (Outing: Homage to Le Nain)*, 1970–75


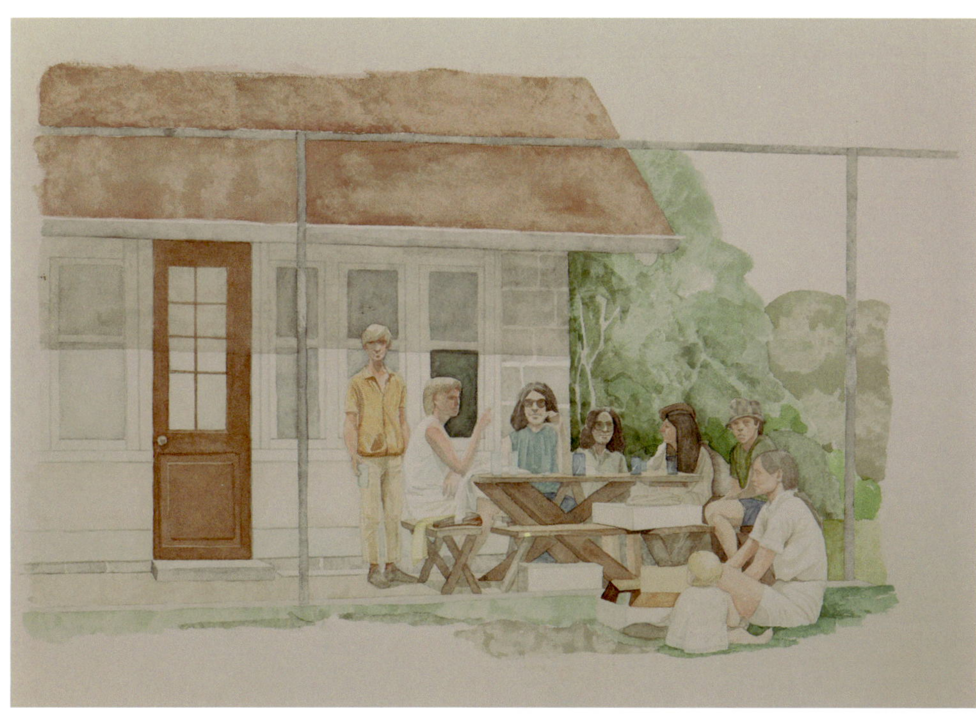


PLATE 9
*Related to "Picnic (Outing: Homage to Le Nain),"* c. 1975

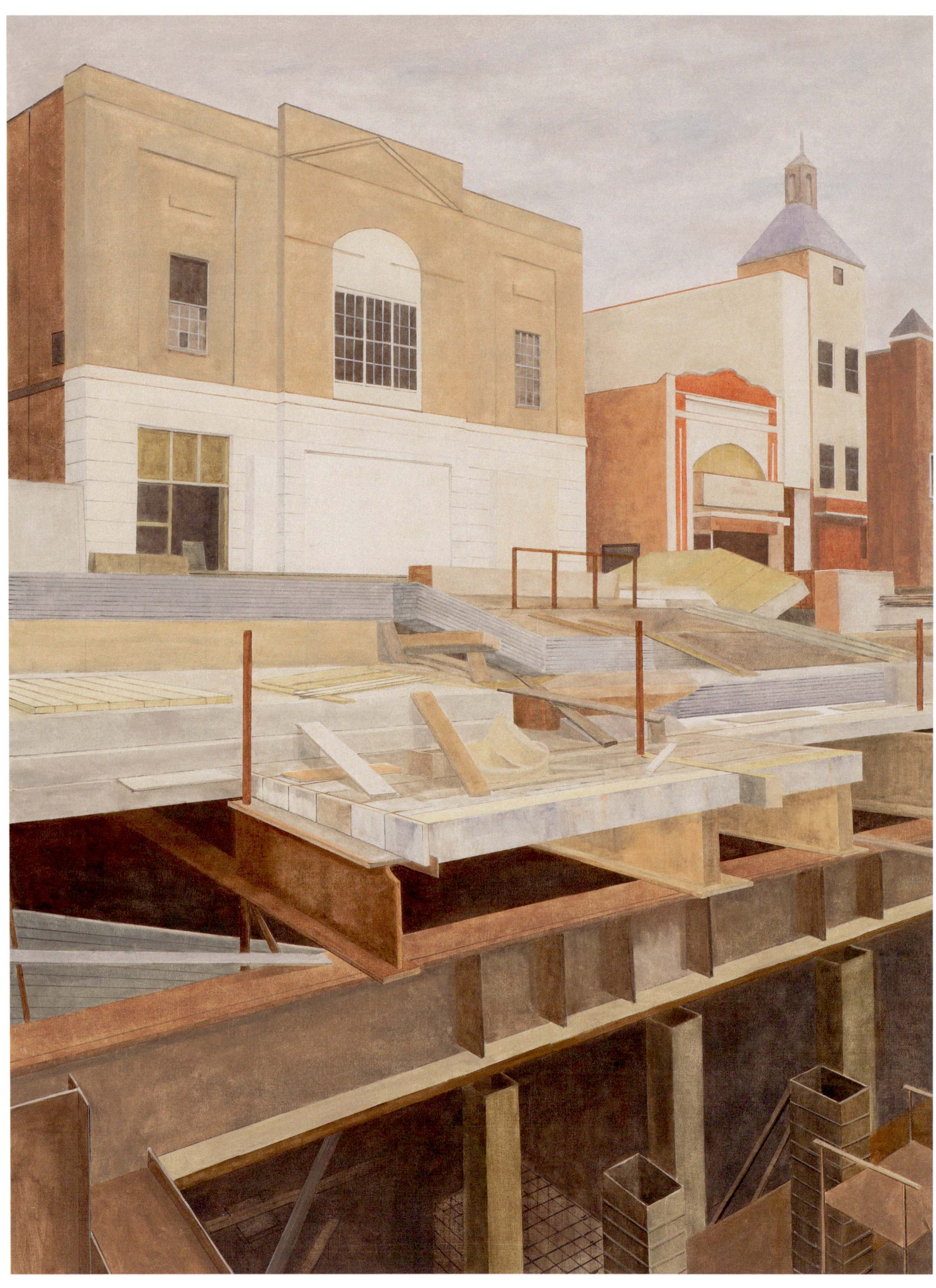

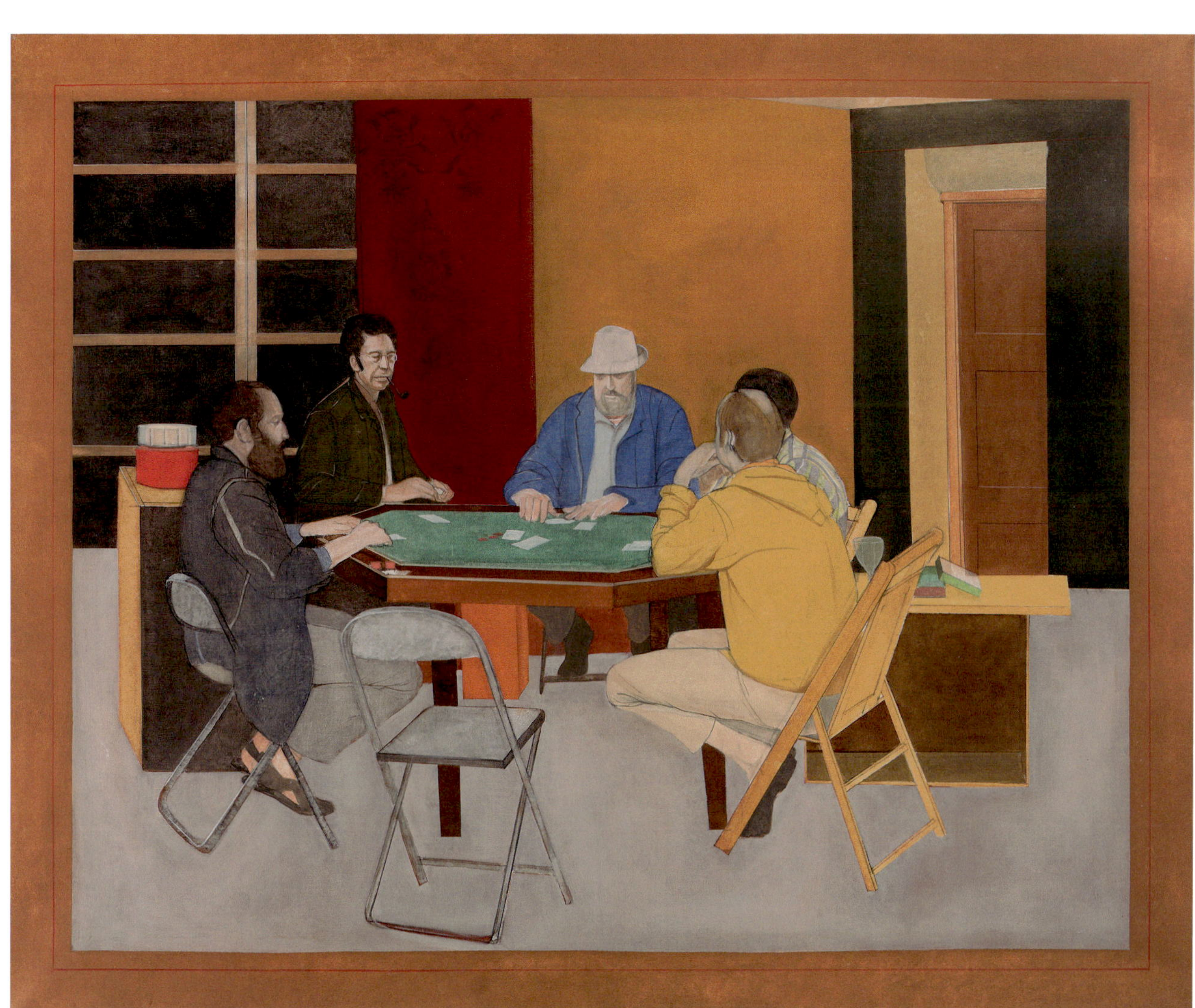

PLATE 11
*Poker Game*, 1970

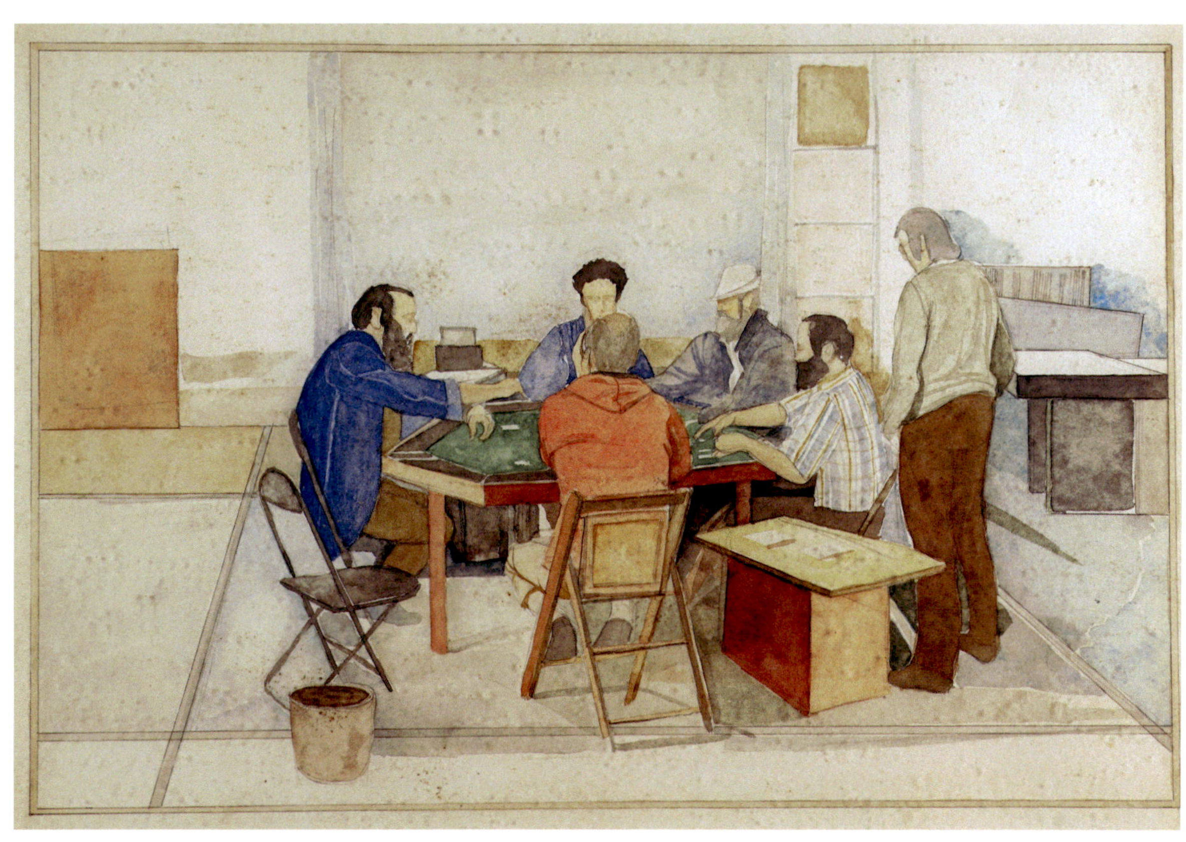

PLATE 12
*(Poker Game)*,
c. 1970

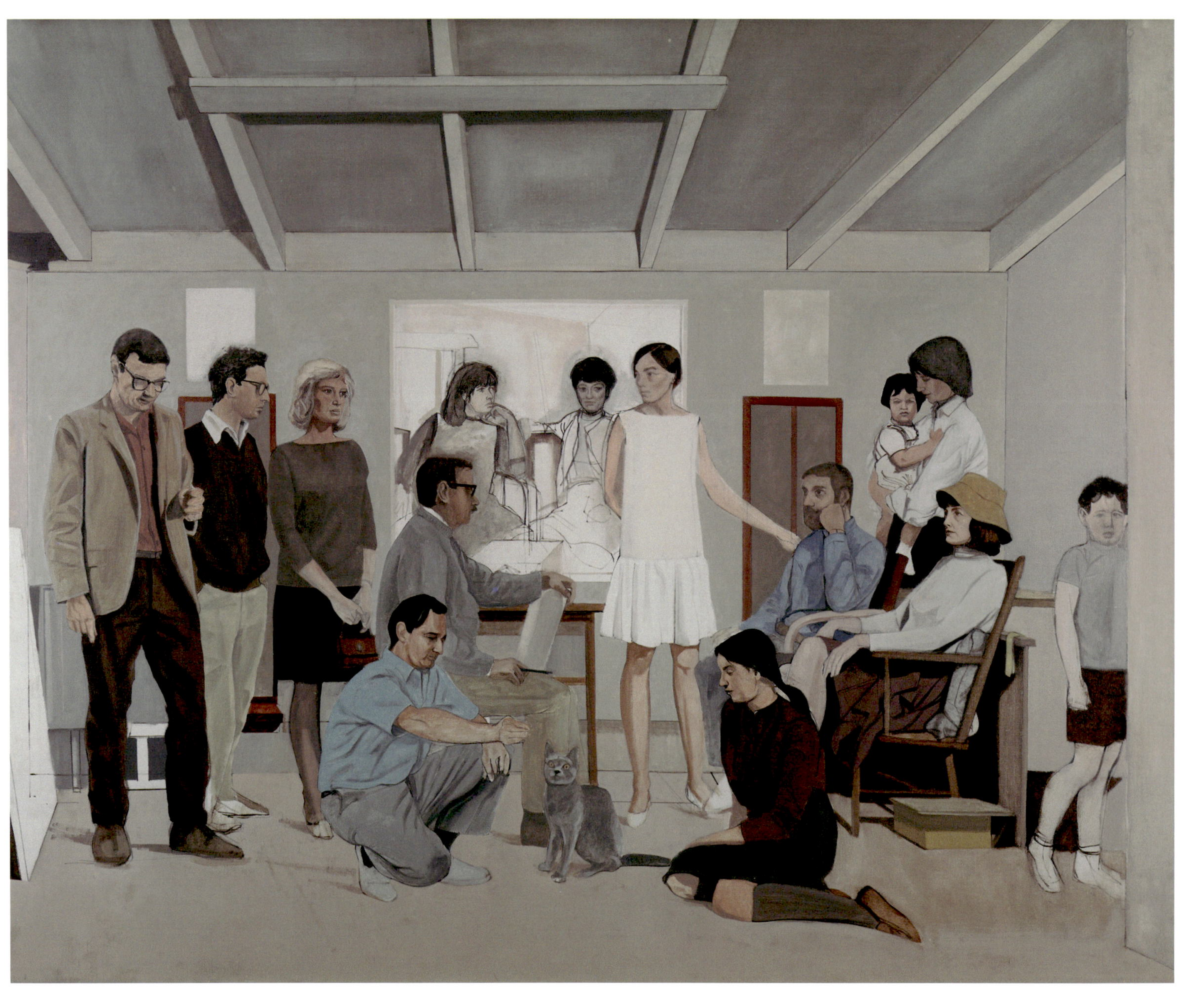

PLATE 13
*Group,* 1967

32

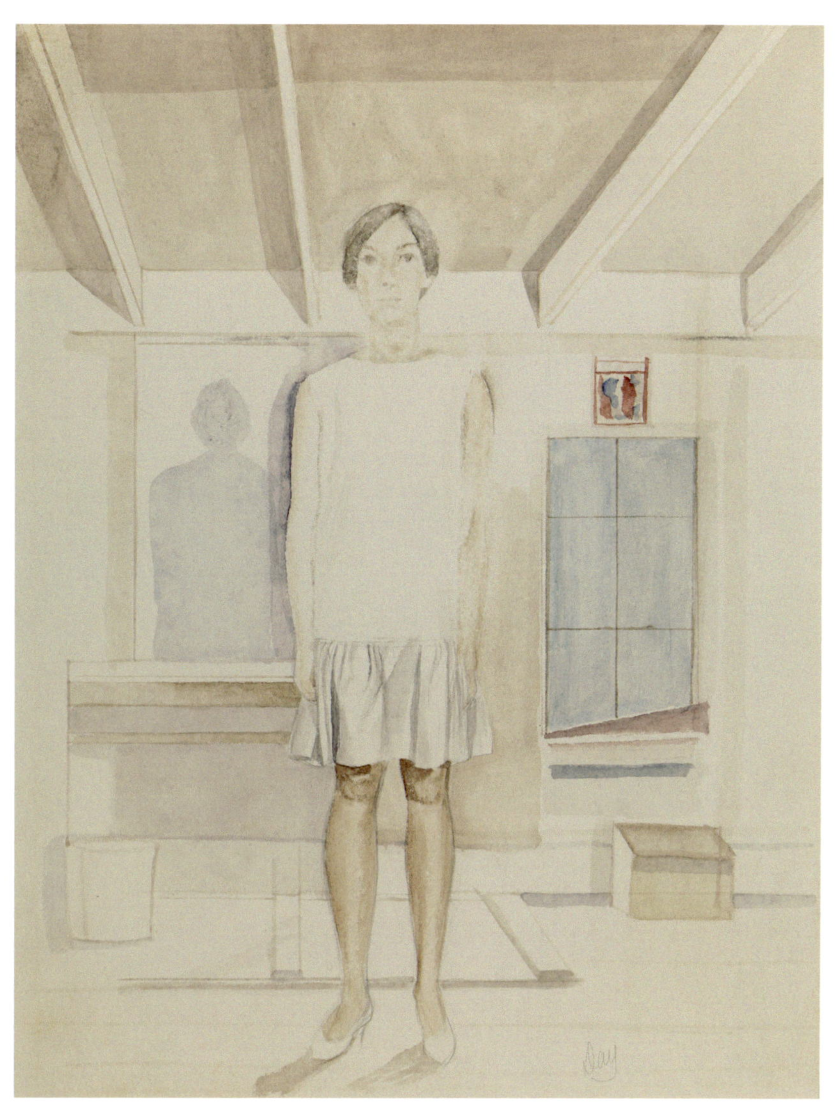

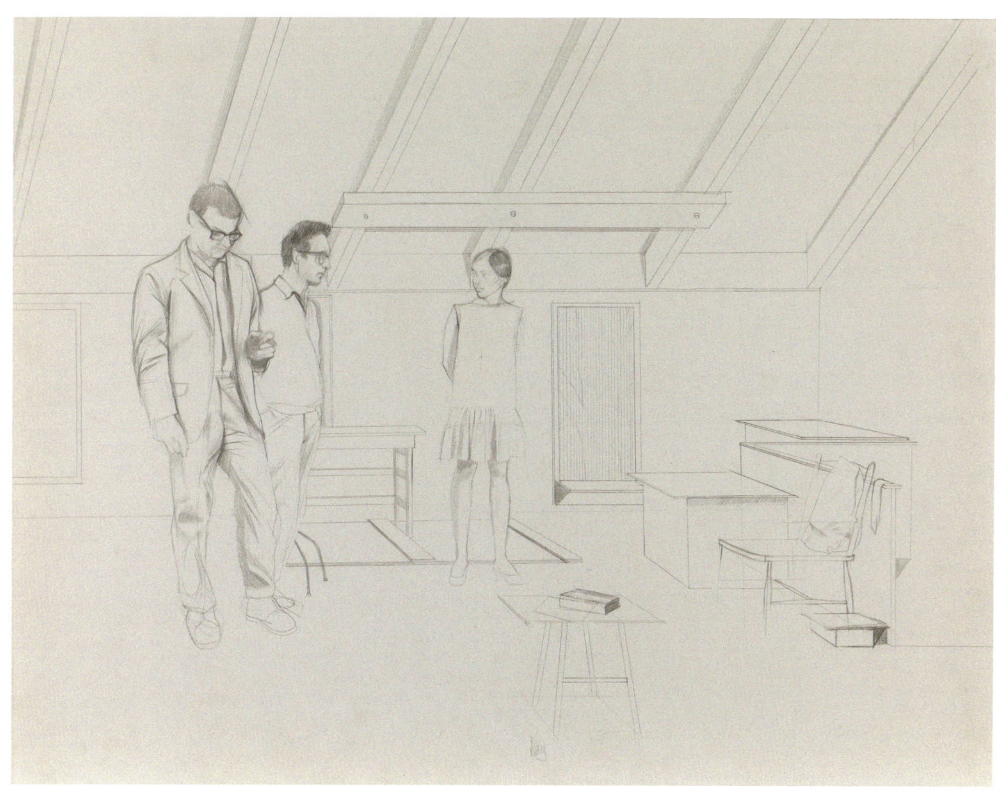

PLATE 14
*Untitled, study for "Group,"* c. 1967

PLATE 15
*In the Studio, study for "Group,"* c. 1967

PLATE 16

*Miss Charkow and
Mrs. Melnicoff*, c. 1967

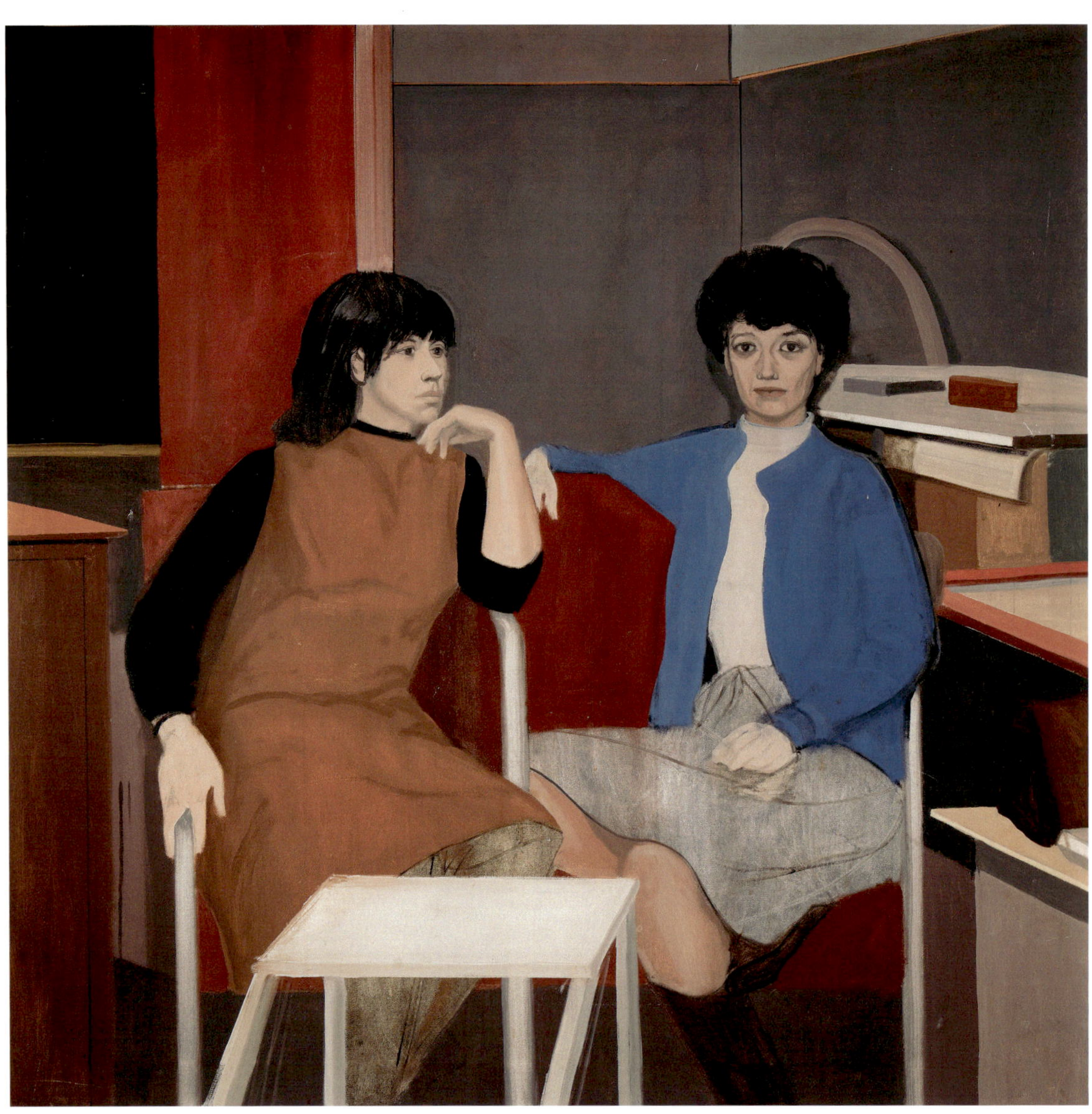

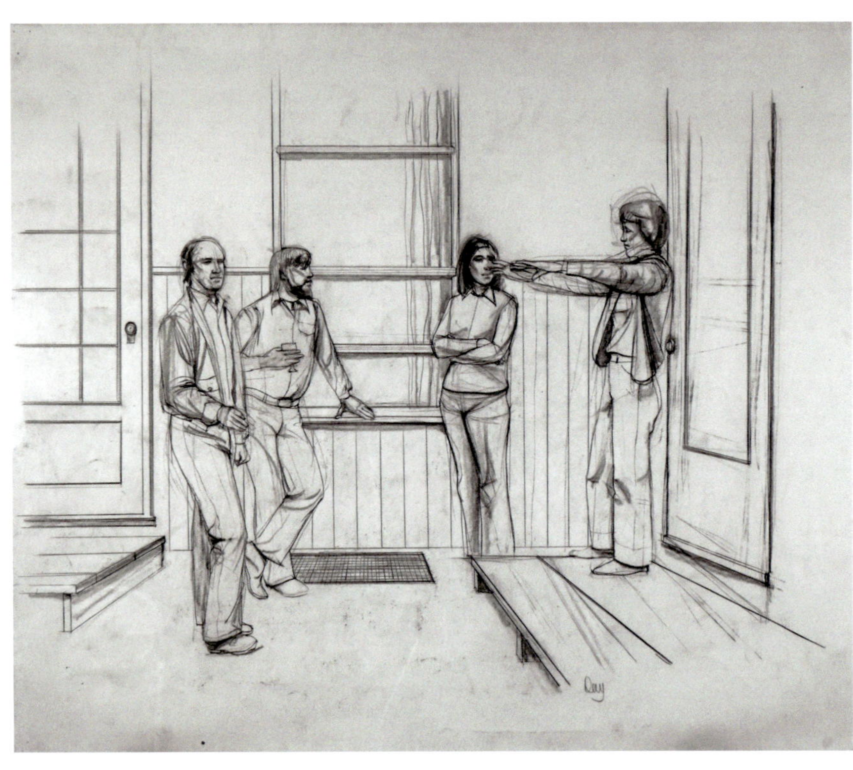

PLATE 17

*(Couples)*, c. 1970

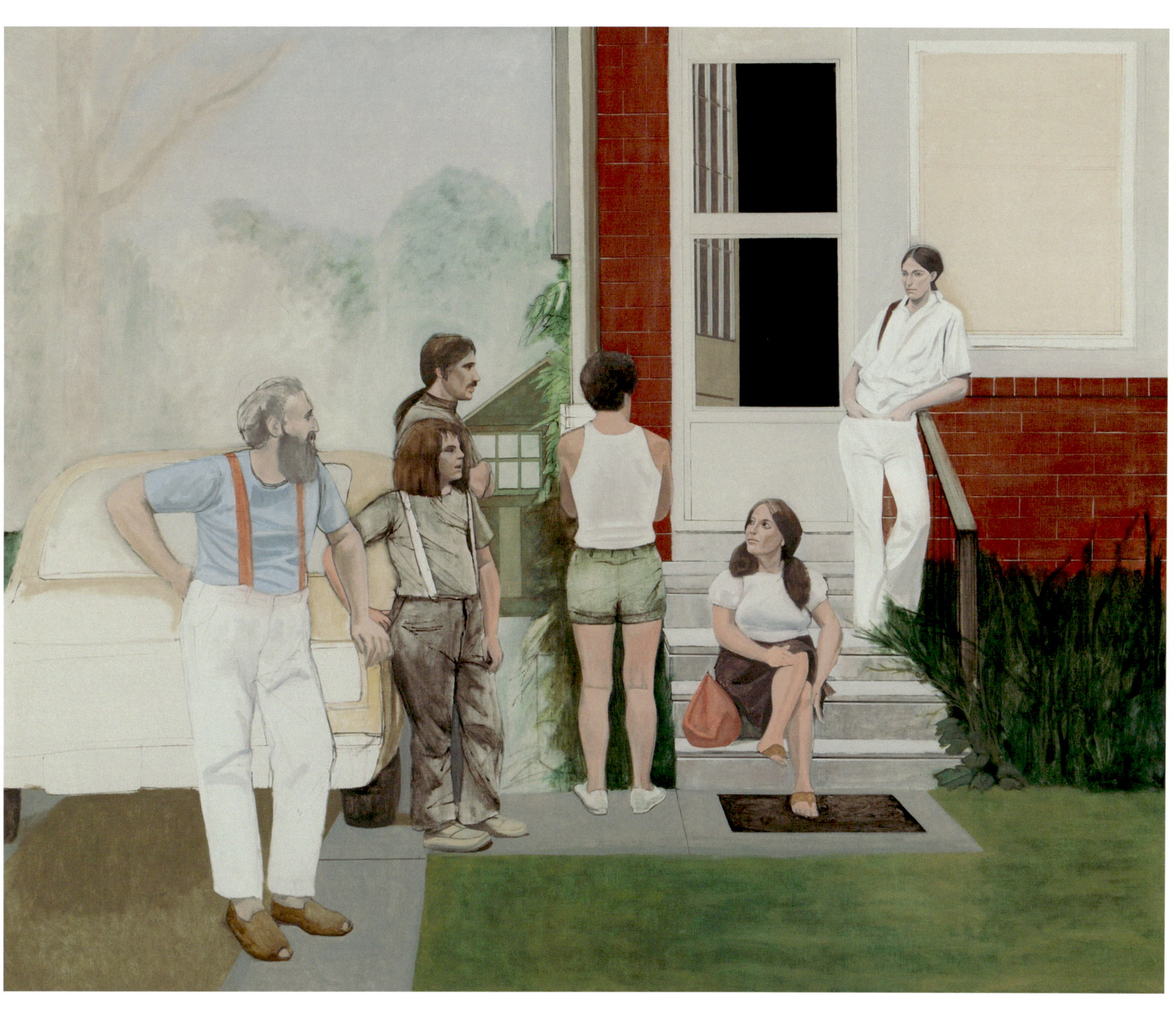

PLATE 18
*Conversation Piece I,*
1973–74

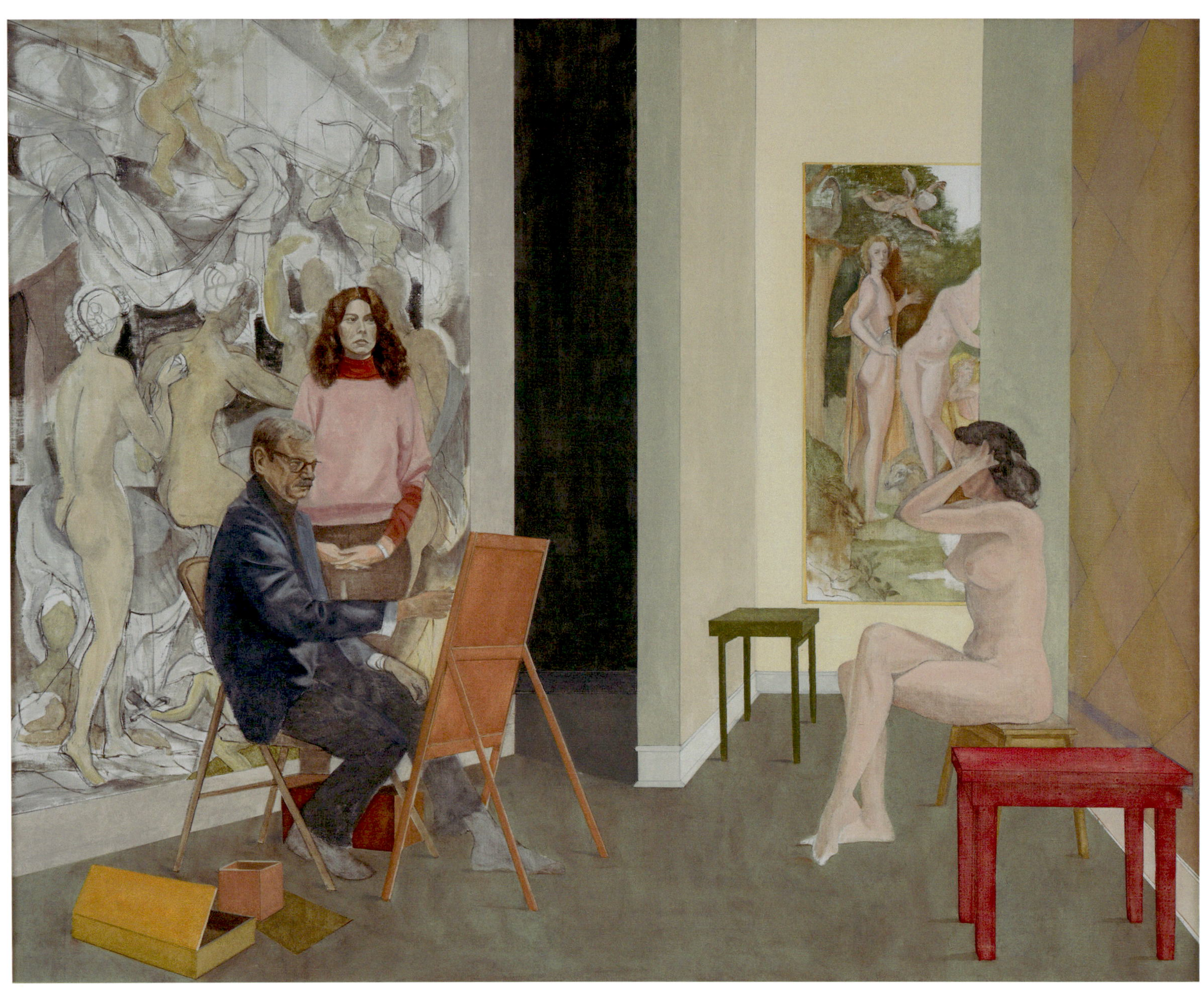

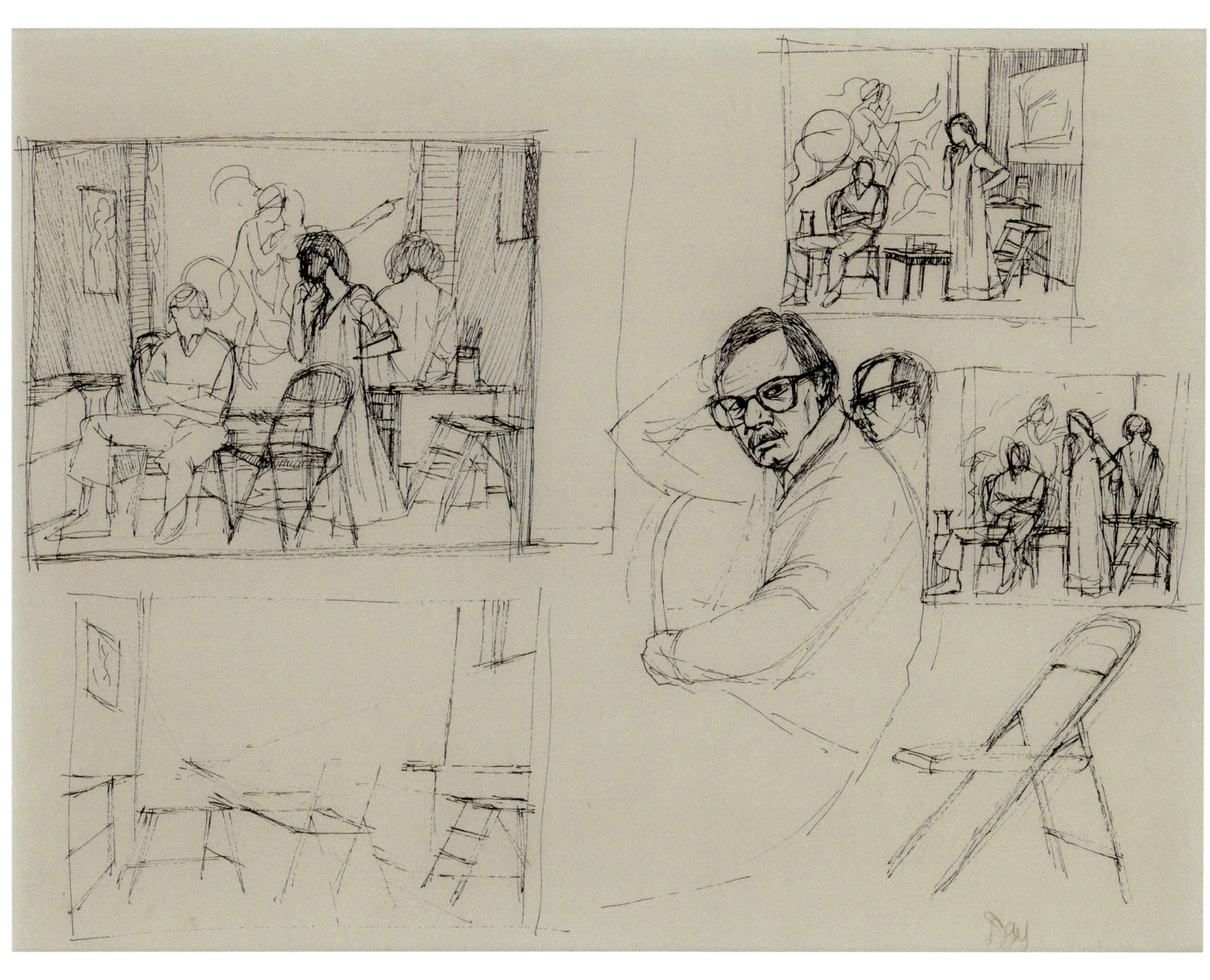



37    *Related to "Break,"* 1981

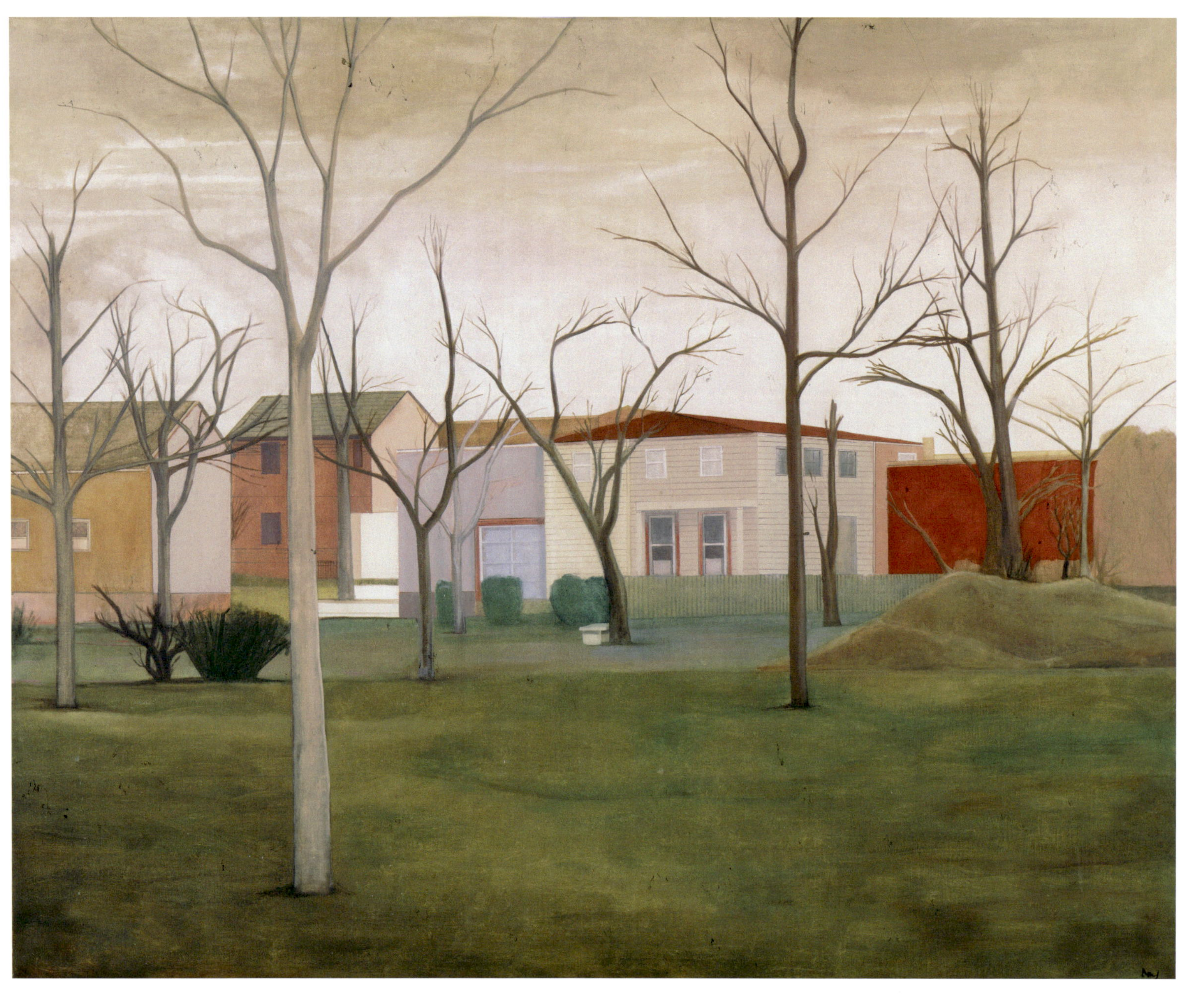

PLATE 22
*Yard II*, 1978

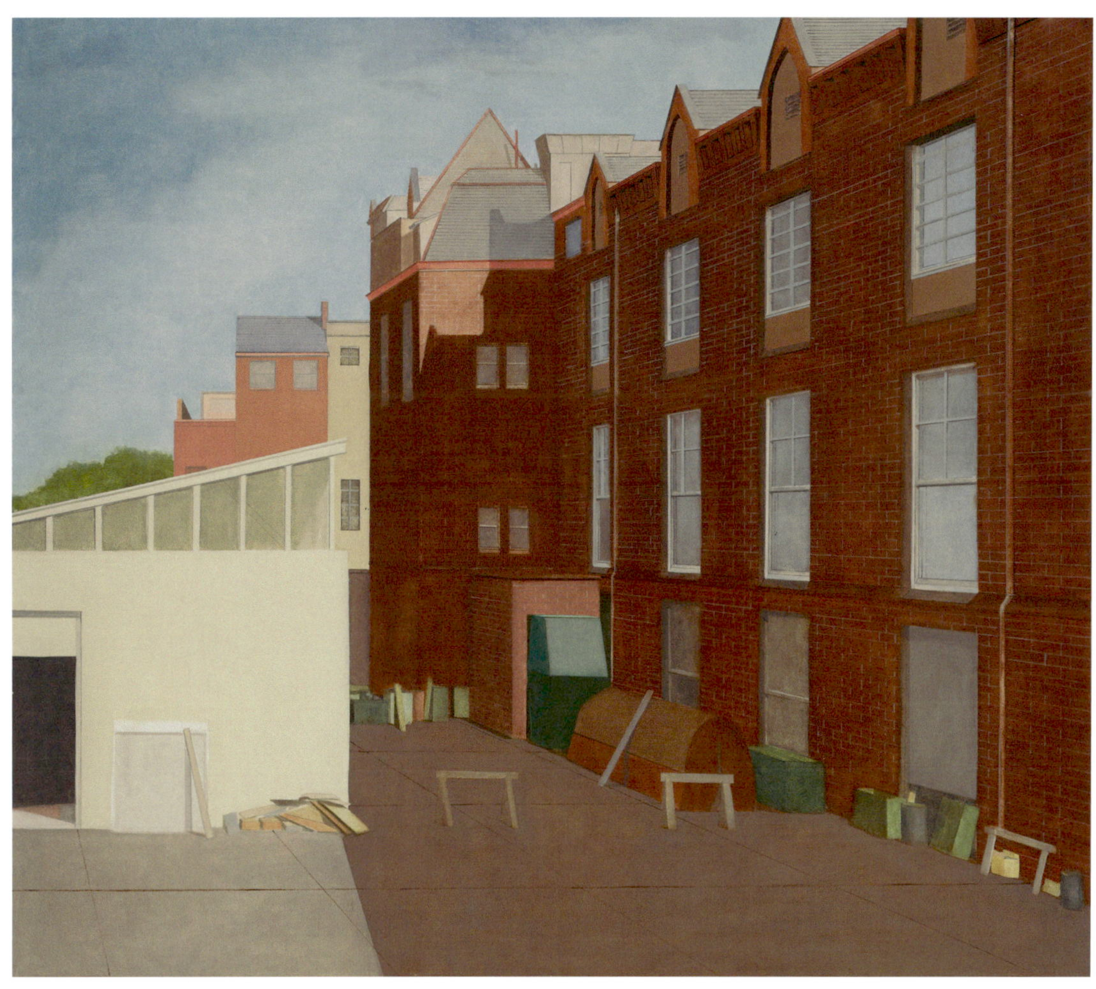

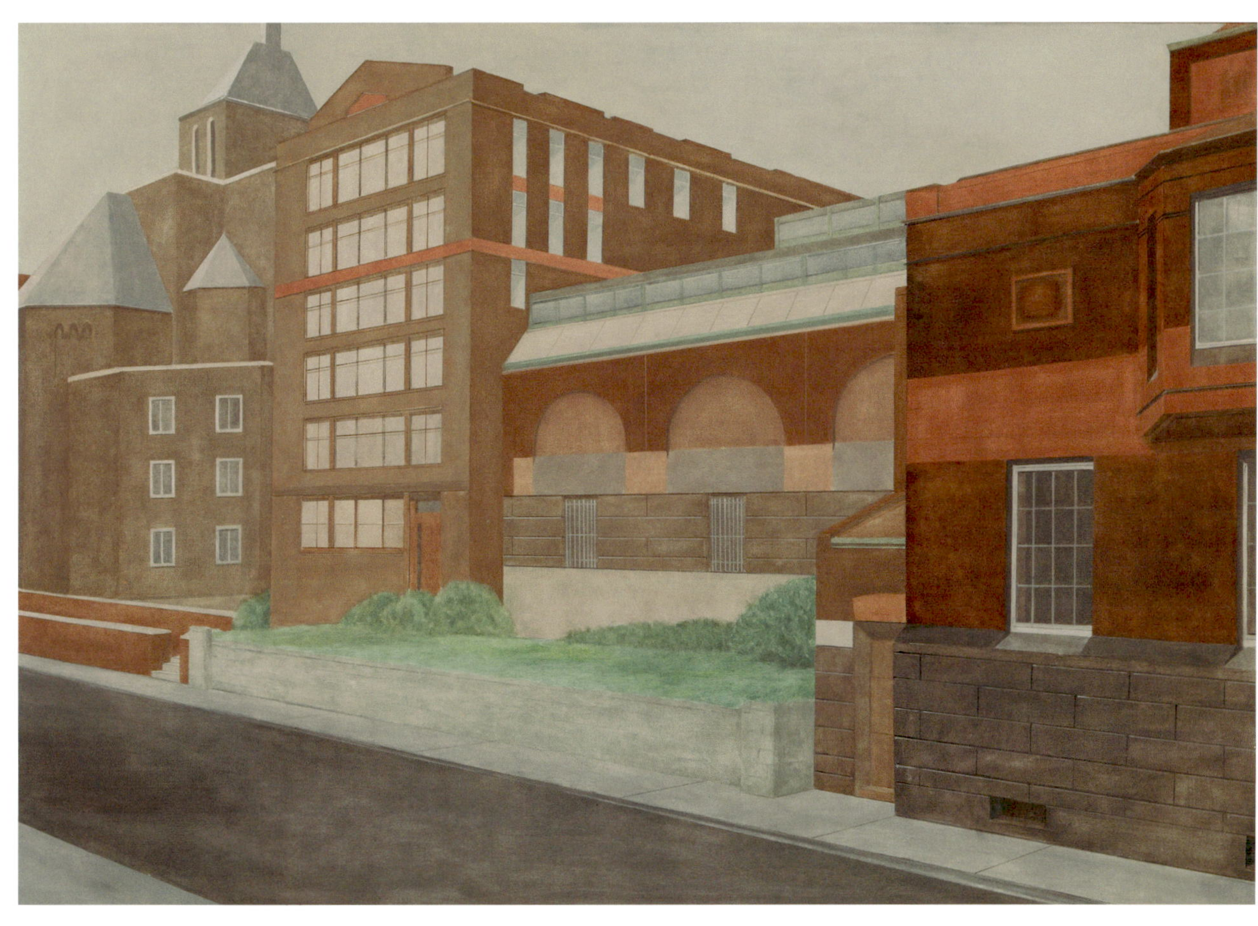

PLATE 23
*34th Street*,
c. 1980

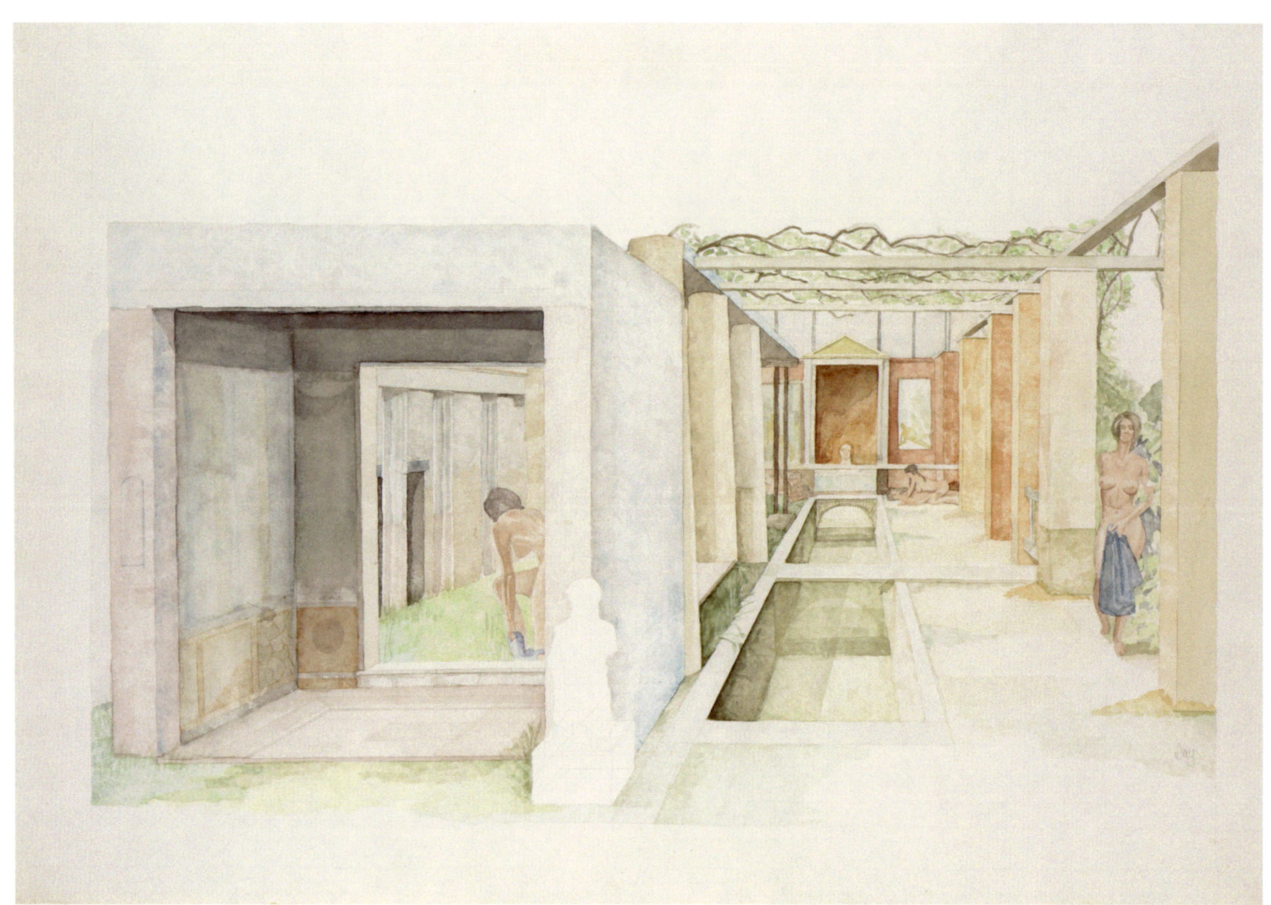

PLATE 24
*The Foundation*

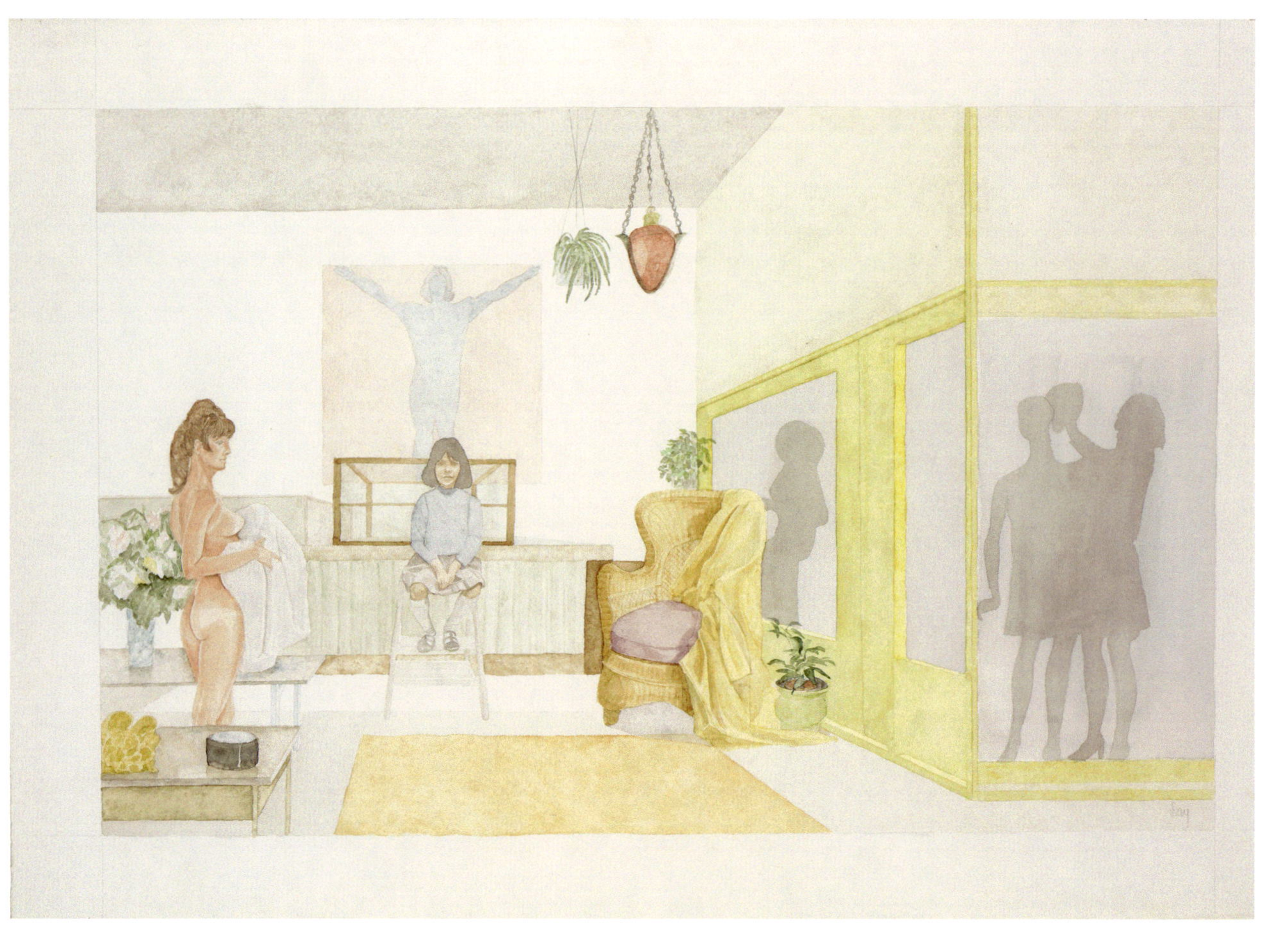

PLATE 25
*The Establishment
of Ritual*

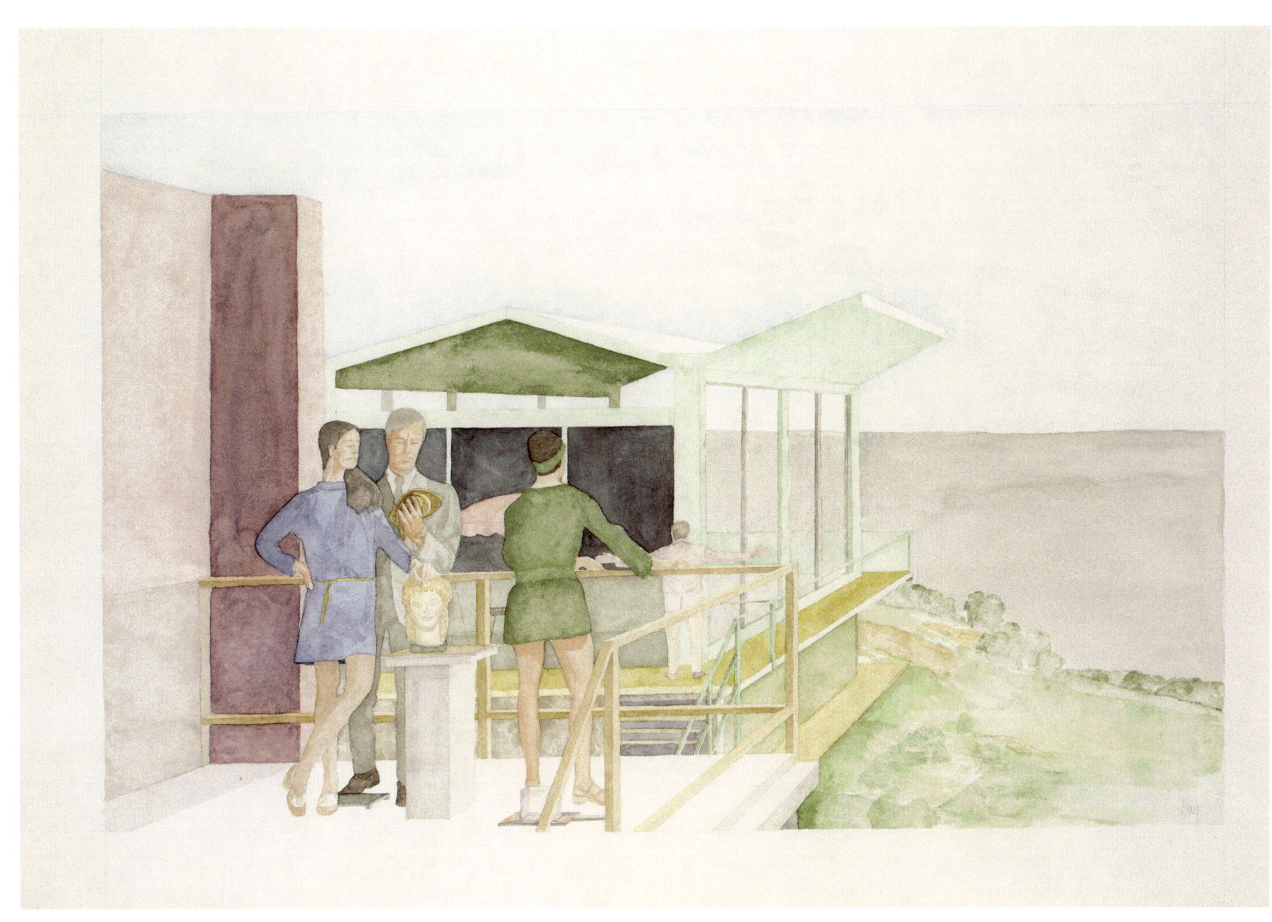

PLATE 26
*The Discovery of
Another Society*

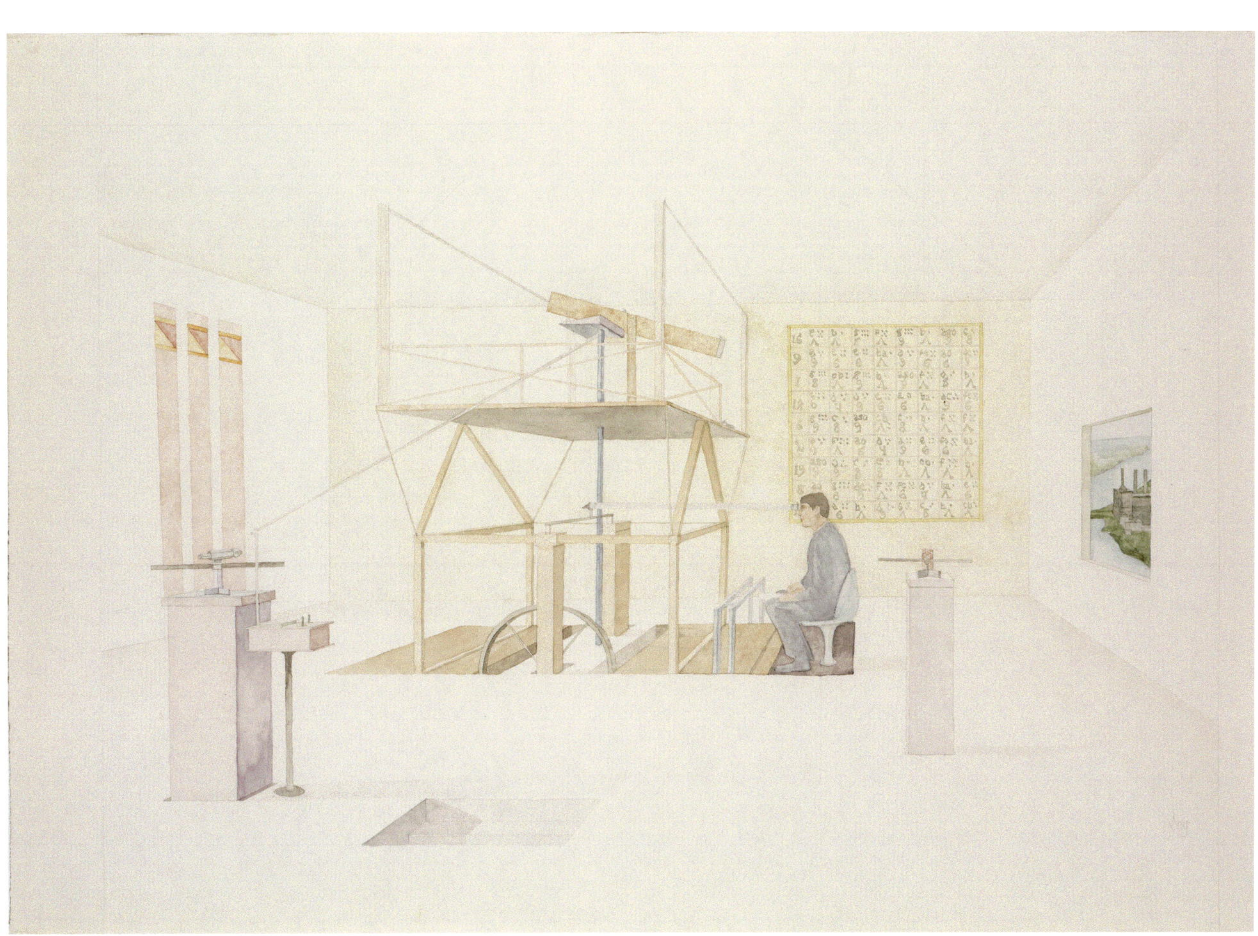

PLATE 27
*The Other
Society's Base*

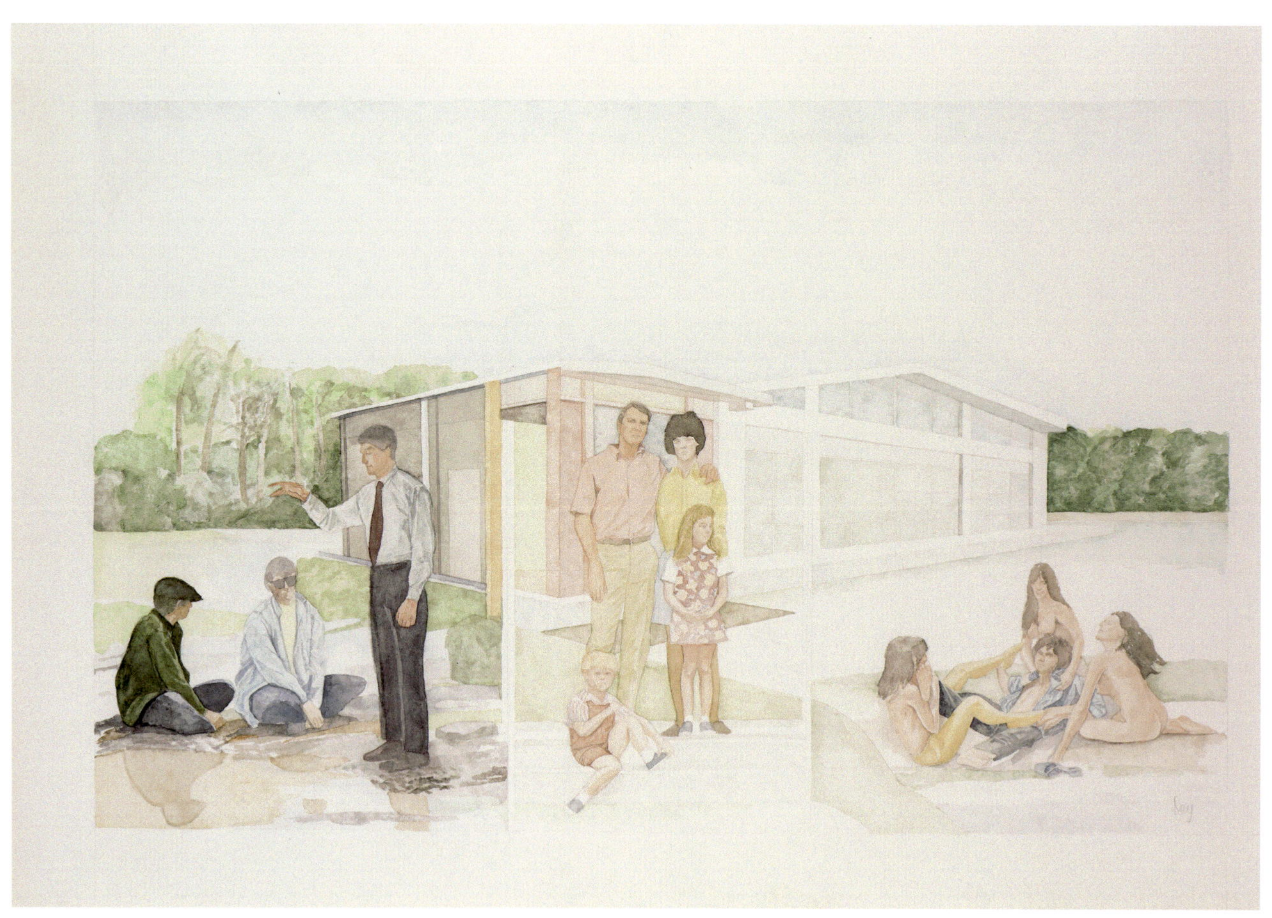

PLATE 28
The Struggle for
the Uncommitted

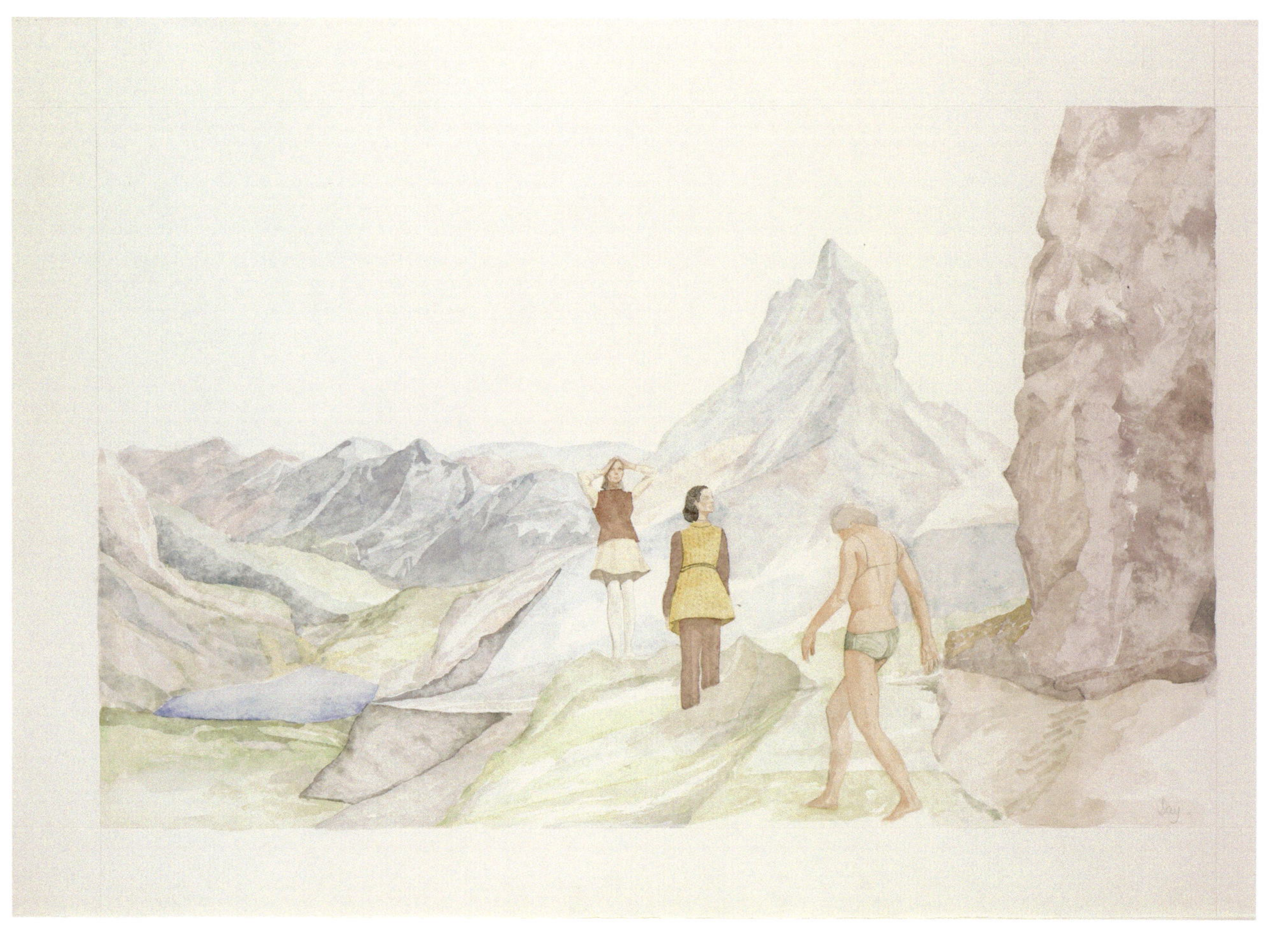

PLATE 29
The Search,
Atonement

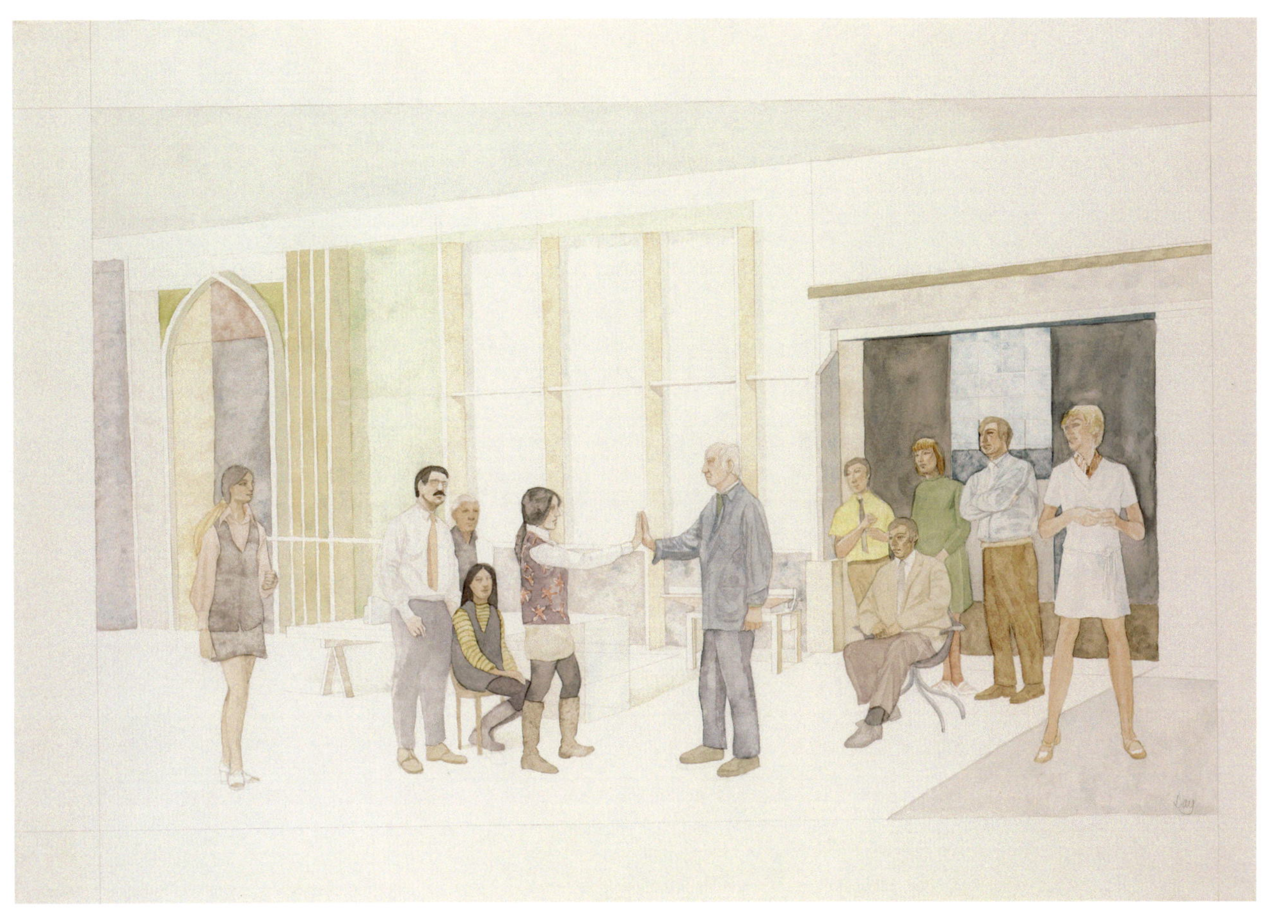

PLATE 30
*The Merger*

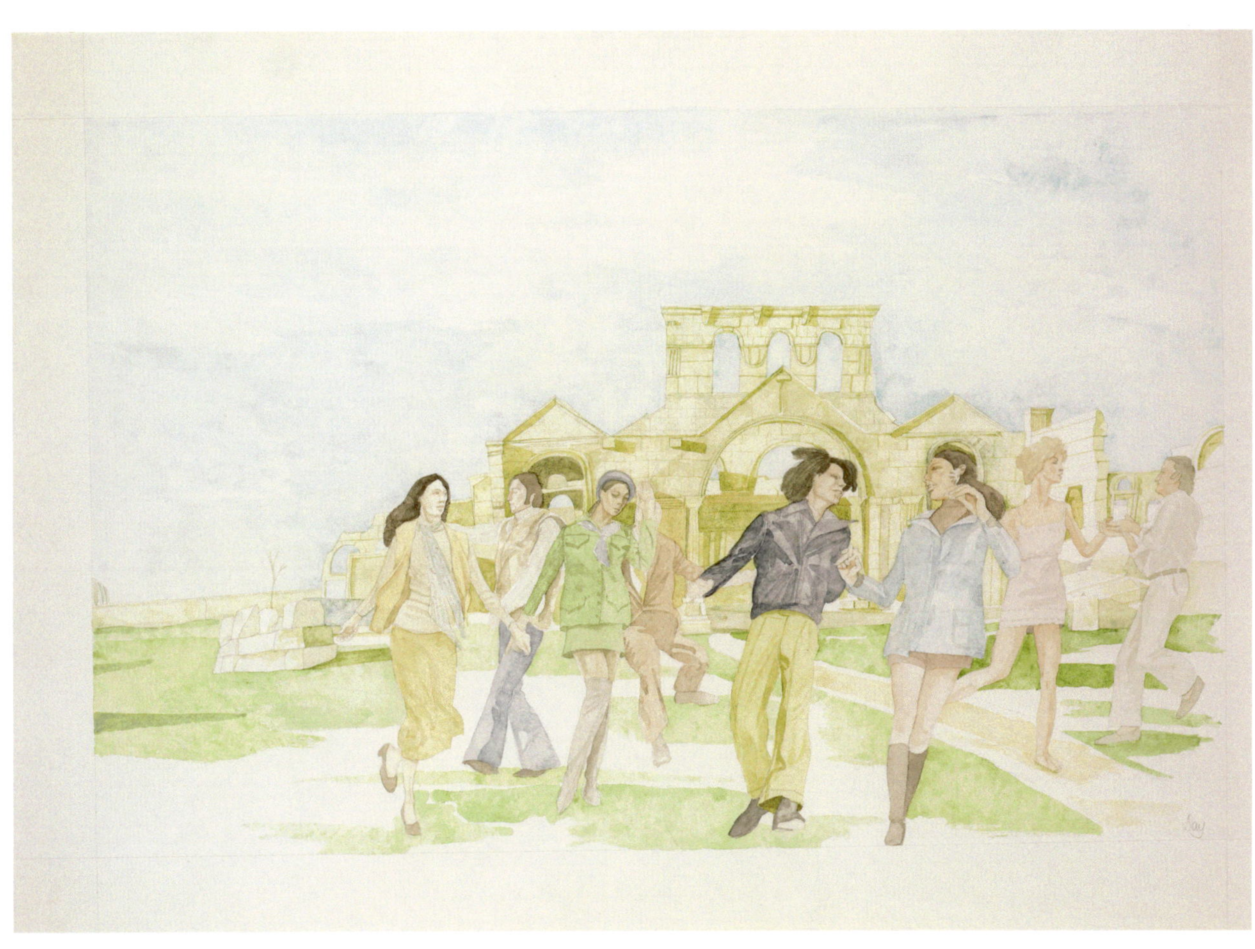

PLATE 31
*The Dance*

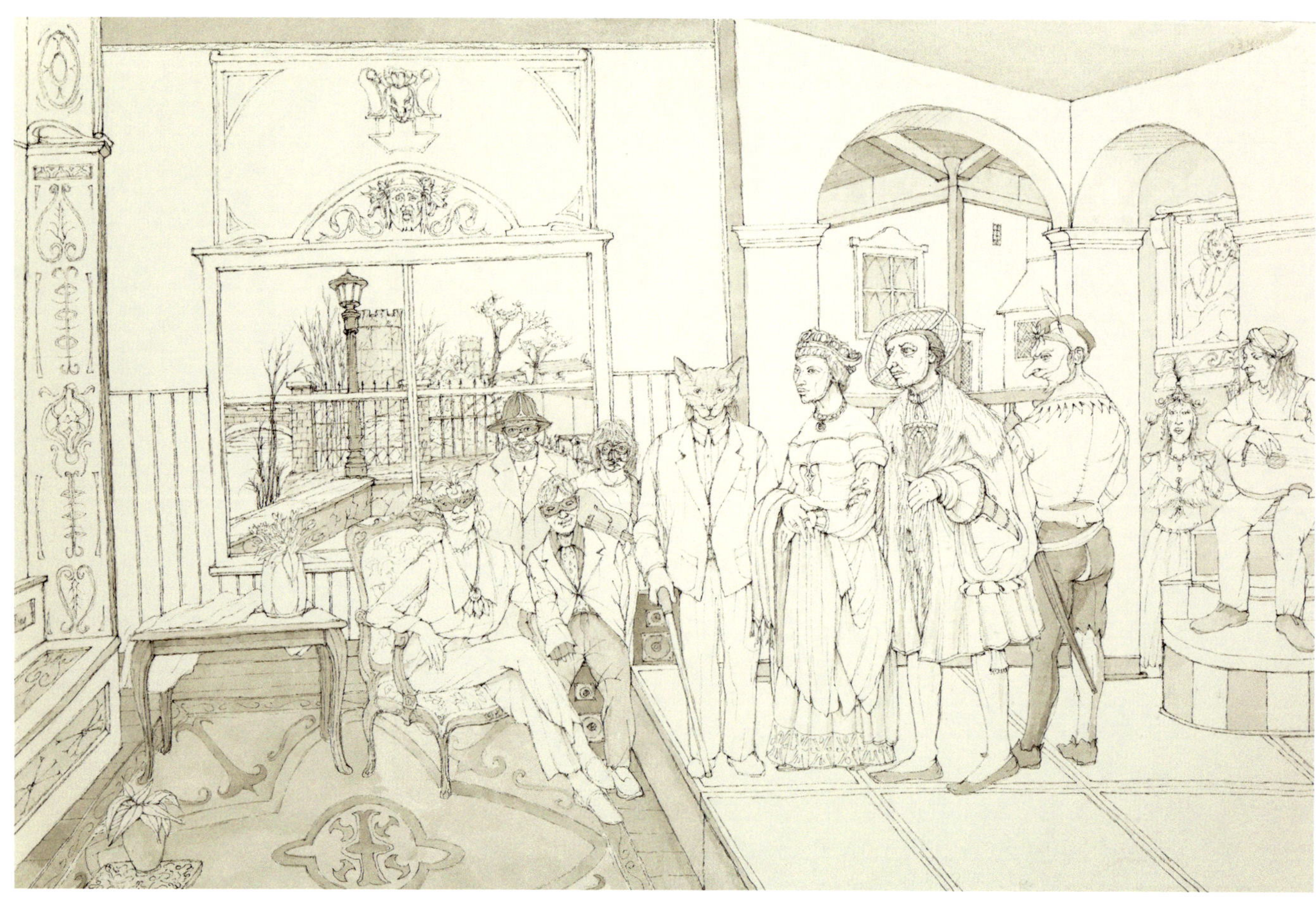

PLATE 32
*(Masquerade),*
c. 1995

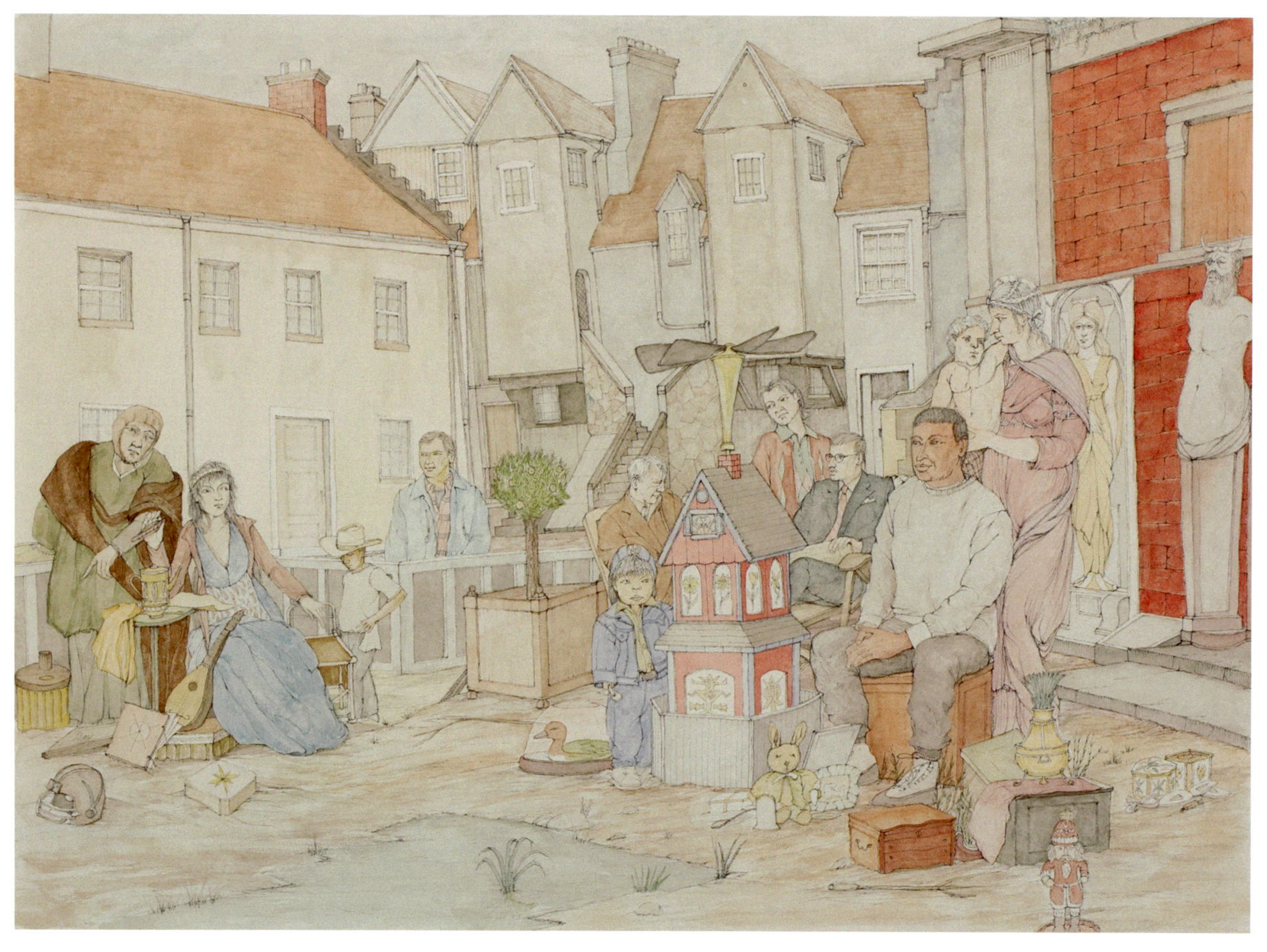

PLATE 33
*(Party),* c. 1995

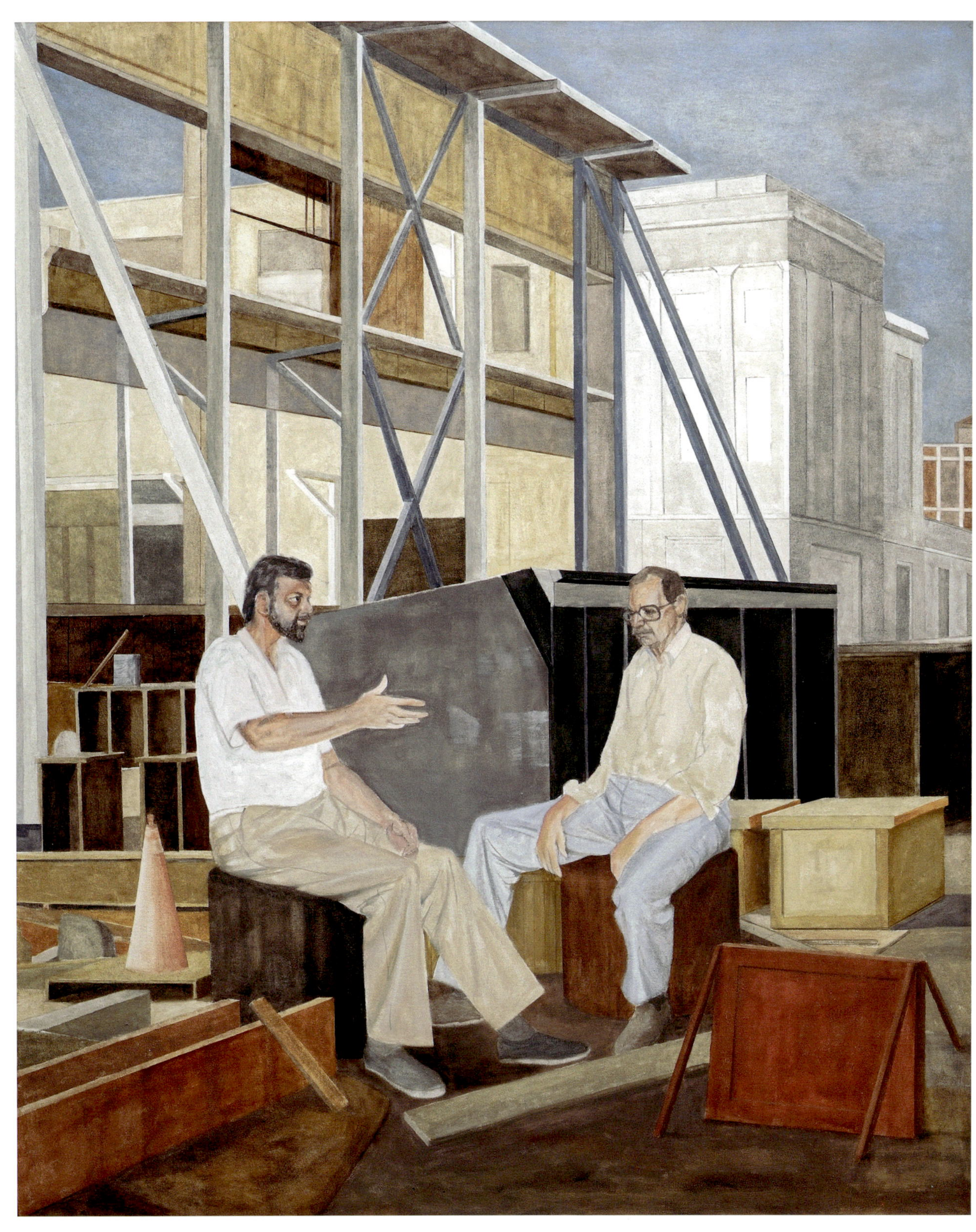

PLATE 34

45     *Dialogue*, 1992

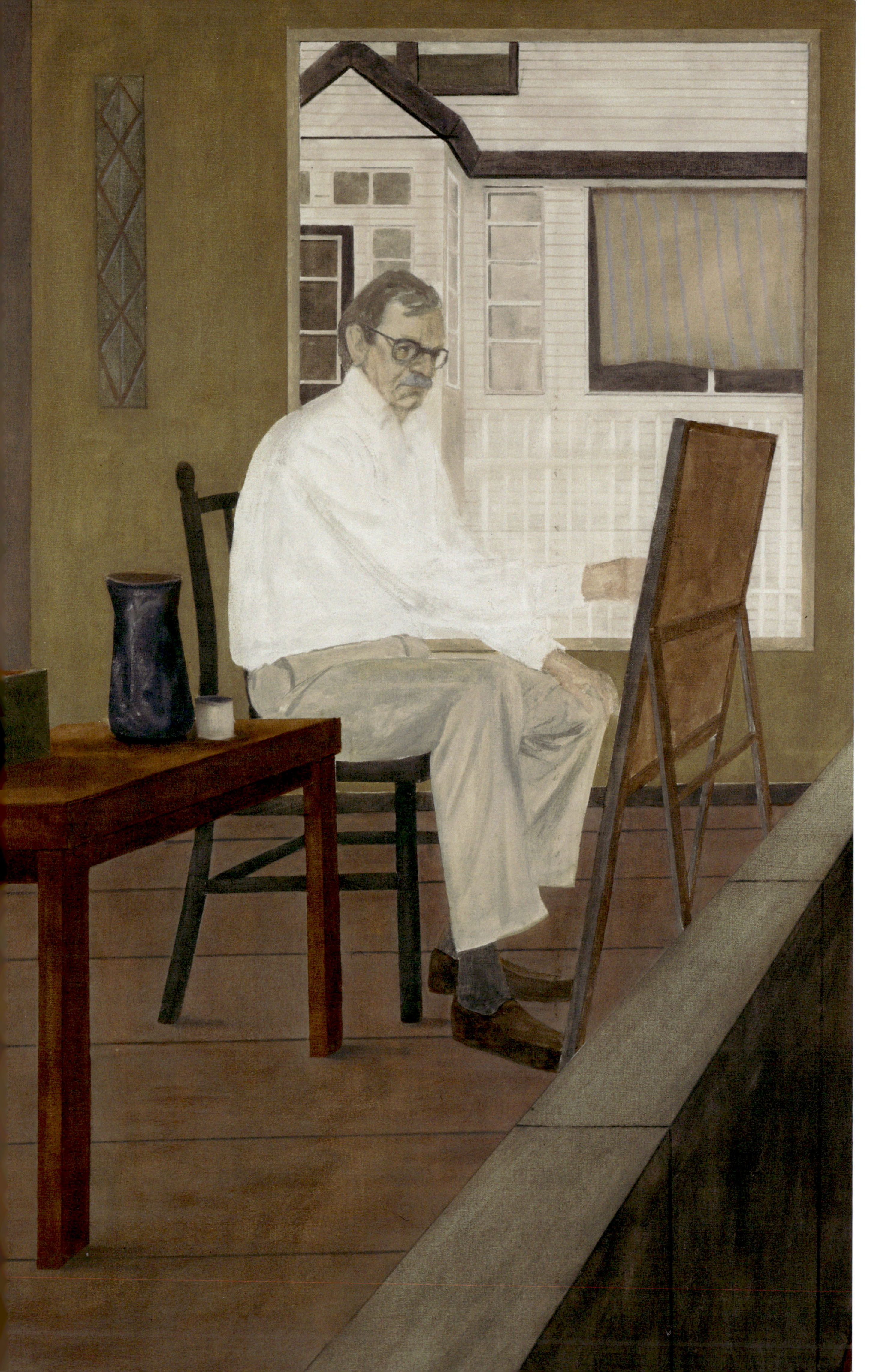

*Eileen Neff*

# A Possible Studio

Description with and without Place[1]

I f we think of the studio as a place where an artist's ideas are envisioned, we might also consider it to be a place where an idea of the artist itself is likewise imagined—if the studio is a place. Interest in the artist in the studio has been extensively recorded, feeding a public curiosity driven by a view of the artist as someone special and, it follows, casting the studio in a privileged light. For the artist, picturing oneself in the studio is a particular form of self-portraiture, a mirror of self-reflection as well as self-projection. This enduring and evolving relationship between the artist and a possible studio, from workshops with their attendant apprentices to the abiding romanticism of a solitary artist at work, has subsequently included a more elusive image of the artist in some studio-less condition, somewhere, anywhere, perhaps just on the phone.

Historically, as the artist/studio relationship unfolded, two distinct images have been repeatedly revisited: the artist has been pictured alone, most often before a canvas, or alternatively, surrounded by friends and admirers (an updated version of its precedent, with apprentices at hand). Among many examples, Rembrandt van Rijn's small but impactful *Artist in His Studio* (fig. 3.1) is exemplary of the lone figure in the studio, while Gustave Courbet's *The Painter's Studio* (fig. 3.2) places the artist at the center of a crowded audience—two opposing portrayals.

Across Larry Day's practice, one recognizes his fascination with these studio representations, manifested variously and over time as significant subjects for his consideration. The image of the artist in the studio seemed to hold mythic proportions as Day related to it, as if it symbolized some vital purpose to which painting is put, offering the ideal configuration for his most inventive pictorial stagings.

Beyond the depiction of the artist in the studio, in individual cases and in several series, Day announced a studio presence, often by including himself as the artist, out of the studio, but pictured in a studio state of mind, and simultaneously or alternatively, by turning otherwise common settings into studio-like sites for engaging models or friends or borrowed figures from art history for his imaginative intentions. (Paradoxically, though not the focus of this essay, Day's figureless cityscapes introduce the importance of the viewer, a subject addressed in his *Ceres* series, who remains as the solitary presence before these works.) As a central representation of Day's deepest thoughts, the figure and its world—with its particular artist/studio

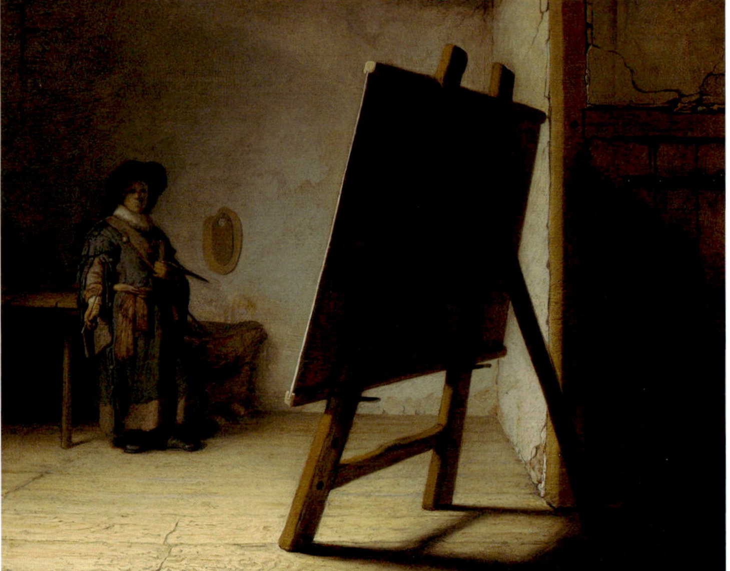

Figure 3.1   Rembrandt van Rijn, *Artist in His Studio*, about 1628, oil on panel, 9¾ × 12½ in. (Museum of Fine Arts Boston: Zoe Oliver Sherman Collection given in memory of Lillie Oliver Poor 38.1838) Photograph © 2021 Museum of Fine Arts, Boston

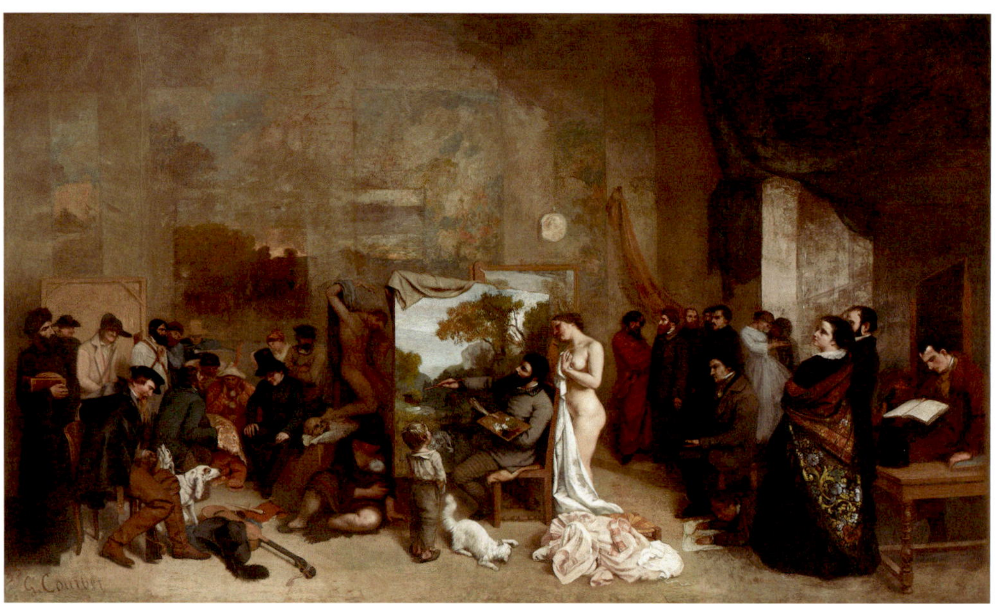

Figure 3.2   Gustave Courbet, *The Painter's Studio: An Allegory*, 1854–55, oil on canvas, 361 × 598 cm. (Musée d'Orsay) © RMN-Grand Palais / Art Resource, NY. Photograph by Hervé Lewandowski

iterations—remained a generative paradigm of his philosophically probing engagement with the nature of imagination itself and how it might be represented. So expressed, the porous relationship between Day's reality and its pictured presence allowed him to create an idea of the artist as he pondered his own role, "as much a witness as an active participant,"[2] and considered his place in the world he would draw, before and around him.

To give a biographical account that actually positions Day in the studio, one would first find him on the third floor of his family home in Cheltenham Township, Pennsylvania, his earliest studio; he would create his last works in a windowed alcove off the sitting room in a small apartment in a neighborhood not far from this original site. There were several other spaces along the way, including a return to a basement studio in his family home that he would picture in *Limit* (fig. 3.3). A significant stretch of time was spent in Takoma Park, Maryland, in a space adjacent to the living room he shared with his wife, Ruth Fine. As factual locations, these images are telling in themselves; as primary sites for the fictions that Day would create, they transport us far beyond their literal frames. At different points within his practice, Day acknowledged the studio traditions named above: the solitary

48

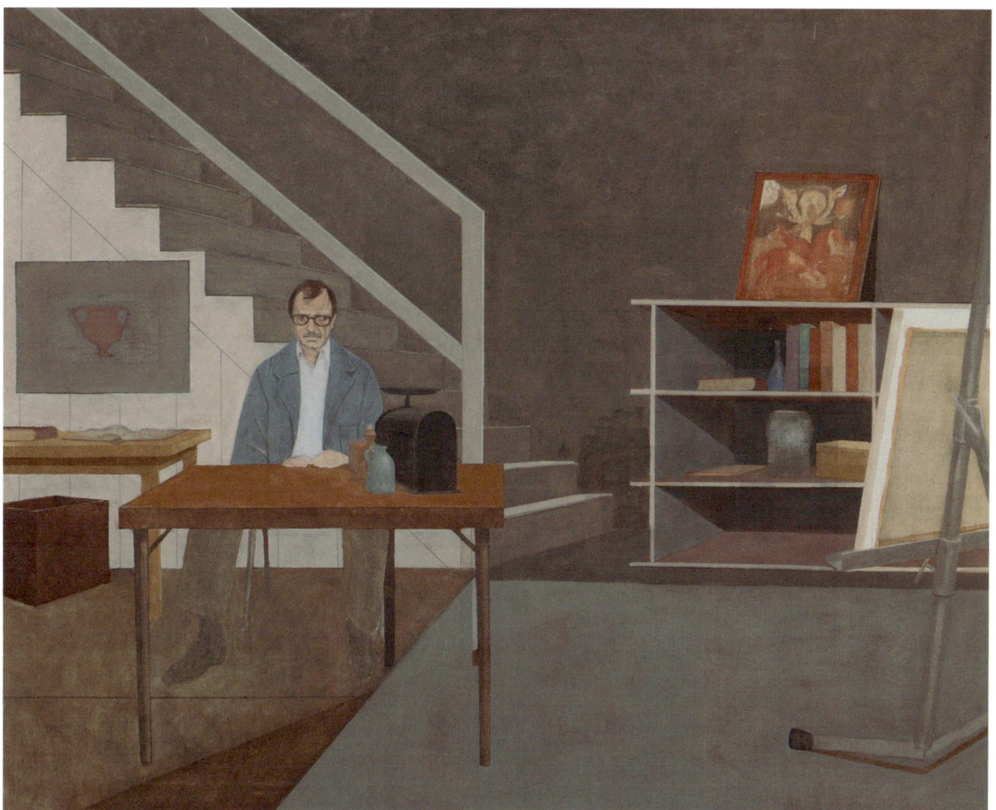

figure in *Limit* and the artist surrounded by others, as in *Group* (plate 13), a kind of prototype for the many gatherings that would appear in his works for decades to come.

Painted in 1983, the year he married Fine, *Limit* is distinctive as an unaccompanied portrait, unique in Day's painted oeuvre. Two other self-portraits from this period, *Break* (Eleanor D. Wilson Museum) and *Changes* (plate 19) have him keeping company with models as well as figures in paintings within these paintings. *Limit* also stands apart for its lineage, two decades after the artist turned to representational painting, and for its location in the artist's familial home, which he would permanently leave in 1985.

As a self-portrait, *Limit* pairs Day's role as subject with that of his canvas, with its back to us (much like Rembrandt's), developed as a recognizable image through many centuries. But Day confounds the familiarity of this conceit with his poker face. While his gaze seems to have his viewers in mind, only his right eye appears to be focused on us; his left looks toward his canvas—the other subject of this portrait—and whatever is or isn't there.

The back of a canvas on a wooden stretcher was the image of choice (conceding the doubled primacy of the lightbulb) of another contemporary artist's idea of self-portraiture in the studio; an amplified depiction of this pictorial trope, Philip Guston's *Reverse* (fig. 3.4) further supports this artist's ironic nod by forgoing the representation of the artist.[3]

## The Others

Contemplating the limits and rewards of the artist in the studio, Guston has been quoted saying: "I believe it was John Cage who once told me, 'When you start working, everybody is in your studio—the past, your friends, enemies, the art world, and above all, your own ideas—all are there. But as you continue painting, they start leaving, one by one, and you are left completely alone. Then, if you're lucky, even you leave.'"[4]

Though commonly repeated, this quotation has an uncommon resonance when considering Day's work, as he seemed to have inverted Cage's premise in his insistence on keeping so many others—friends as well as anonymous figures and historic favorites—in his studio world, populating a wide range of his images, with a distinct sense of his holding on to ever more over time. And with this we recognize that for someone who had a great capacity for the pleasures of solitude, Day also had a great affection for relationships, both personal and historical, and often at the same time, with an in-depth look at the work suggesting that the historical often provided a model for the personal—or the picturing of the personal. It wasn't that he didn't have the satisfaction of real and compelling relationships with his peers; it was more that he was often thinking about the storied images of art history and how they might give shape to the otherwise less remarkable moments of the day.[5]

### The Imagination Wishes to Be Indulged[6]

> The dilemma in realist figurative art is that the image must be recognizable which implies a common ground (and a common ground considerably cuts down imagination) and at the same time the image must be challenging, which implies some assault on commonality.[7]

In 1988, Day was in a fanciful mood when he began *Salome Variations*, an extensive series of drawings, a print, and a single painting at least partially based on photographs of friends he had engaged while they were unsuspecting guests in the artist's Takoma Park home (plates 37–39).[8]

Nearly all the works depict a central female figure as Salome. In one early drawing, her arm is raised as if dancing; in other instances, she's pictured without the fabled stance and often in contemporary dress, suggesting that Day was drawing from fashion magazines, so stylized are the clothing and the poses. Or she's costumed in some unidentifiable way, or nude as an artist's model would be nude—an exuberant array of how a woman might be pictured by a man—or this man, considering Salome.

And always accompanying the title figure, another woman (Herodias, Salome's mother, we're to assume, with Day's wife occasionally taking this role) and a man (Herod, the father, often played by artist Gerald Nichols), both focused on their daughter. That the eyes of the seated man are often parallel with the region of the standing woman's body where the legs join the torso offers an expansion of the original narrative. Among the several dozen drawings and less-evolved sketches initially framed by this domestic space, other variations accumulated. Additional figures were sometimes present or pictured on the walls. Eclectic architectural examples appear as well, sometimes bringing the outside in (and in one case, placing the players outside), evoking the atmosphere of a Victorian parlor game (perhaps charades), where the players enact their parts.[9]

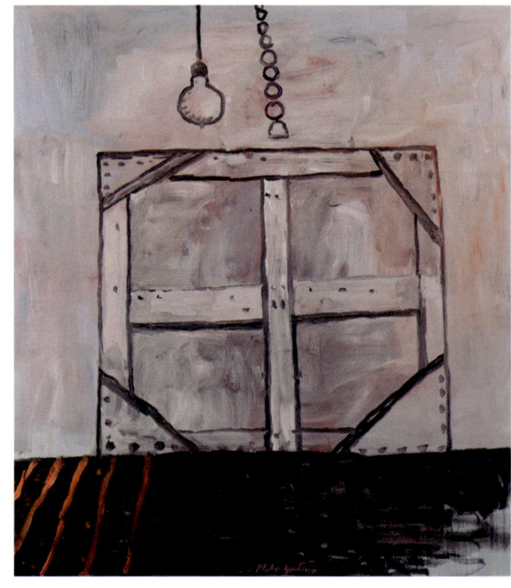

Figure 3.4   Philip Guston, *Reverse*, 1979, oil on canvas, 60 × 52½ in. (Private Collection) © The Estate of Philip Guston

And among those gathered for the occasion, Day pictures himself in two versions, sitting behind an easel. In a graphite drawing, he is positioned on our left and the Salome figure is presented frontally, though her gaze is elsewhere. In an offset lithograph, which appears as a horizontal flip of the image, the artist sits on our right, the Salome figure having turned her back to us and appearing to face the artist, who has switched drawing hands, reinforcing the many transpositions of this pictorial play. For Day, the ongoing activity within these scenarios was apparently too irresistible to keep himself out of, too much mythic opportunity to not be a part of.

## Matisse Among Others

Day was conversant with a wide range of historically significant cultural figures, reflecting his many interests. Before turning to the visual arts, he explored the fields of music, theater, and literature, and was well acquainted with the histories of each.[10] Having focused on painting, he turned from his early abstract investigations (plates 40 and 41) to explore figurative representation in the 1960s, a time when many artists were moving beyond the grip of mid-century Abstract Expressionism, embracing diverse pictorial modes, with Pop, Minimal, and Conceptual Art at the forefront of the alternatives. In Day's recalibration, art history led the way. Proposing what was "probably some hidden desire" as elements of the figure began to enter his abstract paintings, he made an illuminating observation about the role of the past in these new considerations in his 1958 Logbook:

> This is no Renaissance, no rebirth. There is no attempt to relive the past, no glorification. The cracked marbles, the worm-eaten carvings that we accept and see are in the manner that we see and accept them closer to us than to their earlier creators.[11]

Day understood how the past and present needed each other; his matter-of-fact sense of the past as belonging to him was formative, giving him his particular access and allowing so much work that was to come. It wasn't so much a Shakespearean past as prologue, but more of a Faulknerian past that was not even past; it accounted for Day being a confident appropriator before appropriation entered the contemporary art world's common parlance. With the often-acknowledged influence of his painting after *Merry Widow* from Jan Steen's studio (plate 7) and his discovery of Henri Matisse—ultimately instrumental in much that was distinctive about his turn to figurative painting—these initial encouragements supported his representational explorations, even as they were among so many earlier artists he recognized for their boundless source of inspiration. Day's attachment to Matisse persisted, and within the scope of his extensive written musings on art, his *Madame Matisse* essay (see pp. 141–45) is particularly expressive of the imaginative and reflective nature of Day's mind. It helped identify a characteristic feature in the development of his own figurative interests, as it celebrated the possibility of the inscrutable within an otherwise recognizable reality, and provided a guide for the pictorial language to support the world he was creating, so that we might ask of Day the same questions with which he opened his essay: "What was he looking for? What was he looking at?"

## Inseeing[12]

In *Day by Day* (plate 42), the artist has cleared out all the others to once again picture himself, this time in one of his invented architectural interiors, seated at an easel. Doubling up on the idea of self-portraiture in this two-tiered space, Day at first seems to be looking down and through an invisible mirror into an earlier time, at an earlier self, who is pictured with a miniature version of the still life that accompanies the artist on the upper level.

That the young boy appears to be on the same horizontal plane as Day's canvas in this illusory construction suggests that, in fact, the pictured Day couldn't literally be seeing his younger self at all, and adds to the mystery of this overtly psychological work (fig. 3.5). And with the windows opened (or a painting within the painting) and shutters closed, and subtle decorative elements waiting to be discovered, this very considered staging for a reflection on time and memory also suggests an homage to Matisse, in what is a study in deliberate restraint within an imaginary frame, another aspect of Day's complex persona, in contrast, for instance, to the expansive Salome performances created around the same time.

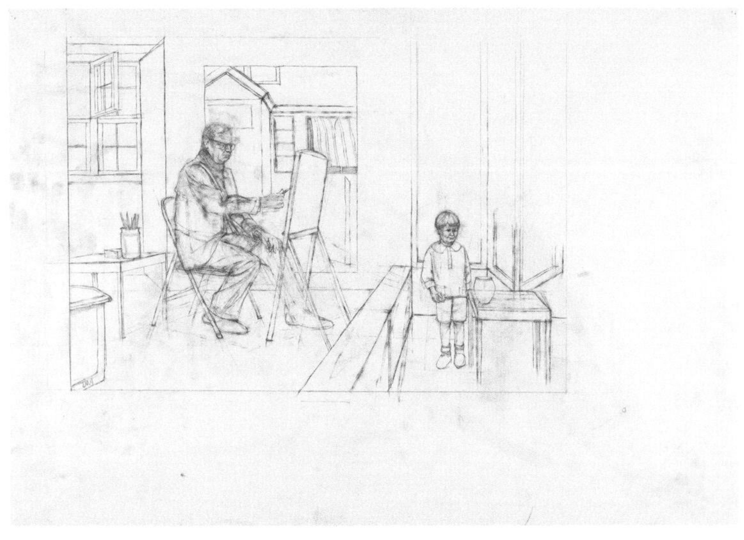

Figure 3.5  *Study related to "Day by Day,"* 1993, graphite on paper, 22 × 29⅞ in. (The Metropolitan Museum of Art, Gift of Susan Lorence, in memory of the artist, 1998) Image copyright © The Metropolitan Museum of Art. Image source: Art Resource, NY

## A Baroque Sensibility and Classical Mind[13]

While Day has otherwise placed himself in multiple studio-suggestive situations, he strikes a particularly studio-reflective pose in the *Ceres* series (plates 44 and 45, figs. 3.6 and 3.8), giving a complex portrayal of his meditations on the art experience: engaging the idea of the artist, the model, other spectators (within the image), and ultimately making a subject of the viewer as well. This series, like *Salome Variations,* is drawing rich, not matching the latter in numbers, but with drawing being the form of its most remarkable inventions. These works also reach what would be considered their more traditional climax in a single painting, that is, if we hold the conventional view that drawings have a more preparatory, provisional nature in relation to painting, and forego what all artists know, that drawing is the most intimate and often the most telling form of expression. While Day has made many masterful paintings, in the case of both of these series, the drawings are where the artist, and therefore the viewer, appears most imaginatively engaged. It is also worth noting that with the dating of Day's works being less than certain, it is probable that some of the drawings followed the execution of the painting.

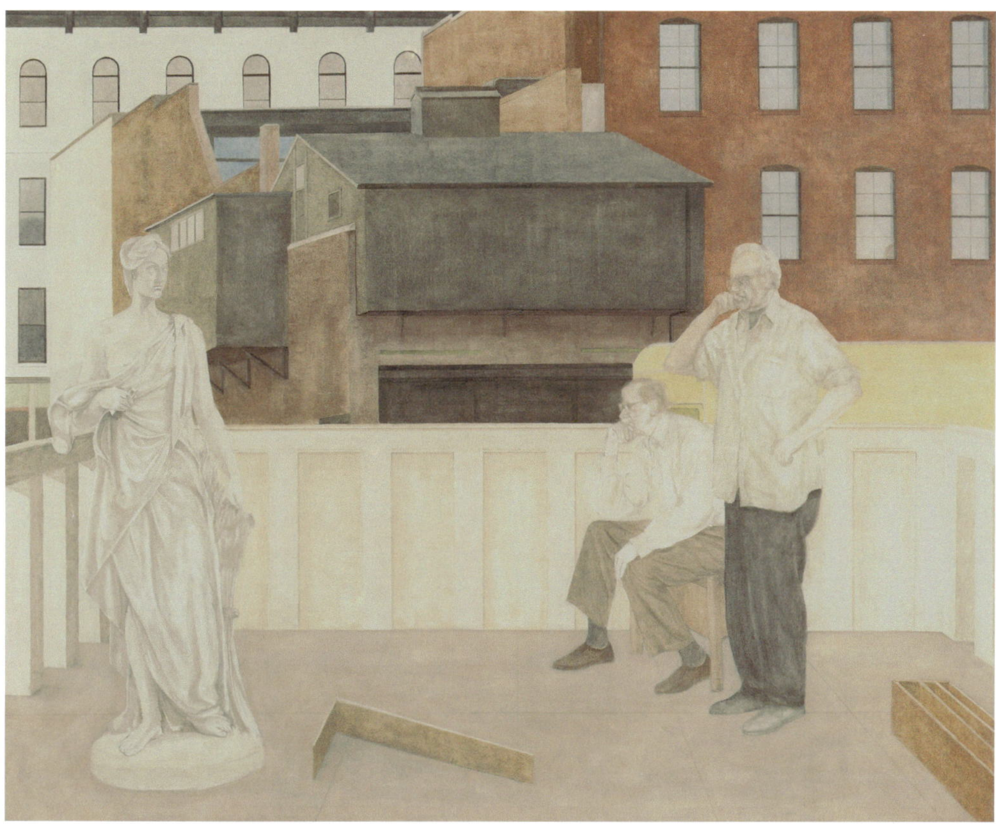

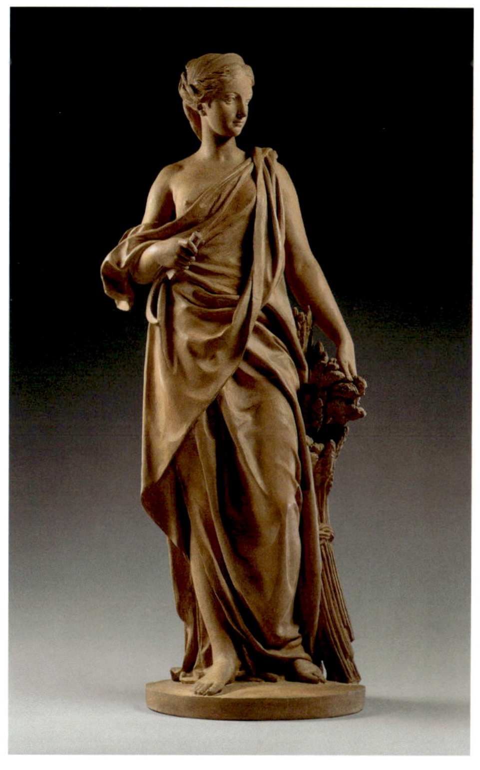

Figure 3.6   *Ceres*, 1992, oil on canvas, 60 × 72 in. (Collection of Ruth Fine)

Figure 3.7   Augustin Pajou, *Ceres*, c. 1768–70, buff terracotta with reddish patination, 24⅝ × 7½ × 7½ in. (The Metropolitan Museum of Art, Purchase, C. Michael Paul Gift, Josephine Bay Paul and C. Michael Paul Foundation Inc. Gift and Charles Ulrick and Josephine Bay Foundation Inc. Gift, 1978) Image copyright © The Metropolitan Museum of Art. Image source: Art Resource, NY

It was a special gift of Day's to conflate elements from different periods of time in the most casual manner, and that happens here. The *Ceres* series takes place in a fictive outdoor space, a frame within a frame, a balcony that feels like a floating studio—a latter-day Édouard Manet painting Claude Monet in his studio boat. Once again, it's *Day by Day*, but Day is accompanied by his artist friend Dennis Leon, suggesting not a mirror image, but another version of the self, a double of sorts, a particular companion in his particular form of contemplation—a sculptor to join him in studying the sculpture of Ceres, the Roman goddess of agriculture, who was also associated with nourishment and human fertility. In the more classical of the drawings picturing Ceres, Day's specific source is Augustin Pajou's ceramic statue (fig. 3.7). Centered between Day and Leon, the resemblance, down to the short, round pedestal, is striking. Her appearance in the painting (fig. 3.6), where she appears in the near left corner of the image, is similarly recognizable, regarding its source. Though with color introduced, we can't help but notice how pale she looks, whited out somehow, as are the top halves of the two men, now pictured together in their consideration of the statue; could they be wondering where her original warm glow has gone, and why its absence is also affecting them? And as a master of enigmatic details, Day introduces what looks like a metal corner, a fragment from another unaccountable metal structure, lying on the floor of the *Ceres* painted stage, while other random forms are displayed in the ground of the series' drawings as well.

It is also worth observing that in the graphite drawings, where there is no color and few if any shadows, we don't question *Ceres*'s temperature, as everything is cast in the paper's light, creating a generally flattening effect, the only emphasis and vari-ations made by the alternating pressure Day applies to his drawn line. We notice, too, that the pictured artist appears on the left side of one *Ceres* drawing, then reappears on the right in another, where he's alongside Leon, his viewing partner. With hand to chin, nearly mimicking the contemplative gesture that Leon holds throughout much of the series, Day proposes a less fluid role for his companion, and leaves no doubt that he is the director, the author of these tales.

And as such, he chooses, in another drawing, to replace the classical Ceres with a more eccentric, whimsical one, with an arm up, as if trying to hold steady the bas-ket of wheat on her head. Now bare breasted and with a pedestal for a lower body, this Ceres is more like a peasant girl who has stumbled out of the wheat fields and, suddenly remembering that she's a goddess, has thought to gather herself together to assume her role.[14] The two men, on the other hand, have hardly changed a hair, as if dumbstruck by what's before them.[15]

And perhaps it is the last drawing associated with this series where Day has taken his imagination on a longer than usual walk; in the same arena, but in place of Ceres, he pictures a nude, nymph-like figure in the arms of a satyr, with one of his hoofed legs resting between hers, and the other raised and securing her in place (fig. 3.8).

While there are several origins for the name "satyr," a common one defines him as a wild animal or lustful man, as suggested here; another identifies its connection to the Roman god Saturn, the root "sat" meaning "to sow," and keeps us in the Ceres mood.[16] Painter Scott Noel has proposed that the nude is a hermaphrodite, and simul-taneously suggested how she appears as a horizontally flipped look-alike of François Boucher's 1751 *Blonde Odalisque*.[17] As an attempt to locate her origin, these proposi-tions adhere to the kind of historic appropriation and strategic inverting that Day was prone to, with the possibility of sexual ambiguity adding to the double nature of the moment (already expressed by the man/animal satyr) that he was keen to engage. Departing from their independent Greek origins, satyrs and nymphs were often pic-tured as consensual lovers by the seventeenth century, the updated mythological status making their seductive pairing more tolerable at the time; likewise, we are prompted by Day and Leon's casual regard of this encounter to experience a similar read of the image as our vision is uniquely locked in time with the moment of this drawing, even as our view of the satyr/nymph embrace differs from theirs. Mean-while, Day is back in the left corner, where he witnessed the classical sculpture of Ceres, and Leon holds firm in the opposite corner we've come to associate with him. The mythological nod with which Day filtered other pictorial decisions in his work is operative here and recommends that we accept the sensual reach of this moment in the *Ceres* series as just another historically rich association, and not as the picture of two contemporary men in their own pornographic fantasy, which, if that thought had any legs, as opposed to some pedestal proxy, would shift our read from a party of three (the trio with Ceres) to a potentially lively foursome.

Ultimately, the perceptual experience becomes a dominant subject, present as another staged character for the viewer to consider. We find ourselves engaged in

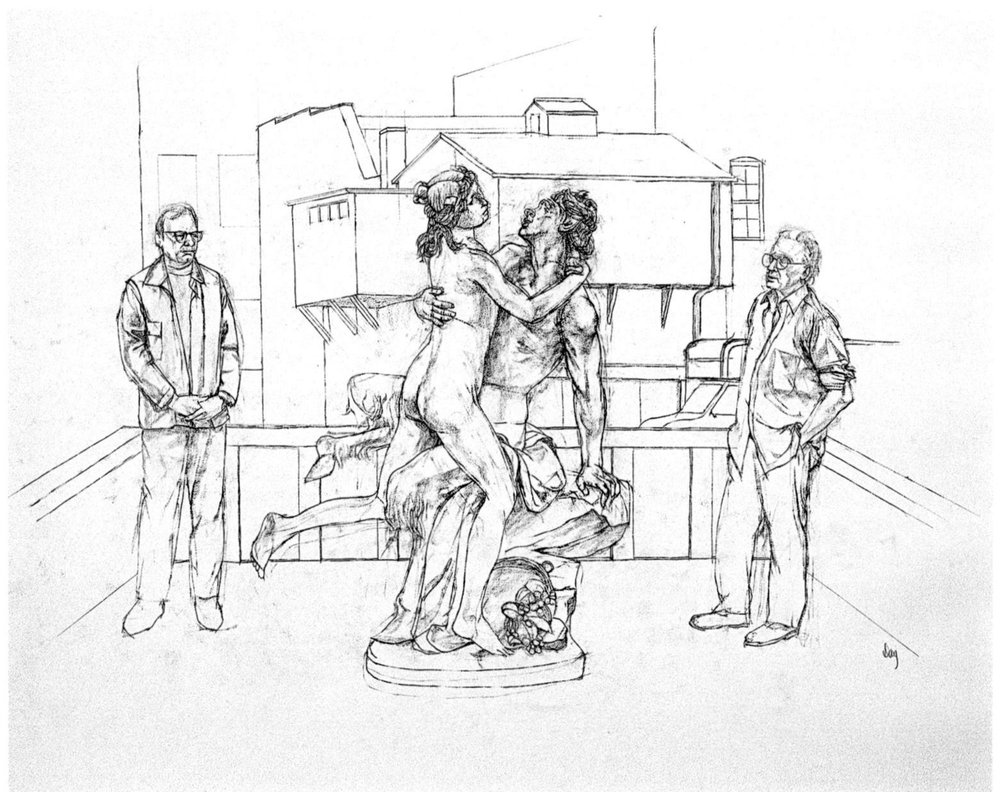

Figure 3.8. *Related to "Ceres,"* c. 1992, graphite on paper, 28 × 33 in. (Courtesy of Bill White)

the inventive possibilities of representation and how what's represented might be perceived, encouraged as we are to identify with the Day and Leon figures; observing from our own vantage point, not seeing exactly what they're seeing, but seeing with them, nonetheless, thus expanding the field of what might be visible. So identified, a correspondence is made with the work of art historian and critical theorist Kaja Silverman and her dynamic consideration of a triangular chiasmus within the visual field, drawing a tight, reciprocal knot between the artist, the object of the artist's gaze, and the viewer.[18] Day has set up his own complex conversation among these elements, with his *Ceres* drawings putting them into play.

## Seeing While Being Seen Continues

In 1992–93, on the heels of the *Ceres* series, Day created *Tempi del Giorno*, a more narratively expansive suite of eighteen drawings that featured the artist and was eloquently addressed by poet John Hollander in a 1994 exhibition catalogue essay. Sometimes picturing himself as the solo spectator in these imagined worlds, Day is seen at other times among those we might recognize from earlier works of his, or from his life.

Roaming around in what we have come to regard as his familiar state of attention—"contemplating, regarding, gazing, listening"—Day ponders the range of selves that each new context, informed by some remote art historical reference, helps evoke.[19] Perhaps the assorted locations offer a more diffused read of Day's posture (regarding the artist in a studio state of mind), compared to how he was perceived in the fixed arena of the *Ceres* series, though it is impossible to forget that it is the artist we're witnessing. A more direct rendering of a studio experience is proposed in two of the drawings: in *The Living Past*, the artist sits at an easel while a scene from a group of Fragonard prints is pictured in an adjoining space before him; and in a Day-like twist, he disappears as an observer in *In the Shop*, only to reappear on the canvas of one of the artists in the sixteenth-century workshop of Johannes Stradanus.[20]

## The Artist Exists: Stage Left

The deliberations of *Tempi del Giorno* seem to have exhausted Day's urge to picture himself, as his final two groups of work were created without his own portrayal. Instead, *Caprices* (figs. 4.9 and 4.10) and *Elegies (Homage to Rilke)* (plates 46–55) offer an array of unidentifiable contemporary figures, surrogates for the artist and his companions, perhaps, mingling with an equally random assembly of art-historical figures, all within a radically complex dismantling of the seams of time.[21] Day's architectural interests also make their most extreme stylistic and temporal leaps and juxtapositions, announcing the past as present in ways he's been insisting all along, and in these last works, most profusely. Without the centrifugal force of Day's presence, we begin to notice Day-like qualities in those remaining. Now many who are pictured, contemporary or otherwise, appear to consider what's before them; contemplation permeates these staged worlds. Moments of conversation and unaccountable narratives suggest that we're witnessing fragments of dreams, or half-remembered memories. "Seeing" is everywhere, before the backdrops, amid the ruins, as a widely embracing figurative exploration extends to include four-legged creatures as well as those who require a pedestal to stay upright, all congregating as they will, as Day would will them. Larry Day's last sweep of interfacing inventions finds its unpredictable though inevitable harmony as it delivers a final glimpse of the visibility of his thought, of his studio state of mind.

## Notes

1   With this variation on the title of Wallace Stevens's poem, *Description without Place*, I'm hoping to establish a link to both Stevens's understanding of the gap between language and its object, and to Stevens himself, a poet of great interest to Larry Day.

2   Larry Day, "Artist's Statement," in *Tempi del Giorno: Eighteen Drawings by Larry Day* (Lawrenceville, NJ: Rider College Art Gallery, 1994).

3   Beyond both having engaged the back side of a stretched canvas, Day and Guston were introduced to each other by Mercedes Matter. When Guston turned to figuration in the late 1960s and he was receiving unfavorable reviews, Day sent him a letter offering his support.

4   Philip Guston, *Philip Guston: Collected Writings, Lectures, and Conversations* (Berkeley: University of California Press, 2011), 30. The recording was made during a 1960 panel at the Philadelphia Museum School of Art (now the University of the Arts). This was during Larry Day's tenure as a professor there (1953–88), suggesting the inevitability that he would have been present. The other panelists included Robert Motherwell, Ad Reinhardt, and Jack Tworkov, with Harold Rosenberg moderating.

5   As he sometimes described as well as pictured himself as a participant and observer in his own images, so, too, does this self-portrayal recall an enduring memory of mine—how I knew Day for many years. Initially he was a professor of mine at the Philadelphia College of Art (PCA, now the University of the Arts); I still have my notebook from his sophomore seminar. Ultimately, we would be colleagues and friends, spending many hours in PCA's painting department, where he often sat among us (the rest of the faculty). It seemed to me he was there but not there, perhaps drawing us in his imagination, arranging and rearranging us in his mind—the artist at work, suggesting a picture that would help shape an idea of a possible studio, a studio state of mind—how I would be considering his work so many years later, in writing this essay.

6   Wallace Stevens, "Adagia," in *Opus Posthumous: Poems, Plays, Prose* (London: Faber and Faber, 1957), 159.

7   Larry Day, "Notes on Figurative Art," in *The Figure in Recent American Painting*, ed. Robert Godfrey (New Wilmington, PA: Westminster College, 1974). The exhibition traveled to four other venues, including PCA.

8   Just after Day retired from teaching at PCA, a few friends and colleagues, including Gerald Nichols and myself, made a visit to his home in Takoma Park. As we sat in the living room off his studio, Day asked if I would stand up and raise an arm; "Think Salome," he said. It never occurred to me to refuse, and the photographs he took led to the (arm raised) drawing, which his widow, Ruth Fine, has gifted to me, and which is pictured here, an early version, perhaps the earliest, of the *Salome Variations*. Nichols went on to be the featured male figure in about half of the dozens of drawings. Fine later told me that she and Day saw a 1990 production of *Salome* at the Washington National Opera, a certain confirmation of a thematic exploration he was already committed to.

9   Day was interested in gaming and its constructions for human gatherings, investigated in *The Bridge Game* works, as well as those of *Poker Game,* included in this exhibition. A drawing and a painting, both entitled *A Game of Charade*s, are also on view.

10   Larry Day's interest in theater was not just as a spectator but as a performer as well. He participated in theatrical productions during his student years at Tyler School of Art, and later at the Cheltenham Art Center. Knowing this history provides a backdrop for understanding his inclination to create such staged encounters in much of the work considered here.

11   Larry Day, "Extracts from a Logbook on a Work in Progress," *Art Education Bulletin* (Eastern Arts Association) 15, no. 4 (April 1958): 11–13.

12   The term *inseeing* (*einsehen*) was often used by poet Rainer Maria Rilke, who had learned it from philosopher Theodor Lipps. Rilke's interest was in its suggestion that seeing could be a deeply penetrating and creative experience. Day felt a great connection to Rilke and acknowledged the bond with *Elegies*, his last group of drawings, with Rilke's monumental *Duino Elegies* certainly in mind.

13   Day, Logbook, 17.

14   One possible source for this Ceres could be found in a Guillaume Coustou sculpture at the Jardin des Tuileries, a more elegant version of Day's figure which nonetheless turns into its own pedestal below the torso.

15   A very similar, basket-on-head version of Ceres is seen in the *Tempi del Giorno* suite of drawings, though in a less eyebrow-raising form, as she's architecturally bound and not subject to anyone's gaze.

16   Adrian Room, *Room's Classical Dictionary: The Origins of the Names of Characters in Classical Mythology* (London, England; Boston, MA; Melbourne, Australia; and Henley, England: Routledge & Kegan Paul, 1983), 271.

17   Scott Noel, email to author, April 22, 2020. Noel is a Philadelphia figurative painter and author of the catalogue essay in *Larry Day: Ironic Realist* (Roanoke, VA: Eleanor D. Wilson Museum, 2008).

18   Kaja Silverman, *The Three-Personed Picture, or the History of Photography, Part II,* forthcoming. (Part I, *The Miracle of Analogy, or the History of Photography* [Stanford: Stanford University Press, 2015].) Speaking about the evolution of the photograph into "picture" status, she says, "Finally, it depends for its existence as much upon the sitter and the beholder as it does upon the author, and it links them to each other through a three-person chiasmus." Her texts and our conversations have been illuminating and confirming in my thinking about Day's work.

19   John Hollander, "Introduction," in *Tempi del Giorno*. The drawings are in the collection of the Philadelphia Museum of Art.

20   See drawings no. 2 and no. 6 in *Tempi del Giorno: Eighteen Drawings by Larry Day.*

21   The *Caprices* series is reproduced in *Larry Day: Ironic Realist* (Roanoke, VA: Eleanor D. Wilson Museum, 2008), https://www.hollins.edu/museum/catalogs/documents/larryday_cat.pdf.

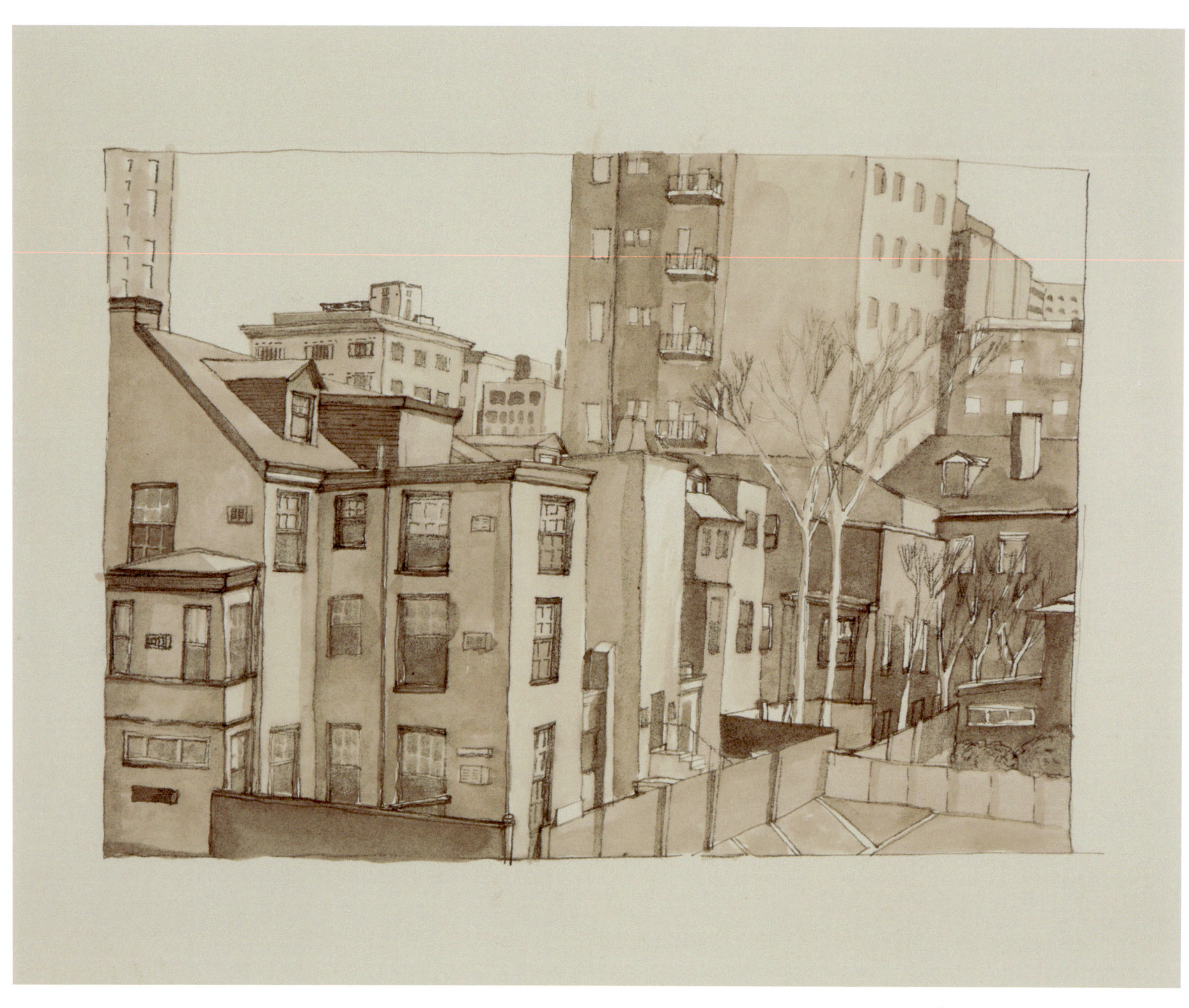

PLATE 35
*(Center City)*, c. 1970

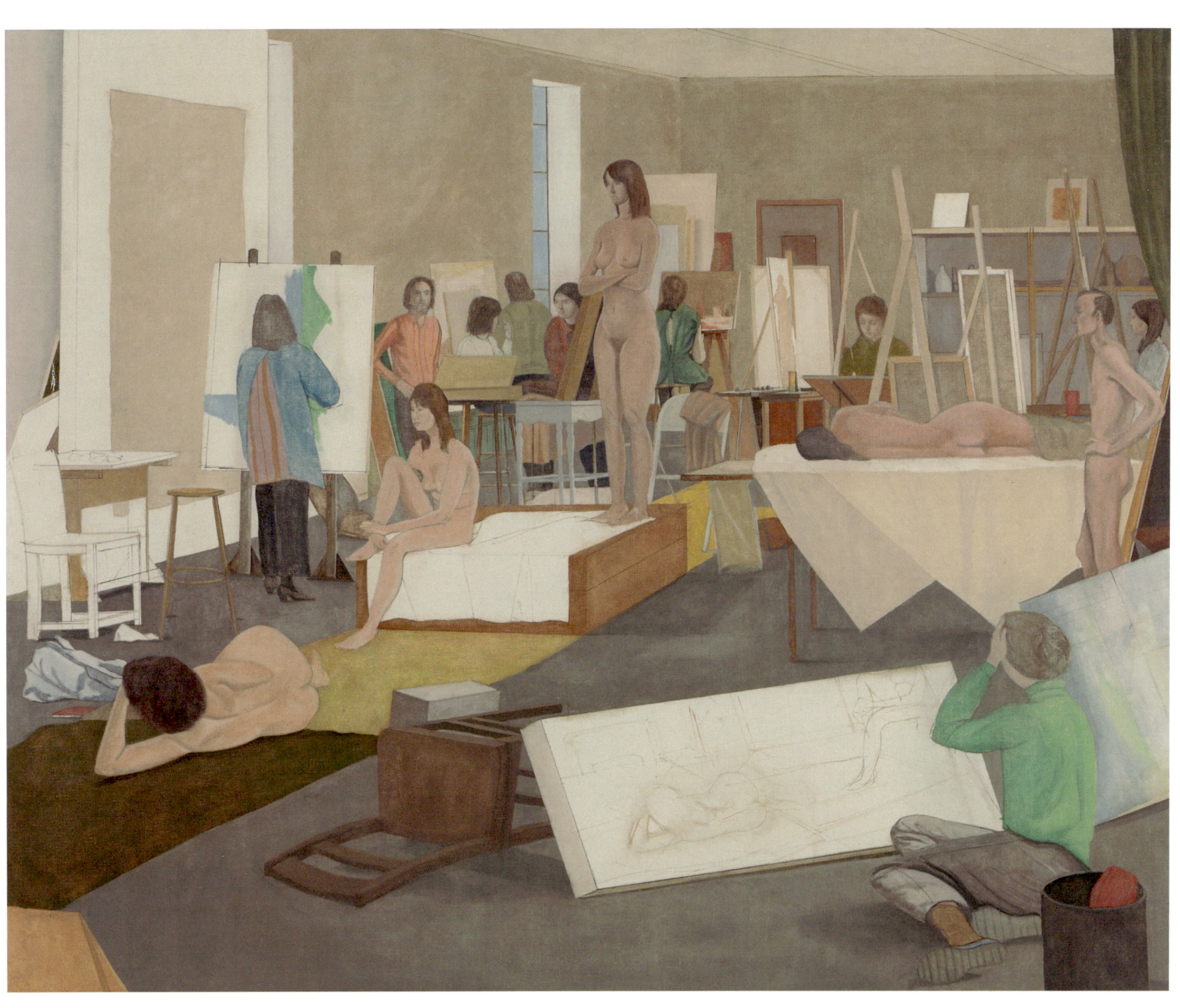

PLATE 36

*Harry's Class*, 1972–73

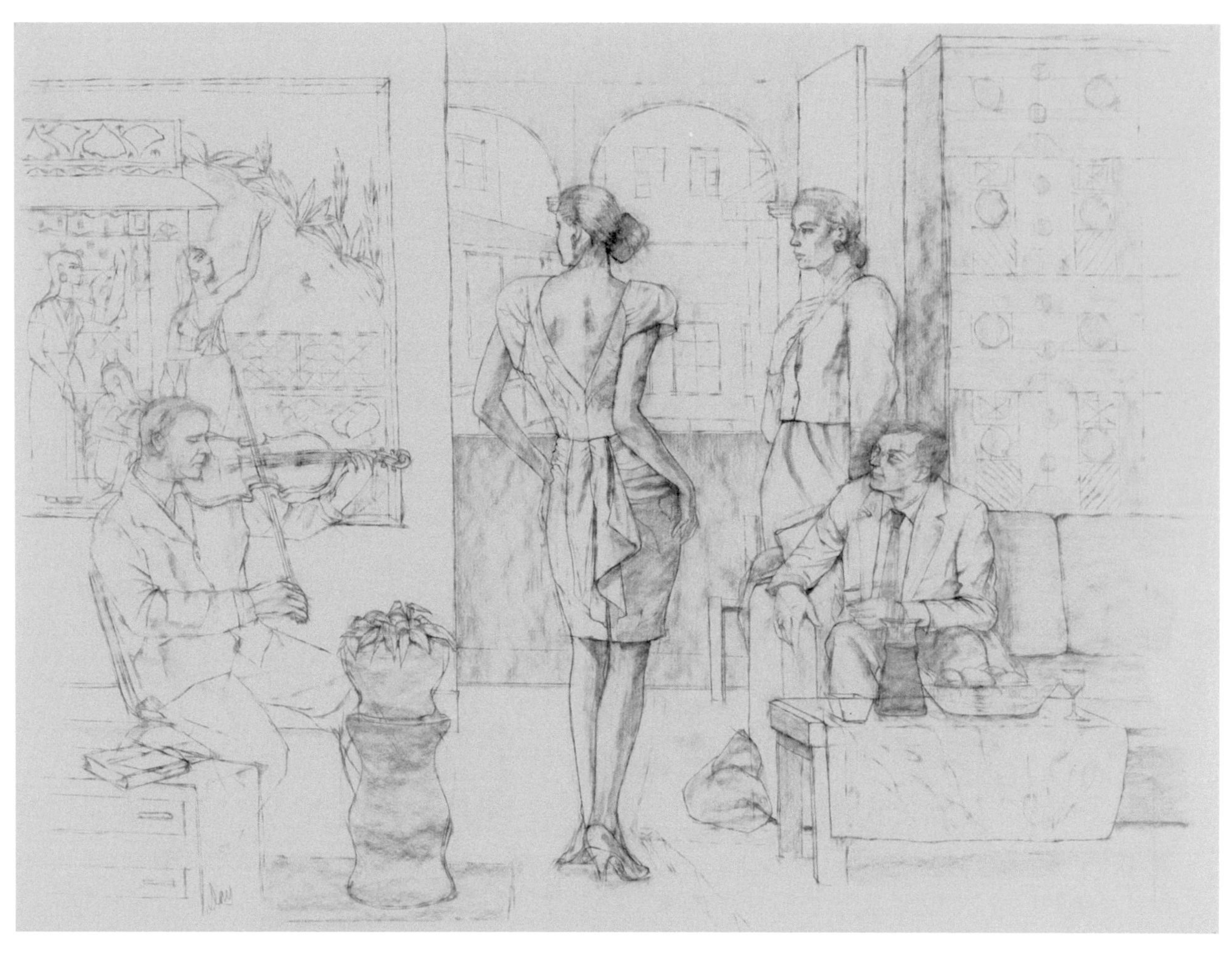

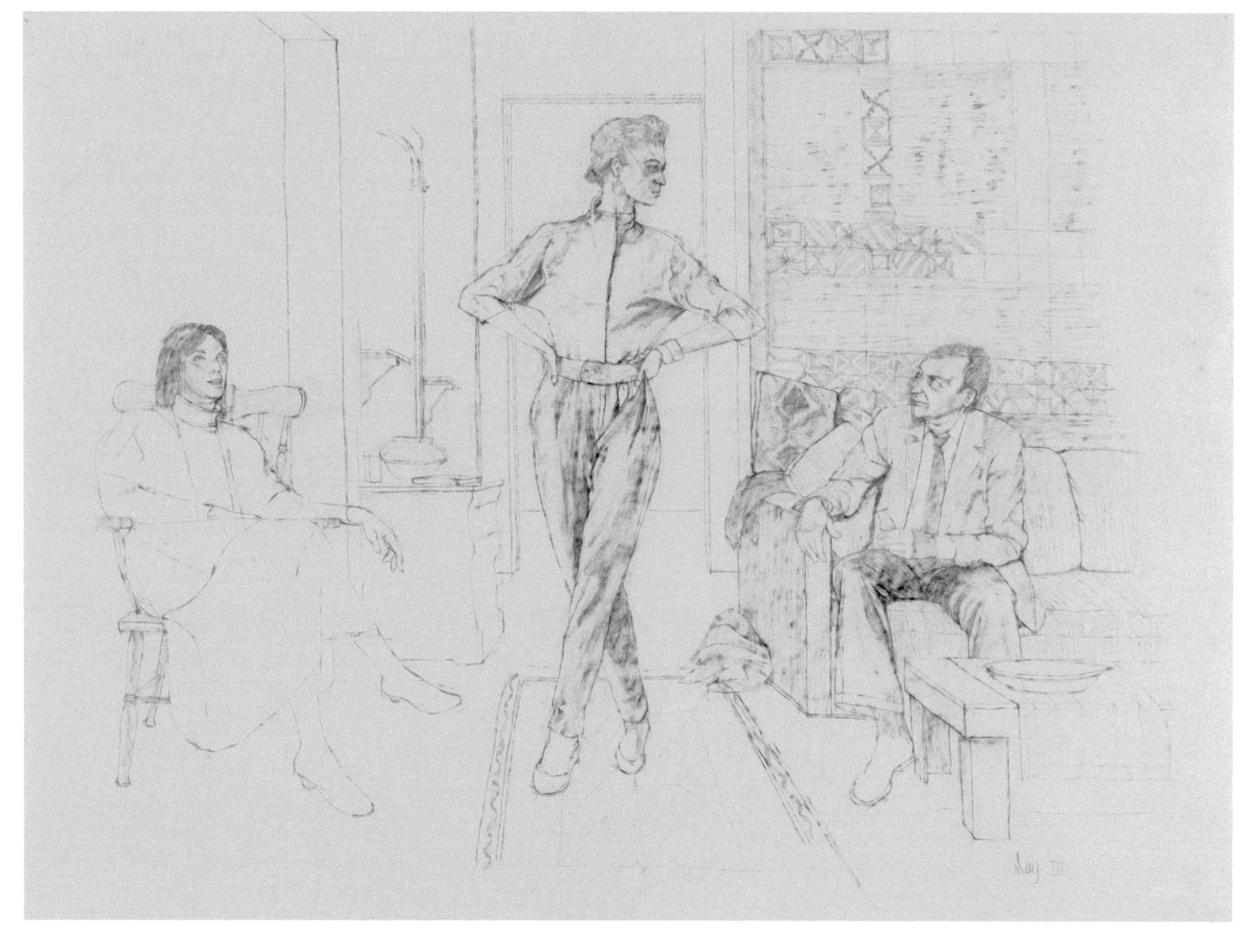

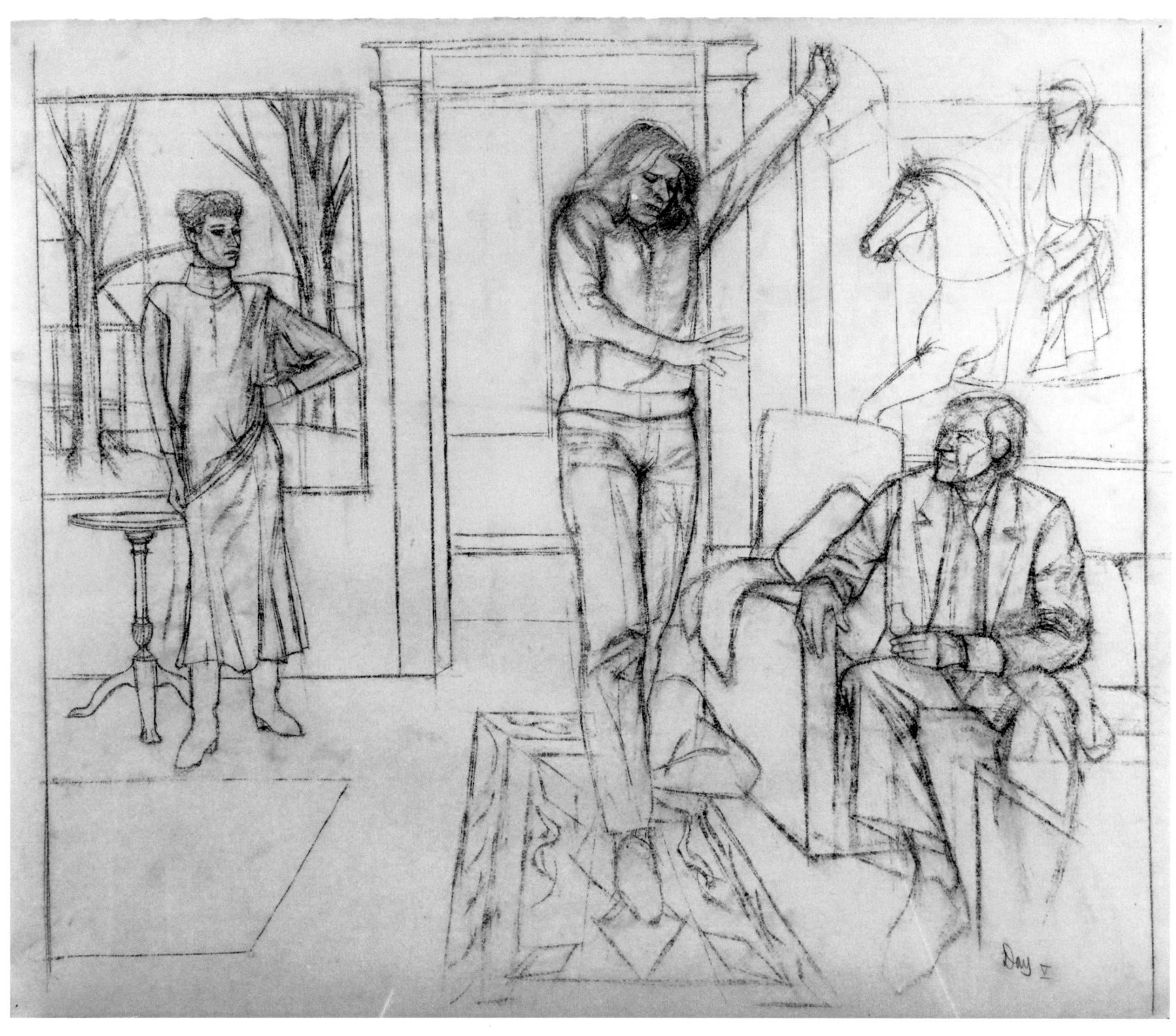

PLATE 37
*Salome Variation A*, 1988

PLATE 39
*Salome Variation K*, 1988

PLATE 38
*Salome Variation B*, 1988

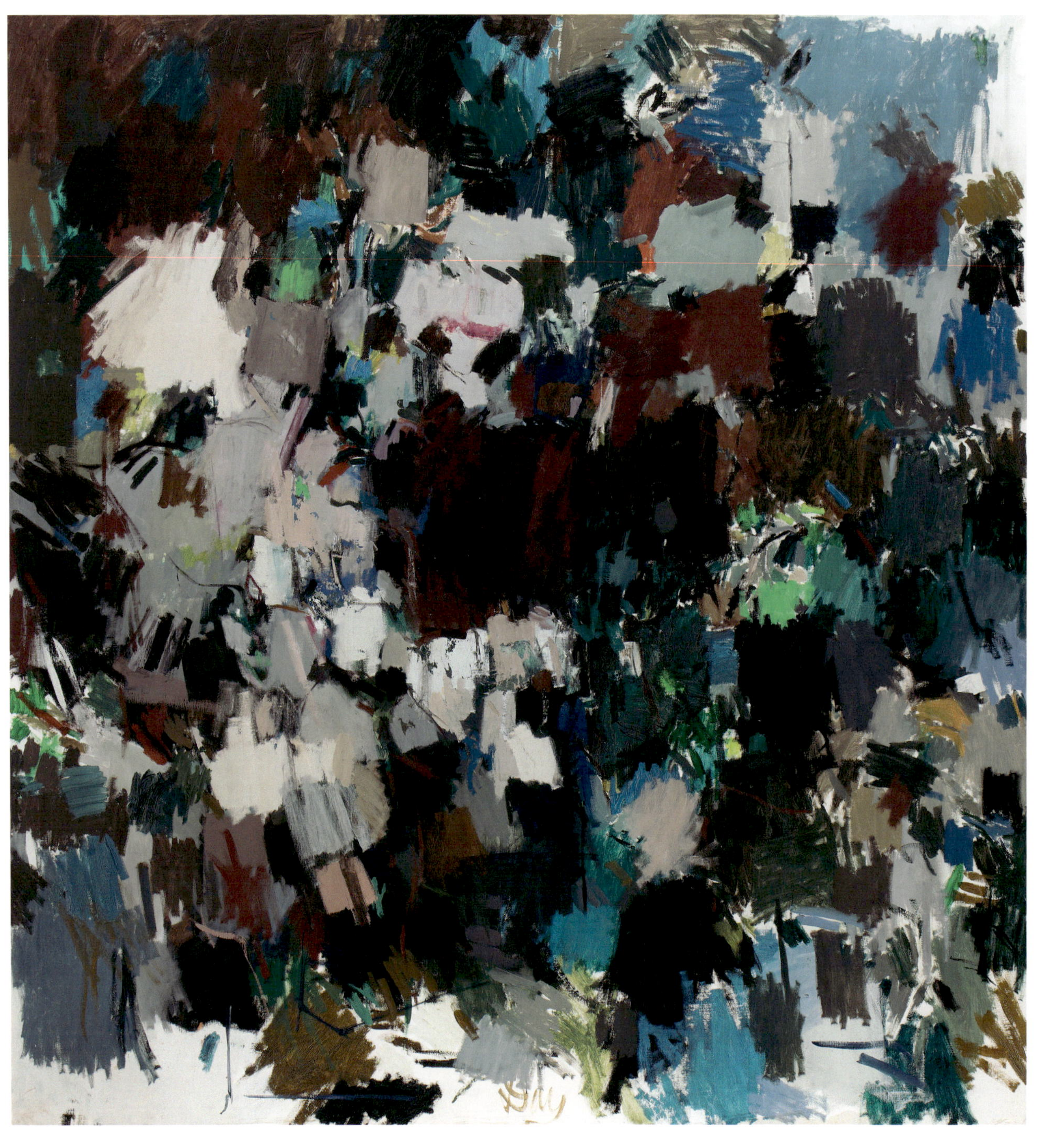

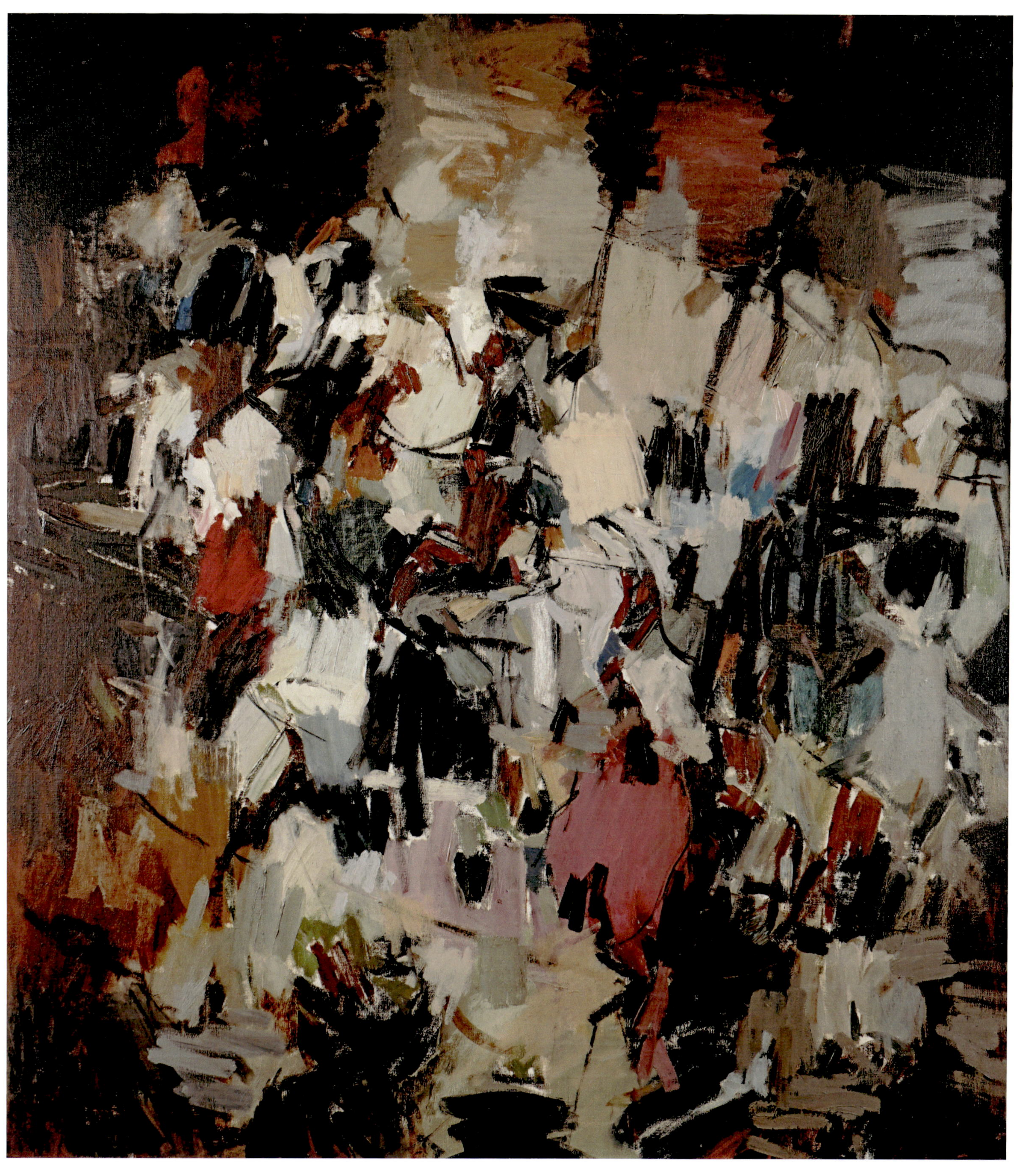

PLATE 41

*(Abstraction)*, c. 1958

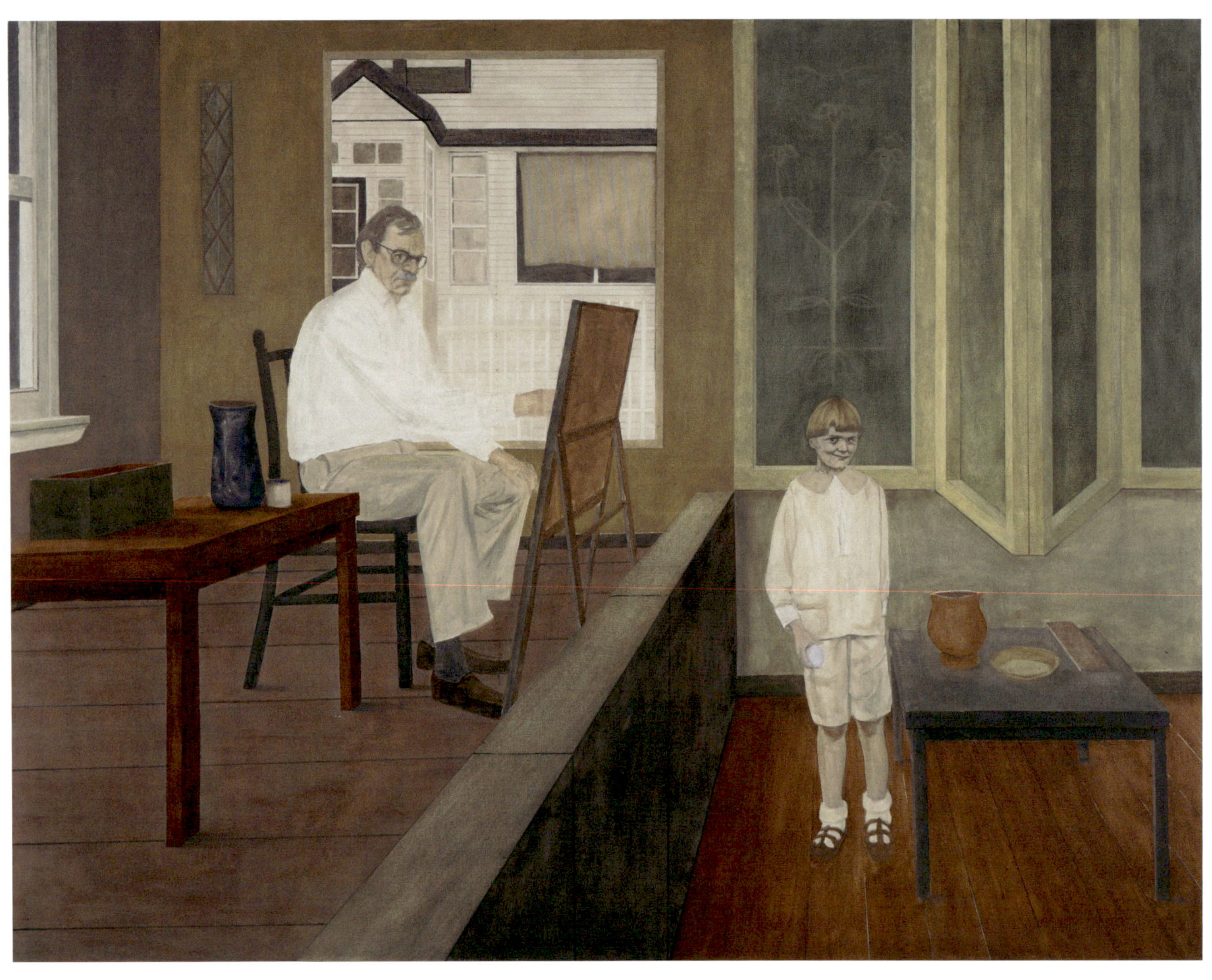

PLATE 42
*Day by Day*, 1991

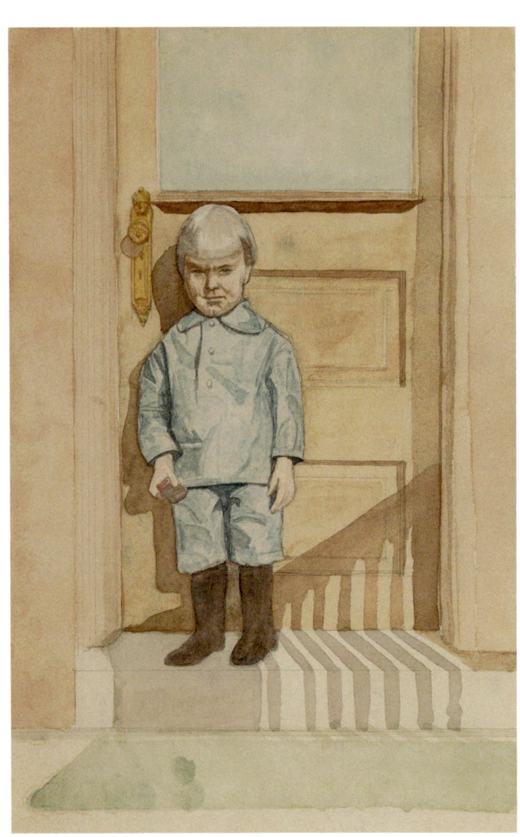

PLATE 43
*(Self-Portrait as a Child)*, c. 1991

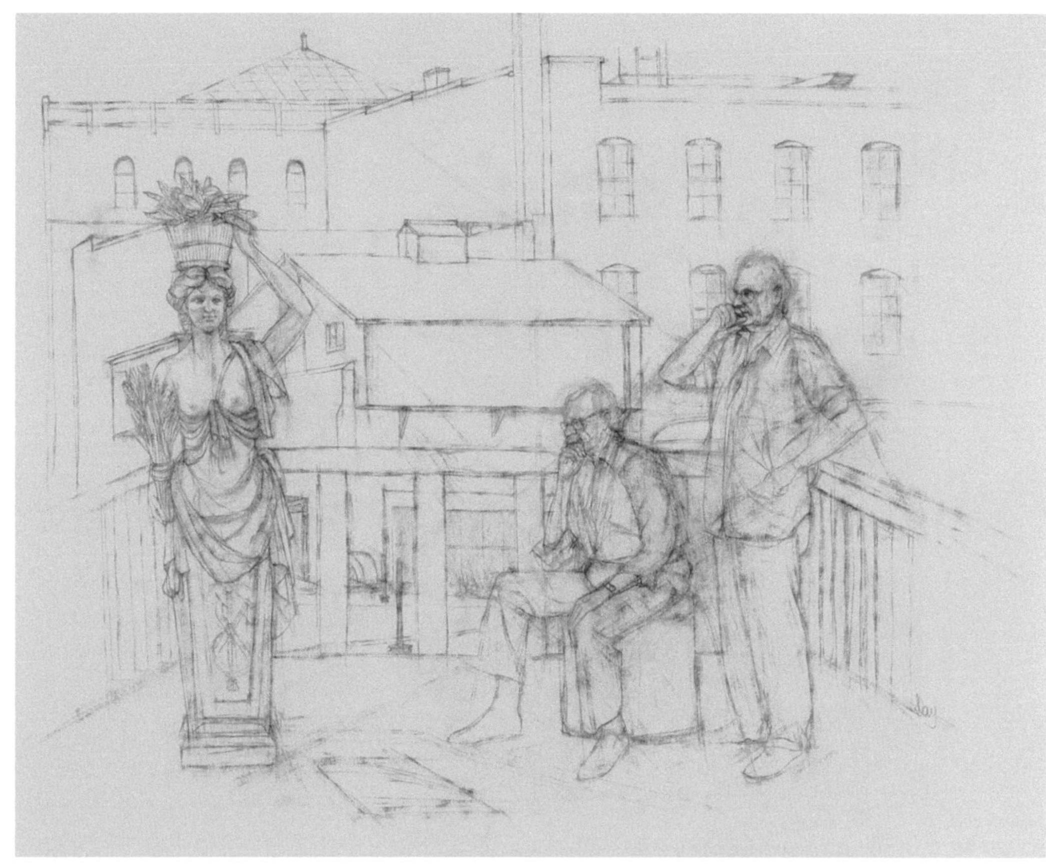

PLATE 44
*Larry and Dennis
(Related to "Ceres"),*
c. 1992

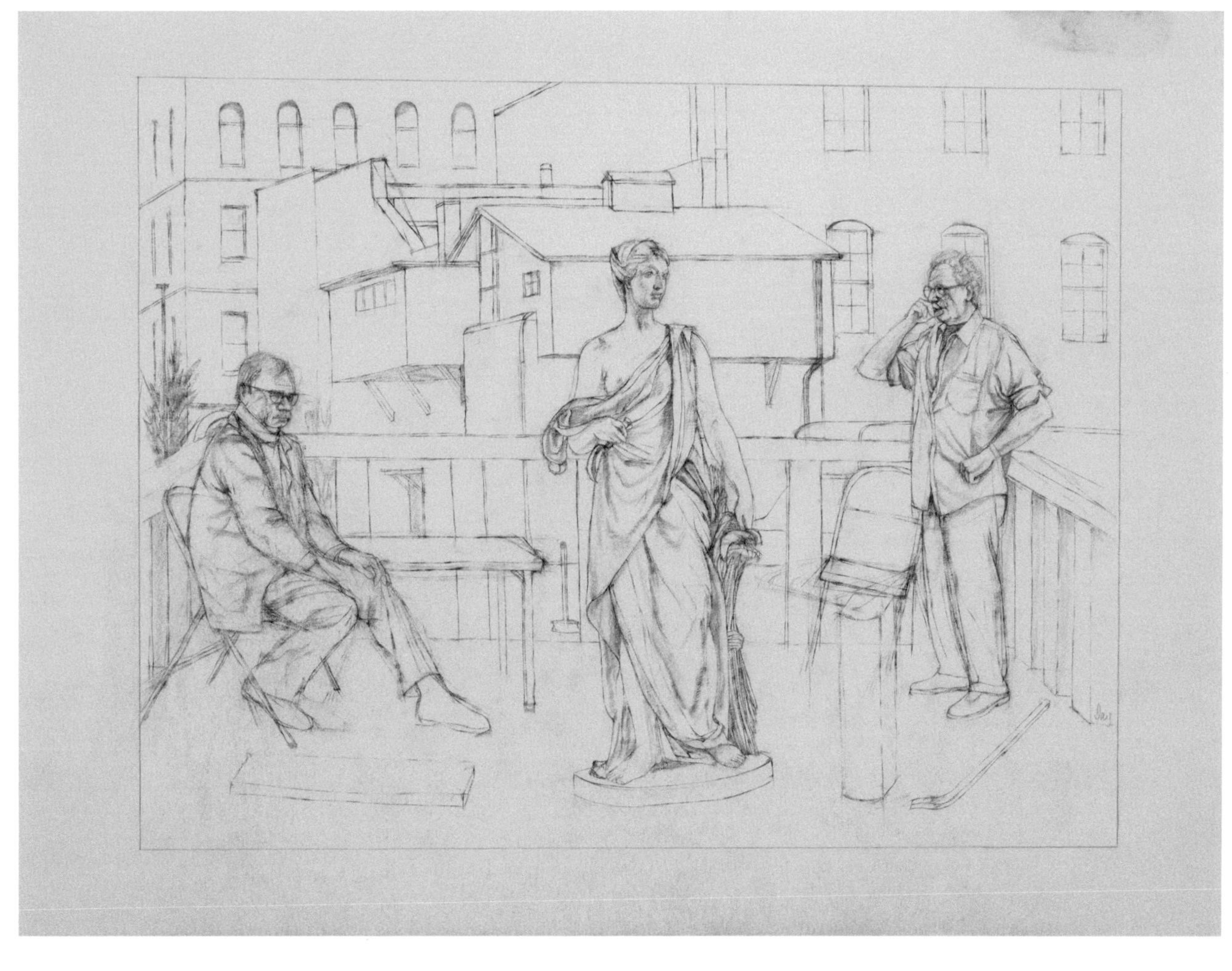

PLATE 45
*Related to "Ceres,"*
c. 1992

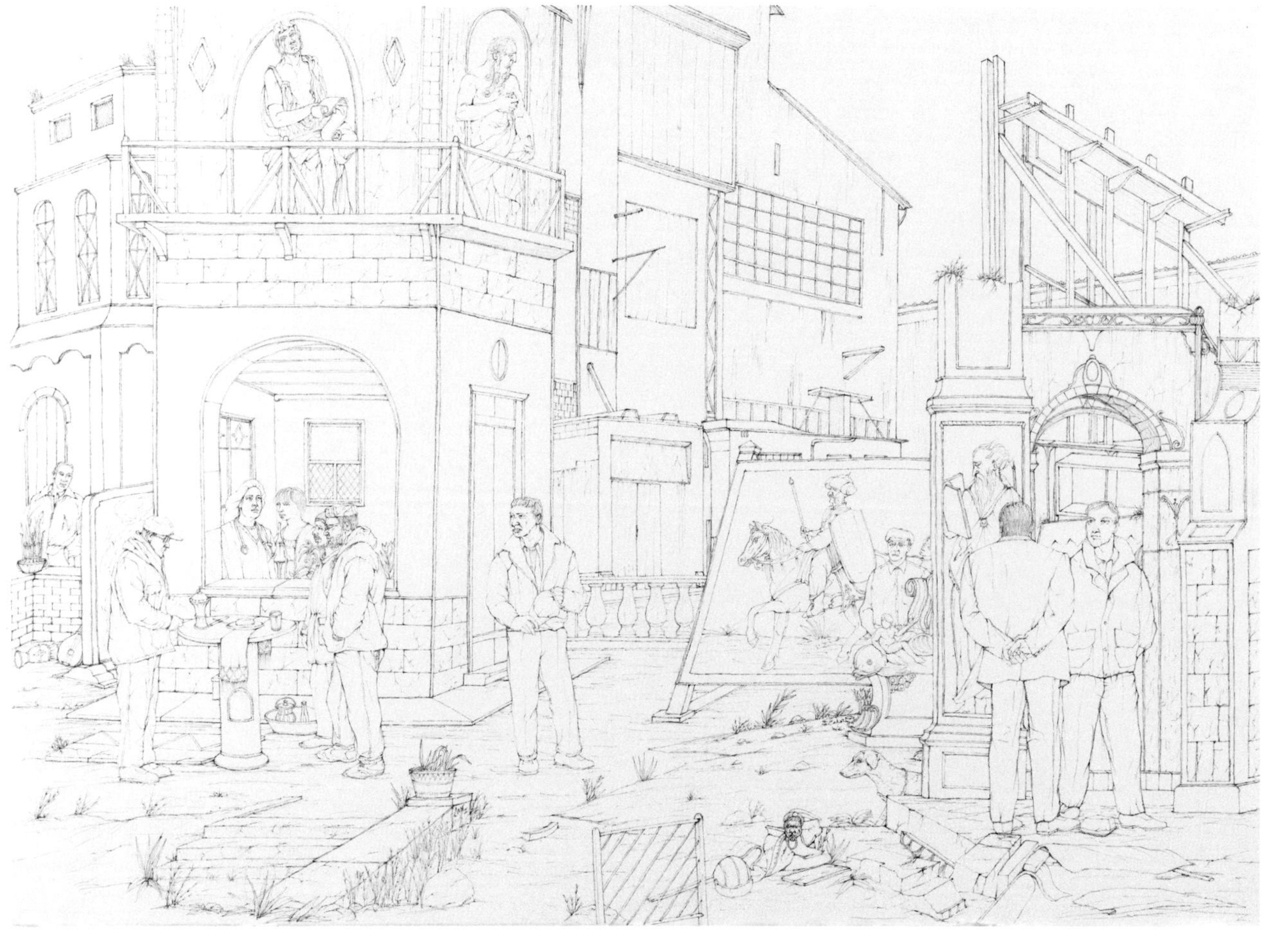

PLATE 46
*Elegy I*

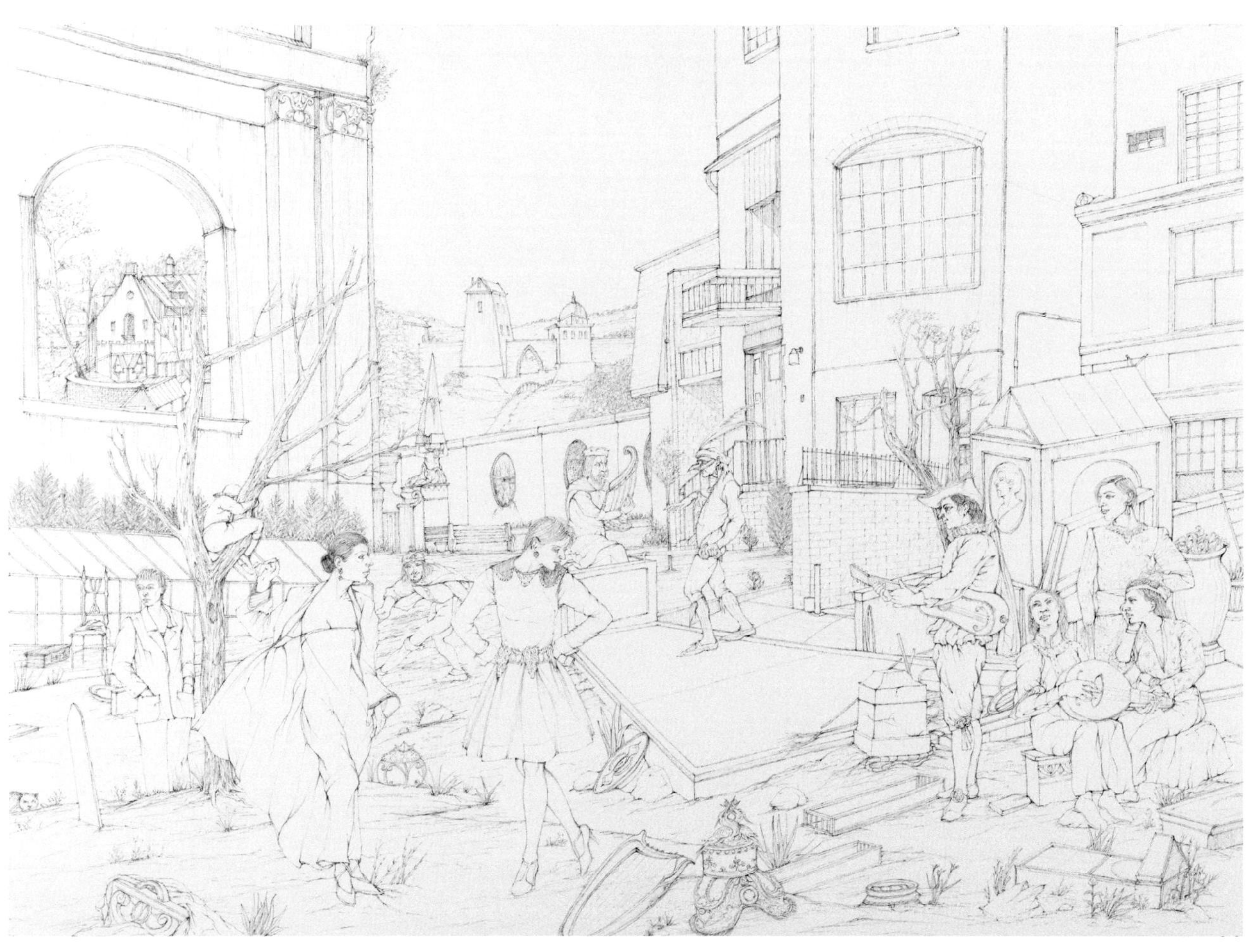

PLATE 47
*Elegy II*

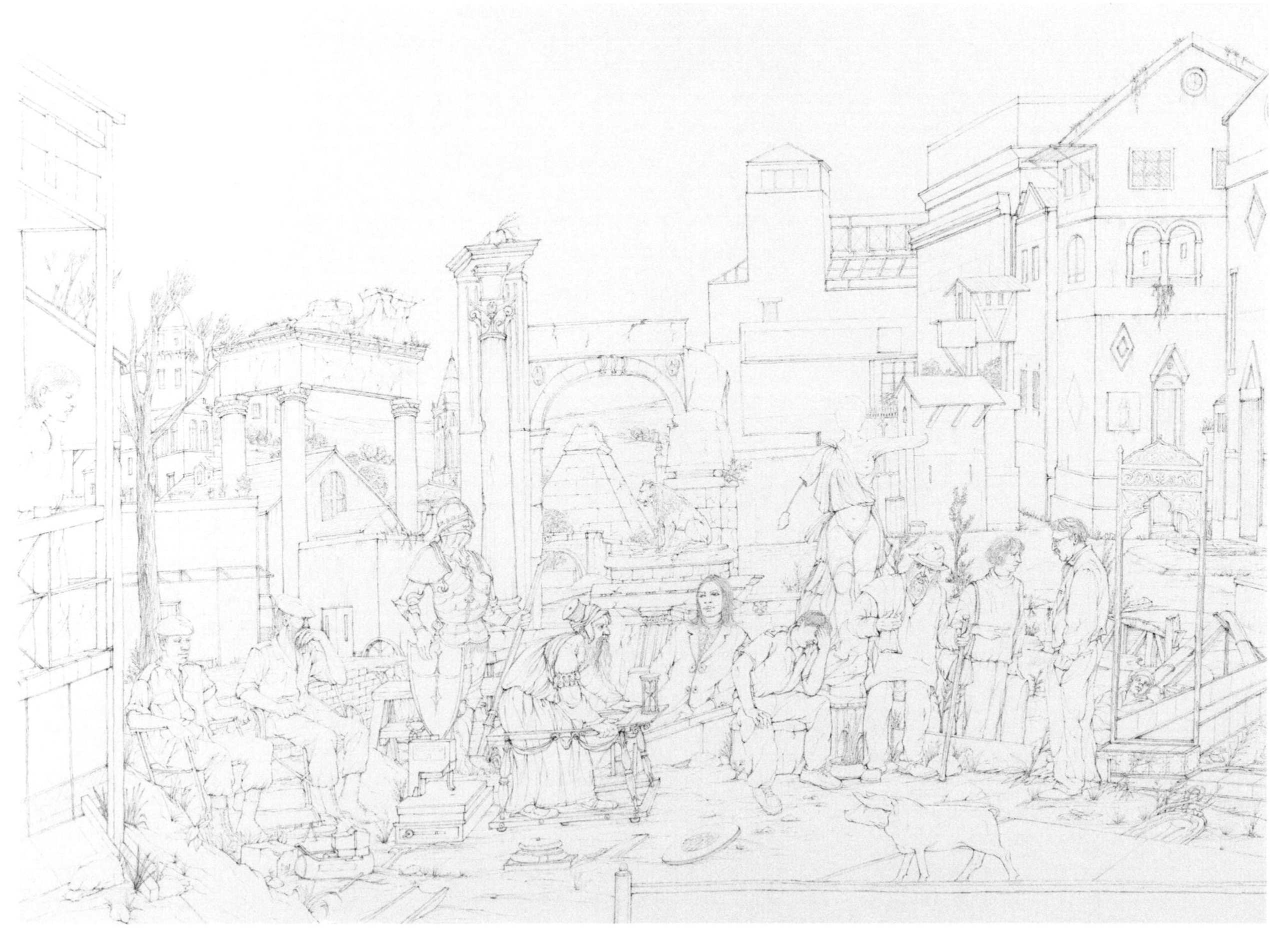

PLATE 48
Elegy III

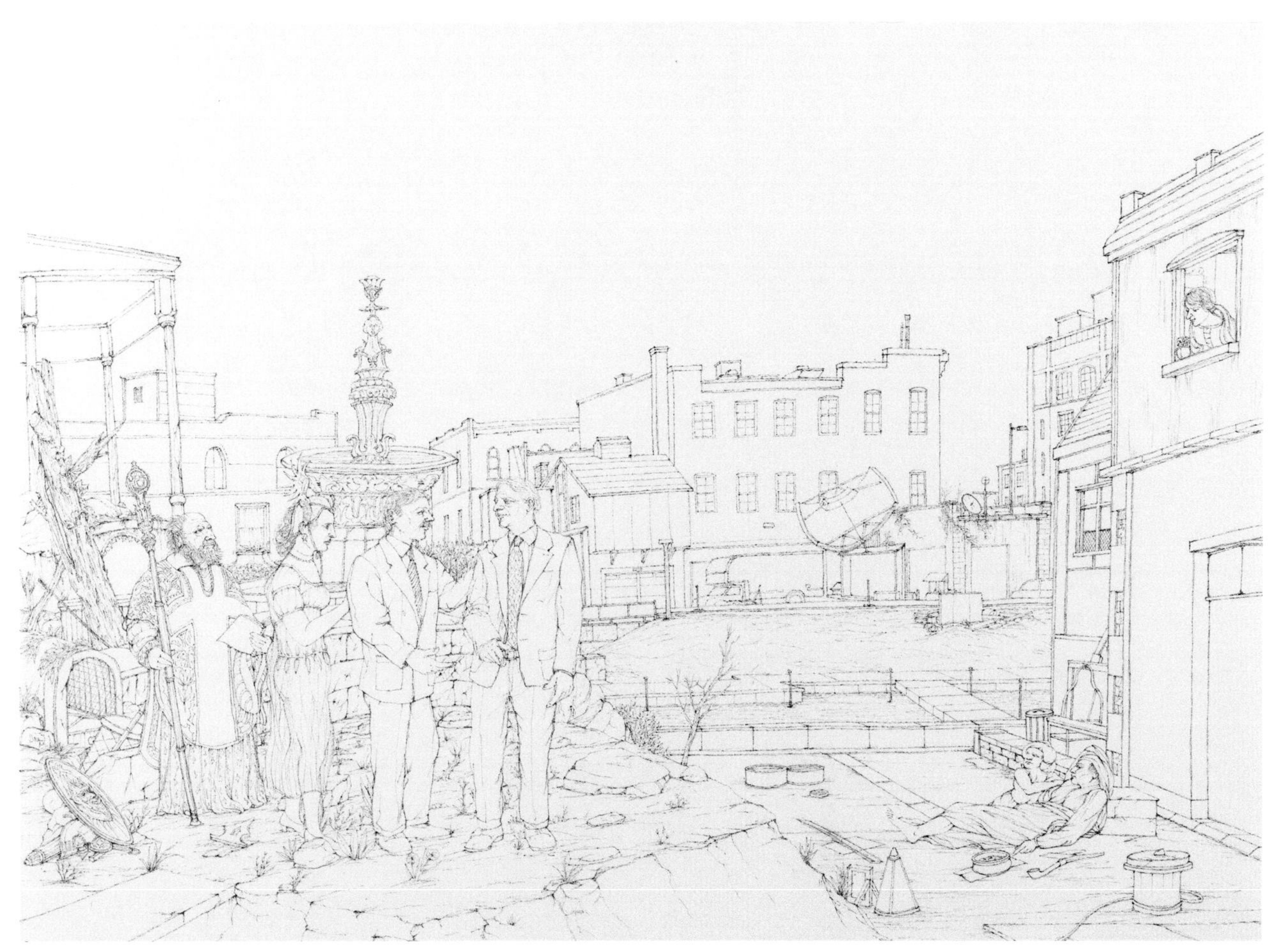

PLATE 49
Elegy IV

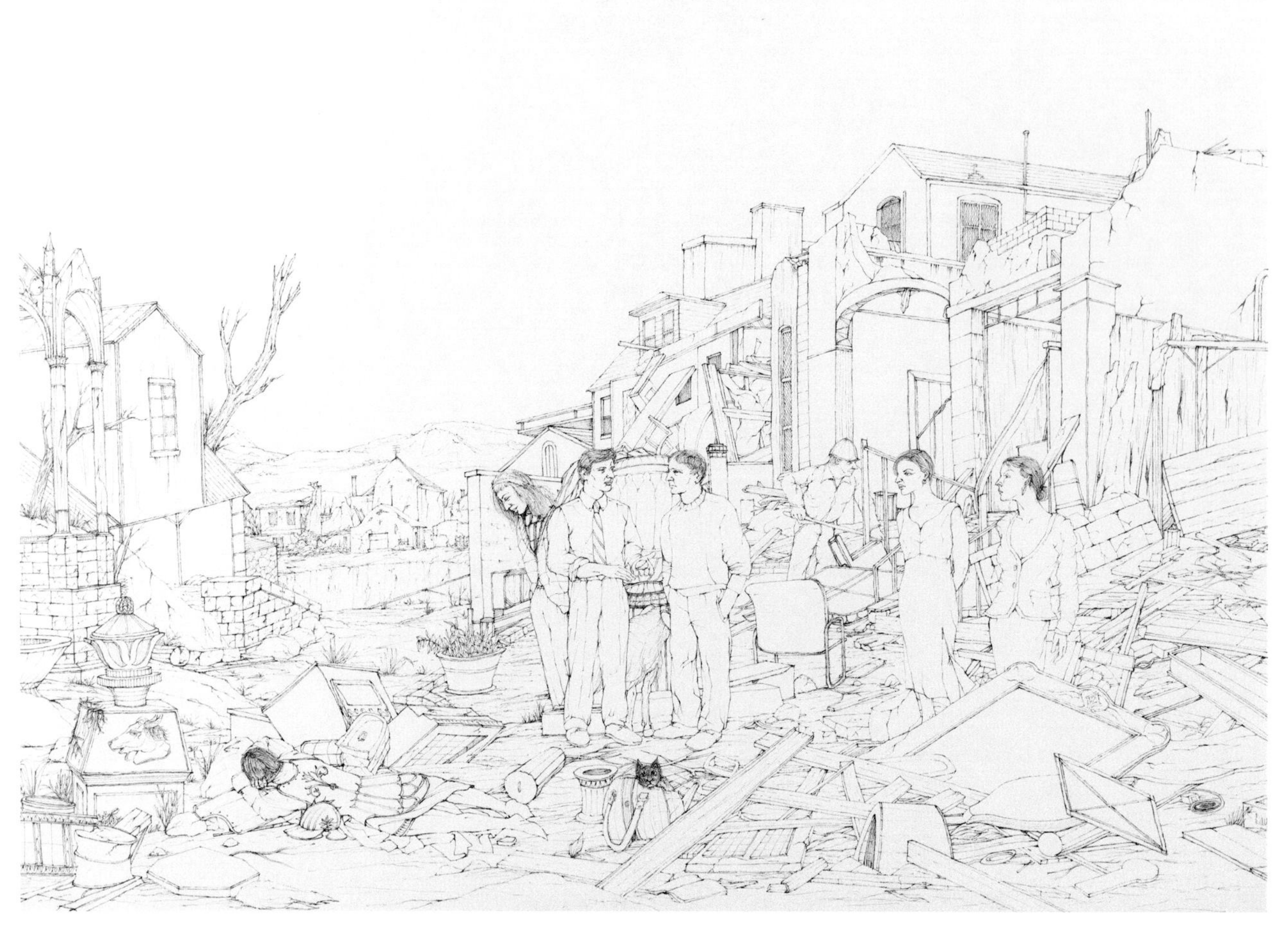

PLATE 50
*Elegy V*

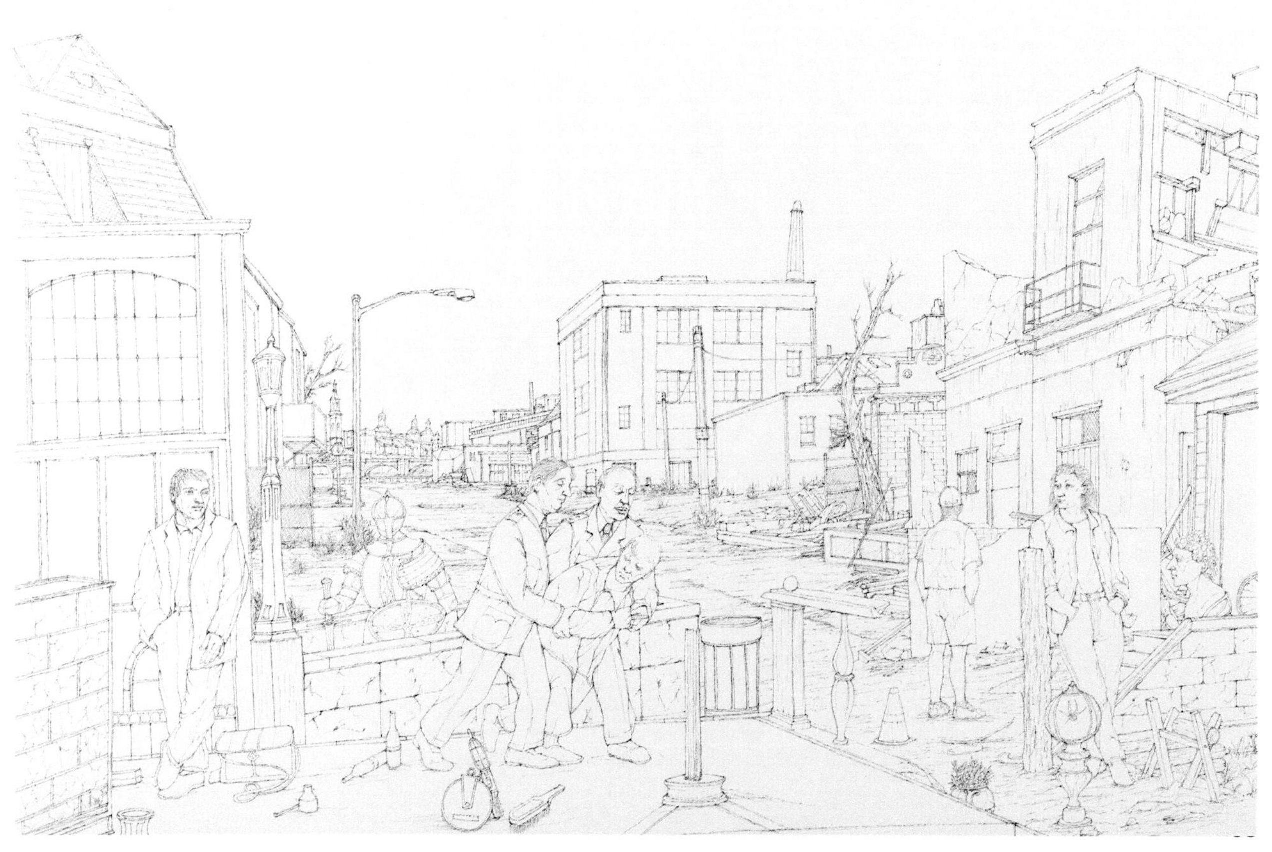

PLATE 51
*Elegy VI*

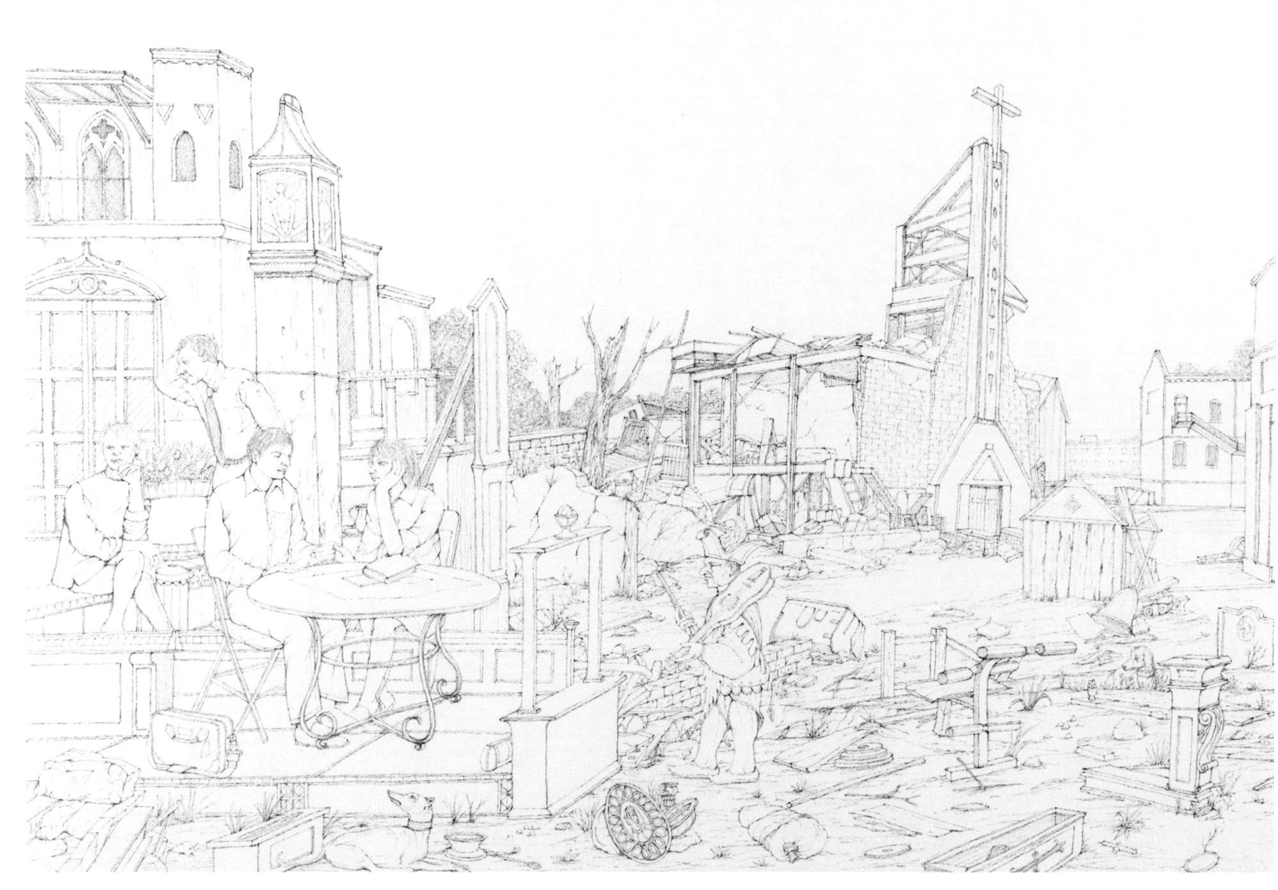

PLATE 52
Elegy VII

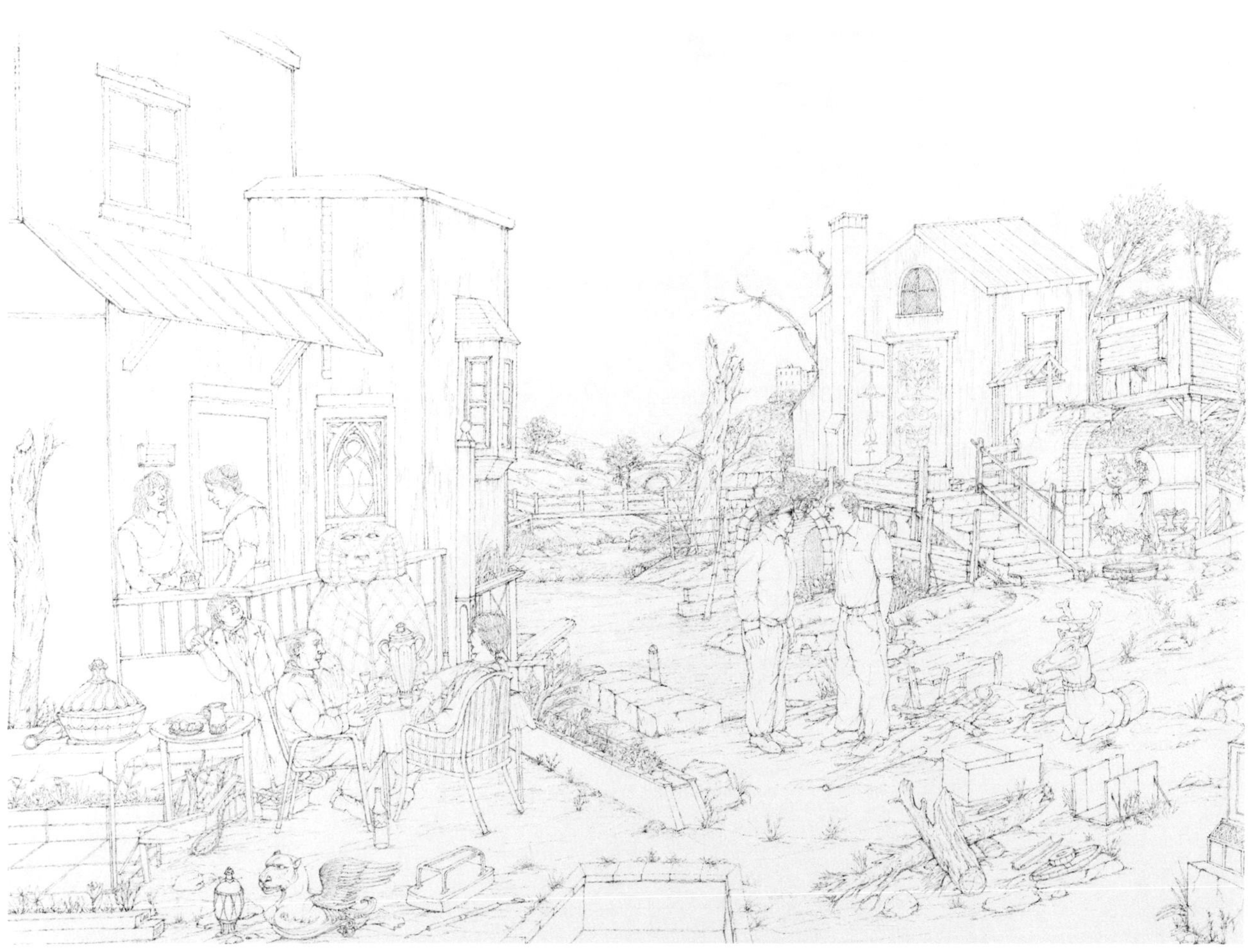

PLATE 53
Elegy VIII

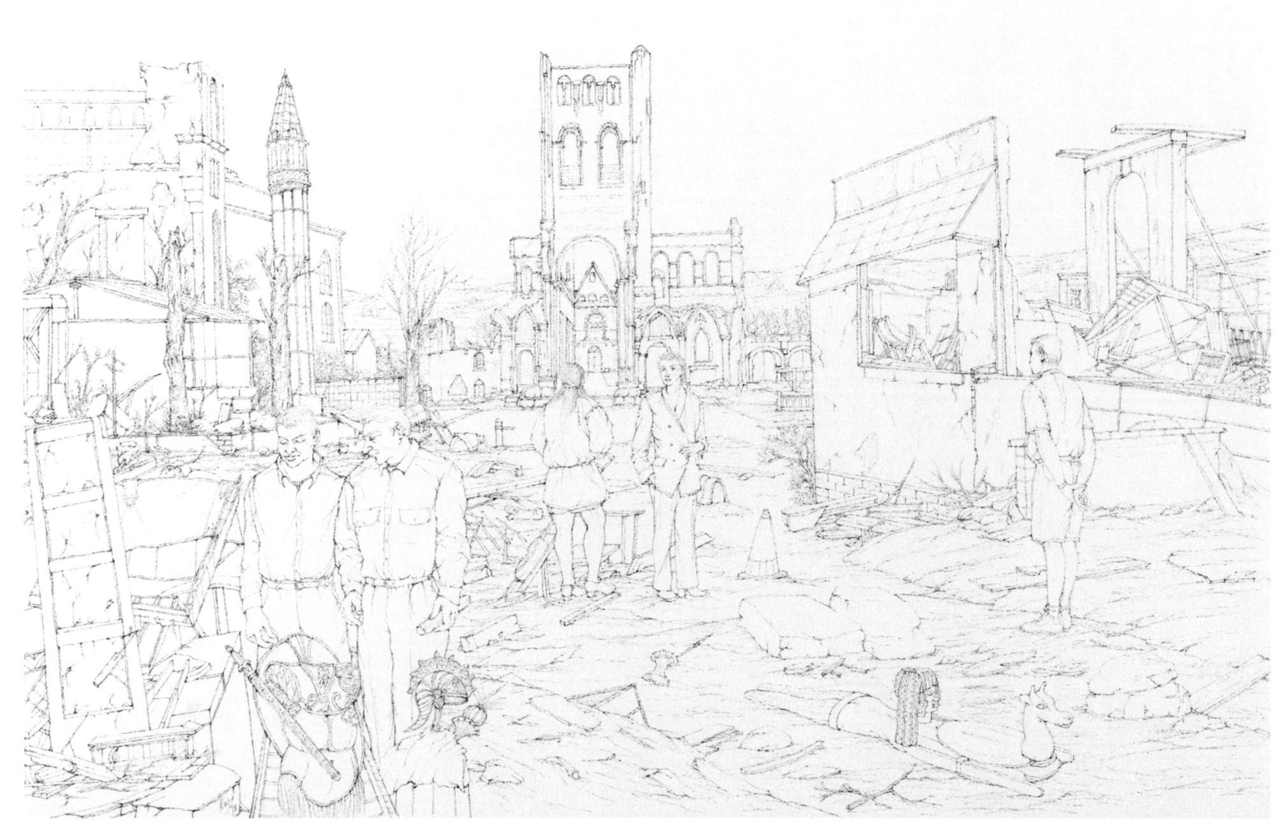

PLATE 54
*Elegy IX*

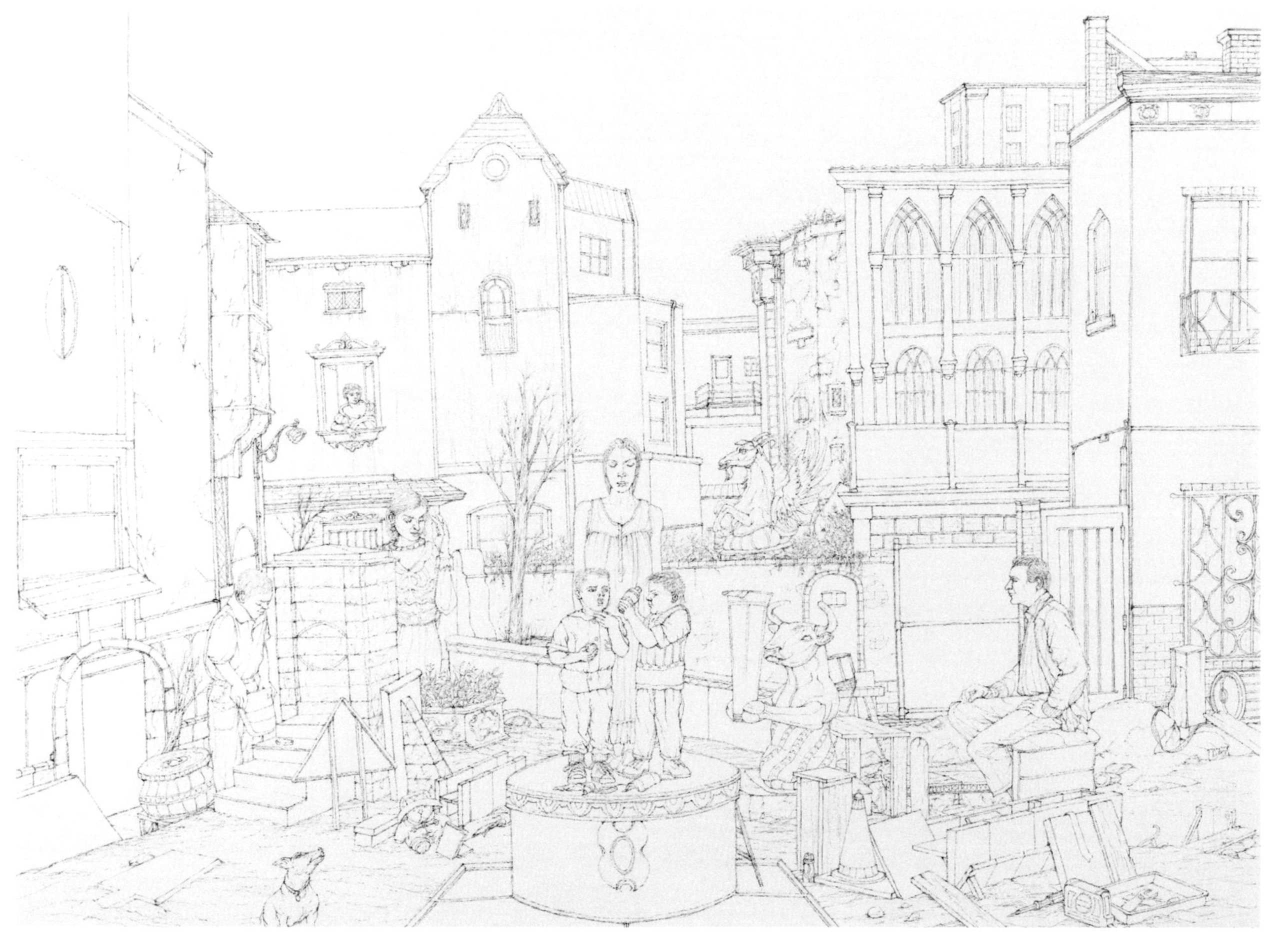

PLATE 55
*Elegy X*

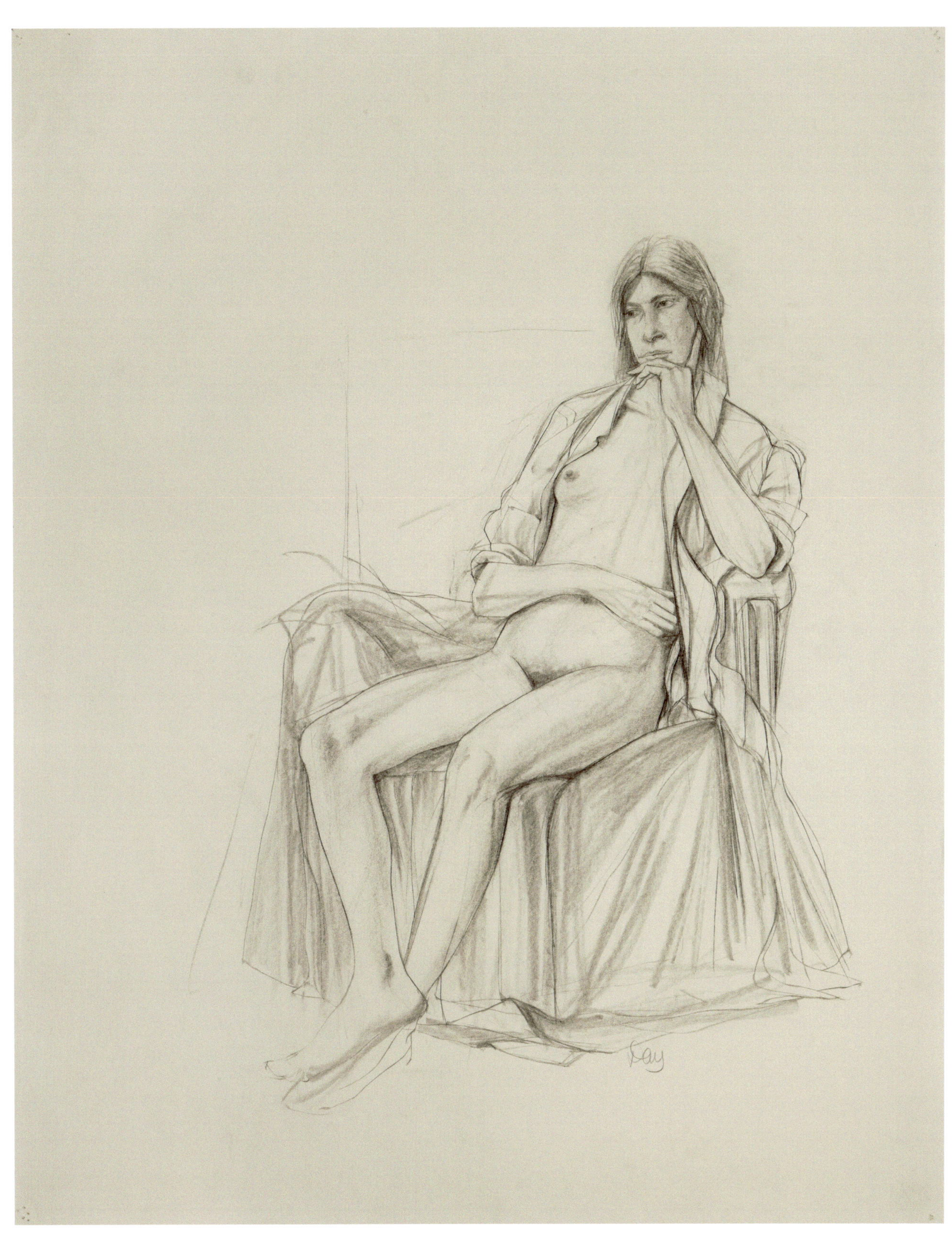

PLATE 56
*(Seated Woman in Robe)*, c. 1980

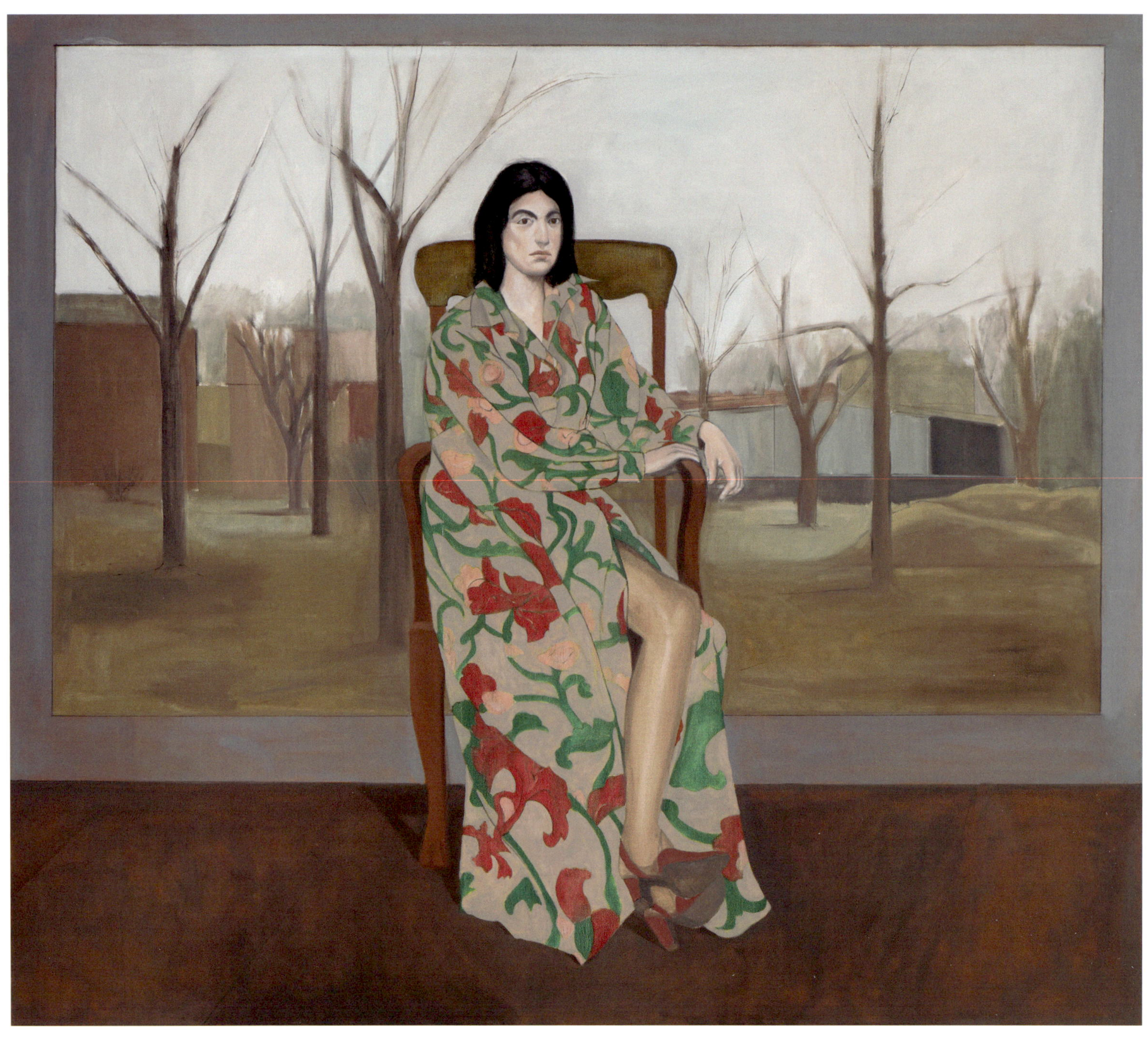

PLATE 57
*Partial Portrait, 1976–77*

72

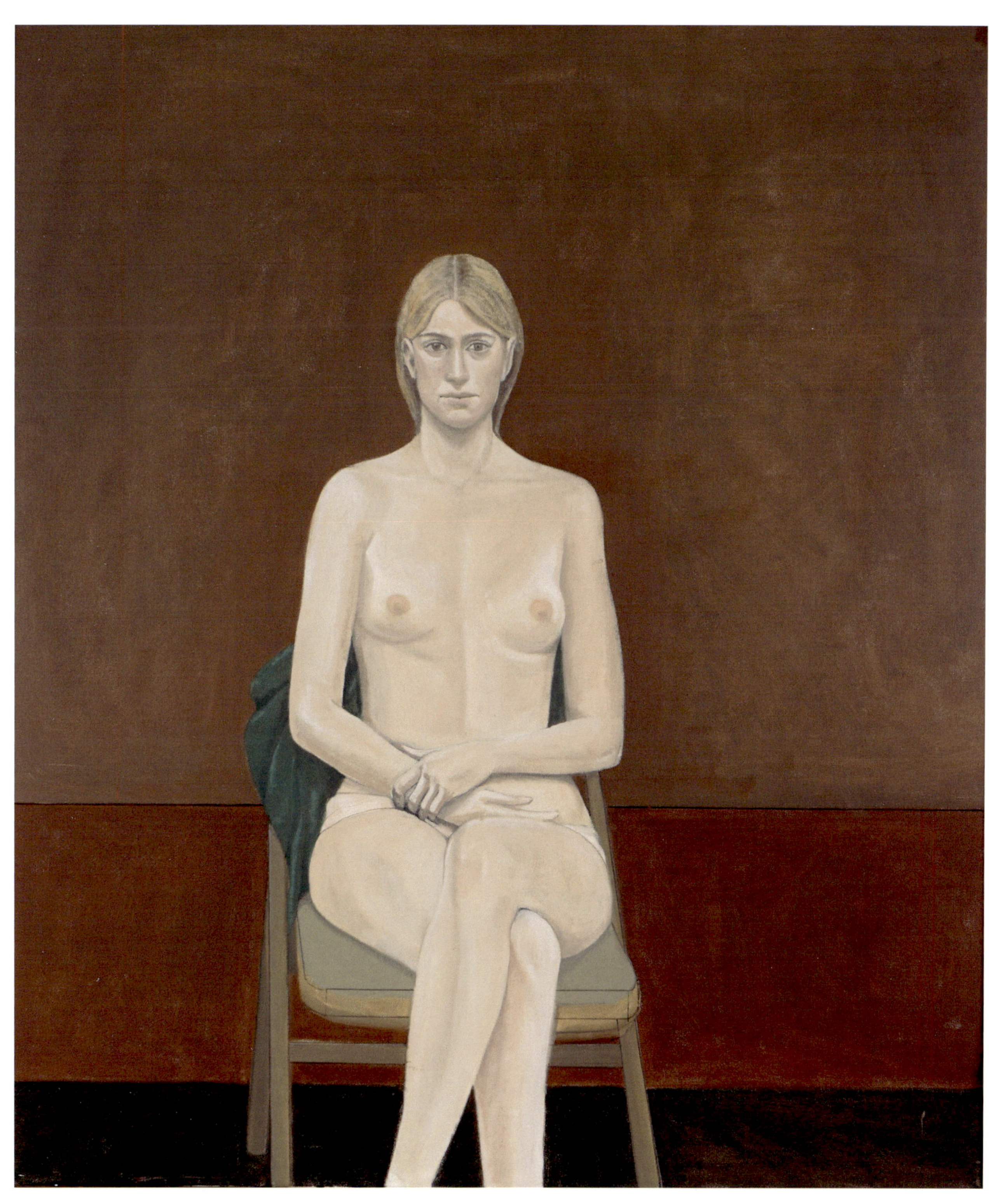

PLATE 58
*Nude*, 1978–79

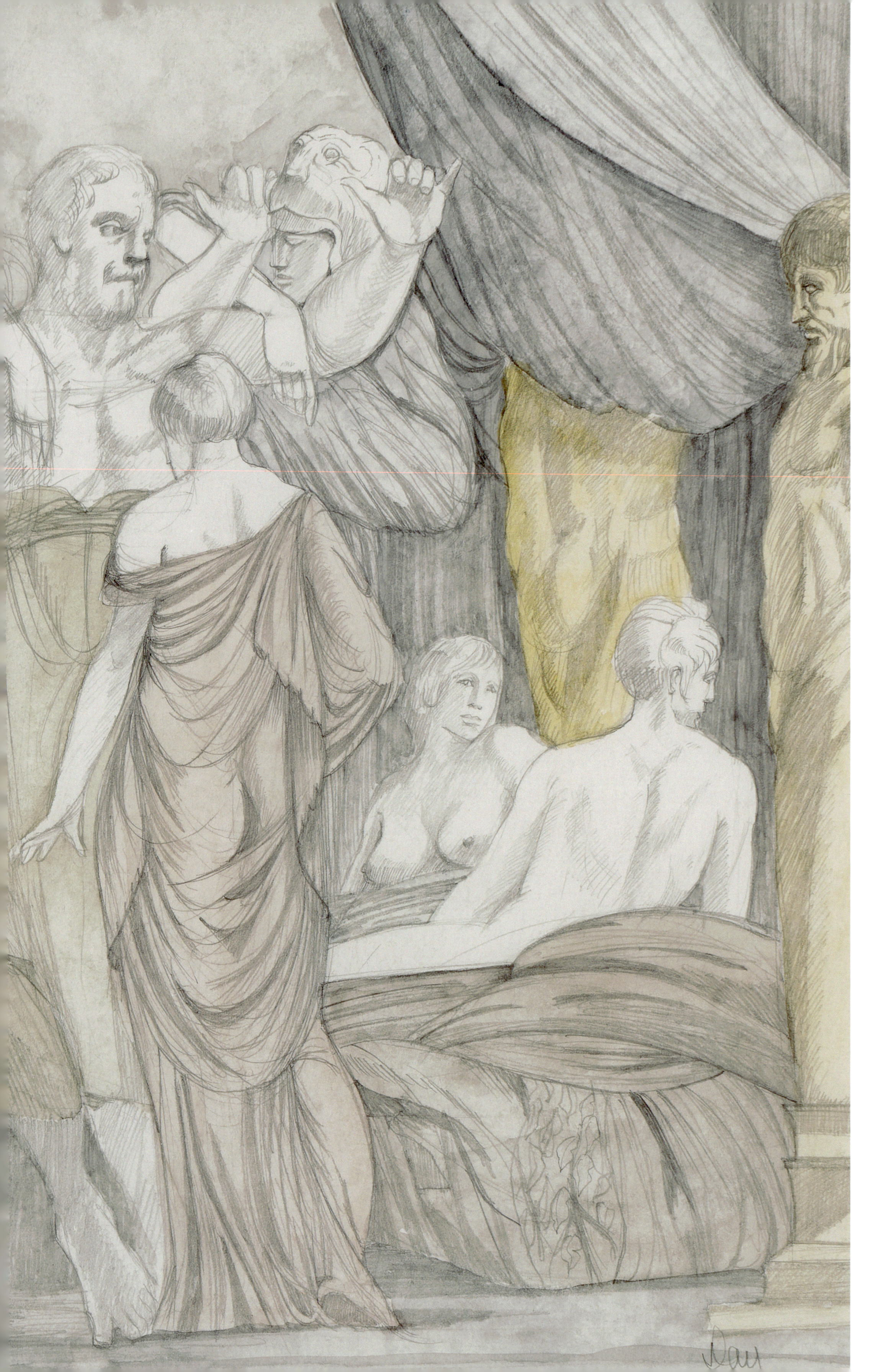

*Jonathan Bober*

# Larry Day Drawing:
# From Copy to Invention

The exhaustion of Abstract Expressionism was among the crises of the early sixties. The intense subjectivity, the plumbing of the depths of interiority for imagery and procedure, had itself become conventional, its language familiar, its products predictable. The most characterized, self-conscious, and polemical responses featured a return to everyday experience and the creation of new forms out of its material. But some artists rediscovered meaning in traditional forms and practices, from the academic to the realist, and in the species of modernism like Surrealism and Social Realism that had kept a certain faith with the figurative.

Larry Day was outstanding among these artists. His conversion from abstraction was consistent in spirit and relative timing with that of Philip Guston and perhaps closest in resemblance to that of Alfred Leslie. Day's, however, would be the purest, the most disciplined, and the most sustained pursuit of a figurative style. Unique, it would be predicated upon a thorough and continuous research of the art of the past. It would aspire to and attain that level of craft. Most conspicuous, and the subject here, Day's art would turn to drawing, not just as an accessory or a byproduct, but as an inspiration and then a principal bearer of personal meaning.

Day's earliest post–art school drawings from the masters, from the 1950s, are copies in the oldest sense of the medium. A study after one of Paolo Veronese's incessant studies of multiple motifs in pen and ink with wash, formerly in the collection of Robert Lehman (plate 60), is typical in conception and function. It recapitulates the entire sheet, honoring its brilliant mise-en-page. The copy dwells on the formal aspects of greatest interest—value structure, rhythmic movement, and activation of interval—and exaggerates them. Elliptic but discrete in Veronese's drawing, individual figures are elided and dissolved. In some other copies of the period, the representational element is so transmuted that the source cannot be identified (plate 61). That Day's work seems so coherent, so beautiful, is due to a fundamental alignment of Veronese's priorities with those of Abstract Expressionism. Like Michelangelo's studies after Masaccio, or a student's in a museum today, the drawing is at once a record of experience (probably through reproduction), a reckoning with its style, and an attempt at its internalization.

Day would persist in such traditional study through copying during the 1960s. His models were all historical works by major masters, mostly concentrated in the sixteenth and seventeenth centuries, and generally in pen and ink. His attention was focused on paintings, such as Titian's glorious *Bacchanal of the Andrians* (plate 62) and Peter Paul Rubens's *Garden of Love*, but he would admit the occasional print, like Rembrandt van Rijn's *Adoration of the Magi*. From this point onward, however, Day excluded drawings as models, later explaining in a note to himself:

> It would be presumptuous to draw from a drawing: that is to draw in the same medium as the object. I think if I did draw from a drawing it would have to be in another medium; a material distancing would be necessary to recognize my contribution and my discovery of what I could not, or would not, or to be true to myself, should not do.

In practically every case, his drawings address the whole composition, not the individual motifs or figures often standard in such copies. While the figurative elements are usually delineated, they are only selectively and summarily elaborated. The principal concern remains intervals, interstices, and the relationship between forms. And the hand in these drawings is chameleonic according to source and interest. The formal weight still favors the model, and the copy is still that, deferential and unsettled. But the direction and basic terms of Day's later drawings—the commitment to comprehensive structure and articulate contour––were already established.

Over the course of the 1970s, Day's drawings found balance and consistency. They continued to be complete compositions, demonstrating an overwhelming concern for structure and pattern, only more carefully controlled and refined, sometimes in a separate study. The figural component is admitted at a regular and legible level of articulation. Often it includes the succinct notation of facial expression—first signs of an emotional content, and sometimes an ambiguity or irony as complex as the formal calculation. How systematic the research, how deliberated the process, is underscored by a series of seventeen studies, identical in size and materials, examining every possible aspect of a surprisingly obscure work: a lithograph of a salon concert by Mariano Andreu (figs. 4.1–4.3), which Day knew from a photograph of an impression in Lessing Rosenwald's vast collection.

A marked preference for certain artists became apparent. Poussin was preeminent (plate 63), the reason, perfect order, and diagrammatic interaction in the paintings of his early maturity offering authoritative templates (see Day's essay on Poussin, pp. 135–38). Reference to the paintings of Jan Steen (fig. 4.4), the most rigorously composed, carefully cadenced, and subtly humorous in seventeenth-century Dutch art, was also frequent. Works by these artists' earlier counterparts also began to appear regularly. The lucid construction and superb craft of Andrea Mantegna and Albrecht Dürer held an obvious appeal (fig. 4.5). If the formal lessons were less relevant, the altered reality and idiosyncratic expression in Hieronymus Bosch proved potent. A copy of

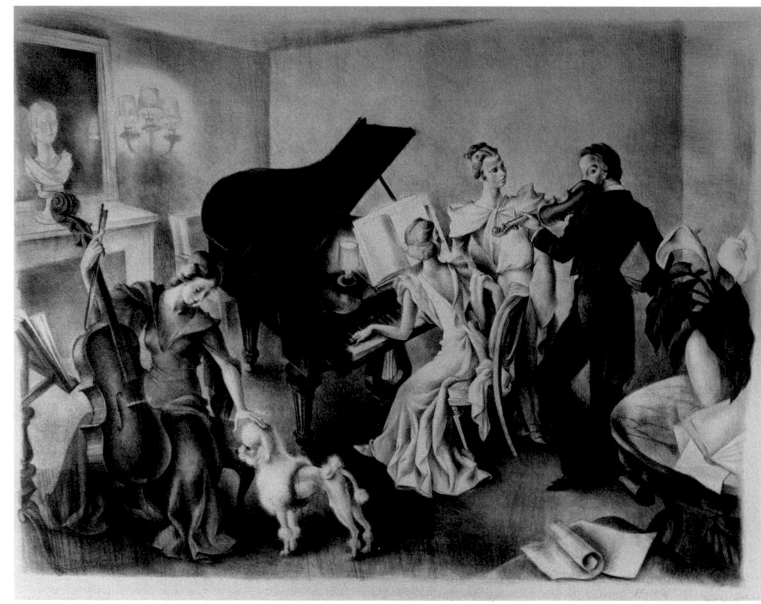

Figure 4.1   Mariano Andreu, *The Concert*, 1934, lithograph on BFK Rives paper, 18⅞ × 24¼ in. (Image courtesy of Ruth Fine)

Figure 4.2    *After "The Concert" 1*, late 1970s, pen and ink, 10⅝ × 14 in. (Larry Day Art Trust)

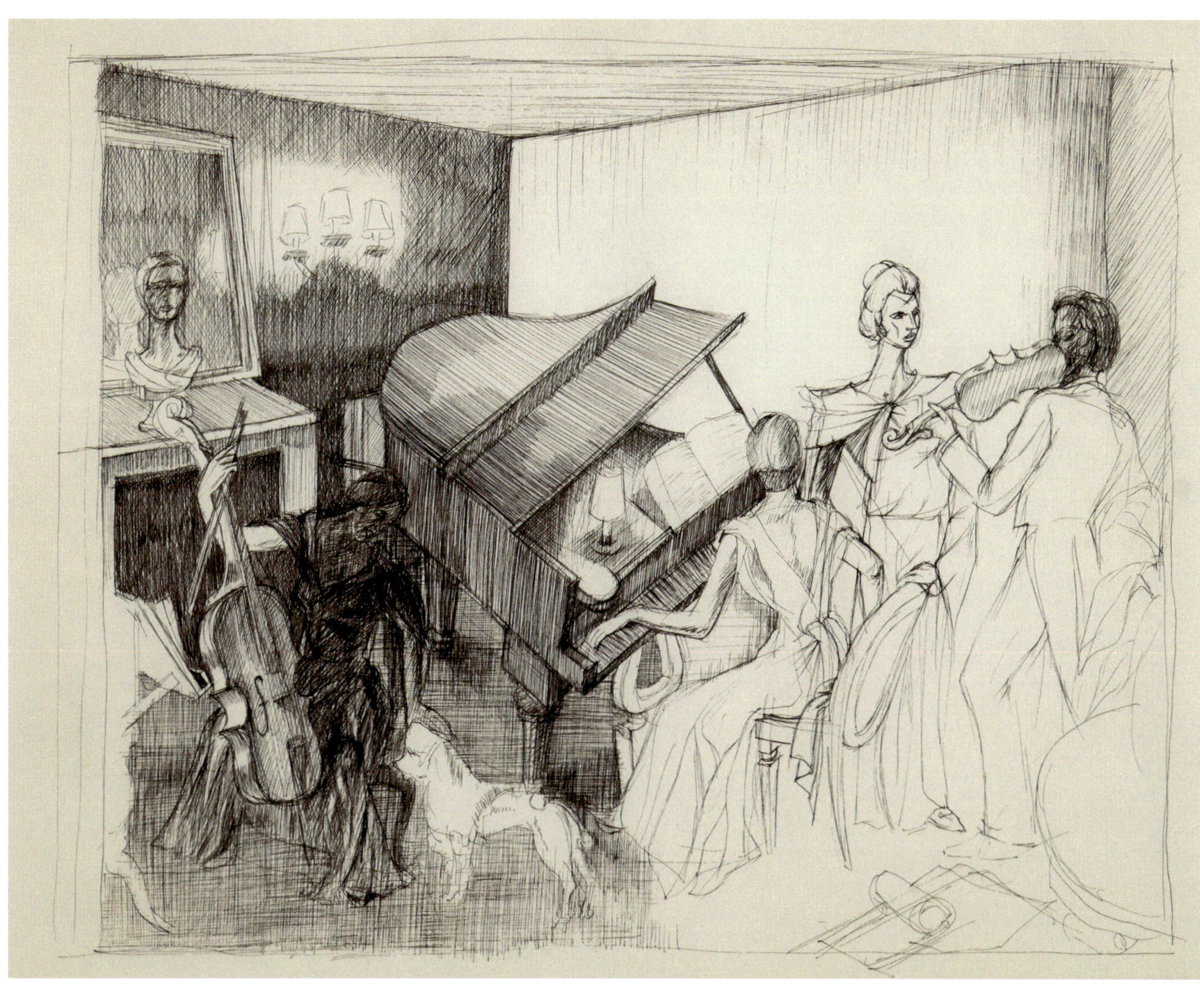

Figure 4.3    *After "The Concert" 17*, late 1970s, pen and ink, 10⅝ × 14 in. (Larry Day Art Trust)

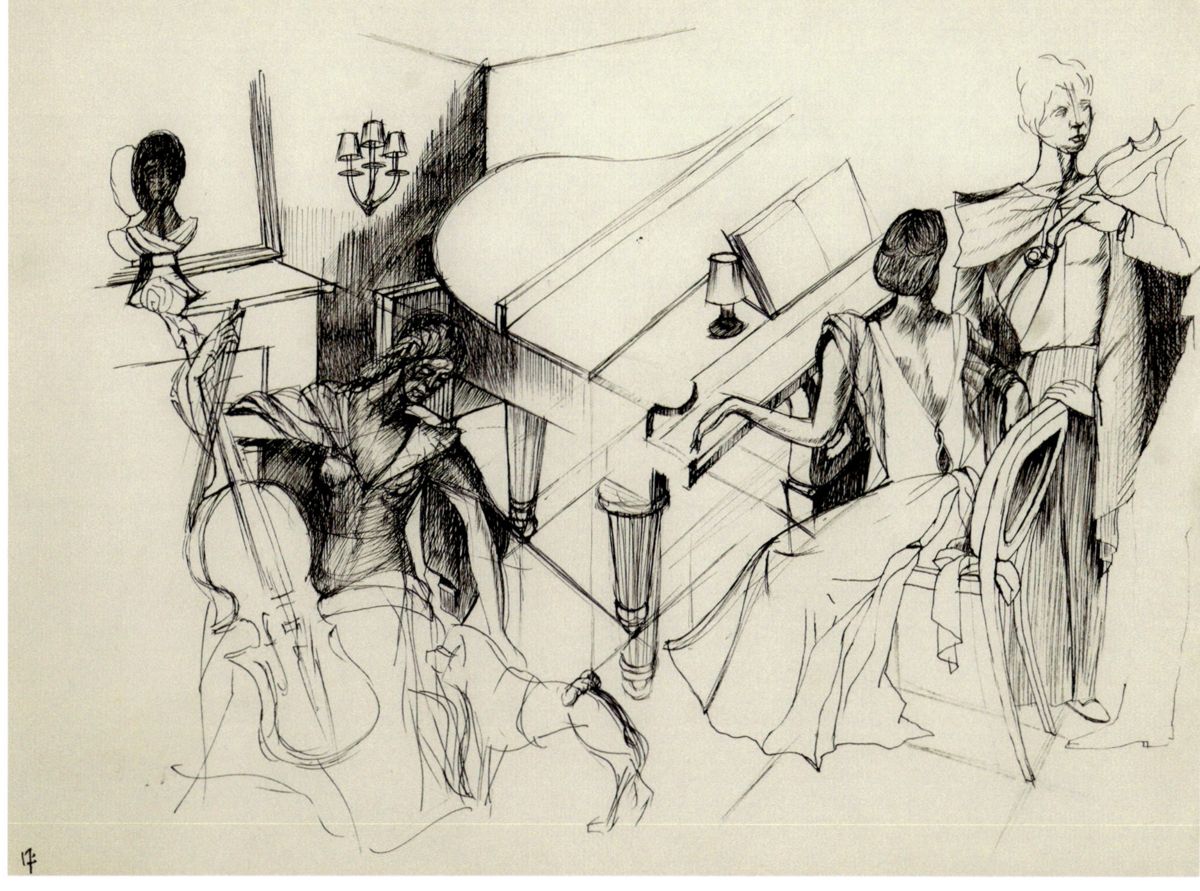

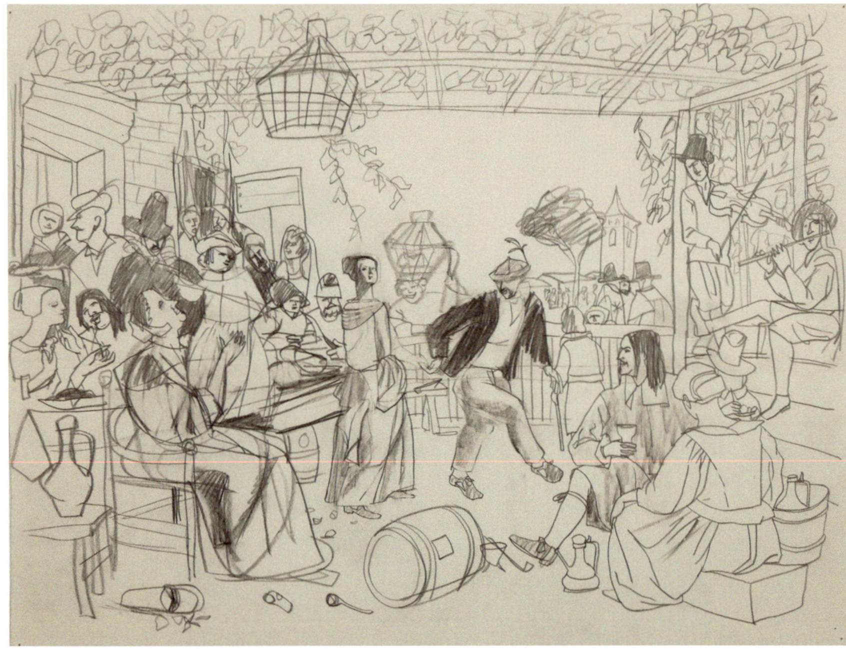

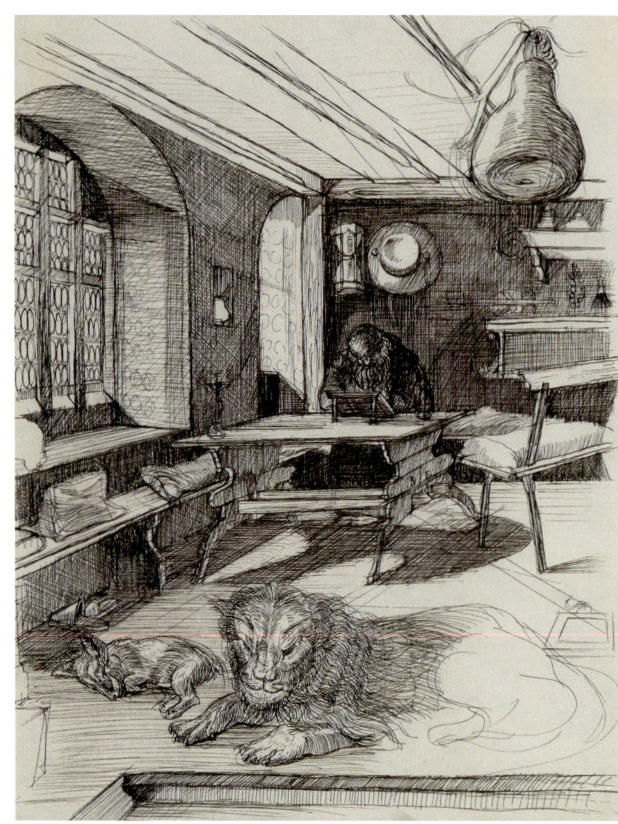

Bosch's *Temptation of Saint Anthony* (fig. 4.6), restricted to the central portion of the main panel, becomes an oneiric enactment on an outdoor stage. These artists and their constellation of styles would remain Day's favorite sources and the basis of others to come. Nearly as telling are the styles that seem never to have held his interest: the full-blown Baroque, with its subtending movement and optical fusion, and, equally, classicism when its ideality and rhetoric were unleavened.

While Day's graphic style would never surrender modal possibilities, during this period there emerged a dominant language. It is overwhelmingly linear and exquisitely responsive to the subject's contours, but only passingly concerned with the description of surfaces and contingent properties. Silhouetting individual forms and transforming entire compositions into elegant lattice work, Day's language gives appropriate shape to the primary concerns that had been steadily emerging. In pen works, occasional accents of densely hatched shadow are distributed according to an original value structure as much as to that of the prototype. Toward the end of the period, his use of graphite became frequent, animating contour, enlivening surface, and imparting a subtle tone to better approximate the model's pictorial properties. There were still the more routine copies. Prints, with their own inescapably linear language, were the most resistant to this evolving interpretation. But by the late 1970s, Day's copies seem resolved in intention and hand, balancing the style of the source and a self-consistent personalization. They begin to function both as works in their own right and as a coherent oeuvre. Indeed, for the first time, some bear signatures.

These developments reached another stage, and Day's graphic style its full flowering, in the early 1980s. The artist's responses to old masters continued apace, now predominantly in graphite. His commitment to Poussin's mythologies (plate 104) and Steen's genre scenes (plate 64) was unwavering. At the same time, his repertoire expanded to paintings of less perfect calculation, richer stuffs, and quieted interactions: later seventeenth-century Dutch artists like Gerard ter Borch and Gabriel Metsu, and early nineteenth-century French artists like Baron Gérard (fig. 4.7). The

Figure 4.4  *(After Steen, Dancing Couple)*, c. 1970, graphite, 14⅜ × 18¾ in. (Collection of Ruth Fine)

Figure 4.5  *After Dürer, Saint Jerome in His Study*, 1974, pen and ink on paper, 11½ × 8⅝ in. (Private Collection)

Figure 4.6 *After Bosch (Temptation of St. Anthony, Central Panel)*, c. 1965, pen and ink on paper, 17 × 13½ in. (Private Collection)

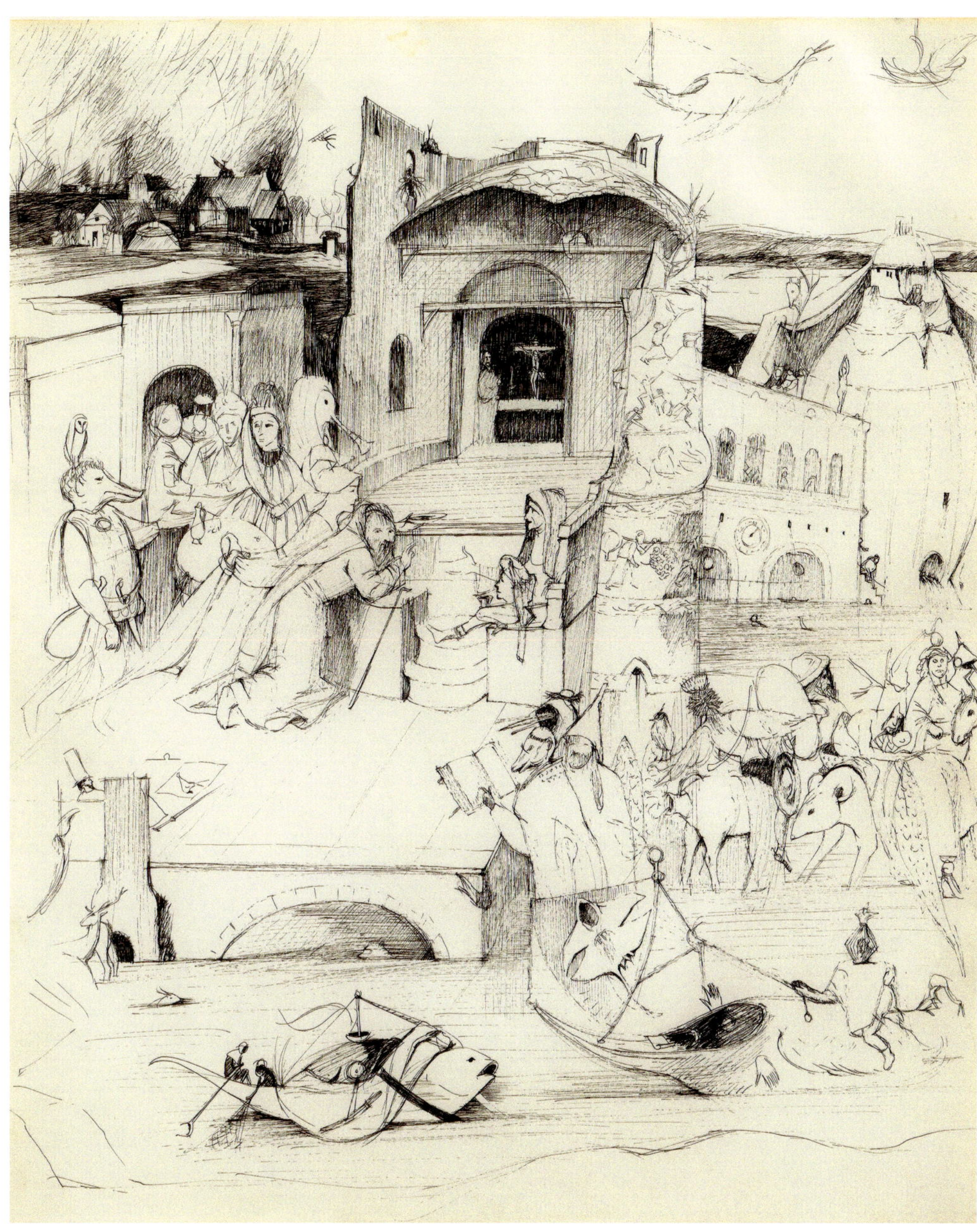

compositions are still largely complete, the emphasis still on clarity of design, but the armatures are now filled with a modeling as exquisite in modulation as the previous line in its movement, and, like it, striking a balance between source and personal vision. Filled with soft pencil, then gently stumped, reserve areas take on a continuous middle tone and metallic sheen, implying surface without defined plasticity. Day certainly knew traditional metal point, and at least one copy seems to refer to an early Florentine example. But it was the technique's closest equivalent among prints, the engravings of Lucas van Leyden, that offered the immediate inspiration. Incomparably delicate in their cutting and sensitive in their assembly (and rapid in their wear), Lucas's plates yielded just such silvery tonality and variegated surfaces. In 1983, the National Gallery of Art in Washington, DC, presented a major exhibition of the engravings. Day's enthusiasm is evident in several copies (fig. 4.8) from around that date.

Tonality was not the only attraction and lesson of Lucas's engravings. Unlike those of Dürer and Marcantonio Raimondi, Lucas's compositions, especially in the larger plates of his mature production, are characterized by an unusually open scansion and a discreteness of part. Interval and incident count more, and carry more

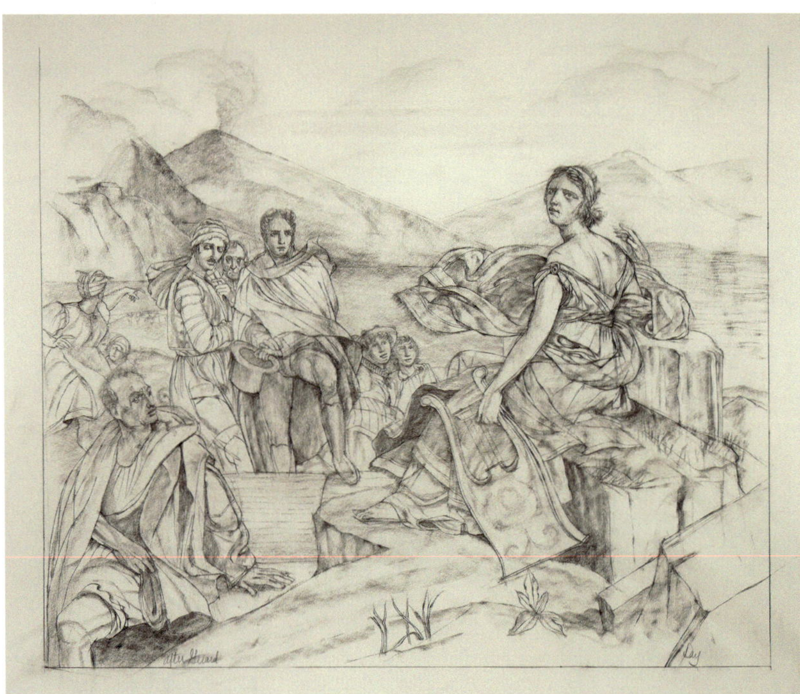

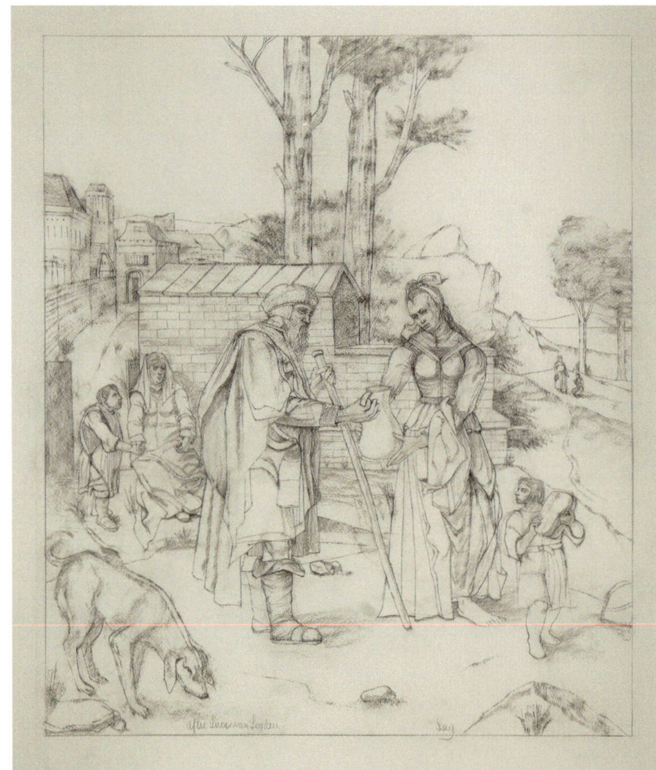

meaning, than rigorous structure or intellectual order. For Day, such examples would have been liberating from the authority of Poussin and Mantegna, and encouraging of a direction already evident in his interest in Steen and interpretation of Bosch. Moreover, even when biblical, Lucas's subjects have an anecdotal flavor and a human content that constantly strains against type, toward the individual in posture and behavior, and toward the oblique and elusive in exchange. Even when embedded in lively narrative, his figures hint at a self-absorption and a disconnection from surroundings. As much as the tonal and compositional directions, Lucas's engravings encouraged the expressive. Thus prepared, Day could engage even the most distilled and ineffable works. His copies of Jacopo Pontormo's early *Supper at Emmaus* in the Uffizi and, the closest he would ever come to copying a single figure, Bosch's haunting *Prodigal Son* amplify dislocation, visual nuance, and existential longing (plate 65). These are masterpieces of this new, integrated style.

More than ever, Day's copies after around 1980 surpass the ostensible intention and transcend the category. Integrated in form, consonant and inextricable in expression, and personalized in both, they are manifestly autonomous works. They often are signed, with the source identified. The mature copies completed his recapitulation of the functions of drawing as a medium, from derivation and induction to independent creation. There had obviously been points of contact between his copies and work in other media. At least one large, two-part canvas is a copy, after Mantegna's *Parnassus* in the Louvre, and rendered much as a drawing of the period around 1970, as a schematic composition. Day's watercolors always depended upon clean boundaries, even zones of thin color, and ambiguous human relationships. From this point on, the aesthetic standing of his copies is equal to that of his other drawings and even paintings. The approaches and terms are practically interchangeable across materials and scales, his style comprehensive and fractal. Day's turning to external models in the figuration of the past may initially have been a response to crisis. His copying had become a dedication to art that maintains a balance and generates greatest meaning between the collective and the individual, between repertory and performance. In that, it correlates further, with his lifelong passion for jazz.

Figure 4.7  *After Baron Gérard, Embarcation,* c. 1980, graphite on paper, 20 × 26 in. (Private Collection)

Figure 4.8  *After Lucas Van Leyden, Return of the Prodigal Son,* late 1980s, graphite on paper, 26⅝ × 20⅝ in. (Private Collection)

Figure 4.9  *Caprice #6,* 1997, pen and ink on paper, 21½ × 26¼ in. (Eleanor D. Wilson Museum at Hollins University, Gift of Larry Day and Ruth Fine, 2005.016) Photograph by Kyra Schmidt

Figure 4.10  *Caprice #1,* 1997, pen and ink on paper, 21¼ × 29 in. (Eleanor D. Wilson Museum at Hollins University, Gift of Larry Day and Ruth Fine, 2005.011) Photograph by Kyra Schmidt

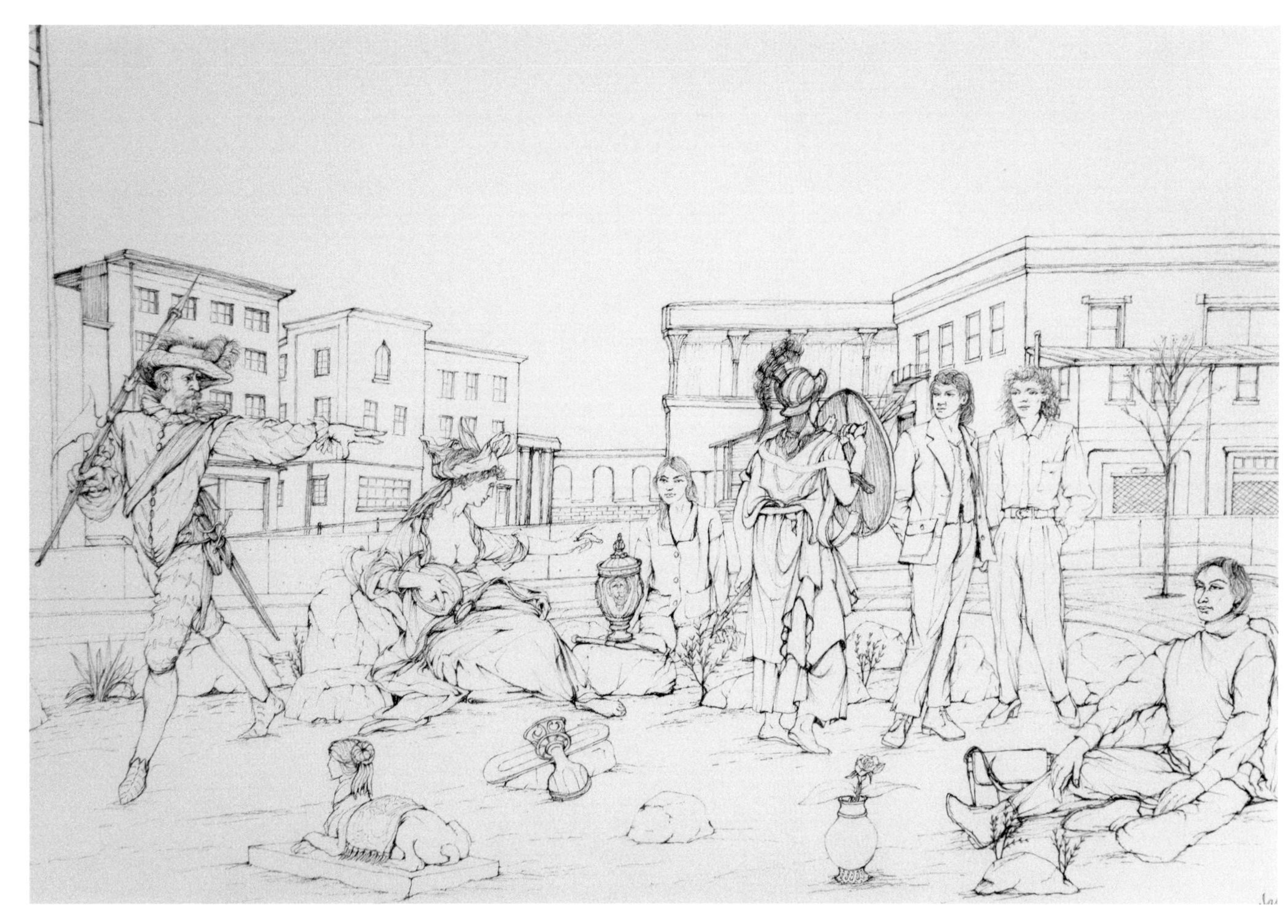

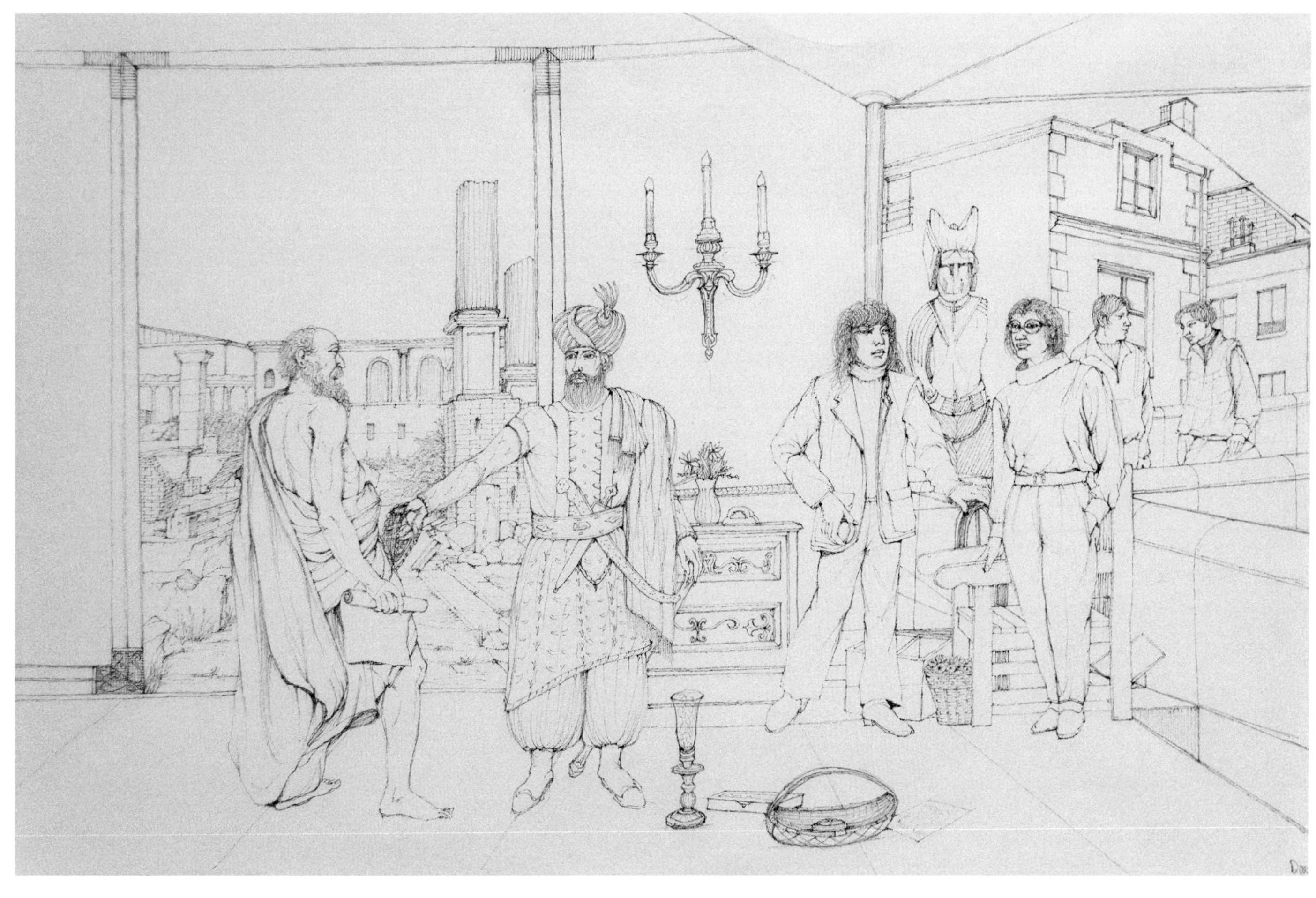

In a final extension and elaboration of drawing, Day moved beyond copying even as a pretext for his own exploration. Some challenges, like the angular fracture and intimate exchange in Antonio Pollaiuolo's *Tobias and the Angel* (plate 59), were too much to resist. But having mastered the syntax, assimilated the vocabulary, and through them found a distinctive voice, he turned to completely independent creations. The series of *Caprices*, employing a lean pen and ink, exemplifies the final development. Each presents an imaginary subject that seemingly comprises day residue. The settings are composites of ruins like those in a Renaissance sketchbook, historical buildings on the threshold of recognizability, and generic fabrications. They momentarily cohere in perspective only to slip askew, proffer temporal unity only to interrupt it. The figures come from the same spectrum, historical costume and stylized pose to modern casual dress and nonchalance. More characterized in their features, some were the artist's friends and acquaintances. Bespectacled and impassive, Day himself attends a few scenes. Distributed across these irrational stages, they seem unperturbed if not oblivious, interacting in small groups, rapt in wordless exchange, or standing in isolation.

In these compositions and relationships, there is a distant echo of the lessons of Steen, Bosch, and especially Lucas. The art of the past, however, is vividly present and essential to any penetration of meaning. It appears in Day's individual figures lifted from original context, now mostly prints and favoring those of Mannerism—long on stylization and disguised in feeling. In *Caprice #1* (fig. 4.10), Saint Jerome from Correggio's great altarpiece of that sobriquet recoils startled from a figure in exotic costume.[1] In *Caprice #3*, pre-Socratic philosopher Empedocles, from an engraving by Réné Boyvin after a design by Rosso Fiorentino, addresses a youth who seems more engaged by a group of revelers, the lead couple excerpted from Hans Sebald Beham's *Peasant Wedding*. In *Caprice #6* (fig. 4.9), youths again in casual dress appear held at bay by an Athena-like figure, while *Vanity* from an engraving by Jan Saenredam and the balletic pike bearer from Jacques de Gheyn's *Company of Rudolf II* gesture as if to caution or remonstrate. Such quotations are not simply recondite. Nor is their action limited to the generation of meaning out of the tension between past and present, art and the everyday. They provoke an equally rich dialogue between Day and the viewer, testing, amusing, welcoming into the workings of his imagination. Beyond Mannerist in preferred source, these quotations are Mannerist in spirit and operation. Like interpolations in the solos of bebop, they proclaim mastery of a tradition and the perennial vitality of its language.

## Note

1    The *Caprices* series is reproduced in *Larry Day: Ironic Realist* (Roanoke, VA: Eleanor D. Wilson Museum, 2008), https://www.hollins .edu/museum/catalogs/documents /larryday_cat.pdf.

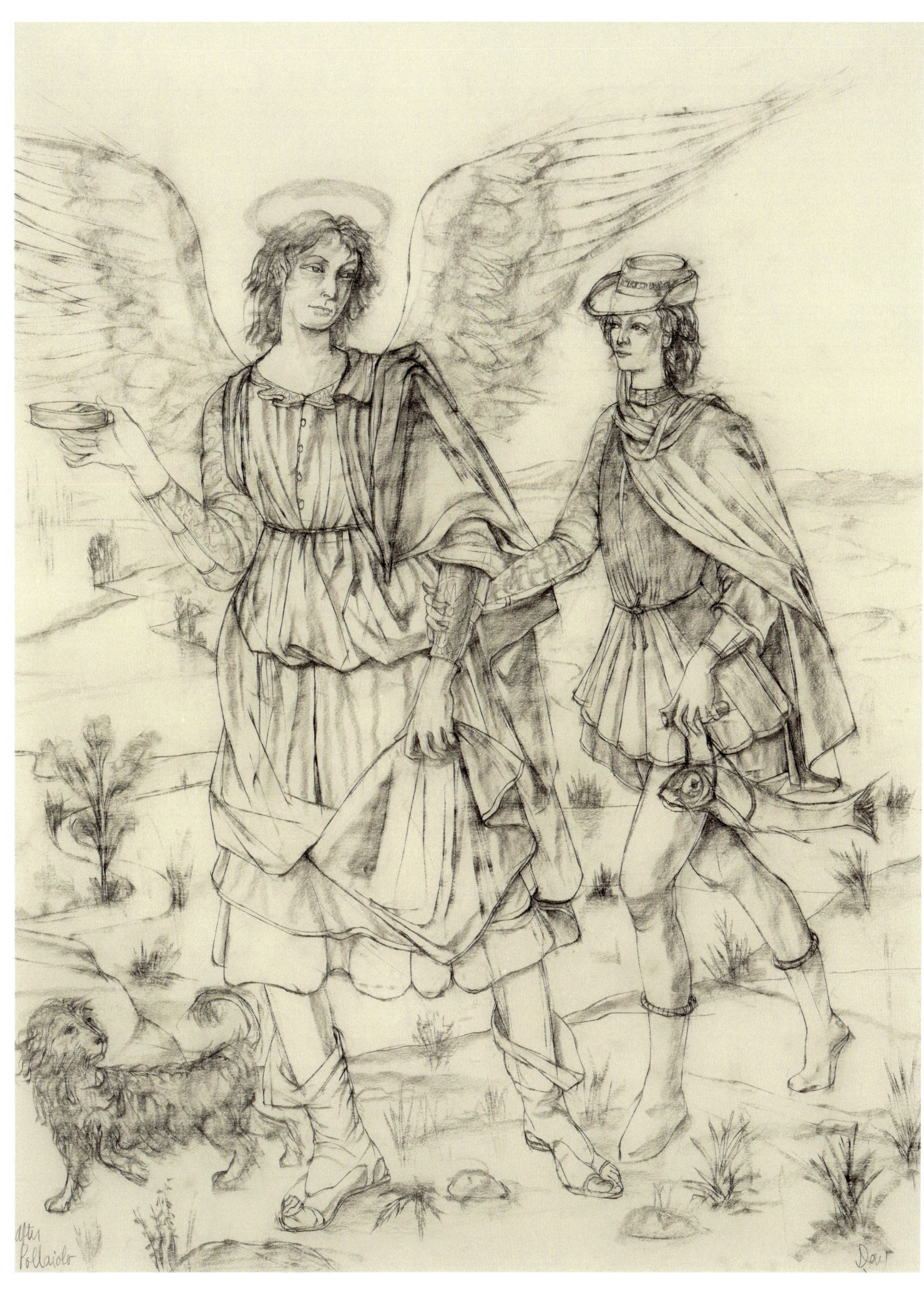


PLATE 59

*After Pollaiuolo*, c. 1985

83

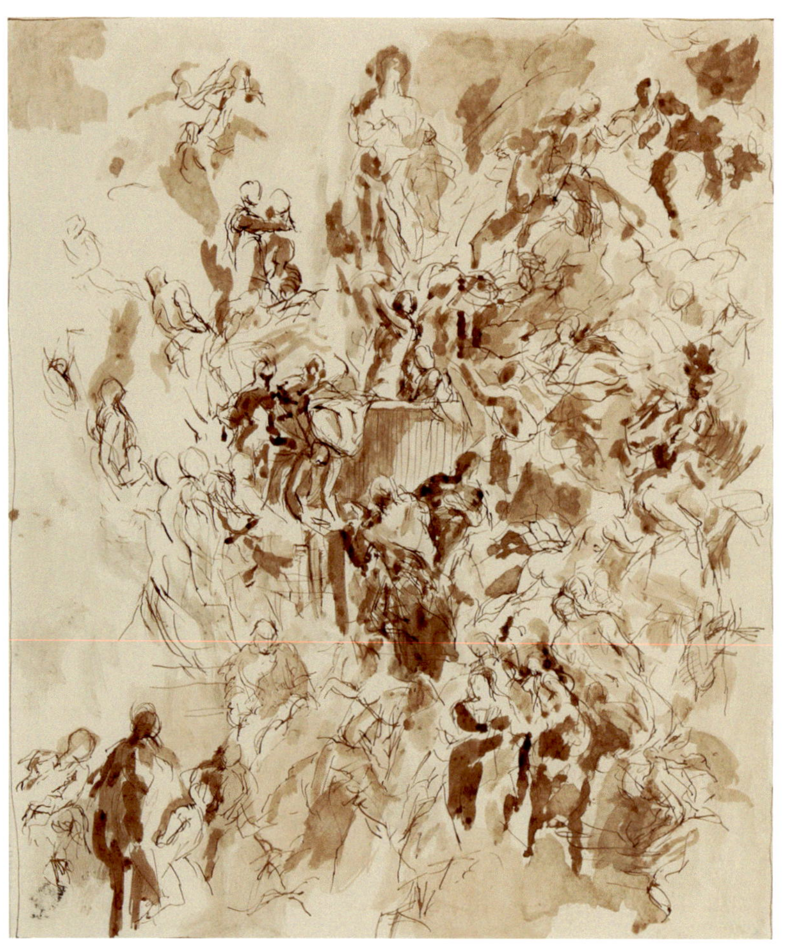

PLATE 60
*After Veronese*, c. 1963

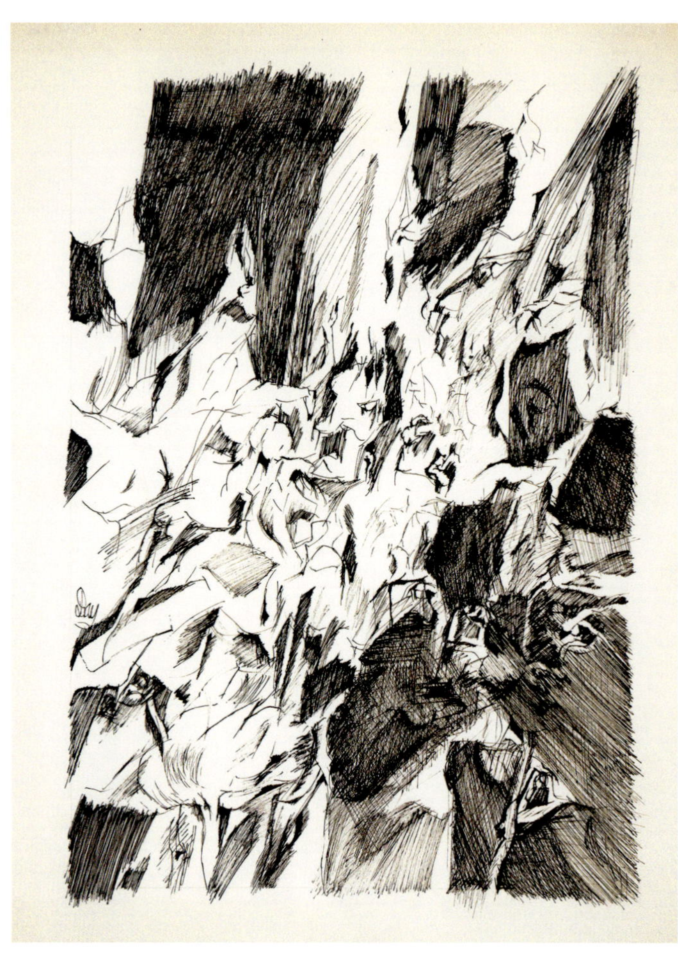

PLATE 61
*After Old Master,*
late 1950s

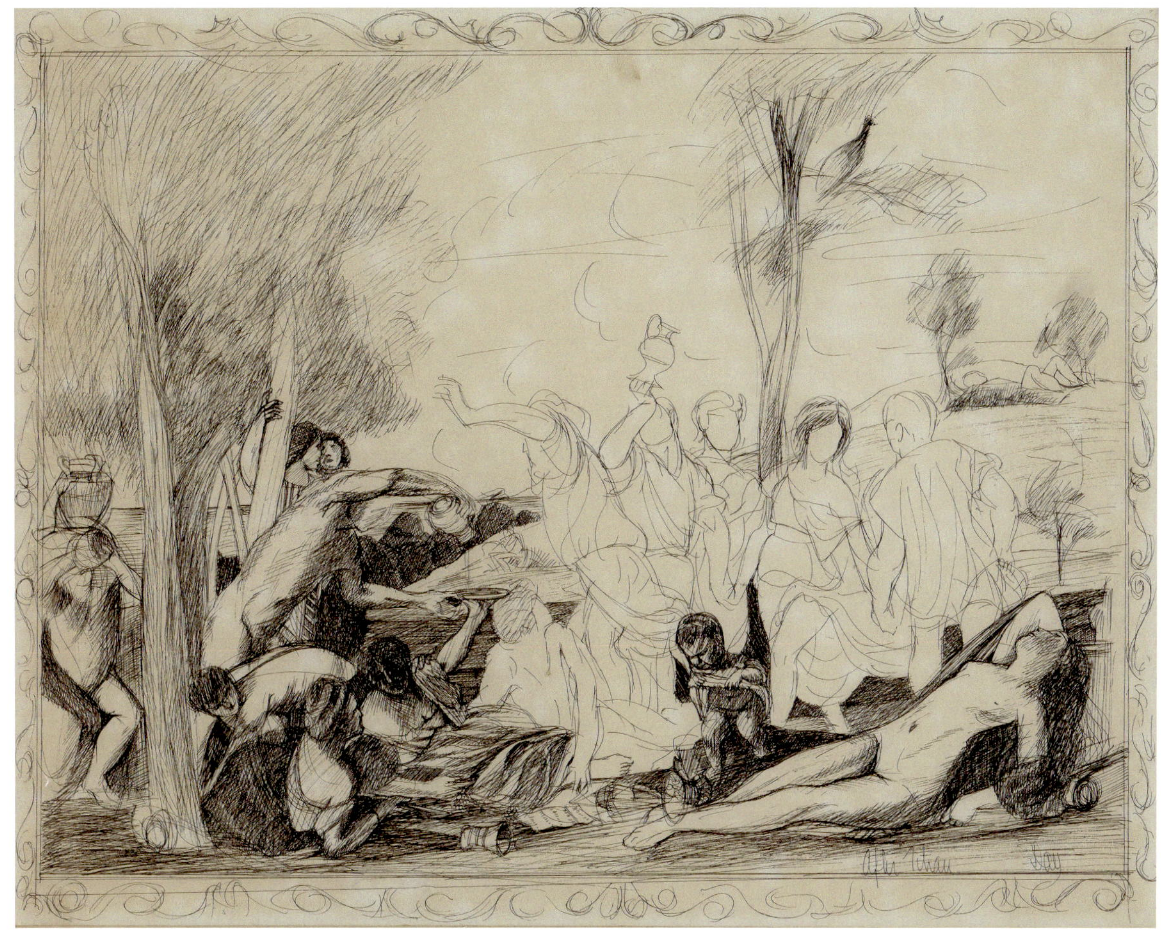


*After Titian*, c. 1970

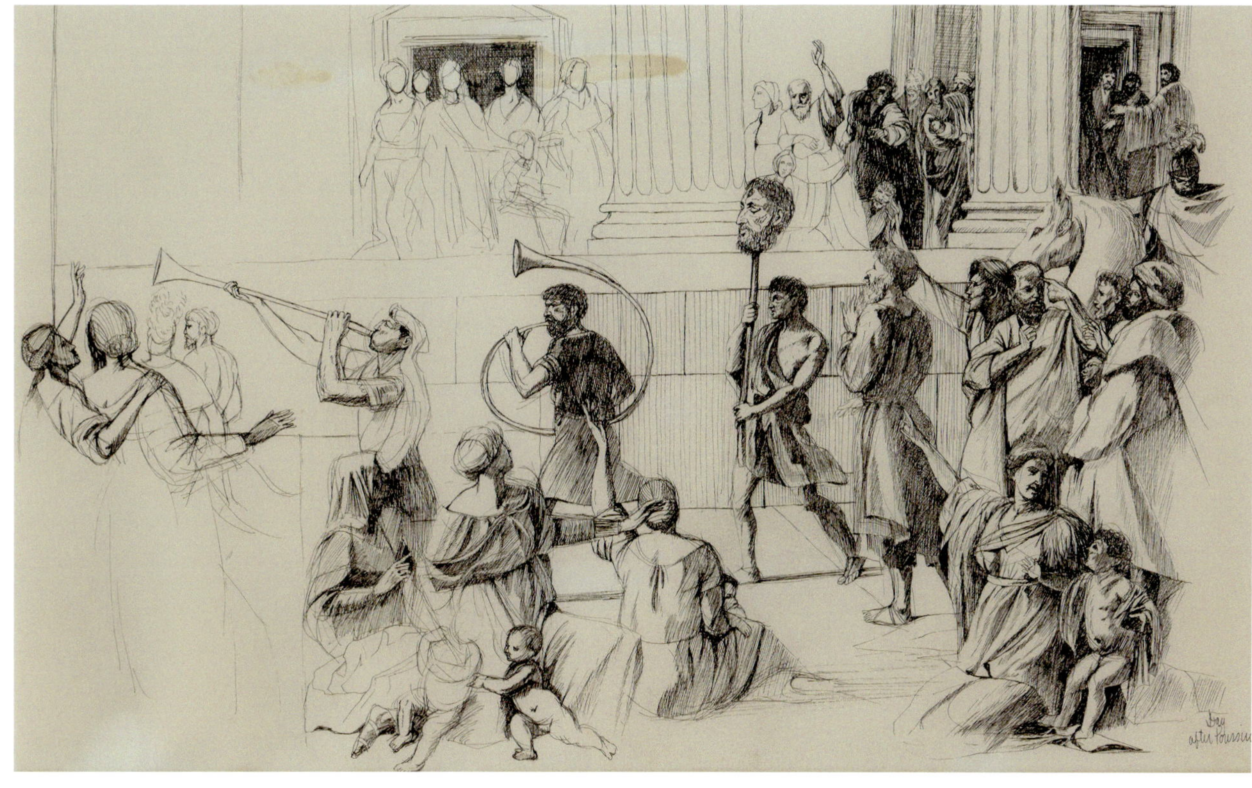

PLATE 63

*After Poussin*, c. 1970

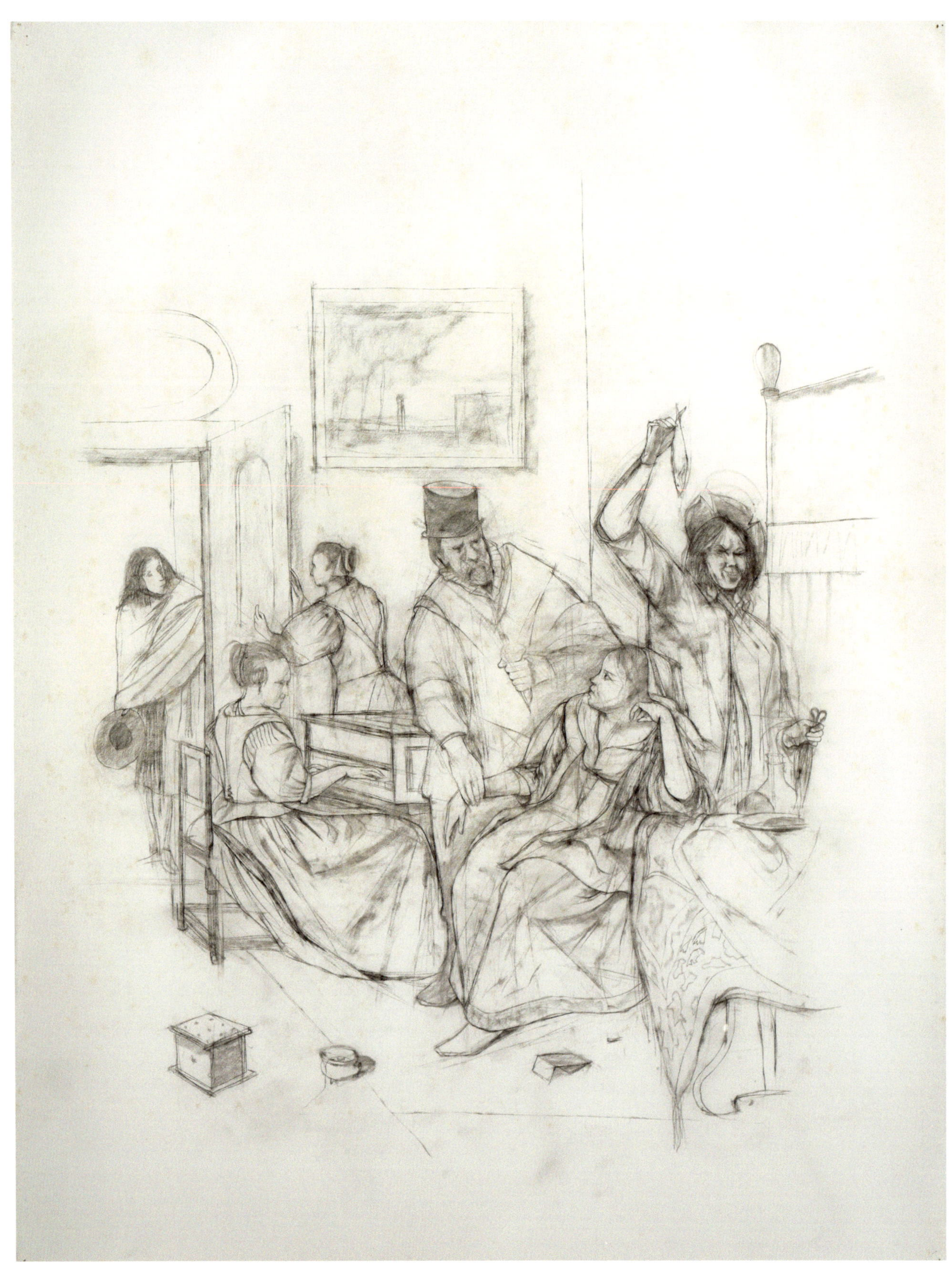



*After Steen (The Doctor's Visit, 1663–65),* 1989

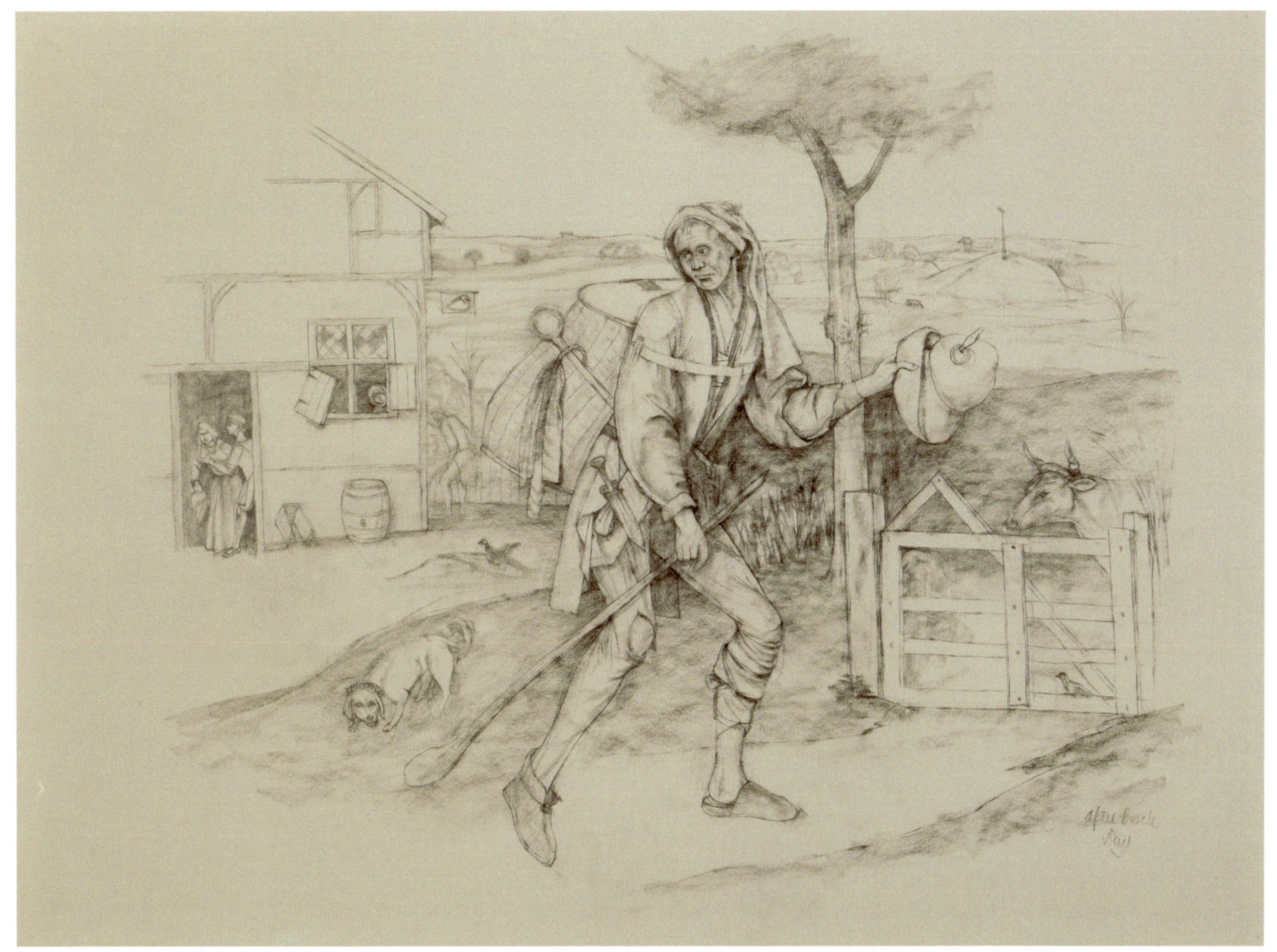

PLATE 65
*After Bosch
(The Wanderer,
1506–16)*, 1991

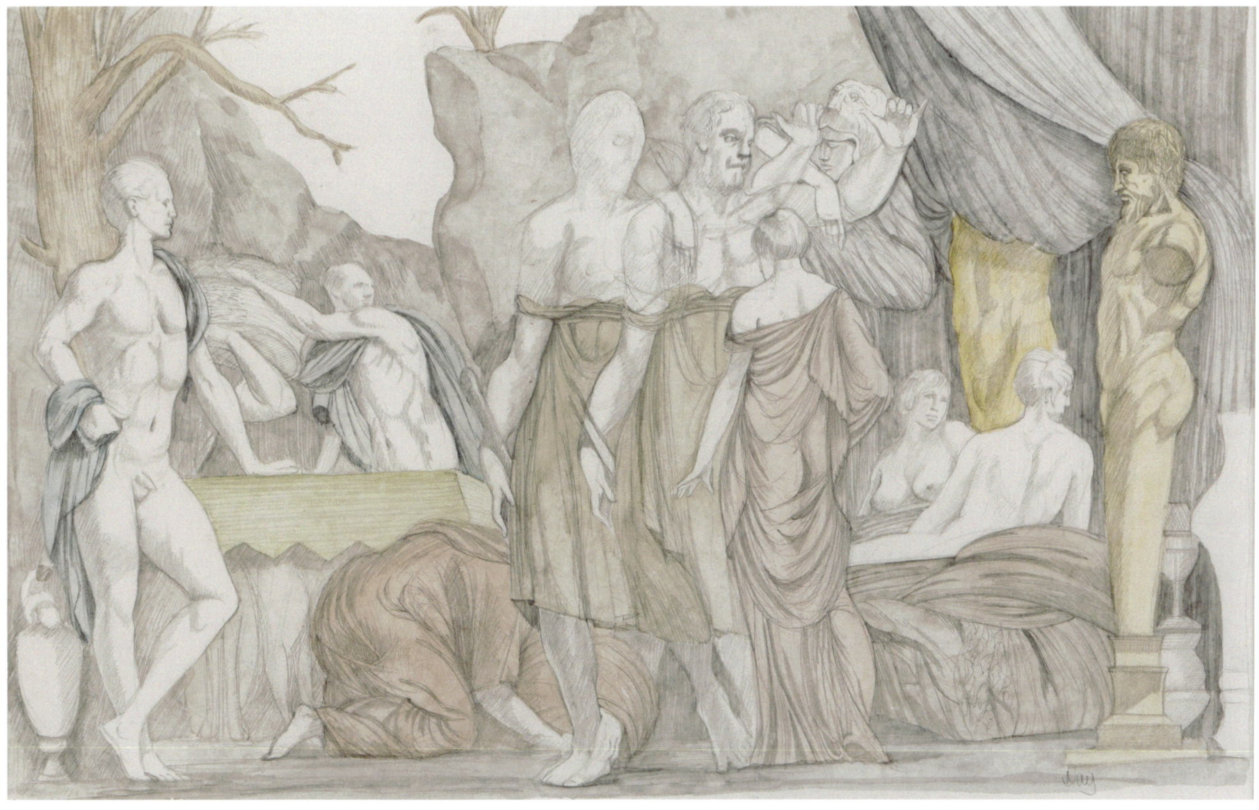

PLATE 66
*Hercules Dressed
as a Woman*,
c. 1990

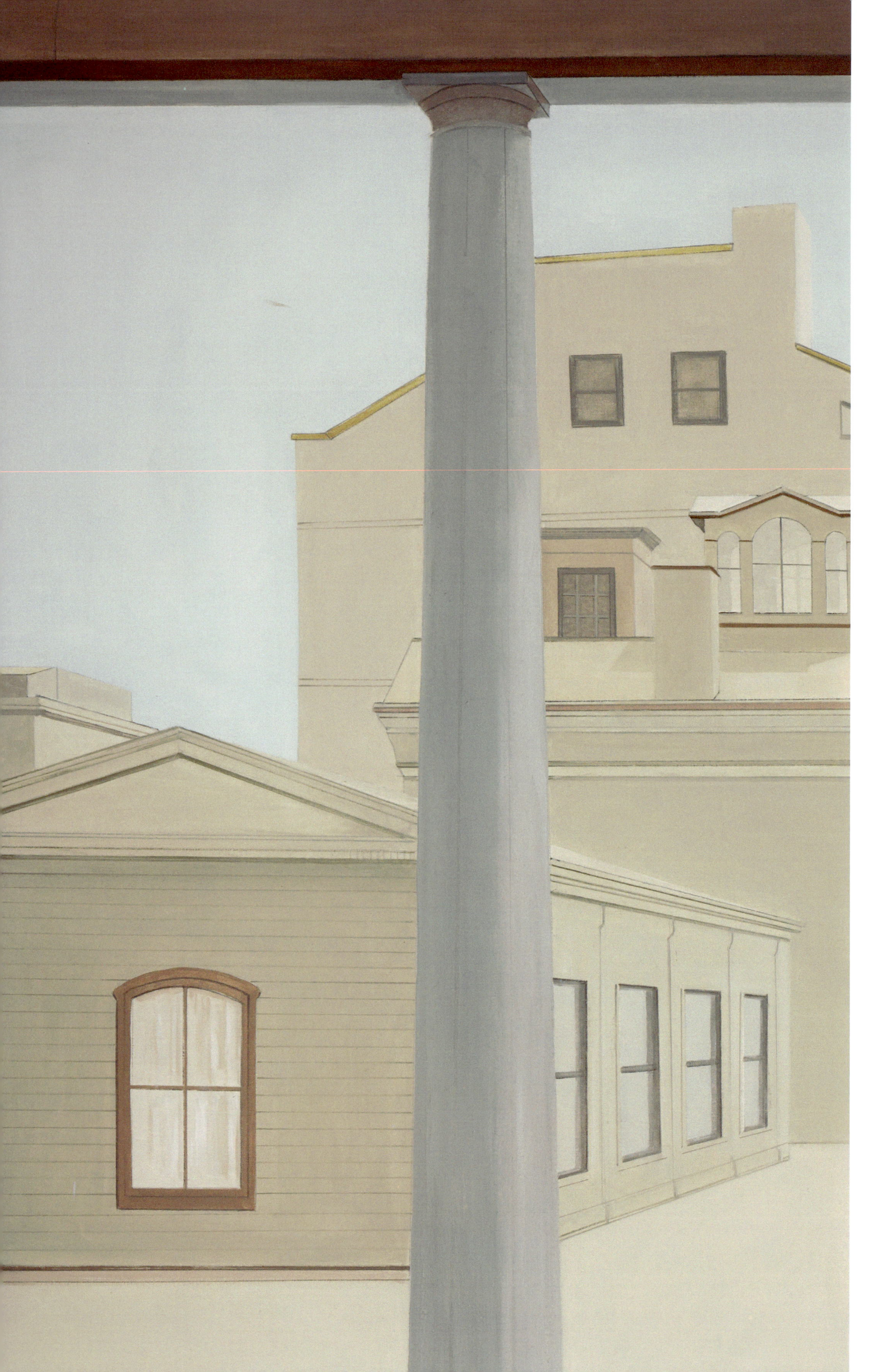

# The Limits of Imagination[1]

In Larry Day's extraordinary afternoons in Philadelphia, the world becomes astounding in the exultations of the painter's vision. When there is no way to get what is ordinarily there, save by letting it tell its extraordinary mythopoetic truth, then urban landscape can transform itself in the highest ways. City-scenes can explore post-modern analogues of the older odes in which landscape painting lit up with meaning: the pastoral and the heroic; the picturesque, beautiful, and sublime; the impressionist seminary of color; the projection of the burning or the building eye; the surrealist *theatrum mundi*; the neo-picturesque of high buildings claiming their slices of sky; the modernist ironies that revealed the dark side of the city after serious painting had been trapped in it—the cosmopolitan as the chaotic, the dense as the airless, the stacking-up of spaces as the emblems of height that can only be reached by suppression. Day's mode of landscape is none of these. Yet it is ever mindful of the ancestry of their possibilities. His fables are not merely epistemological, although they do engage just those stories that modern art has thrust forward in place of a heroic narrative of an older sort, such as the embattled marriage of pictorial flatness with depth, two major characters in the mythology of modern painting, who themselves can play so many roles in its drama (surface can become profound, for example, and deep space trivial).

Larry Day's subject is the world as meditation; his object emerges from a thin, dry paint surface, a carefully guarded tonality, a lyrical geometry. And yet neither these elements of medium, nor the pictorial emptying-out of his public places, constitute denial or retraction of significance, but rather the establishment of it. Like Wallace Stevens's stroller in the streets of imagination, Day is solitary in his walk.

> He skips the journalism of subjects, seeks out
> The prerequisites of sanctity, enjoys
>
> A strong mind in a weak neighborhood . . .
>
> It is a fresh spiritual that he defines,
> A coldness in a long, too constant warmth,
> A thing on the side of a house, not deep in a cloud,
> A difficulty that we predicate:
> The difficulty of the visible
> To the nations of the clear invisible . . . [2]

The spiritual vulgarity of recent, unearned expressionism—it is by its very mod-ishness a prettification—must not distract the serious from the ways in which *démodé* "realism" is a corruption of the real. Realism depends upon a reduction of meaning, most often unwittingly, to formula; the painting of reality, however, is parabolic and represents the inherence of the painter's consciousness in what it scans and surveys. Major art in any mode is always an intellectual act, even though the painter cannot put that act into words; the action is one of revision of some portion of the history to seeing to clear a path through the second-growth scrub of the merely visual to create a space for the visionary. To this degree, the "strong mind" of the painter, the holiness of his set-apart, personal precincts, can make its creations as difficult to characterize as they are (save for those whose eyes have been ruined by bad art and worse counsel) to overlook. Day's private spaces in public places are always generating problems for the viewer's meditation to engage, even as the plein-air scenes engaged, in a different way, that of the artist.

*The Limits of Imagination* (fig. 5.1) is a statement of some of the central relations for all art, between freedom of vision and the restraints which, strangely, give it capability. The enclosure of Day's courtyard, in which things seen become—again in Stevens's words—"things as seen" frames a meditative problem.

The three barred, unaccountable windows in the wall facing the viewer are open rectangles which "in reality" are intercepted by iron grids to protect the foreground from the hideous travesties (violence, wreckage, defacement, and, of course, theft) of community which modern urban life arranges. An earlier American magical tradition would have raised, say with Robert Frost, the question of how every protecting wall also imprisoned. Here, the matter is more subtle and vast: the only canonical, unin-terrupted rectangles in the painting (i.e., those undistorted by perspective, or cut off by the intercession of another form) are those of the barred windows which mediate a view from one place, external yet somehow "inside," into and beyond another such region. The grid of the bars surrenders all of its utility in defense of property to its role as a paradigm of conceptualization. We consider its paradigmatic power with respect to the "picture" each window frames, to the variety of the perspectival sys-tems by which something so ordinarily simple to characterize as "what lies behind them" is revealed. We move across the painting from left to right, from the lower to the higher half of the rectangle, from the most blatant idea of what a vertical grid is for (to be parallel to but out of phase with a vertical-stripe system located as it were "in" and as it were "behind" it), to more problematic ones. Each of these windows tells another story about the eye's possible access to what lies past it; each of them causes the serious viewer of the painting to consider the speaking relationships of other rectangular forms (which ones seem primary, which derived from like ones?). The left-hand "window" is most trivially inviting: a single-point perspective system leads into its heart, a cheerful alternation of red and white stripes, like part of a flag of freedom or a tent of rejoicing, yielding a treasure of drawn incident above it in a diagonal structure, like the prophetic lances in Uccello but, in this case, with con-sequences beyond the frame of the window, where the propped-up boards seem to

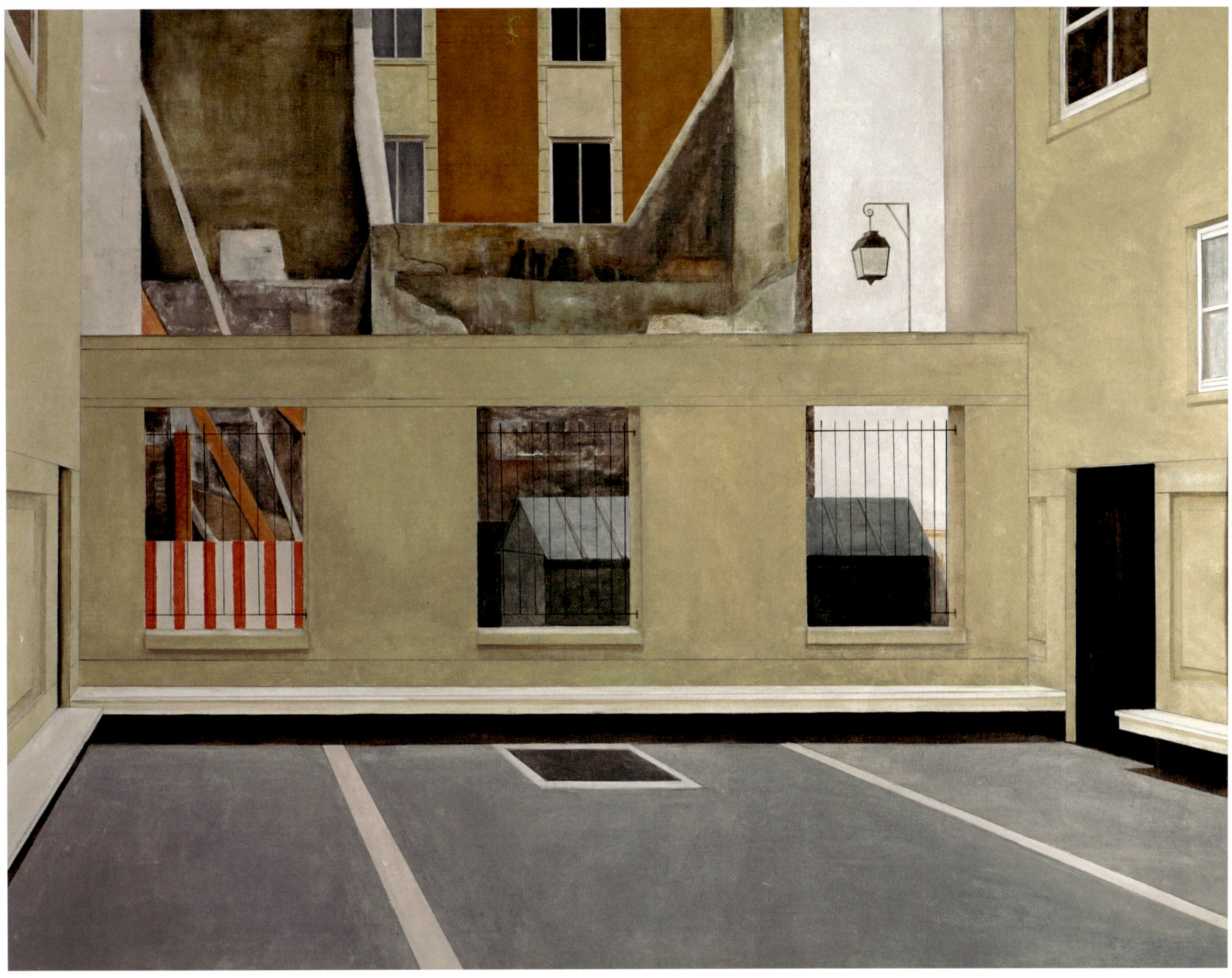



join another world of forms, of long-reaching, framing diagonals of masonry. It is only after the tale of each of these "openings"—each of these complex emblems of conditional glimpse—has been told that the viewer may be invited to consider the puzzles of the vertical strip supporting the lamp on the right (where does it terminate? why is it appropriate to what we do see that we can't quite know?) and of the point of cut-off of the window high on the upper right: what does it mean that just here, now, looking ahead at what we can see and meditating on how our eyes are both imprisoned and nurtured by what faces us, we see only the lower left-hand pane of that window remaining intact, as if it had been built that way? But every framed or enclosed area of this painting is another pictorial event, with a moral of its own and an injunction to the spectator to refresh his or her imaginative life. Nothing is easy here. Nor is anything here easily exhausted, even by endless contemplation. In a sense, this canvas is an allegory of painting.

Such an allegory of painting can explain how, in Day's urban landscapes, presence, and relative closeness or distance, can have at the very simplest an inverse and, more frequently, a dialectical relation . . . space is explored as the object of desire: these buildings are nude figures, in their way, not lolling about in a *bain turque*, but disposed in as much of an arcadian light as we have available.

And as in all of Larry Day's canvases, what the painted world withholds from one part of our visual lives, it returns to others many times over. Their peculiarly American moment is not of Demuth, Sheeler, or Hopper, to which they bear the revisionary relation that, in the case of poetry, Harold Bloom has called "transumptive." Beyond the glib, the operatic, the indignant, the tentative—those tones in which so much painting too easily makes its reports on what there is—these paintings speak with a peculiar wisdom, in voices which do not fade.

## Notes

1   This essay is an edited version of John Hollander's undated, unpublished essay in the Larry Day Archives, published with the permission of Natalie Charkow Hollander.
2   Excerpted from Wallace Stevens's *An Ordinary Evening in New Haven,* Section XIII.

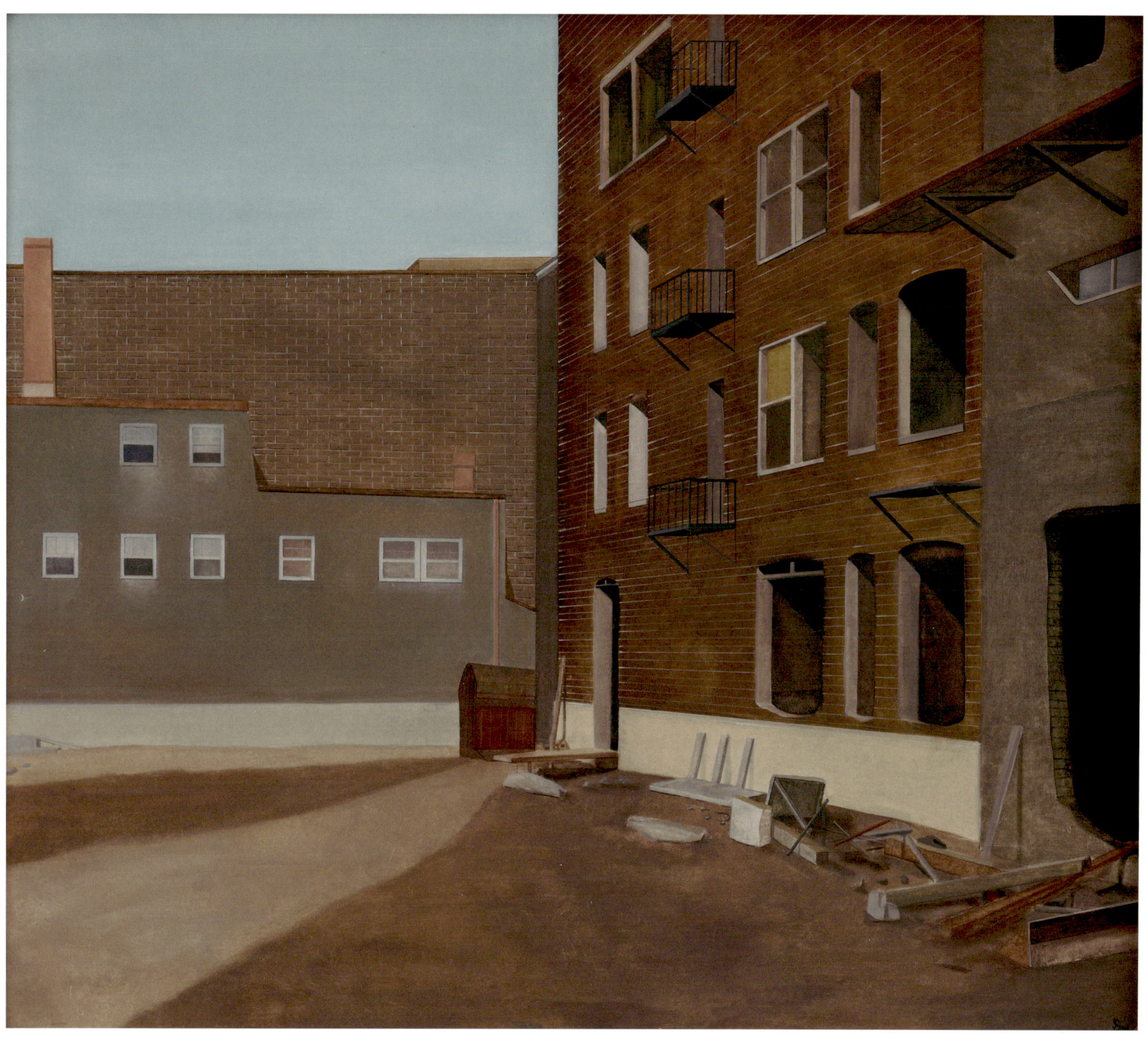

PLATE 67
*End*, 1975

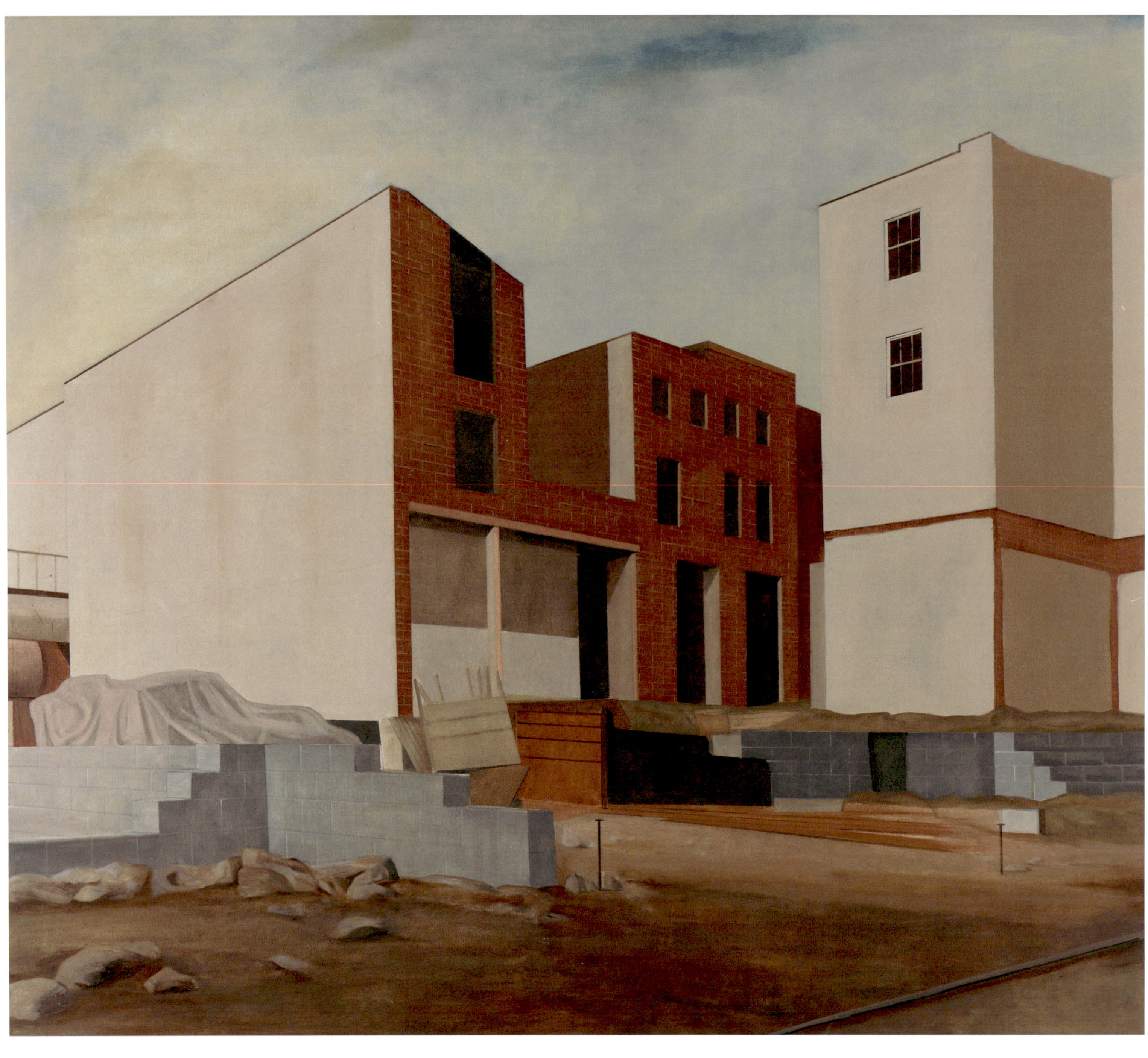

PLATE 68
*Construction Site*, 1979

94

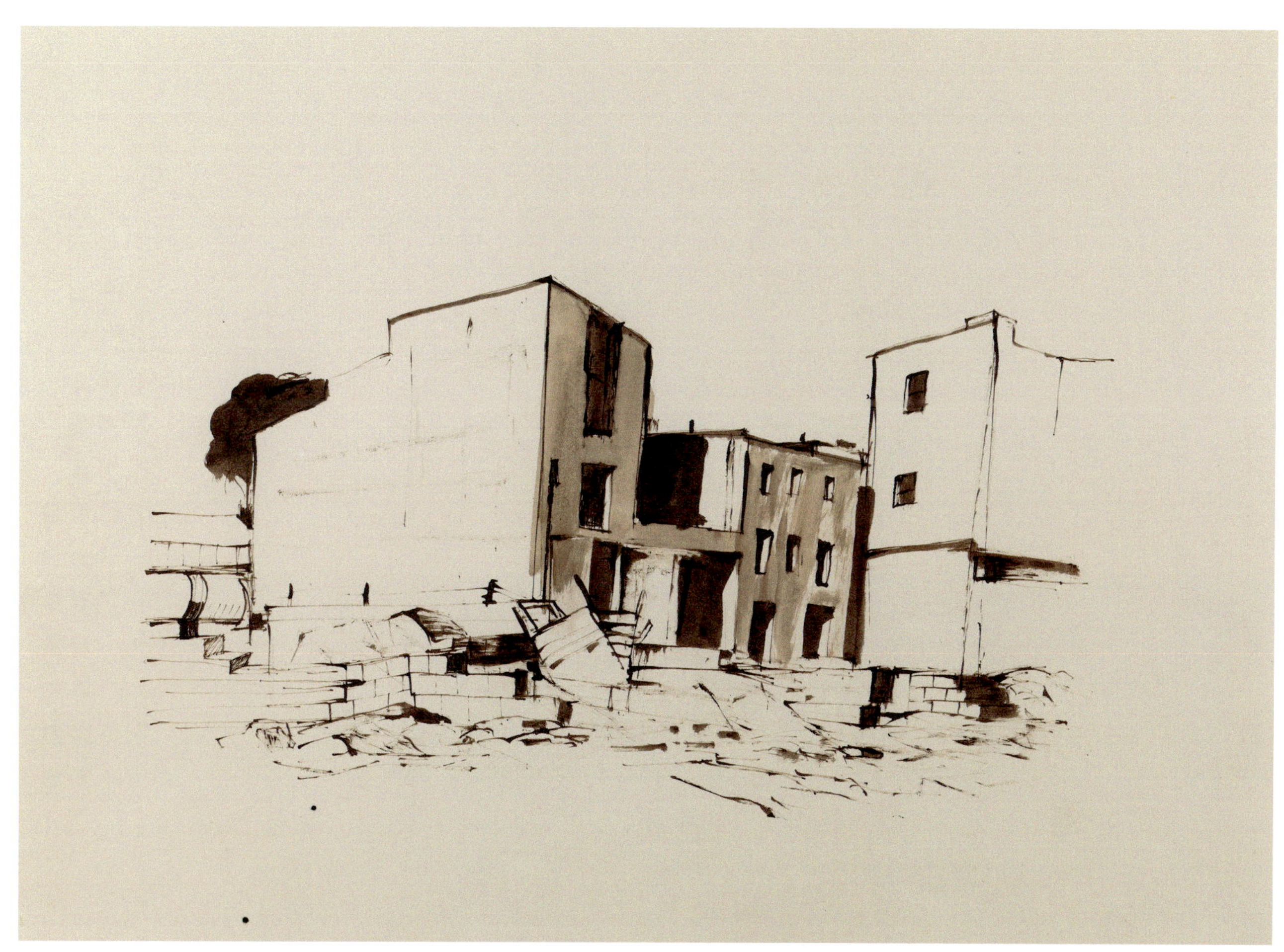

PLATE 69
*Untitled, study for
"Construction Site,"*
c. 1979

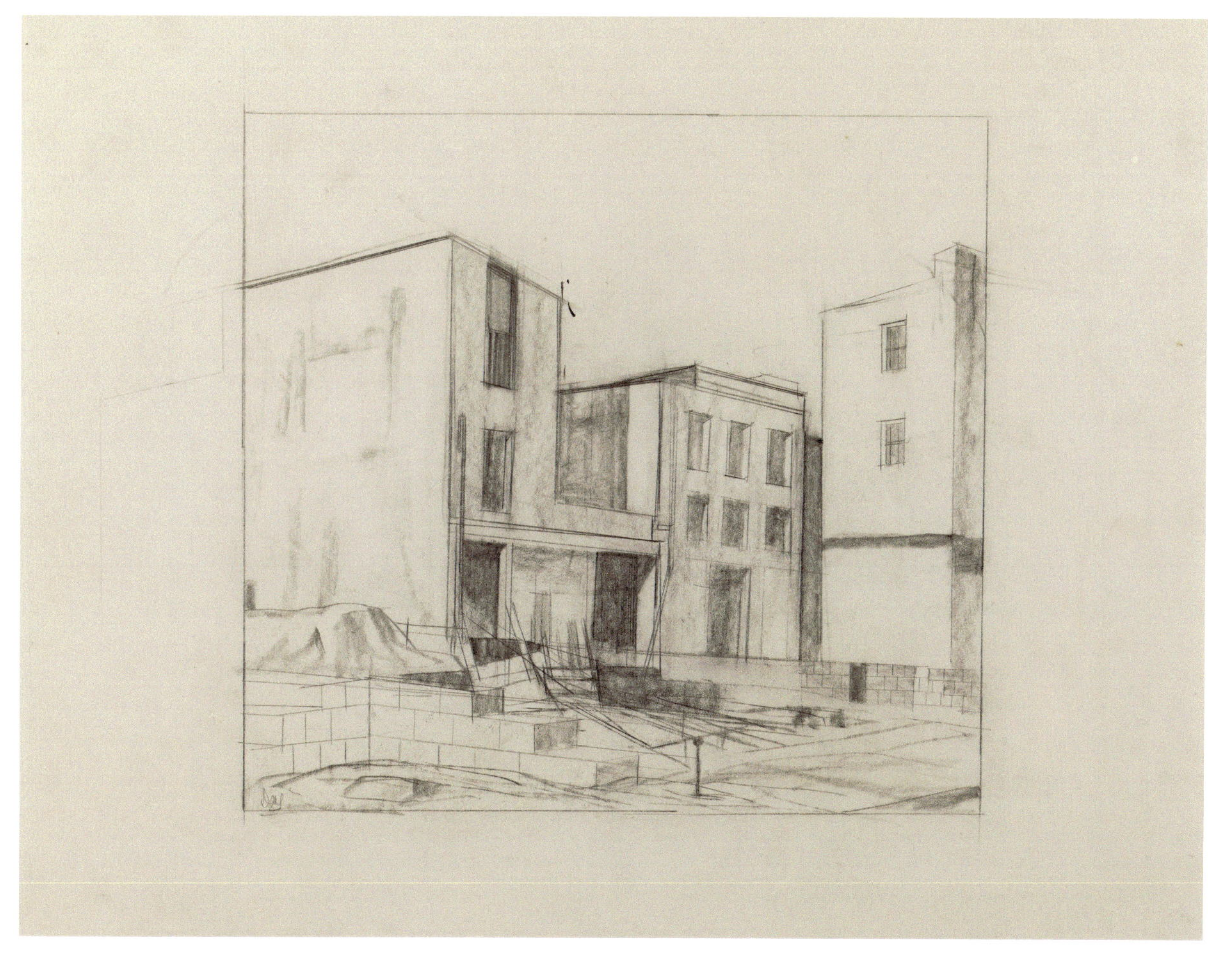

PLATE 70
*Untitled, study for
"Construction Site,"*
c. 1979

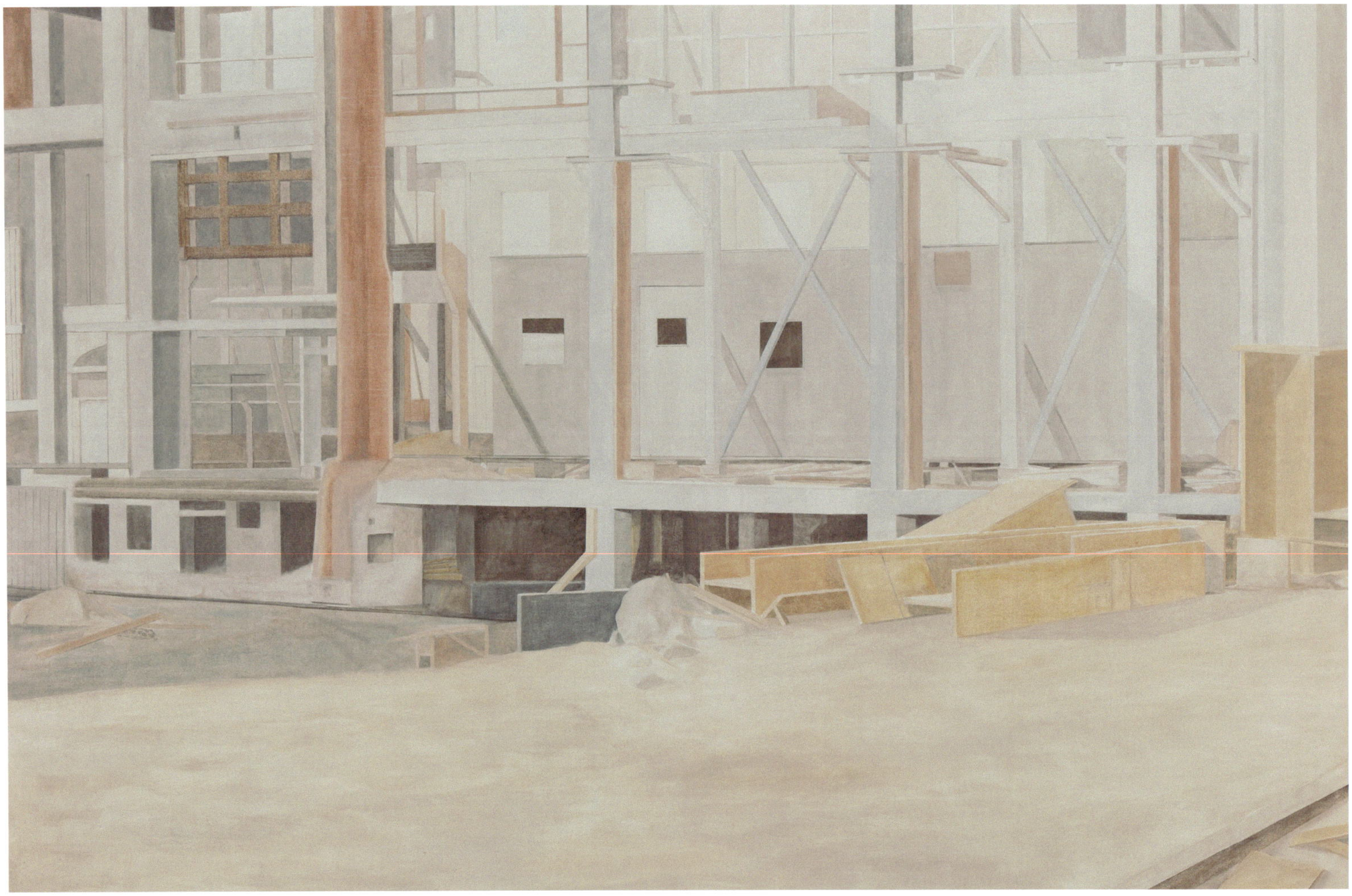

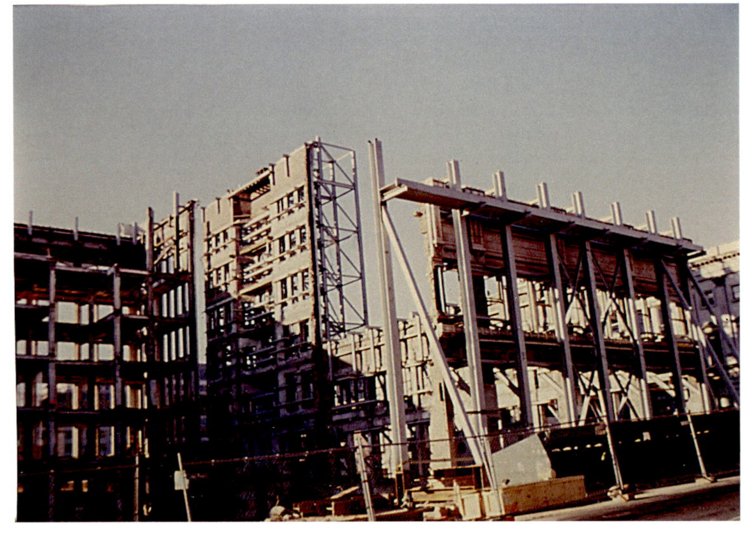

Figure 5.2   Larry Day, photographic source for *Construction* and other works (Larry Day Archives)

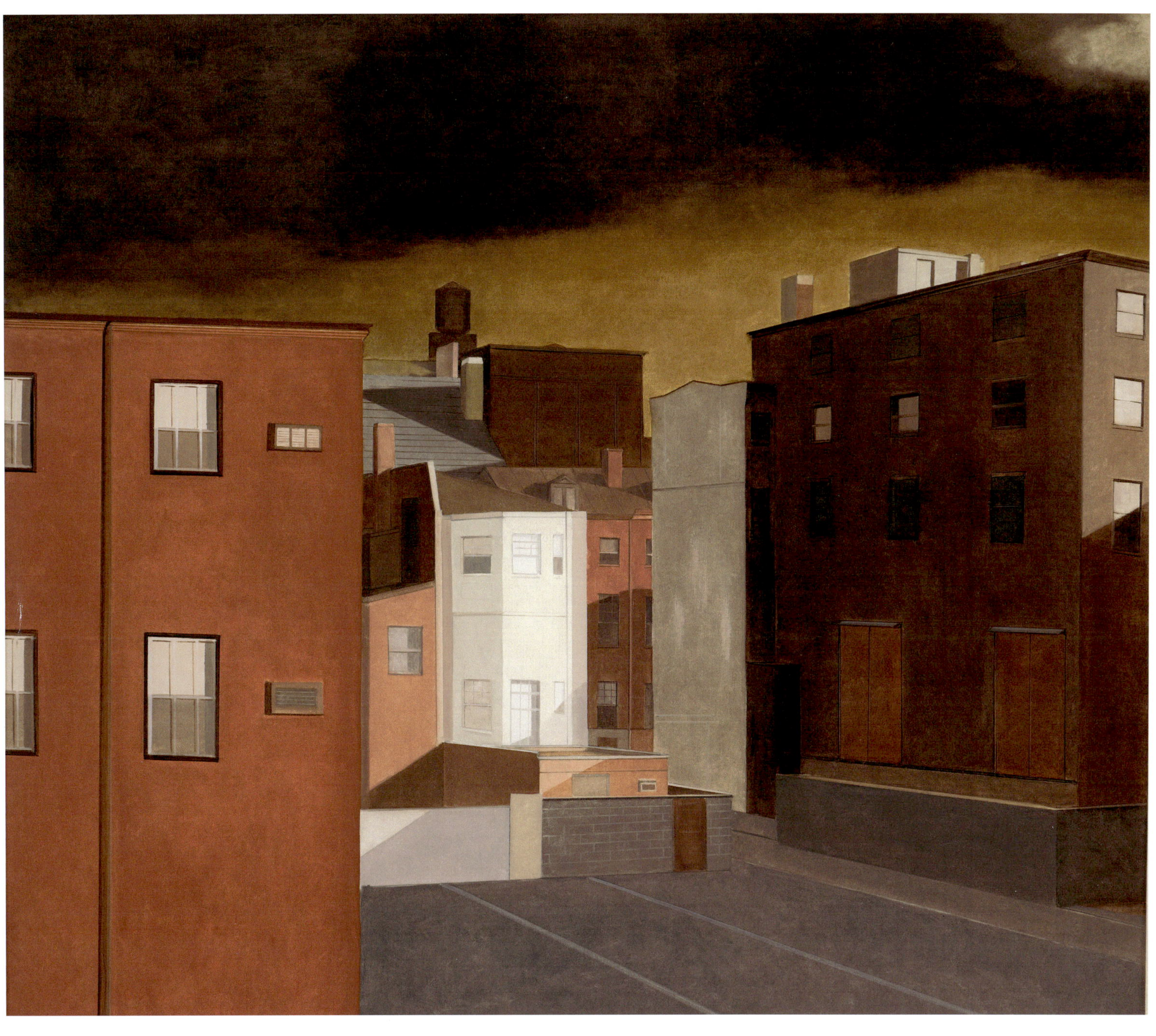



PLATE 72

*Zone, 1976*

*Aquarium,* 1977

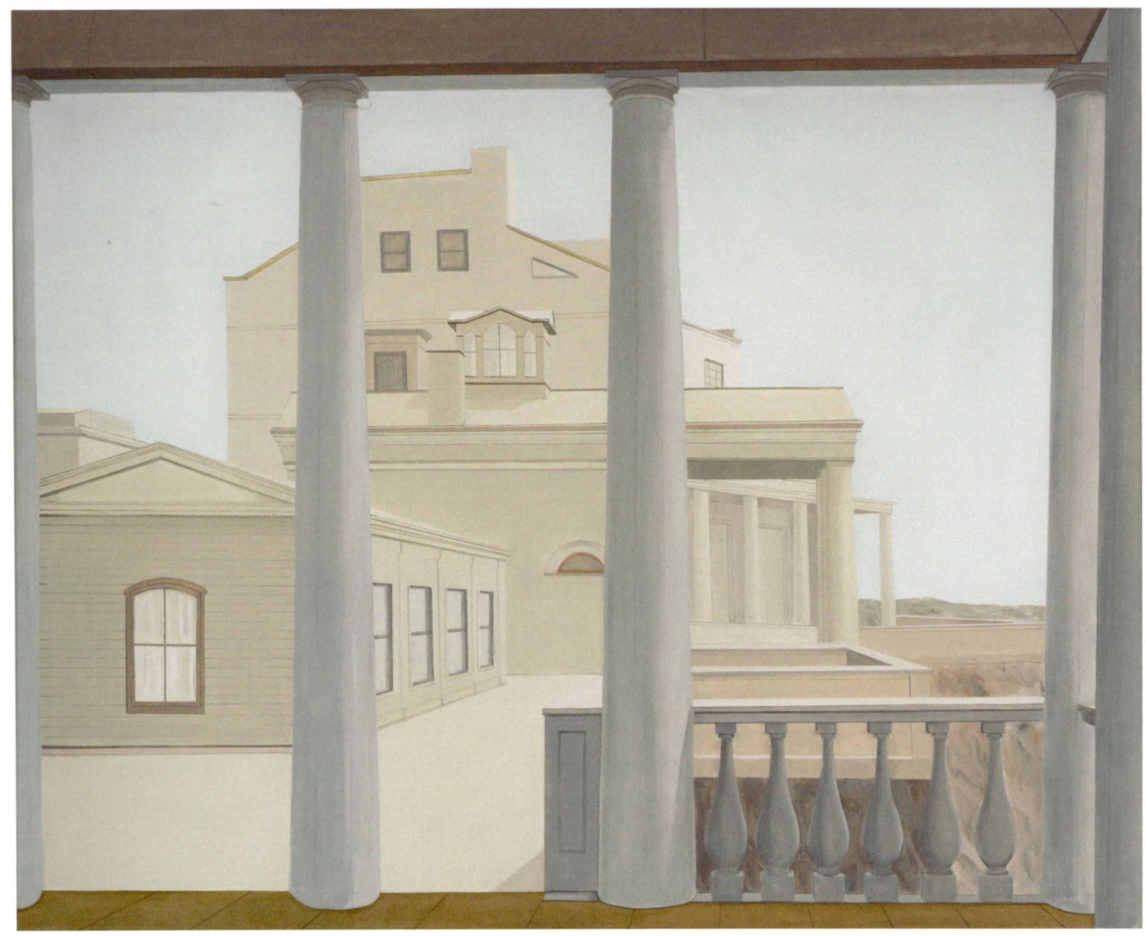

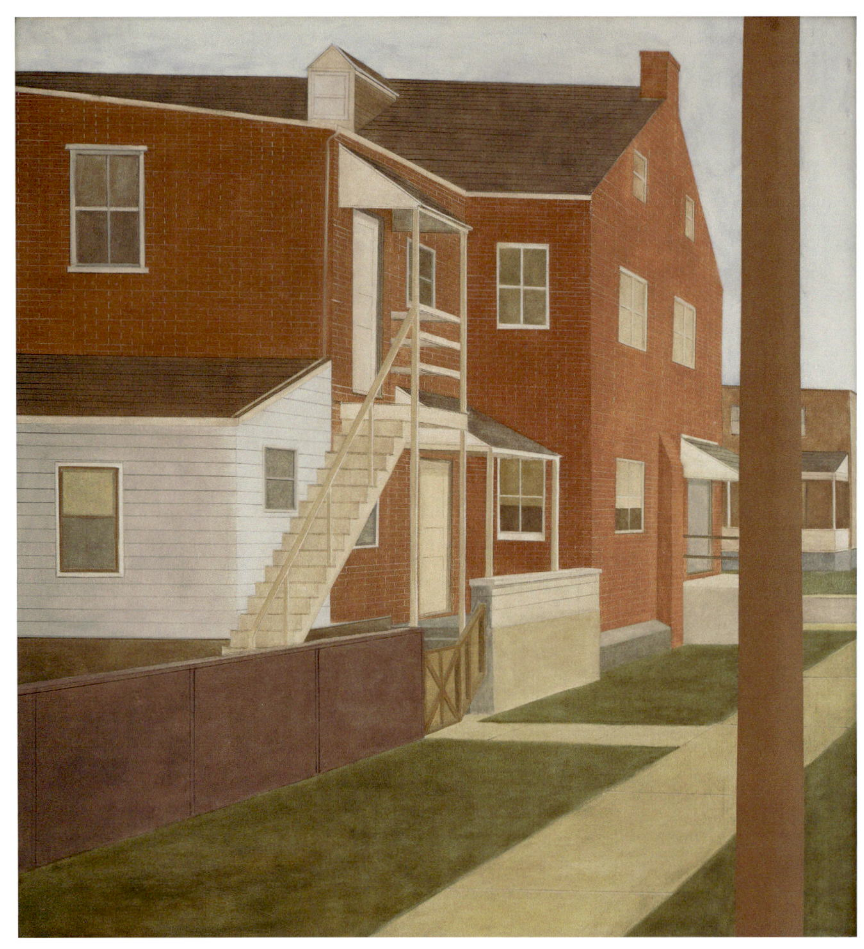

PLATE 74
*Lancaster,* c. 1982

*Building Reflected* (aka
*Reflection*), probably 1985

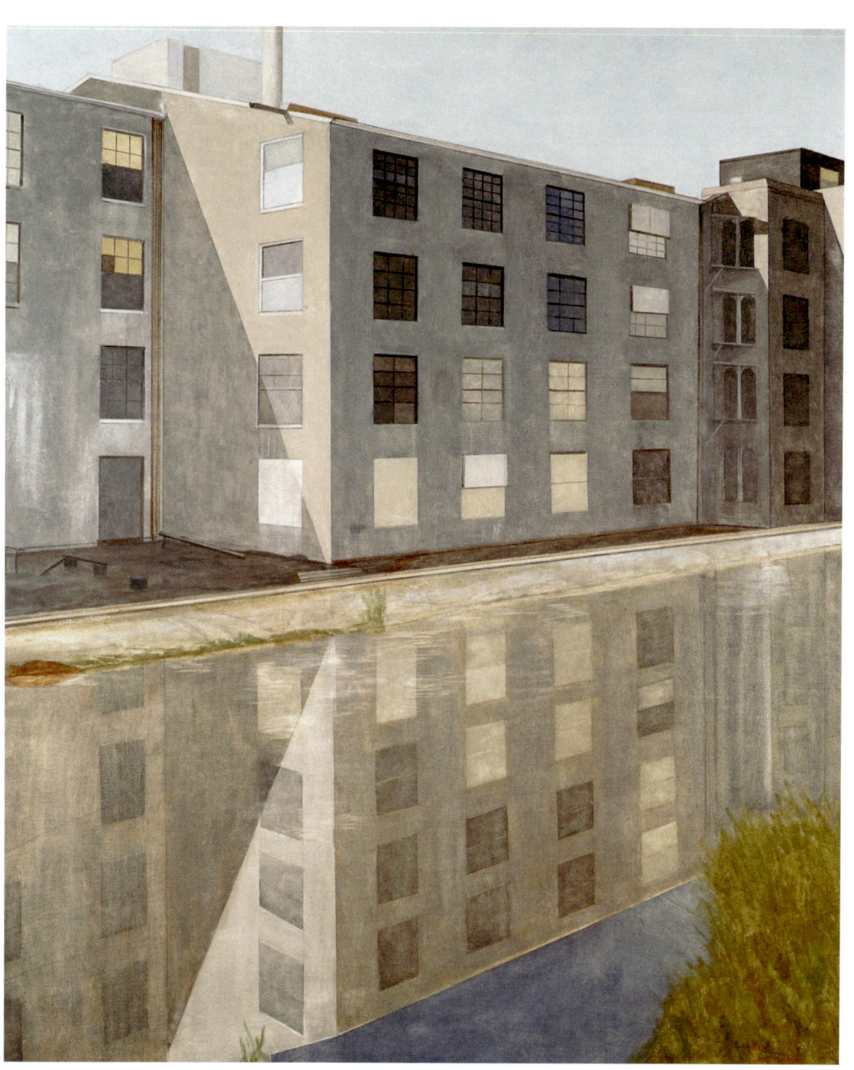

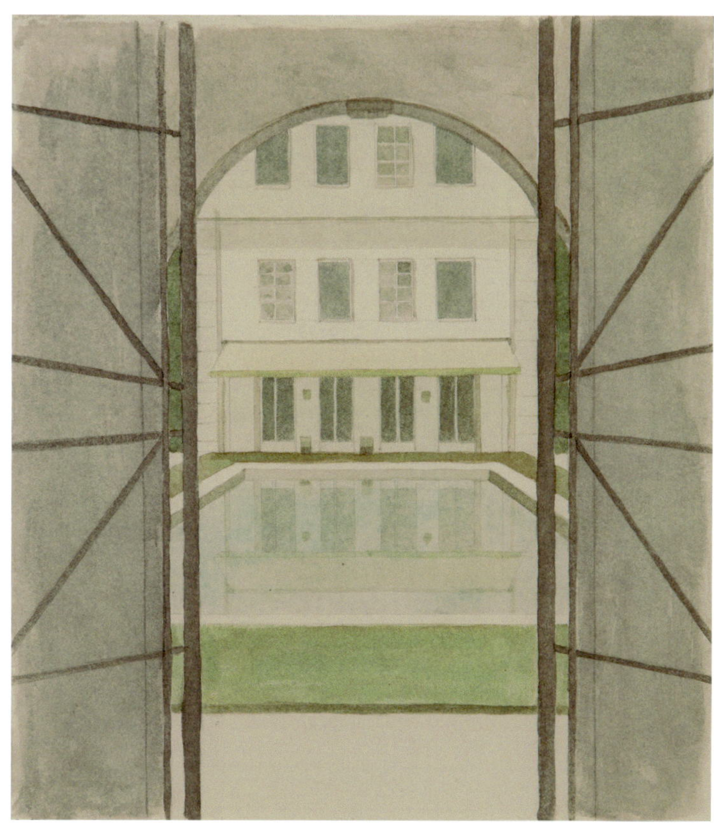



*Related to "Terrace,"* c. 1970

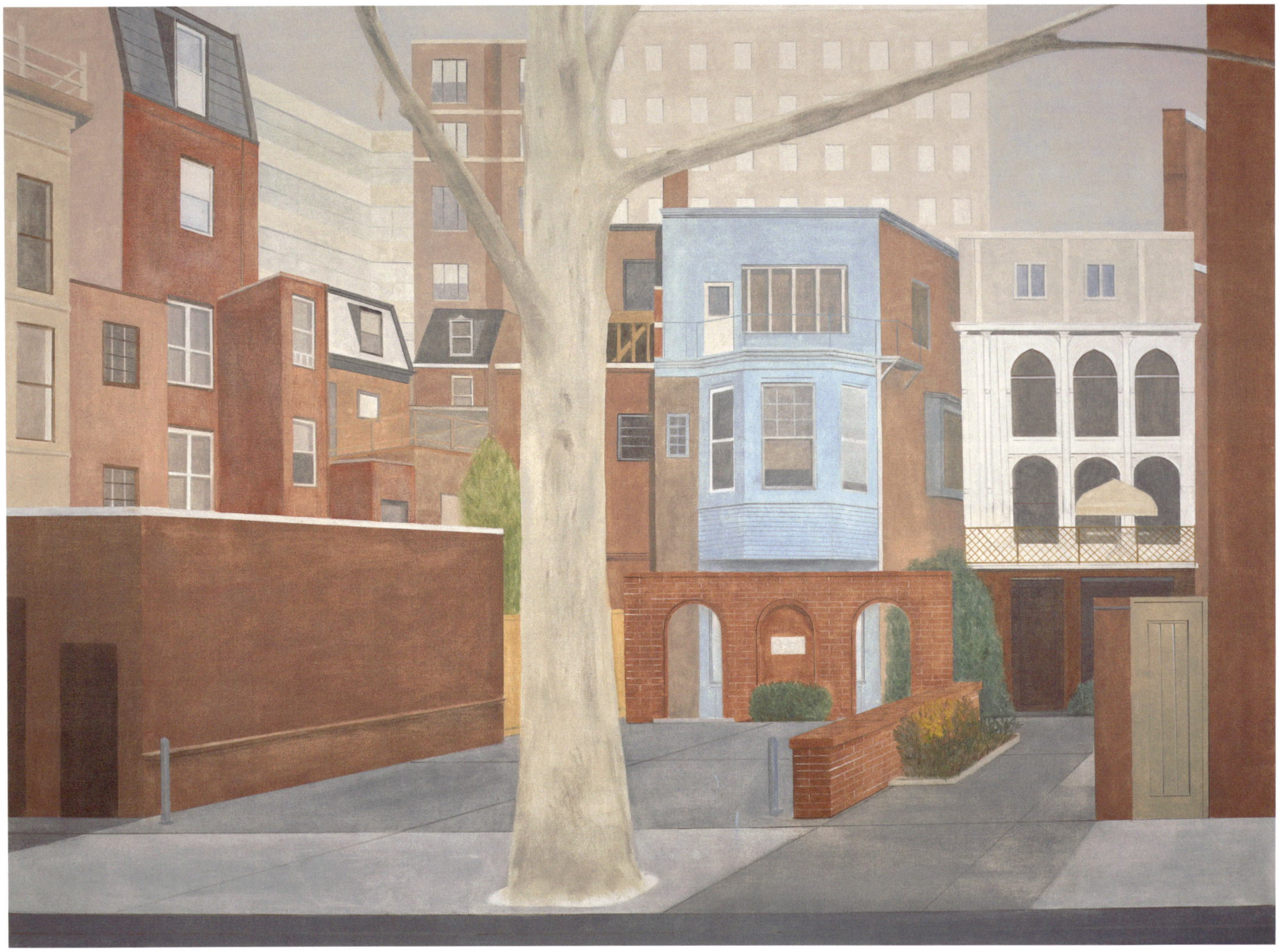

PLATE 77
*Tree in the City* (aka *City Tree*),
1987–88

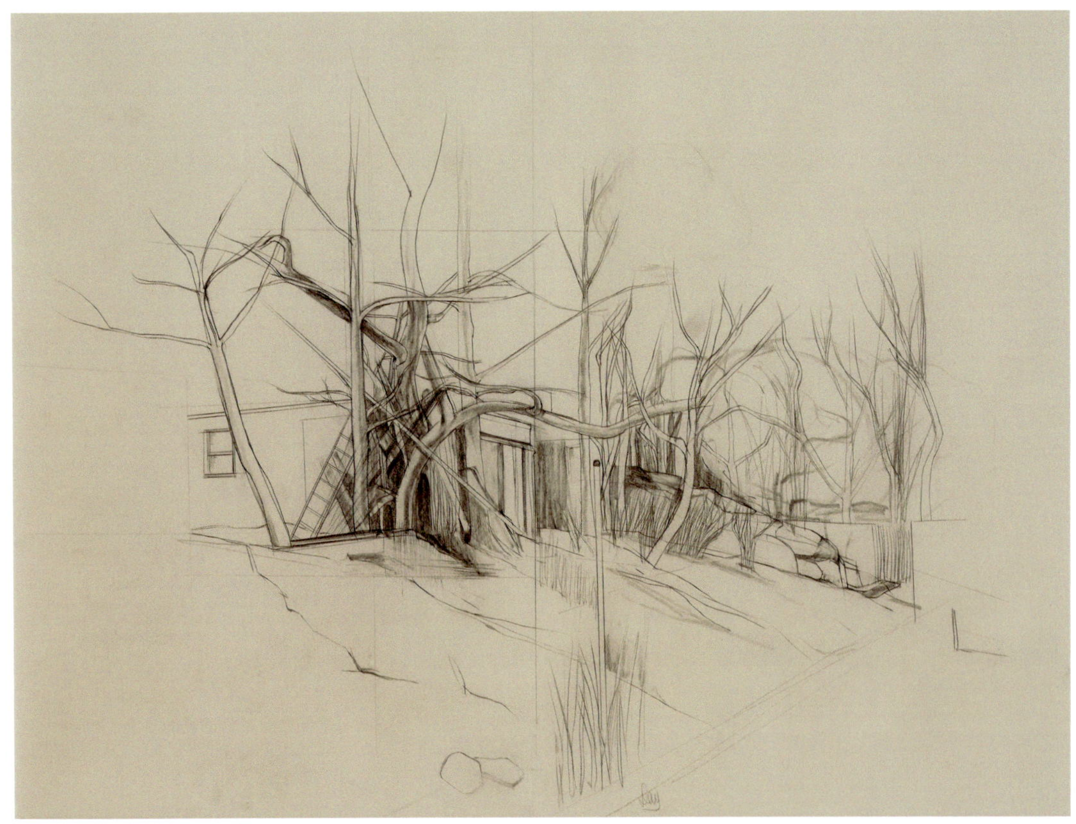

PLATE 78
*Yard II*, c. 1975

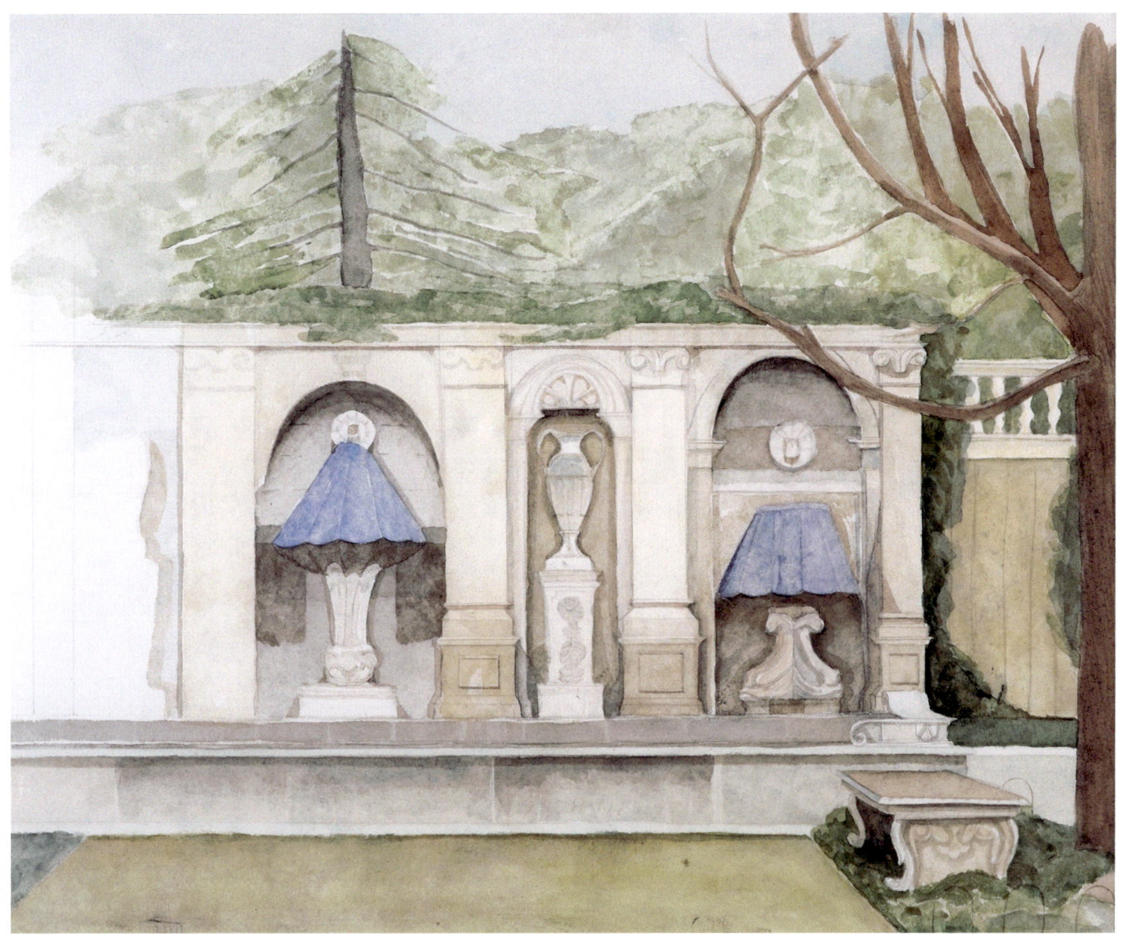

PLATE 79
*(Arboretum)*, c. 1984

PLATE 80
*Study for "Suburban Church,"*
1979

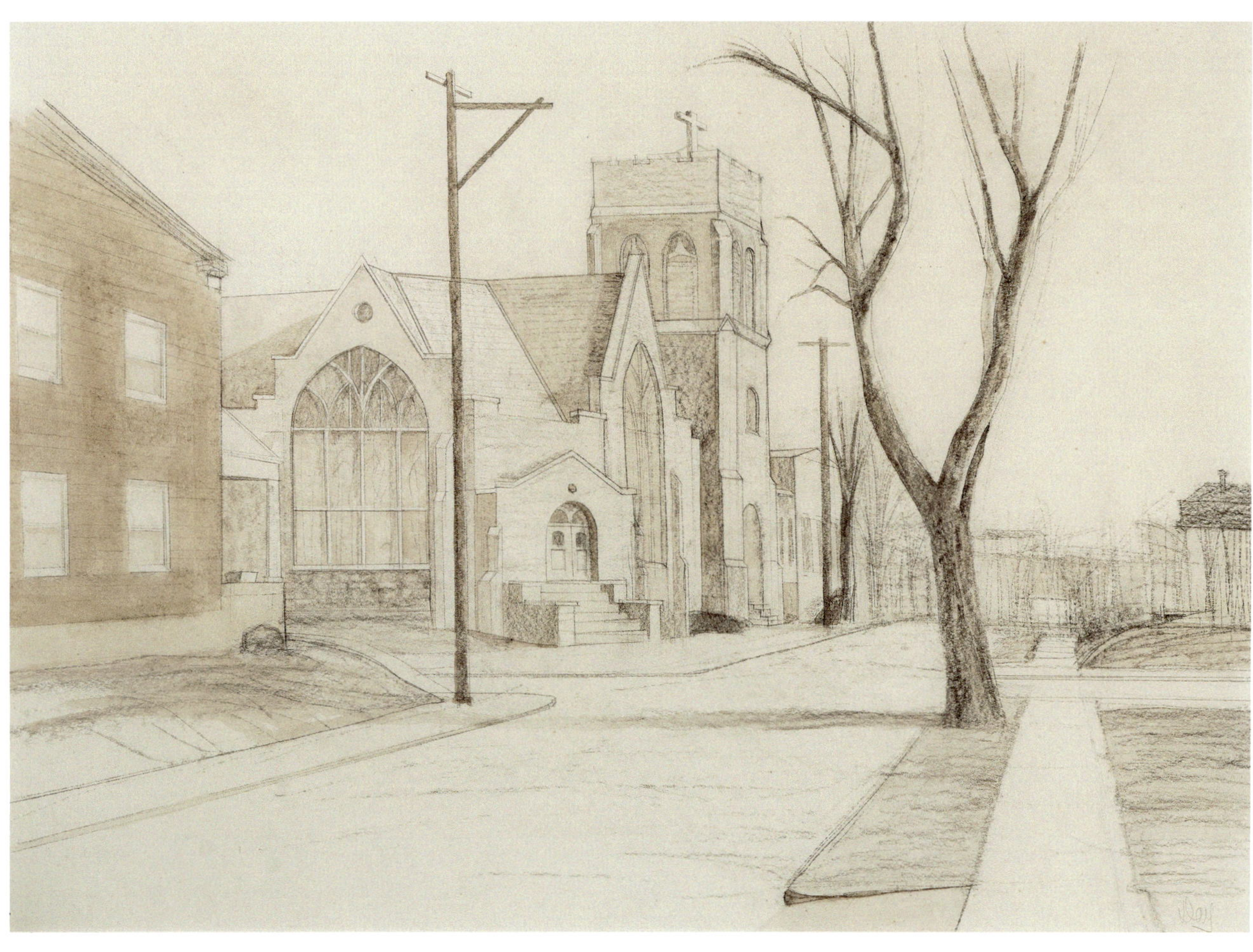

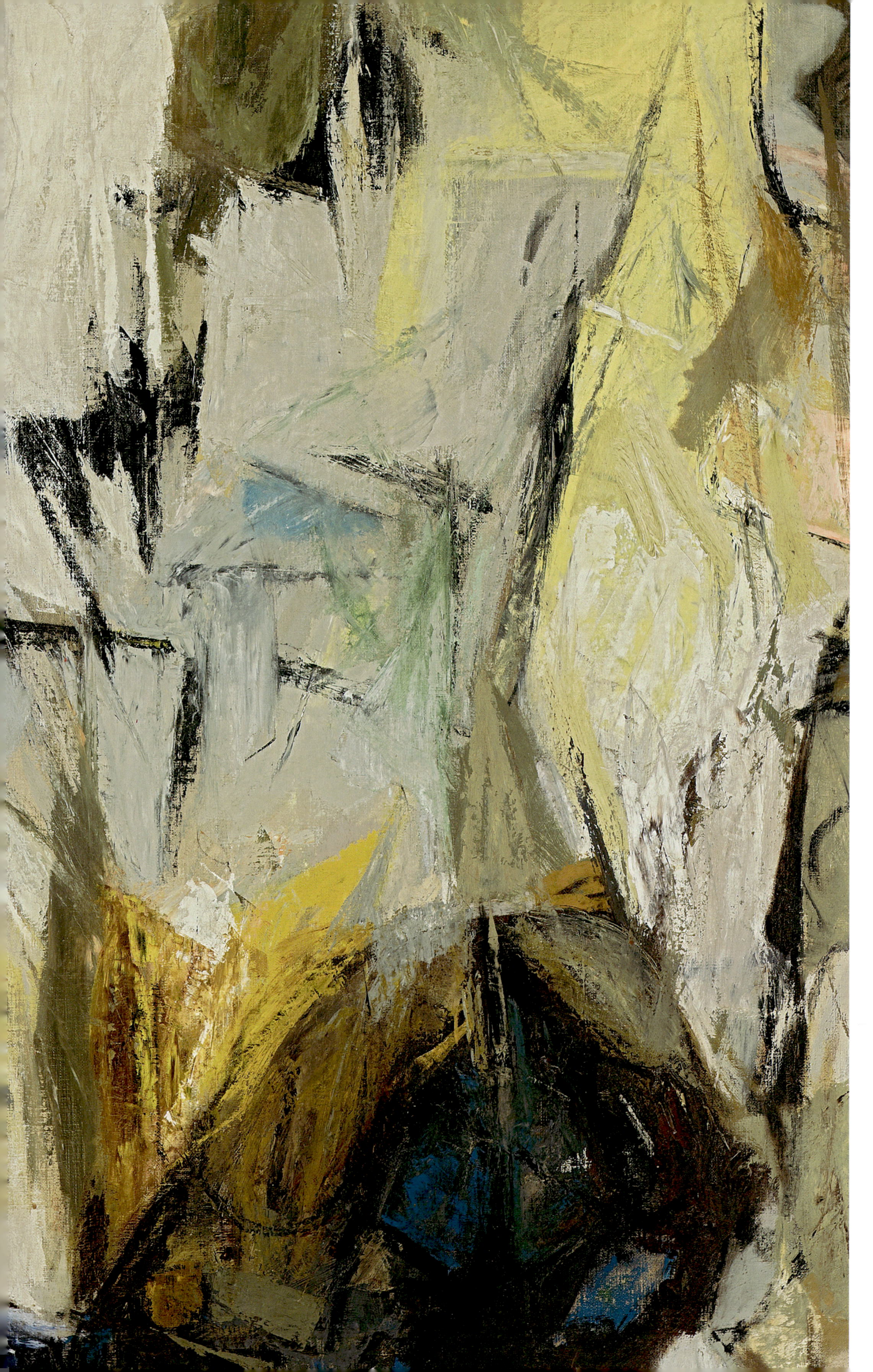

# Larry Day and the Philadelphia School

Larry Day was the quintessential Philadelphia painter. Born there in 1921, his entire career was shaped by his times, and he in turn shaped the ever-evolving art world in that city. As an artist and an educator, he left his mark indelibly on Philadelphia and the region; and through his many students who taught in universities and art schools across the United States and elsewhere, Day's ideas were shared widely.

Day grew up in Cheltenham Township, north of the city, and first studied art informally with Albert Urban, who had been a student of Max Beckmann in Frankfurt before immigrating to the United States in 1940.[1] The budding artist's lifelong passions included literature and music, and he was widely acknowledged for his nous. Indeed, after serving in the Army in World War II (fig. 6.1), torn between his interest in the visual arts and writing, he initially planned to study writing at Kenyon College. With a semester's delay from matriculating in Ohio, he went instead to Temple University's Tyler School of Art, not far from his parents' home. Although intending this interruption to be brief, Day was soon thoroughly immersed in the arts at Tyler, which included dance and theater as well as the plastic arts. He stayed there rather than transferring to Kenyon, but throughout his life his commitment to the written word remained strong.

Tyler in the late 1940s was a relatively new academic institution. Day studied traditional paint glazing techniques with Alexander Abels, but abandoned this pursuit after seeing the 1948 Matisse retrospective at the Philadelphia Museum of Art.[2] This inspired him to work alla prima, directly on his canvases, and to make prints as well (plates 82–85, 87, and 90).

His Tyler schoolmates included Adair Chambers, Roy Davis, George Dunbar, Raymond Hendler, Paul Keene, Robert Kulicke, Bertha Hanstein (later Leonard), David Levine (fig. 6.2), and Aaron Shikler. After graduation, Day worked at sundry enterprises to make money. With classmates Hanstein, Phyllis Pitegoff, and Iris Cohen he started a greeting card business called Hanco-Piday, which produced silk-screened cards for one season. More important was his brief partnership in Kulicke's picture frame business, started in Day's basement. He, along with Kulicke and Kulicke's wife, Barbara, would build frames, then hawk the samples in New York, going door to door, including a stop at the studio of Reginald Marsh.[3]

Soon, Day began selling small portraits through Pearl Fox Gallery in Melrose Park, where Fox worked from her home.[4] She also organized exhibitions for the

Cheltenham Art Center; among the artist-jurors she invited to participate were Milton Avery, Isabel Bishop, Adolph Gottlieb, Loren MacIver, Ben Shahn, and Jack Tworkov.[5] Day taught at the center and had a brief stint at Abraham Lincoln High School. So impressive were the young artist's paintings that his work was shown in the *1950 Annual Exhibition of Painting and Sculpture* at the Pennsylvania Academy of the Fine Arts (PAFA). At that time, these exhibitions were regarded nationally and internationally on the level of the Whitney Museum of American Art annuals and its current biennials. Day's still life *Paul Revere Coffee Pot* was recognized in Thomas Hess's *Art News* review.[6] Through this consequential exposure, Day was invited to have his first one-person show at Philadelphia's Dubin Gallery, opened by Hank Dubin in the 1940s, and one of the foremost outposts of modern art in the city through the 1950s. Day would go on to have five solo exhibitions there.[7]

Traveling to Europe in the summer of 1952, he encountered Paul Dufour, a Philadelphia book dealer/publisher, with whom he went on a grand tour to the Netherlands and London; with Tyler acquaintance Chambers, he also visited Herman Gundersheimer in southern France.[8] In Paris, works by Balthus (Balthasar Klossowski de Rola), Nicolas de Stael, Alberto Giacometti, and Pierre Tal-Coat impressed him, as did his visit to Galerie Huit, the first American cooperative gallery in Europe.[9] Day later recalled, "I knew some of the people who showed there."[10] By this, he was referring to Tyler classmates Hendler and Keene, who graduated the year before Day. Hendler, a founding member of Paris's Galerie Huit, later promoted abstraction through his eponymous gallery in Philadelphia. Upon returning to his native city, Day taught at Germantown High School for one semester. In the fall of 1953, however, Emmanuel M. Benson recruited him to teach at the Pennsylvania Museum School of Art (PMSA).[11]

In the 1950s, the most advanced American art was Abstract Expressionism, an amalgam of Cubism and surrealist automatism with the large scale of Mexican murals and public art projects. In Philadelphia, Abstract Expressionism was showcased prominently at both Dubin and Hendler Galleries. Hendler, located a block from PMSA, exhibited both Europeans and Americans and, like Dubin, became a cultural nexus.[12] Moreover, the PAFA annuals presented all of the New York School, as well as other national tendencies.[13]

Because of New York's proximity, artists reciprocally exchanged ideas along the Eastern corridor. Franz Kline briefly taught at PMSA, staying overnight in Hendler's apartment. Kulicke was friends with both Kline and Robert Motherwell. When Kline left the PMSA, his replacement was Mercedes Matter, originally from Philadelphia.[14] Through them, Day was introduced to New York's Cedar Tavern, whose patrons included Charles Cajori, John Ferren, and Philip Guston.[15] Years later, under Piero Dorazio's direction, other New Yorkers taught at the University of Pennsylvania.[16]

Day's sensitive endeavors were never totally nonobjective, but allied with figurative and landscape motifs influenced by De Kooning. As early as 1950, Day saw De Kooning's *Attic,* its linear, biomorphic shapes defined like drawings in black and

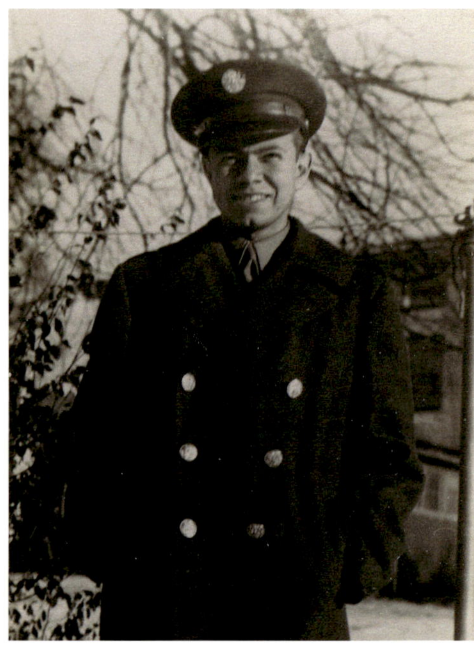

Figure 6.1   Day in his Army uniform, c. 1943, photographer unknown (Larry Day Archives)

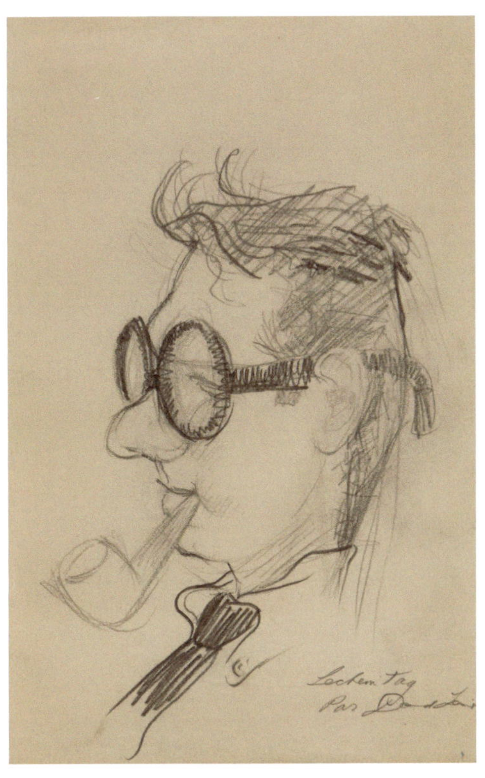

Figure 6.2  David Levine, *Lechem Tag*, c. 1947, graphite on loose-leaf paper, 9 × 5¾ in. (Collection of Ruth Fine)

white with small passages of red and yellow.[17] Day fell further under his spell after a De Kooning drawing exhibition at the PMSA.[18]

Day's New York debut, entitled *Nudes and Angels* with a nod to Rilke, was held at the Parma Gallery in 1954.[19] But shortly thereafter he stylistically embraced a lyrical painting style called Abstract Impressionism, which he explored in paintings and works on paper for some years (plates 84 and 85). Day's ambitious abstract endeavors were not appreciably smaller than his New York counterparts. For example, his *Untitled* (plate 40) was the same size as, if not larger than,[20] classic examples of Abstract Expressionism.[21]

Day's painting approach was physically individual nevertheless. Although Day was influenced by De Kooning's model, he didn't slavishly mimic him. De Kooning's paintings involved the haptic slashing staccato action of the entire arm, creating contours and edges through drawing. Moreover, Day's were made by the wrist, creating delicate marks that defined localized tectonic plates distributed across the picture plane. Day's paintings project meaning through color and mood, and many works are poetically dark and shadowy. Indeed, his works of the 1950s are closer to those chthonic efforts of Guston or Bradley Walker Tomlin in tone and facture. *Landscape for St. John of the Cross* (plate 92), for example, with profound reverence for the Spanish Counter-Reformation mystic, portends a dark night of the soul. *Wiegenlied* (1958), German for lullaby, however, is a lighter-hued verdant landscape, all vegetal spring green.

Still, by the early 1960s, Day's involvement with gestural action painting was over.[22] Thoughtful and Apollonian, Day was uncomfortable with spontaneous improvisation, a major tenet of Abstract Expressionism. Considering his education, it is perhaps not surprising that this revelation came in the process of painting an homage to Jan Steen's *Merry Company* (plate 7).[23] His epiphany, that abstract modalities remained in transcription, facilitated his easy return to representation.

Day was in the forefront of the transition from the Abstract Expressionist hegemony when artists began incorporating veristic scenes and new images of man.[24] In 1966, Neil Welliver became department chair at the University of Pennsylvania, hiring Rudy Burckhardt, John Button, and Rackstraw Downes; Walter and Martha Erlebacher arrived to teach at what was by then called the Philadelphia College of Art (PCA). Swarthmore College also participated in this sea change; Button and Downes taught there, while painter Harriet Shorr ran the gallery, exhibiting, for example, Alex Katz and the Wyeths. Two years later, in 1968, recent Yale graduate John Moore came to teach at Tyler. At PAFA, where Barkley Hendricks studied, Sidney Goodman, Yvonne Jacquette, and Edith Neff were instructors for decades, and Eileen Neff still is. One could say that Philadelphia was the center of a major realist revival.

Representational painting was newly supported by Philadelphia venues in the 1960s. Gladys Myers's Gallery 1015 represented Day (plate 93).[25] Marlin McCleaf Gallery showed Welliver, Downes, Red Grooms, and Fairfield Porter. The gallery was renamed Gross McCleaf in 1960, under the directorship of Estelle Gross.[26] Later, Marian Locks Gallery (now Locks Gallery) promoted representational painters Diane

Burko, Noel Mahaffey, and Elizabeth Osborne. Vick Gallery briefly provided similar artists, such as John Moore.[27] In the 1980s, Charles More opened The More Gallery, which showed Frank Galuska and Sarah McEneaney. Day had three solo exhibitions there in the last decade of his life, as well as participating in simultaneous two-person shows with Frank Hyder at The More Gallery and at the Art Alliance in 1995.[28]

Day was the doyen of the Philadelphia realists. His intellectual stamina and aesthetic integrity influenced both students and colleagues. In the classroom, Day's legendary comments were supportive through subtle means. He didn't critique destructively but guided his students through pedagogical ideas, didn't demand acolytes but rather developed diversity. "An amazing teacher,"[29] he taught undergraduates including Raymond Allen, Marvin Brown, Wendy Edwards, Beverly Fishman, Joe Fyfe, Eileen Goodman, Sidney Goodman, Eileen Neff, Marc Salz, Herbert Schiffrin, and Dan Walsh. Alan Turner studied with him at the Aspen School of Contemporary Art in Colorado.[30] Because many of these practicing artists went on to teach, his wide impact is still felt throughout the United States.[31] To colleagues, Day was known as empathetic, erudite, and well read. Pragmatically anti-dogmatic, his catholic teaching hires broadened the scope of PCA. These included Cynthia Carlson and Robert Storr, among many others.[32]

Called an ironic realist,[33] Day was a modernist of his time. Based on direct observation, photographs, and even contemporary magazine illustrations,[34] as well as countless loosely wrought preparatory drawings (apart from his hundreds of highly finished sheets), his works were honed, clarified, and idealized. This eclecticism allowed Day to absorb the lessons of the past without Renaissance recidivism. Day mixed Matisse's directness with symbolism, the poetic meaning of poses, and Balthus's and Poussin's classicism. Surely, his *Poker Game* (plate 11) resonated with Paul Cézanne's masterpieces in the Barnes and the Philadelphia Museum of Art.

Although Day also lived in Takoma Park, Maryland, for a decade and depicted scenes in Washington, DC, on several occasions, he was defined by Philadelphia. His works epitomize the dry grit of the city and its artists. By his own admission, Day did not sell a lot of artwork until later in his career. He was an artist's artist, recognized and admired by his students and a coterie of friends. "Ninety percent of the drawings I've sold have been to other artists. I like it when an artist buys a work of mine."[35] Among works in the exhibition owned by artists are *Heidelberg Park* (plate 81), *(Factory)* (plate 94), and *Picnic* (plate 95). A chronicler of his milieu, Day produced deft depictions of his inner circle that defined Philadelphia's culturati as succinctly as any historic canvas (plates 13 and 19).[36]

Philadelphia's local light and color significantly affected Day's quiet evocations.[37] His excavation sites, parking lots, brick facades, and stucco walls delineated stark cityscapes as empty as Eugène Atget, as metaphysically mysterious and beguiling as Giorgio de Chirico. Although he worked directly, he approached the easel only after thorough study. Day was always drawing, and relevant sketches were tucked like bookmarks in his many books. His paint was fresco thin, arrived at only after many adjustments. Like Cézanne, Day seemed to have doubts. His drawings, which have been compared to those of Jean-Auguste-Dominique Ingres, were less sure. Day deliberately finessed his contours through staccato strokes to secure edges. In this too, he was like Cézanne and Alberto Giacometti. The world is a projection of the mind.

Because his canvases followed from empirical observations, Day's work never devolved into a formulaic style. The artist's sensibilities were larger than his city, larger than the limitations of stretchers and canvas. His paintings were of the world.

## Notes

1   Urban showed silk-screen prints at the Philadelphia Art Alliance, November 19–December 8, 1945 and later exhibited in *Sixteen Americans* at the Museum of Modern Art.

2   The exhibition was *Henri Matisse: Retrospective Exhibition of Paintings, Drawings, and Sculpture, Organized in Collaboration with the Artist*, April 3–May 9, 1948. This was prior to the Philadelphia Museum of Art's acquisitions of the Gallatin and Arensberg collections, which provided more Matisses to view locally. Day also would have been aware of the deep Matisse offerings in the Barnes Foundation.

3   Larry Day, oral history with Marina Pacini, February 21, 1991, 42–43, Archives of American Art, Smithsonian Institution, Washington, DC. As Day was not a good salesman, he soon departed the partnership, which became one of the largest and most advanced in history. Kulicke's innovations in narrow striping, welded aluminum frames, and Plexiglas boxes defined and dominated American frame design for decades. After retiring from the business, Kulicke went on to paint Morandi-inflected canvases and create historicist gold jewelry.

4   In 1948, Pearl Fox Gallery was established at 103 Windsor Avenue. Day may have worked for her. Fox's stable included Paul Gorka, Ben Kamihira, Seymour Remenick, and Harry Sefarbi.

5   Others included Al Blaustein, Philip Evergood, Lee Gatch, John Heliker, Joseph Hirsch, Morris Kantor, Dong Kingman, Karl Knaths, David Levine, Loren MacIver, William Palmer, Beverly Pepper, Gregorio Prestopino, James Johnson Sweeney, Robert Vickrey, and Max Weber. Archives of American Art, Smithsonian Institution, Pearl Fox letters from artists, 1954–61.

6   This was three years before the publication of Hess's influential "De Kooning Paints a Picture" in the March 1953 issue of *Art News*, chronicling the creation of *Woman I* (1950–52).

7   Abstract painters associated with Group '55 held their soirees at Dubin Gallery. Woodmere Art Museum presented an exhibition devoted to this group from September 24, 2020 through January 21, 2021.

8   Day, oral history, 45 and 62.

9   Members included Carmen D'Avino, Sam Francis, Sidney Geist, Burt Hasen, Al Held, Shirley Jaffe, Herbert Katzman, Jules Olitski, Robert Rosenwald (son of the great Philadelphia print and rare book collector), and Haywood Rivers. The gallery was in Rosenwald's studio. Day, oral history, 65–66.

10   Day, oral history, 65–66.

11   Benson had been a consultant for the WPA Federal Art Project and chief of education at the Philadelphia Museum of Art from 1932 to 1953, as well as dean of its art school from 1953 to 1965. Benson was influential in the emancipation of the Philadelphia Museum School of Art (PMSA, which has had several names over time and is now part of the University of the Arts) from the museum and the incorporation of the Philadelphia College of Art. He later started the Benson Gallery in Bridgehampton, Long Island, with his second wife, Elaine, which showcased Lenore Tawney, Toshiko Takaezu, and the young Dale Chihuly in his first one-person exhibition. Day had a solo show there also, in 1963.

12   "[T]here was also another artist who I knew from Tyler named Ray Hendler. Ray Hendler started a gallery in Philly. The Hendler Gallery. And I think it was every Thursday or Friday night, a group of us would get together there, and talk. It included— besides painters, writers, musicians— George Rochberg, the composer. . . . At one point, we made a newspaper . . .

called Re-Art." Day, oral history, 70. Day contributed an article to the single issue of *Re-Art*. Hendler's gallery was at 1429 Spruce Street, where he showed artists including Paul-Émile Borduas, Willem de Kooning, Philip Guston, Sam Feinstein, Sam Francis, Sanford Greenberg, Shirley Jaffe, Hugh Kappel, Robert Keyser, Franz Kline, George McNeil, Albert Newbill, Stephen Pace, Jackson Pollock, Melville Price, Milton Resnick, Robert Richenburg, Jean-Paul Riopelle, Joseph Stefanelli, Yvonne Thomas, and Jack Tworkov. Hendler was the first to introduce Francis and Riopelle to the US and presented the first one-person shows for Pace, Richenburg, and Stefanelli.

13   For more information, see Sid Sachs, *Invisible City: Philadelphia and the Vernacular Avant-Garde* (Philadelphia: University of the Arts, 2020), 49, n18.

14   Matter knew Philadelphia as the daughter of Arthur B. Carles and Mercedes de Cordova. She taught for a decade at PMSA and founded the New York Studio School in 1964.

15   Matter's circle included Pollock, Krasner, Kline, Guston, Alexander Calder, and Willem de Kooning.

16   Day, oral history, 71, 74. Abstract Expressionists who taught at the University of Pennsylvania during Piero Dorazio's tenure included Helen Frankenthaler, Robert Motherwell, Barnett Newman, Ad Reinhardt, David Smith, and Clyfford Still. Garner Tullis, email to author, October 10, 2017. Also see *Invisible City*, 25–26.

17   *Attic* (1949) was shown in the *Annual Exhibition of Contemporary American Painting*, December 16, 1949–February 5, 1950 at the Whitney Museum of American Art, then on 8th Street. Attic is now in the collection of the Metropolitan Museum of Art.

18   "Week's Art Listing: Philadelphia Museum School of Art, de Kooning, Jacques Lipchitz, and Martinelli," *Philadelphia Inquirer,* January 30, 1955, 7. Day, oral history, 88–89.

19   Robert Keyser, whose small landscape abstractions with glyphs also showed at Parma Gallery in 1955.

20   This painting was shown in the Philadelphia Museum of Art's bicentennial exhibition, *Three Centuries of American Art.*

21   Day's *Abstraction* for example, is larger than Willem de Kooning's *Attic* and *Woman I* (1950–52, MoMA) and *January 1st* (1956, Glenstone), Mark Rothko's *Untitled (Purple, White, and Red)* (1953, Art Institute of Chicago) or Robert Motherwell's *Catalonia* (1951, Saint Louis Art Museum).

22   "Abstract Impressionism" was a term coined by Elaine de Kooning and developed further by Louis Finkelstein, another PCA colleague. It encompassed more lyrical genres of Abstract Expressionism, such as Guston, as well as versions of abstracted landscapes by Nell Blaine, for example. See Finkelstein "New Look; Abstract-Impressionism," *Art News* 55 (March 1956): 36.

23   The Steen is in the collection of the Philadelphia Museum of Art. At Tyler in the late 1960s, Education majors were required to grind their own paints and replicate a painting in the Philadelphia Museum of Art. If this was so under the more progressive era of Dean Charles LeClair, I am assuming that Day's experience a decade before would have been comparable as curricula evolve slowly in academia.

24   See Peter Selz, *New Images of Man* (New York: Museum of Modern Art, 1959); and Judith Stein and Paul Schimmel, *The Figurative Fifties: New York Figurative Expressionism* (Newport Beach, CA: Newport Harbor Art Museum, 1988). In various ways, these included Jean Dubuffet, Francis Bacon, Eduardo Paolozzi, Richard Diebenkorn, Leonard Baskin, H. C. Westermann, Bob Thompson, Jan Muller, Larry Rivers, Lester Johnson, Elaine de Kooning, Grace Hartigan, Red Grooms, Alex Katz, Wolf Kahn, Louise Dodd, and even more strictly representational artists Leland Bell, Albert York, William Bailey, Philip Pearlstein, Yvonne Jacquette, Rudy Burckhardt, John Button, Alfred Leslie, and Sylvia Mangold. Neil Blaine showed at the Art Alliance, February 2–March 5, 1961.

25   Myers ran Gallery 1015 out of her home at 1015 Greenwood Avenue in Wyncote from 1958 to 1967 and exhibited Day's work along with that of David Pease, sculptors Dennis Leon and Natalie Charkow, and ceramists William Daley and Rudolf Staffel.

26   By the early 1970s, the gallery showed a mix of abstract and representational artists. Philadelphia artists who exhibited there included Martha Armstrong, Day, Jane Eisenstat, Eileen Goodman, Humbert Howard, Steve Jaffe, Bertha Leonard, Jimmy Lueders, Edith Neff, Leonard Nelson, Jane Piper, Bruce Samuelson, and Doris Staffel. In the 1980s, Bill Scott organized a Louisa Matthíasdóttir exhibit there. Email from Scott, September 4, 2020.

27   Under the direction of Cheltenham native Aladar Marberger, New York's Fischbach Gallery "changed its programming from abstraction such as Lucy Lippard's *Eccentric Abstraction* show to representational work." Connie Vick's gallery was affiliated with this later iteration of Fischbach.

28   Both exhibitions were entitled *Two Approaches to the Figure*.

29   David Goerk, email to author, June 9, 2010.

30   Marvin Brown, email to author, August 5, 2020.

31   Among them are Allen at Portland College of Art and the Maryland Institute College of Art; Edwards at University of New Mexico and University of Wisconsin before spending four decades at Brown University, where Marvin Brown had preceded her; Matthew Girson, who was in Day's last PCA class, at DePaul University; Robert Godfrey at Westminster College and Western Carolina University; Harry Naar at Rider University; and Eileen Neff at the Pennsylvania Academy of the Fine Arts.

32   In the contentious 1960s, Cynthia Carlson, Ree Morton, and Rafael Ferrer were perhaps perceived as radical. "Day, [Doris] Staffel, [Harry] Soviak, [Robert] Keyser, and [Steven] Jaffe were on the other side of the line but equally important to the overall climate of the school at the time," Goerk, email to author. Still, PCA held some kind of rapprochement, with Ferrer and even Walter Erlebacher being civil (at least for a time). Such was Day's legacy. It also is worth noting that Day and Ferrer were friends and that Day wrote an exhibition review about Ferrer's new paintings in the November 1985 issue of *Arts* magazine.

33   "Ironic realism" was the designation of National Gallery curator Nan Rosenthal. Day, oral history interview, 124.

34   Such as sources from *Vogue* magazine. Ruth Fine, email to author, August 5, 2020.

35   Day, oral history, 135.

36   For example, Henri Fantin-Latour's *By the Table* (1872) and Maurice Denis's *Homage to Cézanne* (1900), both in the collection of the Musée d'Orsay, Paris, and Max Ernst's *A Friends' Reunion* (1922) in the collection of the Museum Ludwig, Cologne.

37   Day, oral history, 133.

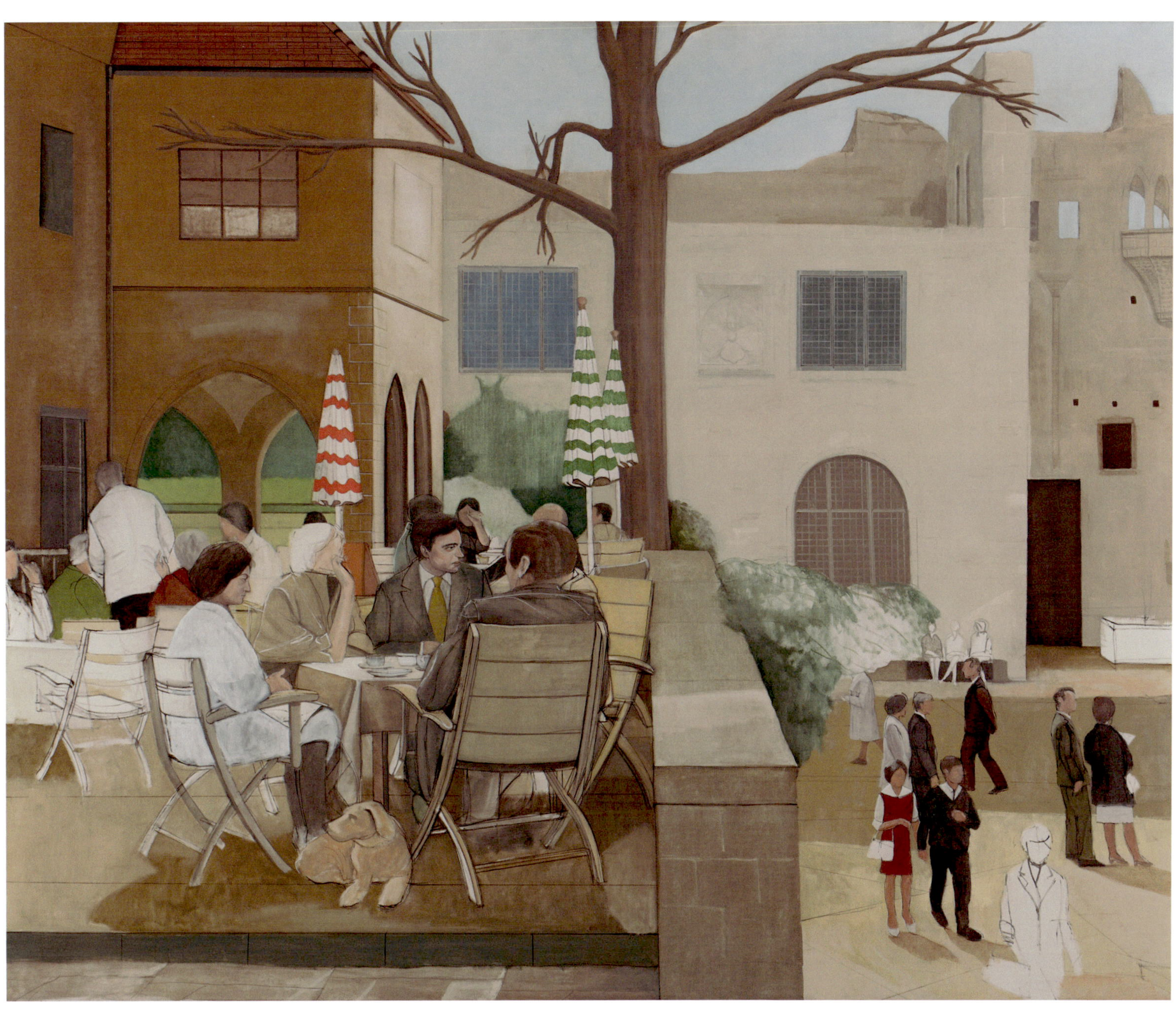

PLATE 81

*Heidelberg Park*, 1972

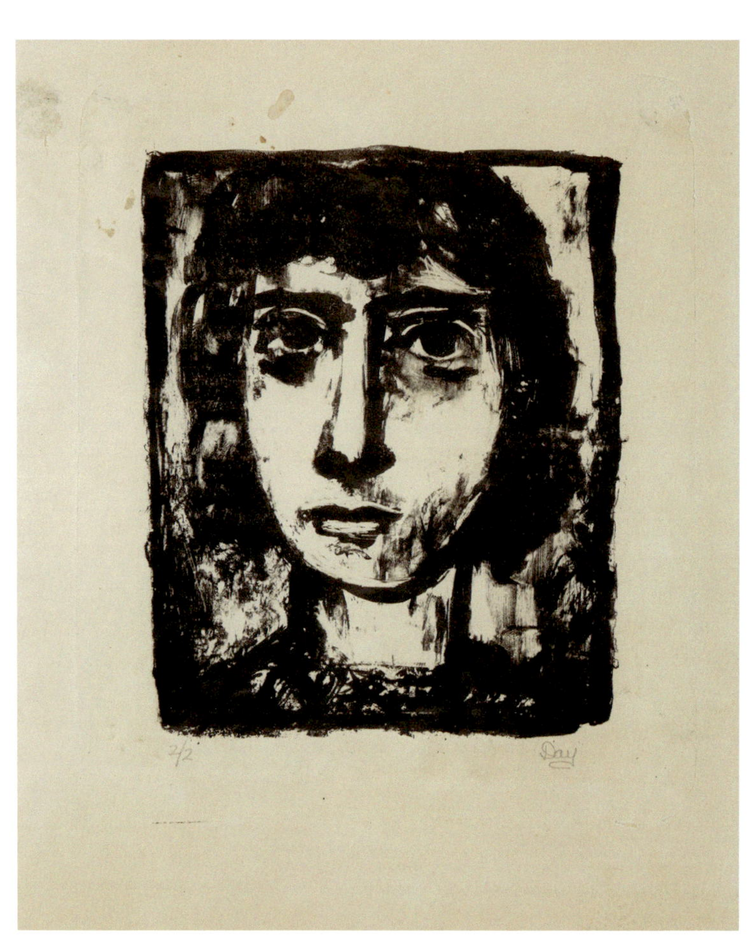

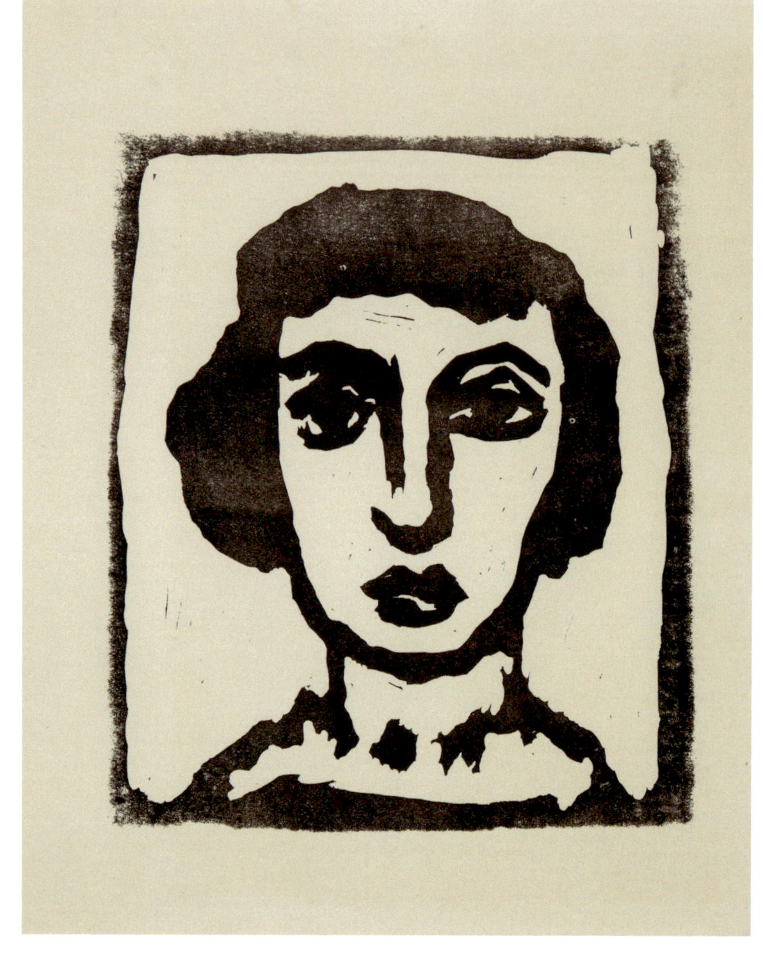

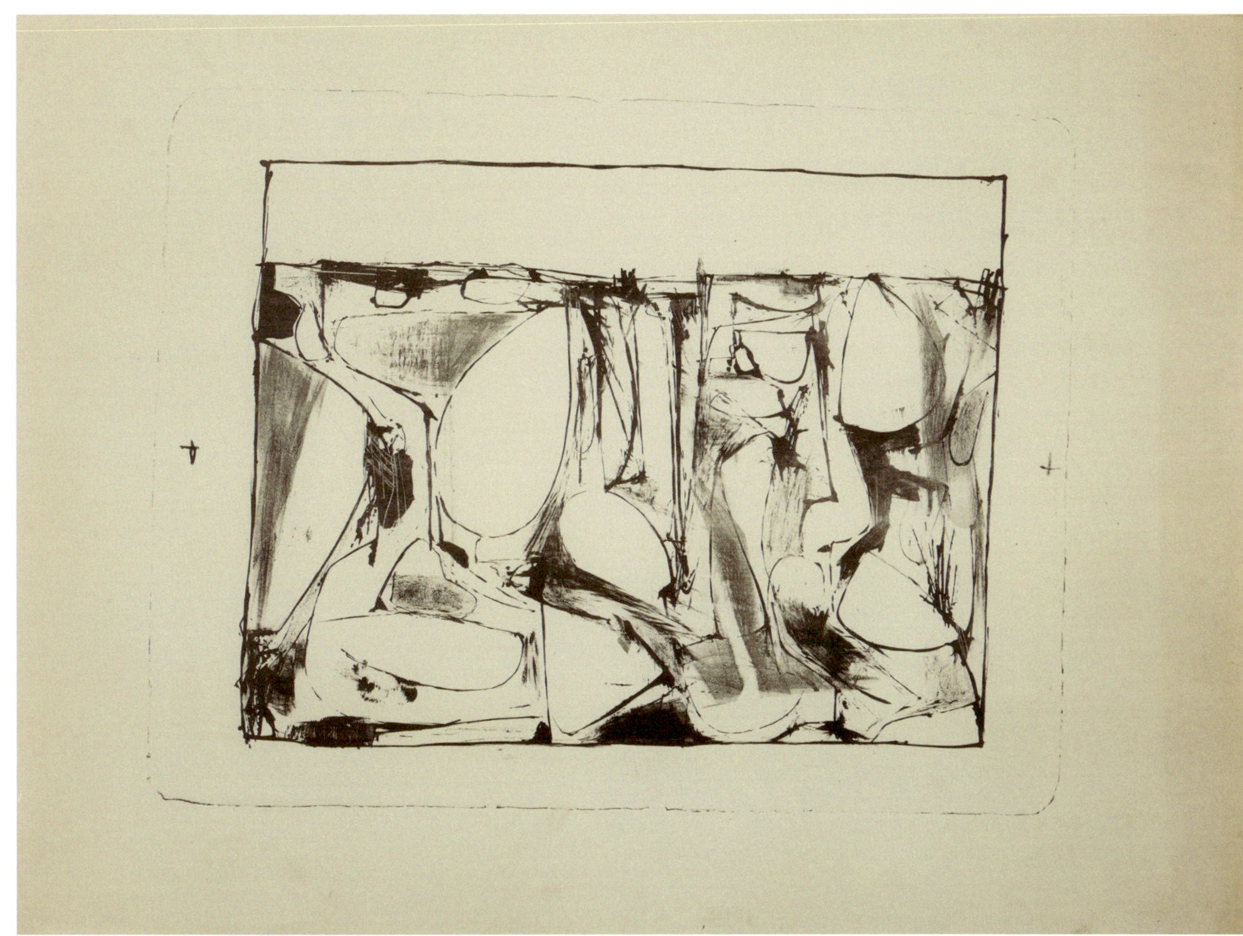

PLATE 84
(Abstract Land-
scape), c. 1956

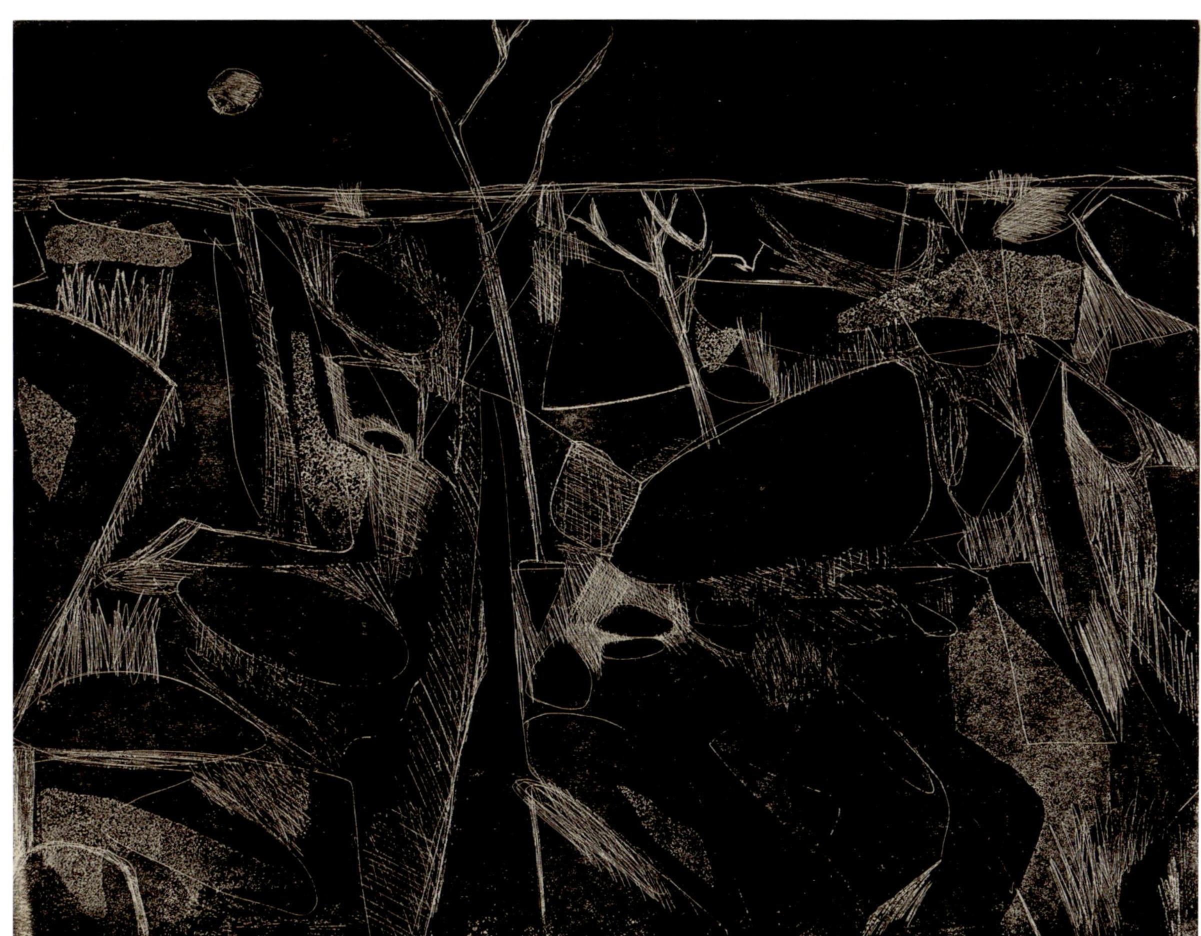

PLATE 85
(Abstract Landscape
with Tree, State 2),
c. 1956

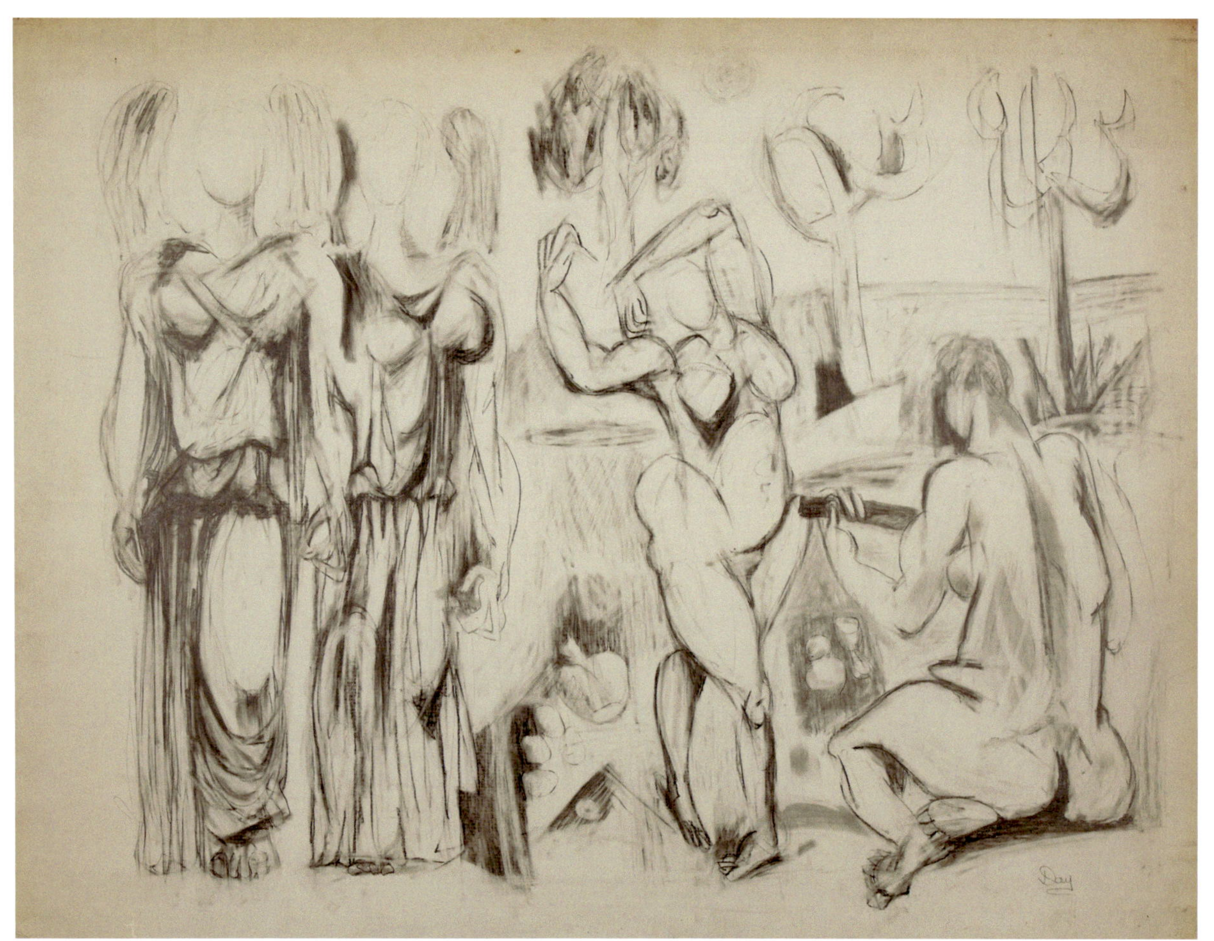

PLATE 86
Sacred and Profane,
C. 1955

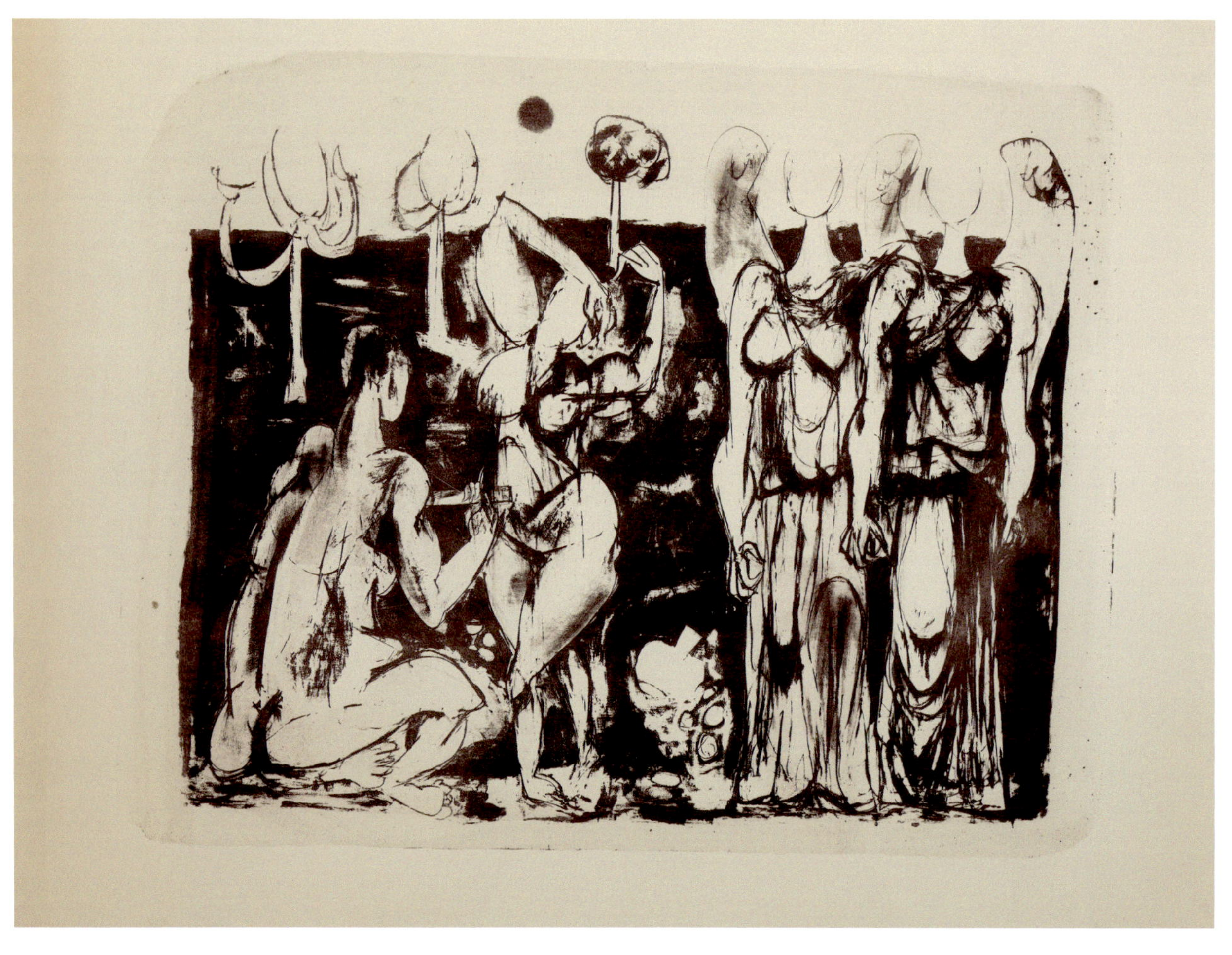

PLATE 87
Sacred and Profane,
State 1, C. 1955

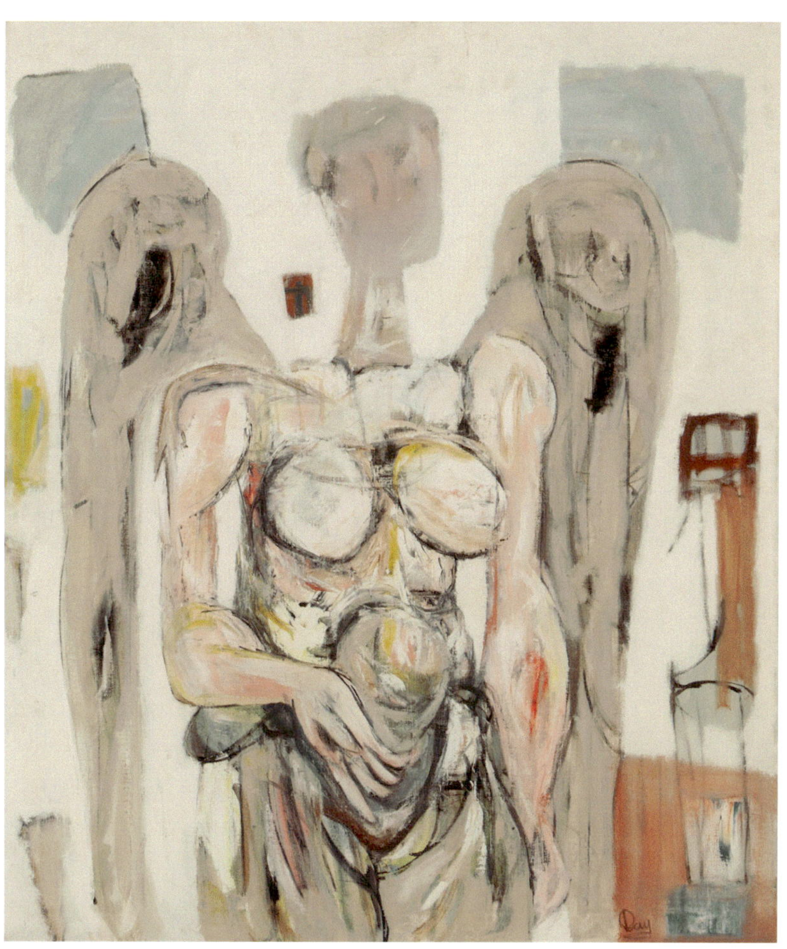


PLATE 88
*Standing Angel,*
c. 1955


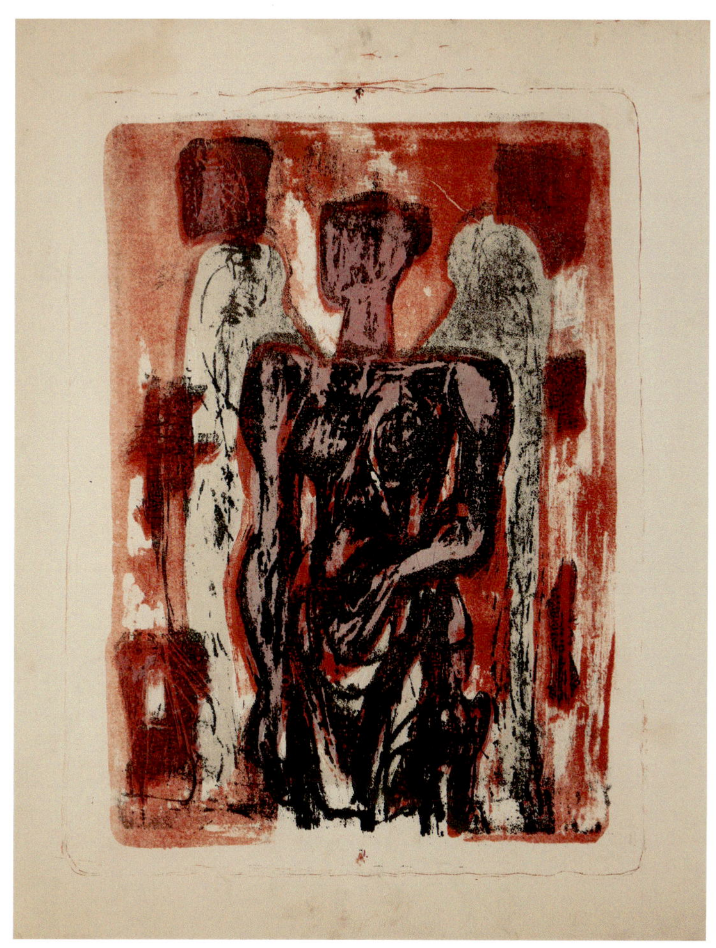


PLATE 89
*Standing Angel,*
*State 2,* c. 1955

PLATE 90
*Aspen Variation,*
c. 1960

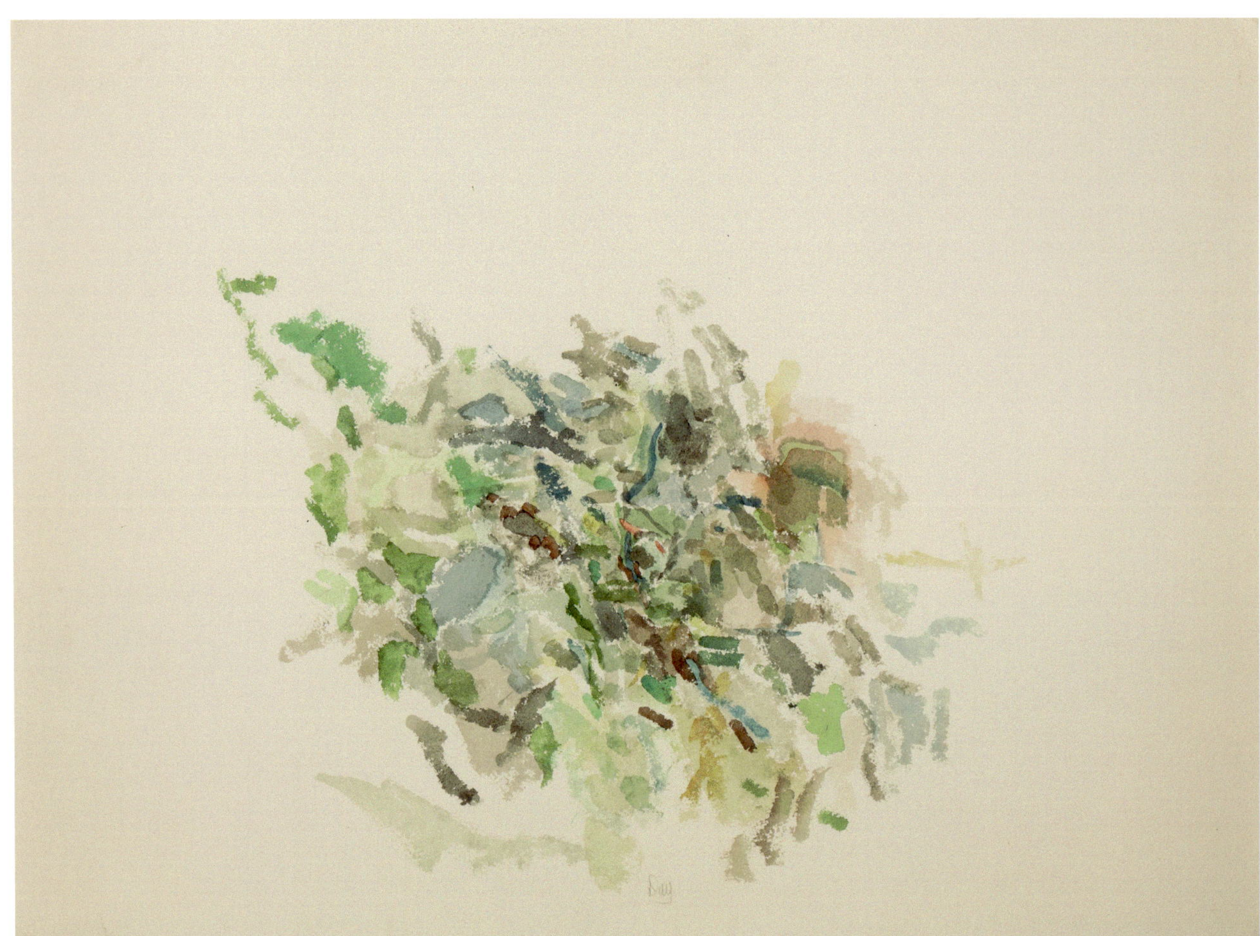

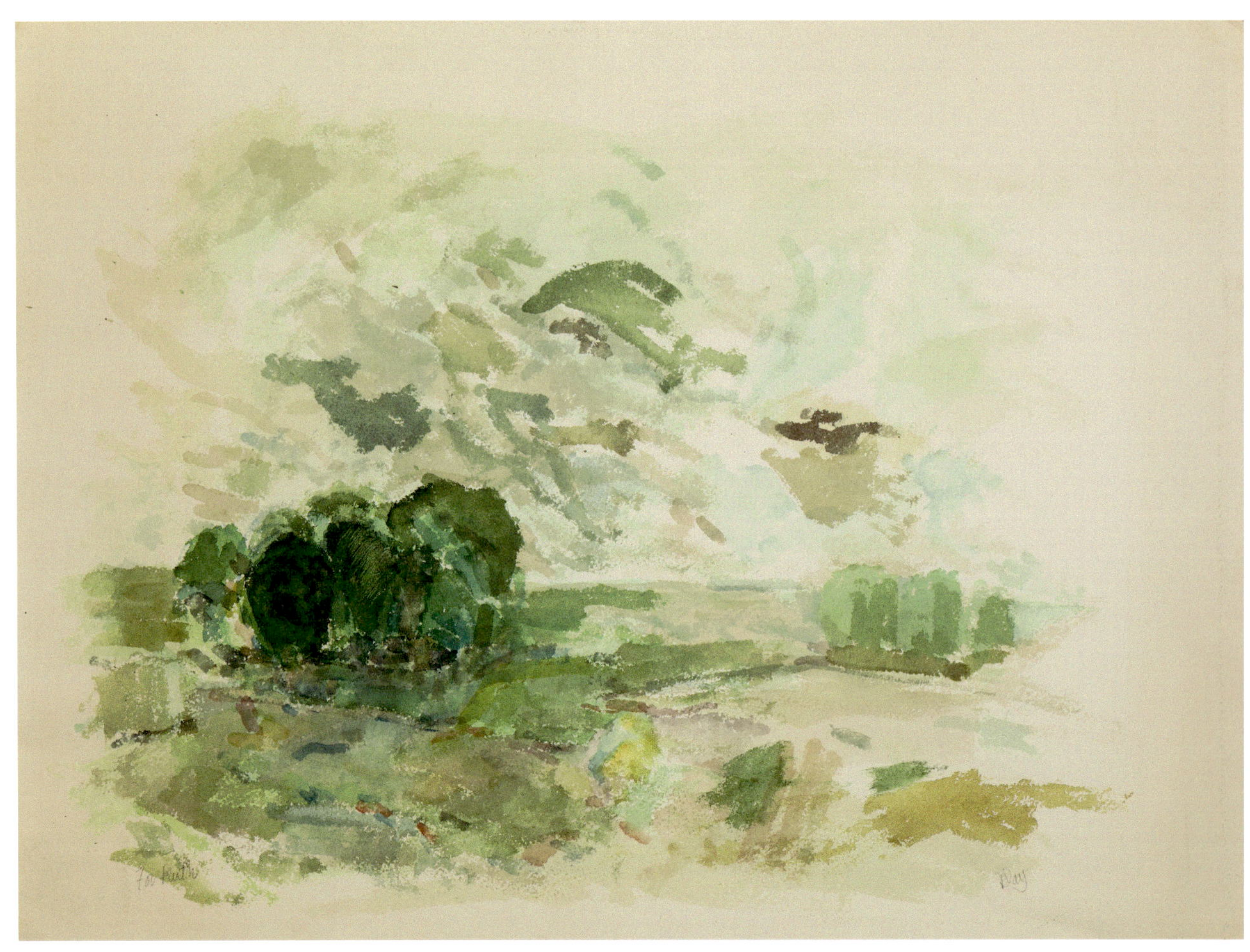

PLATE 91
*(Landscape),*
c. 1960

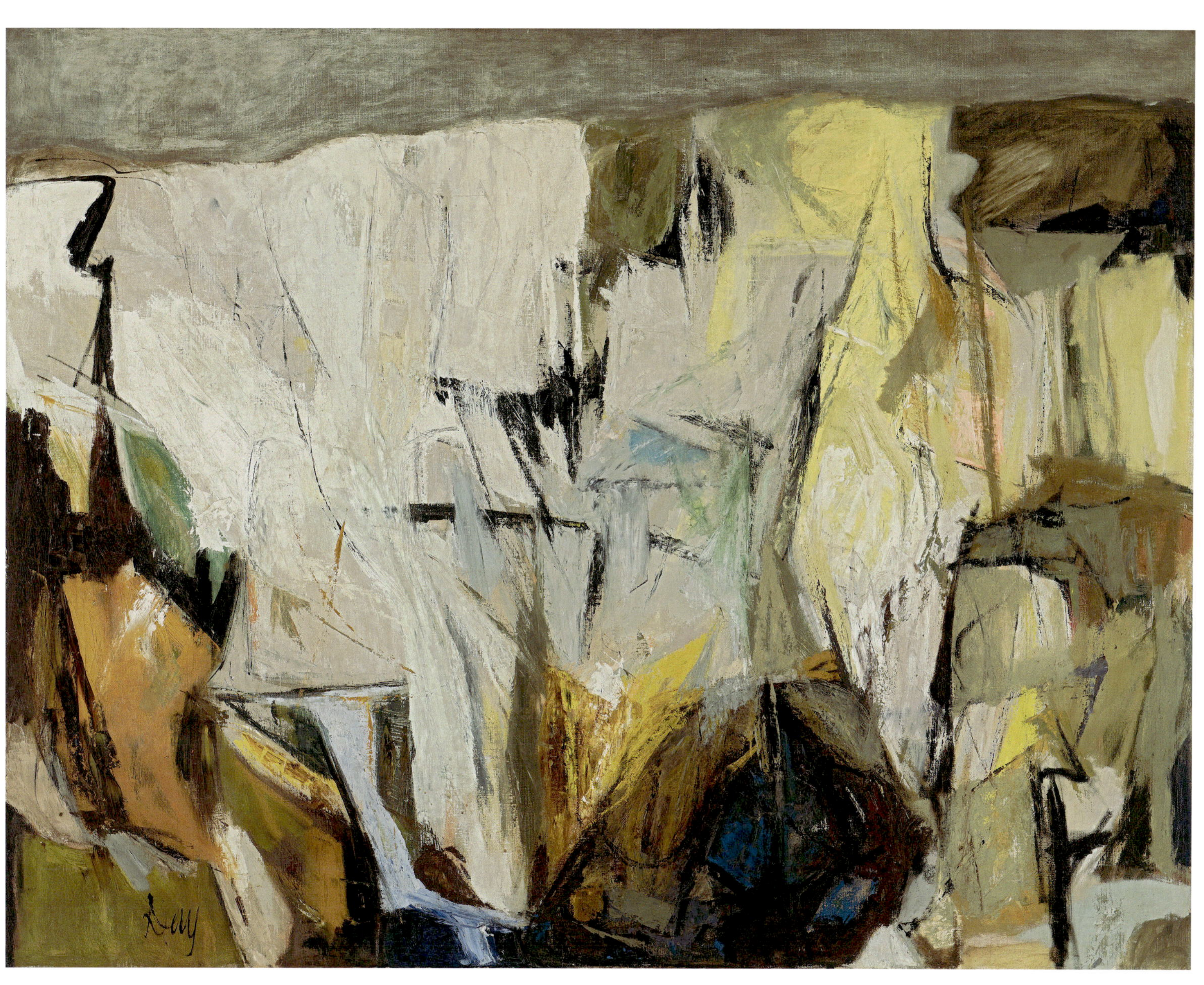

PLATE 92

*Landscape for St. John of the Cross*, 1955

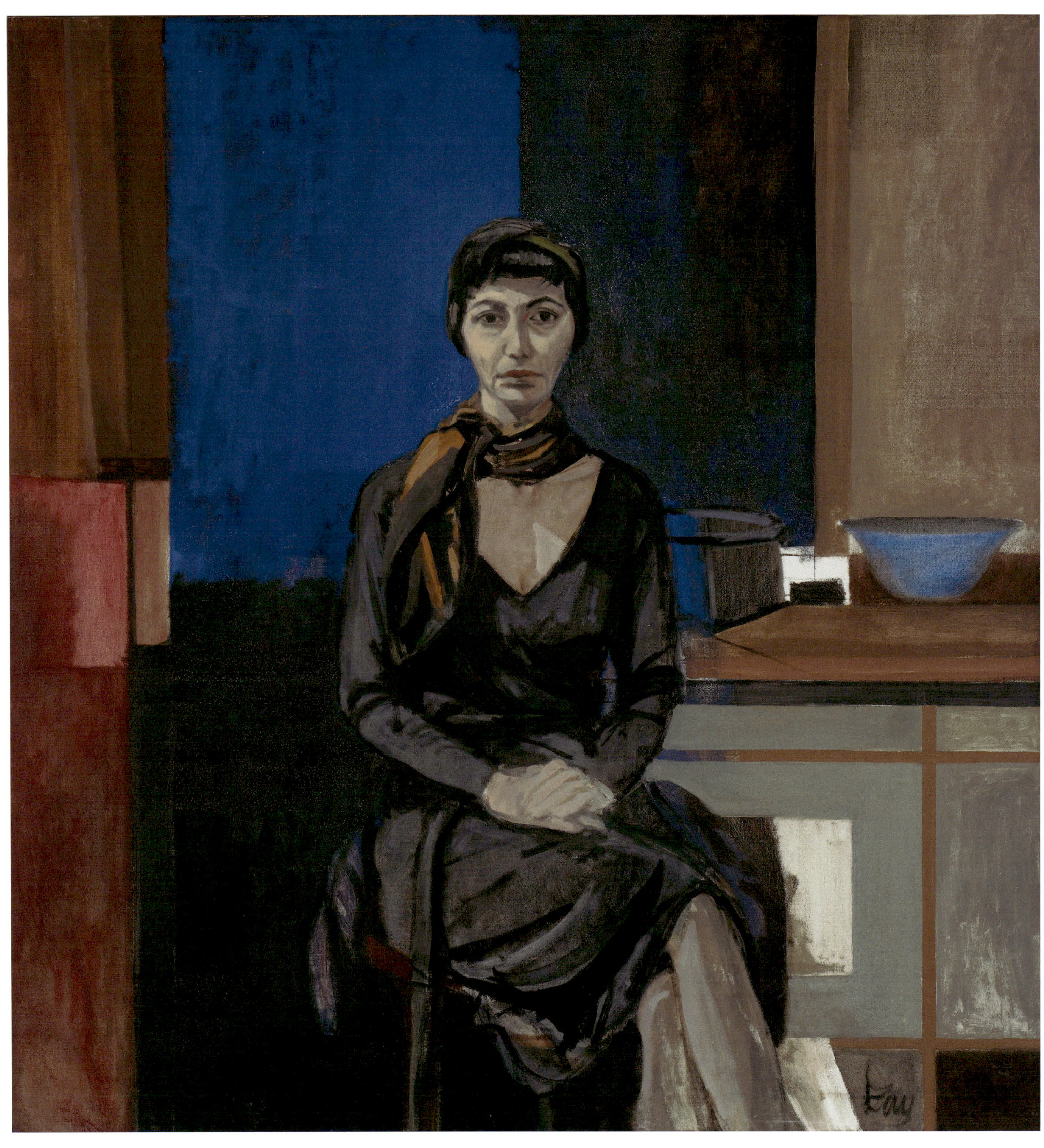

PLATE 93
*Mrs. Myers*, 1964

PLATE 94
(Factory), c. 1970

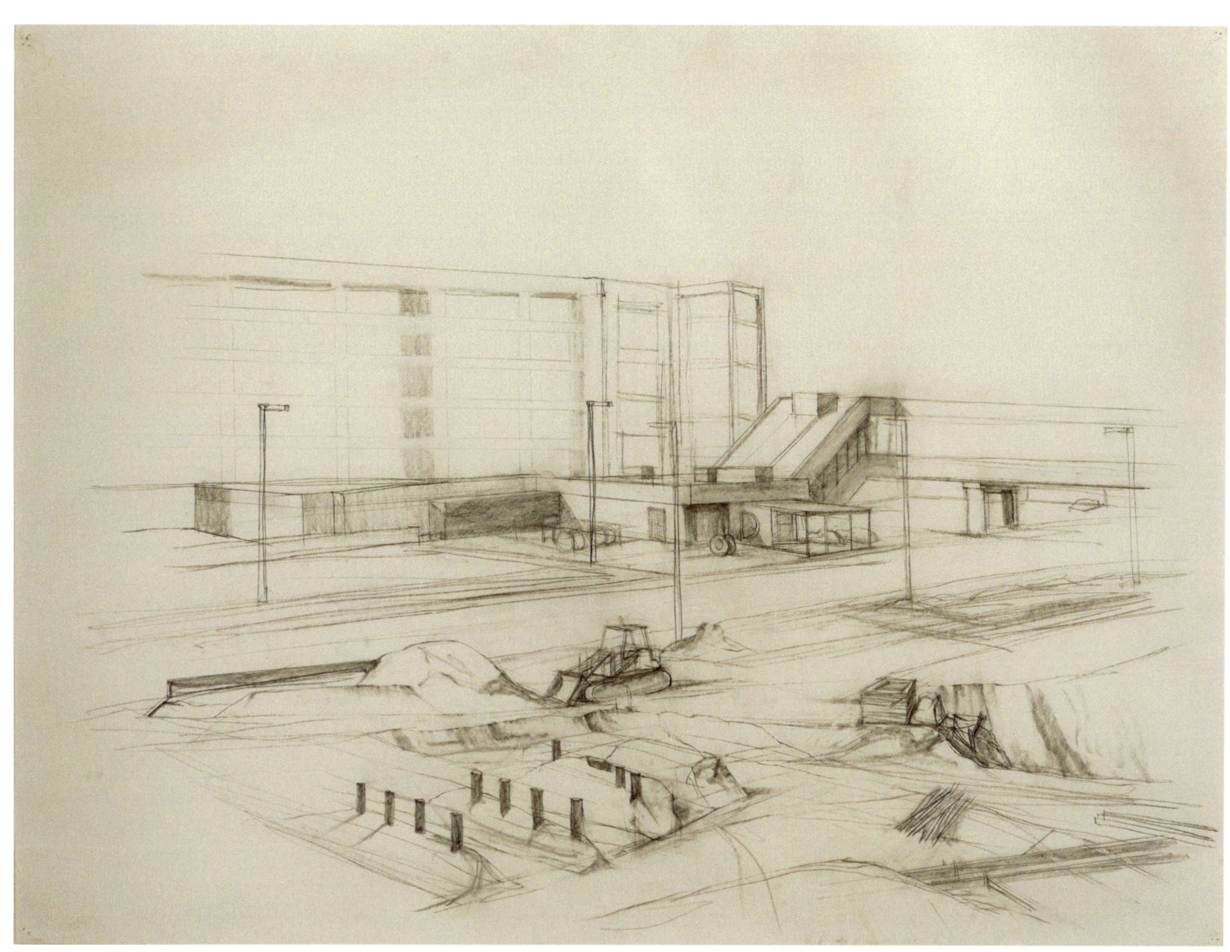

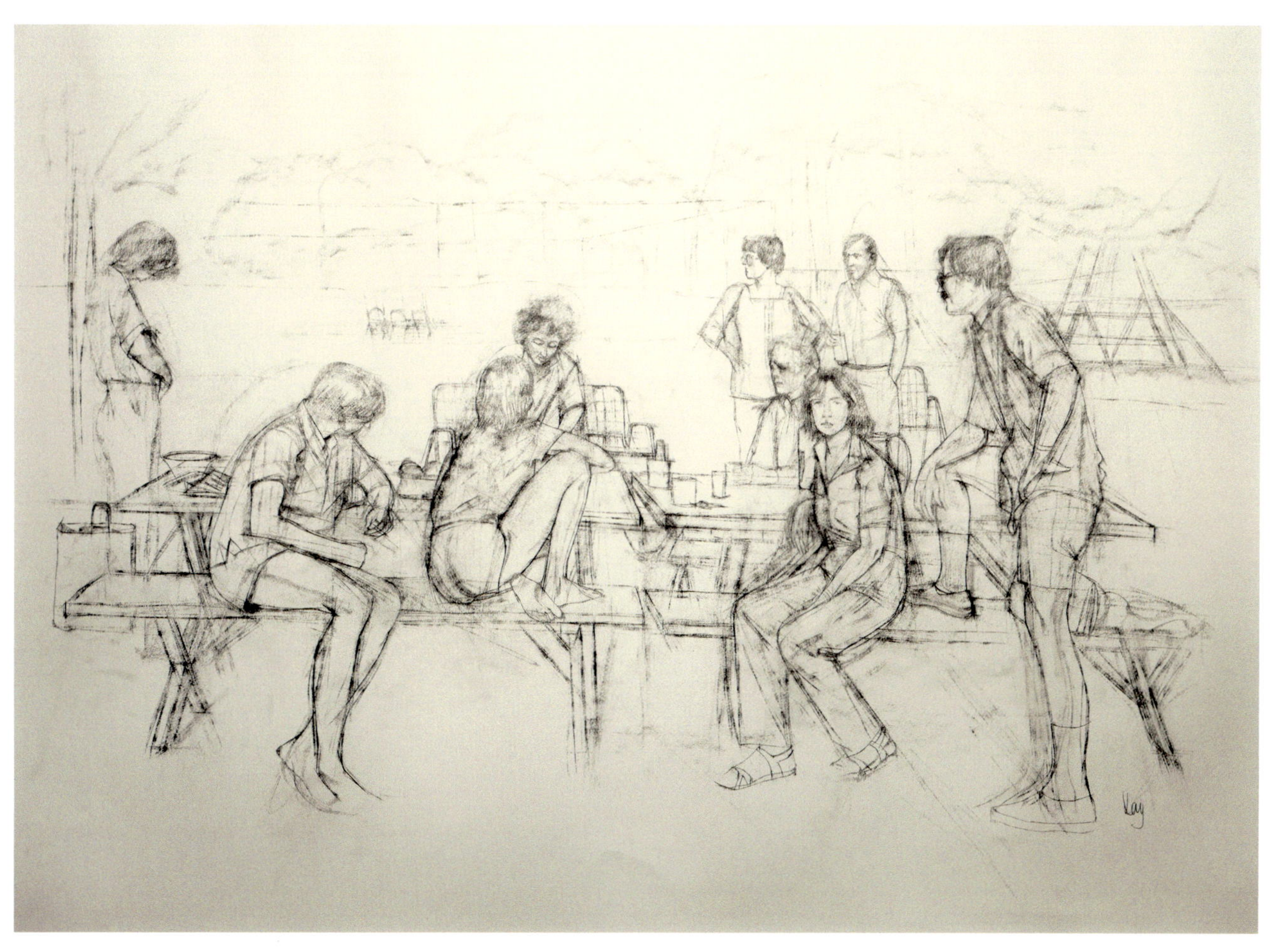

PLATE 95
Picnic,
late 1970s

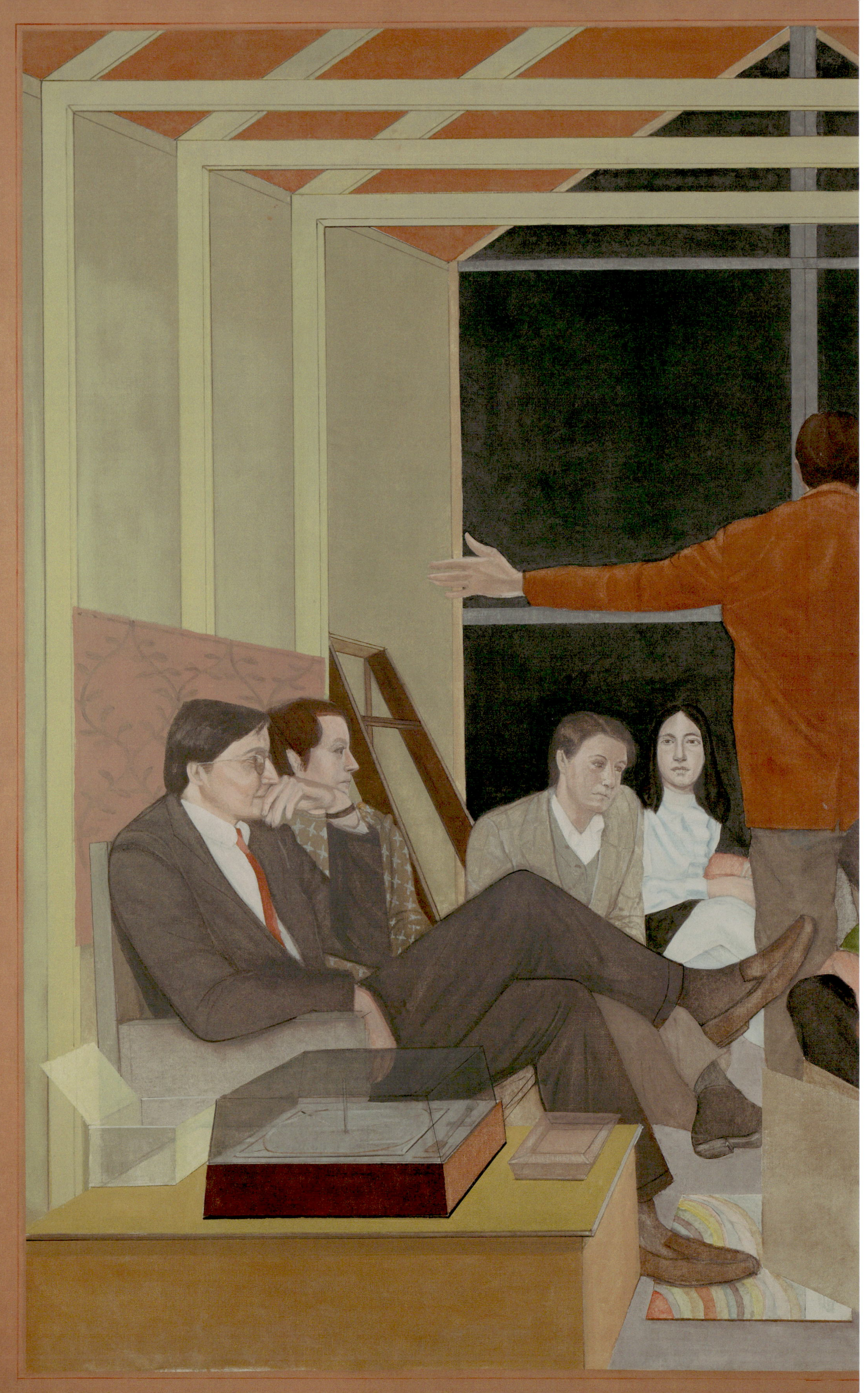

# Memory Portrait

There are two kinds of simplicity: a naïve, pre-conscious simplicity, untouched by the experience of the immense complexity of the phenomena of life, and a post-conscious simplicity which is the result of an extreme artistic effort to master this complexity, and in whose accomplishment we still sense the vibration of this experience and this laboring. It is in this awareness, and this struggle to cope with it, rudimentary as it may be, that true artistic endeavor begins.[1]

The above quotation is one that my husband, Larry Day, highlighted in his copy of Erich Kahler's *The Disintegration of Form in the Arts*, a record of three 1967 lectures delivered at Princeton University and the State University of New York at Stony Brook. Larry's consistent way of noting what he thought important in many of his books was to pencil a light line in the outer margin next to the text. He never read without a pencil nearby, either for use in this ritual or to make a note of the writer's words on a loose sheet of paper or in one of his ever-present notebooks.

Among the dozens of file folders Larry compiled of loose, usually undated, sheets of paper (containing both writing and images), I recently came across his comment that he had almost a "psychopathic fear of living an unimaginative life." I believe he saw the alternative to this, which he so vigorously sought, as a life of profound and unrelenting consciousness of every action he undertook and observed, and of their potential consequences. To my knowledge, even in the drug-enthusiastic decades in which he lived, Larry never was tempted to try them, not even marijuana. In the last weeks of his life, when he was suffering the pain brought on by terminal bone cancer (following several other cancer battles), he refused to accept the morphine that would more fully have alleviated his pain.

This consciousness was emphasized throughout his life in word, mark, and deed. The title of the 2016 exhibition at the Metropolitan Museum of Art, *Unfinished: Thoughts Left Visible*, troubled me, and likely would have disturbed Larry as well given that it seems to assume an impossible knowledge of artistic intention. I departed the Met Breuer thinking a more apt subtitle might have been *Finished Enough,* which strikes me as an alternative possibility for Larry's retrospective subtitle as well. Larry's method was to draw or paint until his investigations in each work were accomplished. He never aimed at conventional notions of finish, which Cézanne, in any case, had redefined for subsequent generations. Larry worked for clarity and unity, engaging however much complexity and refinement were essential to that goal. This is so in his abstractions, for example, in their manner of hovering in a central place on the field; and reflected in his figure paintings through, for example, the expressive character of a head or the materiality of clothing; and in the geometry of his architecture in which, again for example, each window in each building is defined or left undefined in a unique fashion. This commitment may be seen throughout both figurative and architectural elements in *Narrative: To the Memory of Matteo Giovannetti* (plates 96 and 97). It also marks flower watercolors that he painted throughout his life (fig. 9.1), often based on bouquets picked especially for him from the sumptuous garden of ceramists William and Catherine Daley.

A solitary man himself, Larry regarded as his heroes other solitaries, including Henry James, Franz Kafka, and Rainer Maria Rilke. He placed every other aspect of life around the primary foci of his art and his teaching, which were bonded to each other. This meant that before we married when he was sixty-two, he consistently did laundry on Monday, food shopping on Tuesday, and so forth. In other words, he scheduled these tasks of living so they required as little attention as possible. They *merely* were necessary habits. His mind-demanding pleasures were reading, working in the studio, listening to music, and engaging in conversation with others about every aspect of these central categories of life's activity.

Like his library, Larry's record collection was massive, especially in the classical and jazz realms, but also show tunes, a comprehensive collection of Gilbert and Sullivan (for me this paralleled his complete works by P. G. Wodehouse), and popular music from many decades, especially sounds to which his students introduced him. During his last illness, if he was not in the hospital or rehab, more than anything else we listened to Frank Sinatra singing jazz tunes. At other times, Bach and Haydn were high on his list.

Larry also was an avid filmgoer, interested in all genres and committed to Pauline Kael in the *New Yorker*, as well as other critics, to help determine which of the too many offerings were worth his time. This is not to say he necessarily followed the advice of reviewers, so much as gleaned information to use in making his own decisions about what to see. Occasionally he went to the theater, but far less frequently during the last decades of his life than his nascent acting career of the late 1940s and 1950s might suggest. The only play for which I remember *him* getting tickets was a revival of the 1920s Broadway musical *No, No, Nanette*, in which "Tea for Two" and "I Want to Be Happy" are among its most famous songs.

Occasionally Larry reached out in unexpected directions, like the time in the early 1970s when he took private cooking lessons. Among his books are the carefully maintained notes with recipes for the meals on which the class collaborated (often with the French flair then popular). In the back of the notebook, he tucked additional recipes and food-related images and articles cut from magazines and newspapers. Among the clippings, from the January 1, 1973, issue of *Esquire*, is a photograph titled "Cole Porter's Dinner for Edward VIII."[2] The appetizer course is pictured, including

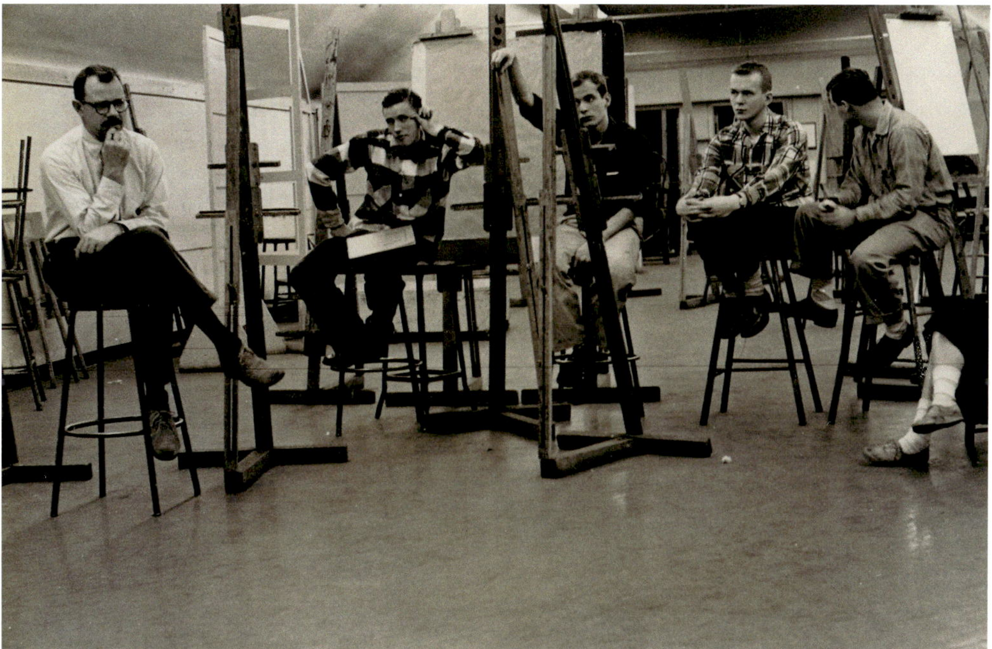



bottles of two favorite beverages of Larry's: dry sherry and a 1969 Sancerre. He always was serious about his wine and food, happy to try new restaurants, and to be either lead or sous-chef in the kitchen. Preferred recipes from the cooking course, which he often annotated with additions and other changes, were spinach soup, beef in red wine sauce, St. Tropez chicken, homemade mayonnaise, carrot flan, and Grand Marnier soufflé.

Larry was absolutely punctual. If invited for dinner at 6:00 p.m., he would arrive on the dot of the hour, though in later years I may have slowed him down a bit. He adored cats and cared for them rigorously when they needed such attention. He also gave great gifts. Many of mine are drawings with special meaning. Other treasures I have from him are a fragment of a Coptic textile and a spectacular Japanese robe. He often talked about dignity and propriety, ironically dismissing short-sleeved shirts as too informal for dining out, for example. My memory, confirmed by others, is that he always wore a tie when teaching. And like most of us at that time, he smoked a lot. When the news of smoking's evils surfaced, however, he bought a cigarette case that held only a half pack, which he made his daily limit (I think he was a Marlboro man); and he stopped inhaling. He was the only person I know who believed Bill Clinton when he said he didn't inhale the marijuana he admitted using as a young man. When Larry's illness eliminated cigarettes from his life, in years when he was feeling relatively healthy, he continued to enjoy as the finale to his birthday dinners the highest-quality cigar he could find. Most special among such dinners were those at the Willard Hotel in Washington, DC, where the waiters conducted a cigar cutting, smoking, and lighting ceremony with all of its many bells and whistles. Starting the meal with a very dry martini was perfection.

The archival materials Larry left behind vividly reveal his major concerns, evident in the extensive notes he kept of his own thoughts and of quotations from others. File folders are labeled, for example, "Morality," "On Quality," and "The Artist in Society." Several files of "Lecture Notes" cover similar topics. For the most part, these are notes for his sustained tenure at the Philadelphia College of Art (PCA, now the University of the Arts), not for lectures he gave throughout the country. Those other one-off presentations were generally delivered using bullet points addressing slides he had carefully organized. He assembled works that took on enhanced relationships owing to his discussion of them, combinations such as Giotto and Max Beckmann.

Teaching was no less compelling for Larry than painting and drawing. His practice was to discuss with students the important artistic, philosophical, and social issues that were in his thoughts when he was in his studio, and to encourage them to explore with him what was on their minds regarding their individual lives and work. To all of their concerns he offered his deepest, personalized attention. I met Larry in 1959 as a sophomore at PCA. My experience was that I could spend hours discussing my work with him and come away with a clear idea of what my direction seemed to be, what might enrich it, where to probe more deeply, and so forth. I also had a heightened awareness of what I might read, look at, and think about, and of possible moves to make when I went back to work on one of the pieces we discussed. By contrast, I had absolutely no idea what he thought of any specific work, or the direction in which I was moving. Larry's teaching was never about building a coterie of disciples, but instead to have each student discover and follow her or his own path.

Larry was a listmaker, not of lists of tasks he needed to complete on a given day, but of categories that were on his mind: kinds of figurative painting, for example, which he designated as narrative, emblem, and tableau. In his file marked "On Quality," one sheet lists:

Theory: Concerning the principles, categories, functions, and criteria of art in general (also poetics)

Practical Criticism: To describe, analyze, characterize, interpret, and evaluate individual works or groups of works, such as one artist or one genre.

Art History: Relating art to, and part of, political, social, and intellectual history (a subgenre being biography)

In this same file is a 1972 proposal for examining the methods by which his students were being taught. It suggests a full reconsideration of the educational process and content for those who would later join the three major pipelines fed by art schools: "Art for the Community; Art for Industry; Art for Culture." Its context further questions the false notion that "people are all alike," indicating how that leads to misjudging the usefulness of statistics in all categories, such as the effect of good or bad reviews on a film and how they impact who would or would not go to see it. His thinking always was interdisciplinary, including quotations from the sports pages in a mention of aggression.

Games were essential to Larry, in both art and life. The art aspect is well-documented in this exhibition, as is the life aspect, in that it is reflected in paintings and drawings such as *A Game of Charades* (plate 98) and *Poker Game* (plate 11). It is significant that his first works upon returning to figuration in 1962 were the *Bridge Game* drawings (plates 102 and 103) and painting (location unknown). Among his studio supplies are games of pick-up sticks and cribbage. He was also a fan of Scrabble. Rules, structure, and comradeship came together in his art and in the games he played alone and with others. Games were critical to what Larry held dear, personified by Sunday morning softball that took place in Elkins Park through the sixties and into

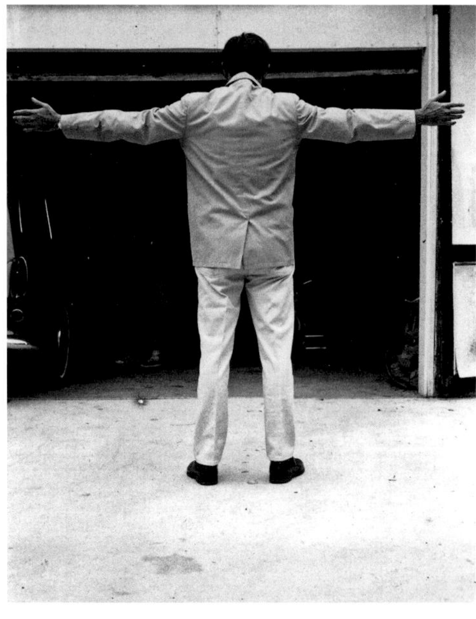

Figure 7.2  Day posed as in *A Game of Charades* (plate 98), probably 1967, photographer unknown (Larry Day Archives)

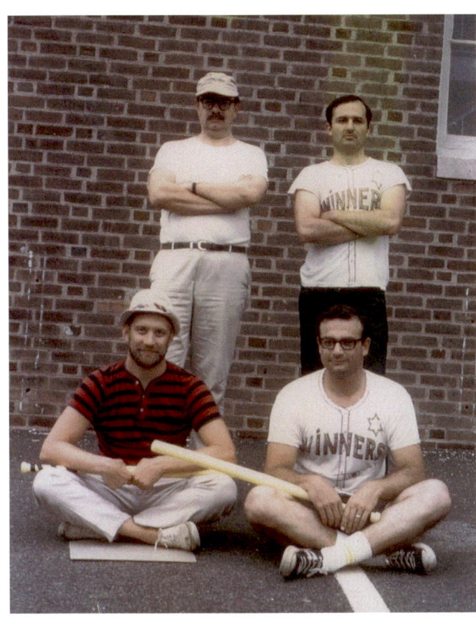

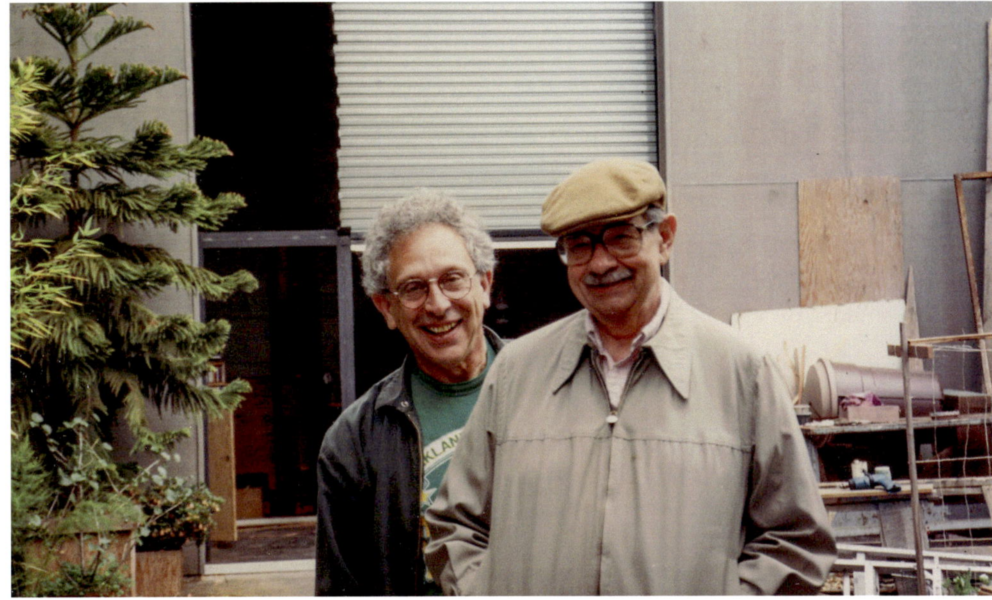

Figure 7.3   Wiffle ball teams, 1960s, photographer unknown (Gift from David Pease to Larry Day Archives)

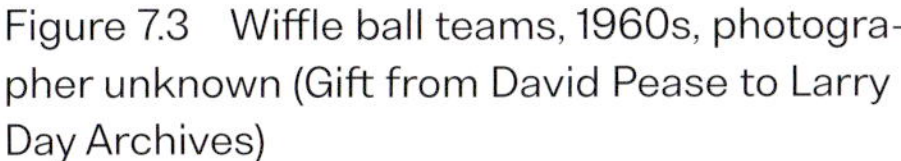

Figure 7.4   Day and Dennis Leon, c. 1992, photograph by Ruth Fine (Larry Day Archives)

the seventies. Tyler School of Art and PCA faculty and students were the players. There also was the Wiffle ball game (fig. 7.3), in which the All Stars (Larry and David Pease) played against the Winners (Sidney Goodman and Leonard Lehrer). In both competitions, Larry usually was the one who shouted the loudest at what he saw as umpire miscalls, or whatever else he saw as worth ranting about.

He rarely reached out for comradeship, however. I think that is what made teaching the perfect form for him. Class situations offered designated partners for conversation and opportunities to form friendships. Among his closest friends was Dennis Leon (they shared a studio in the early sixties), who moved to Oakland, California, in the mid-1970s and died six months after Larry. They remained solidly connected after Dennis's move to the West Coast, and their wry banter was spectacular. But Larry was a banterer in general, with an unparalleled sense of humor that permitted him to discuss what he referred to as his rear-guard sensibility with a smile, as he watched the avant-garde get louder and more blinkered. His commitment to his art and to his students, current and former alike, never wavered. Larry spent his life working to know, understand, and contextualize himself and his world, something he achieved with a clarity and complexity that is rare at any moment in time.

## Notes

1   Erich Kahler, *The Disintegration of Form in the Arts* (New York: George Braziller, 1968), 10.
2   Roy Andries de Groot, "Cole Porter's Dinner for Edward VIII," *Esquire,* January 1, 1973, https://classic.esquire.com/article/1973/1/1/cole-porters-dinner-for-edward-viii.

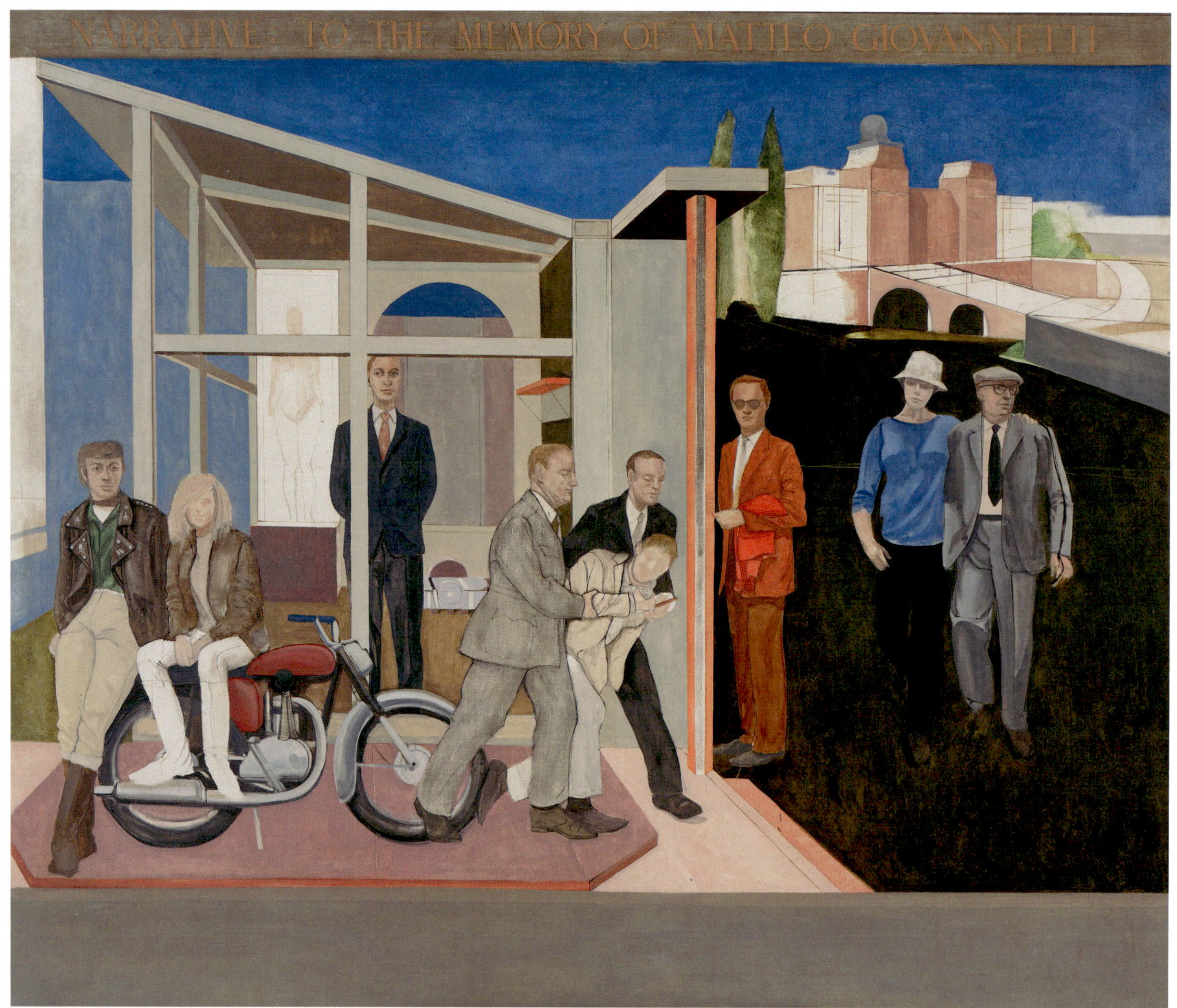



PLATE 96

*Narrative: To the Memory of Matteo Giovannetti,* 1967

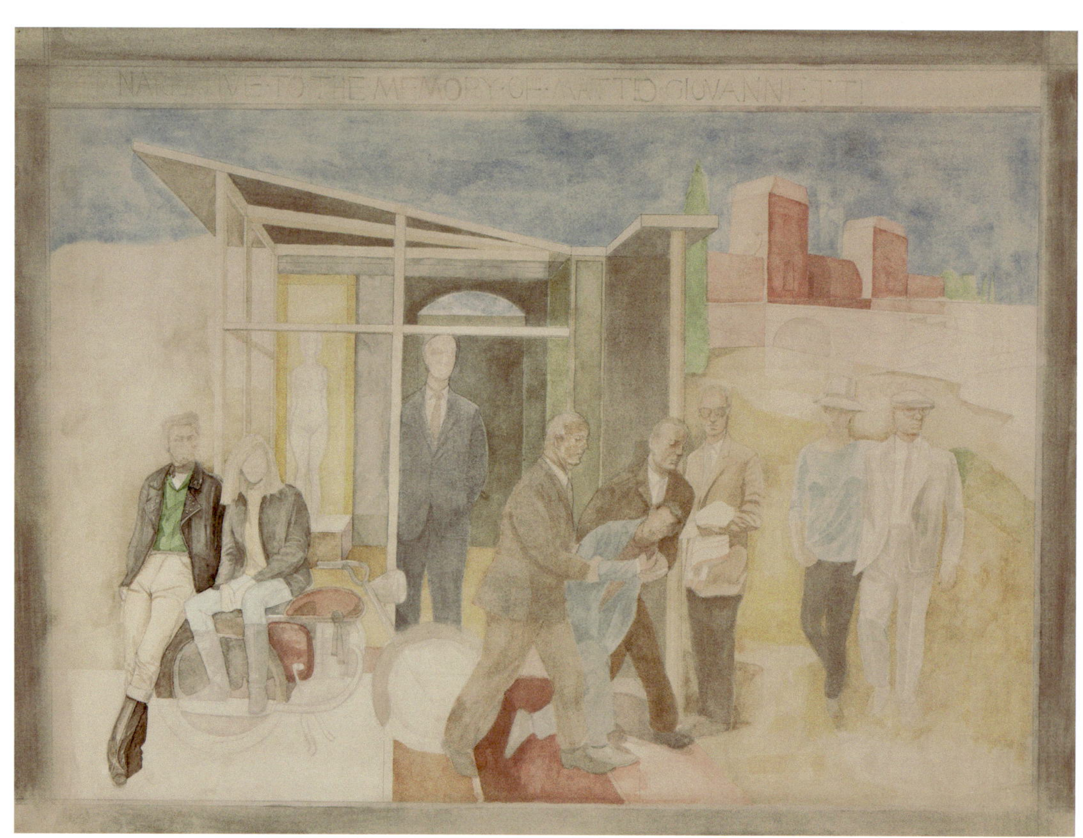



PLATE 97

*Related to "Narrative: To the Memory of Matteo Giovannetti,"* c. 1967

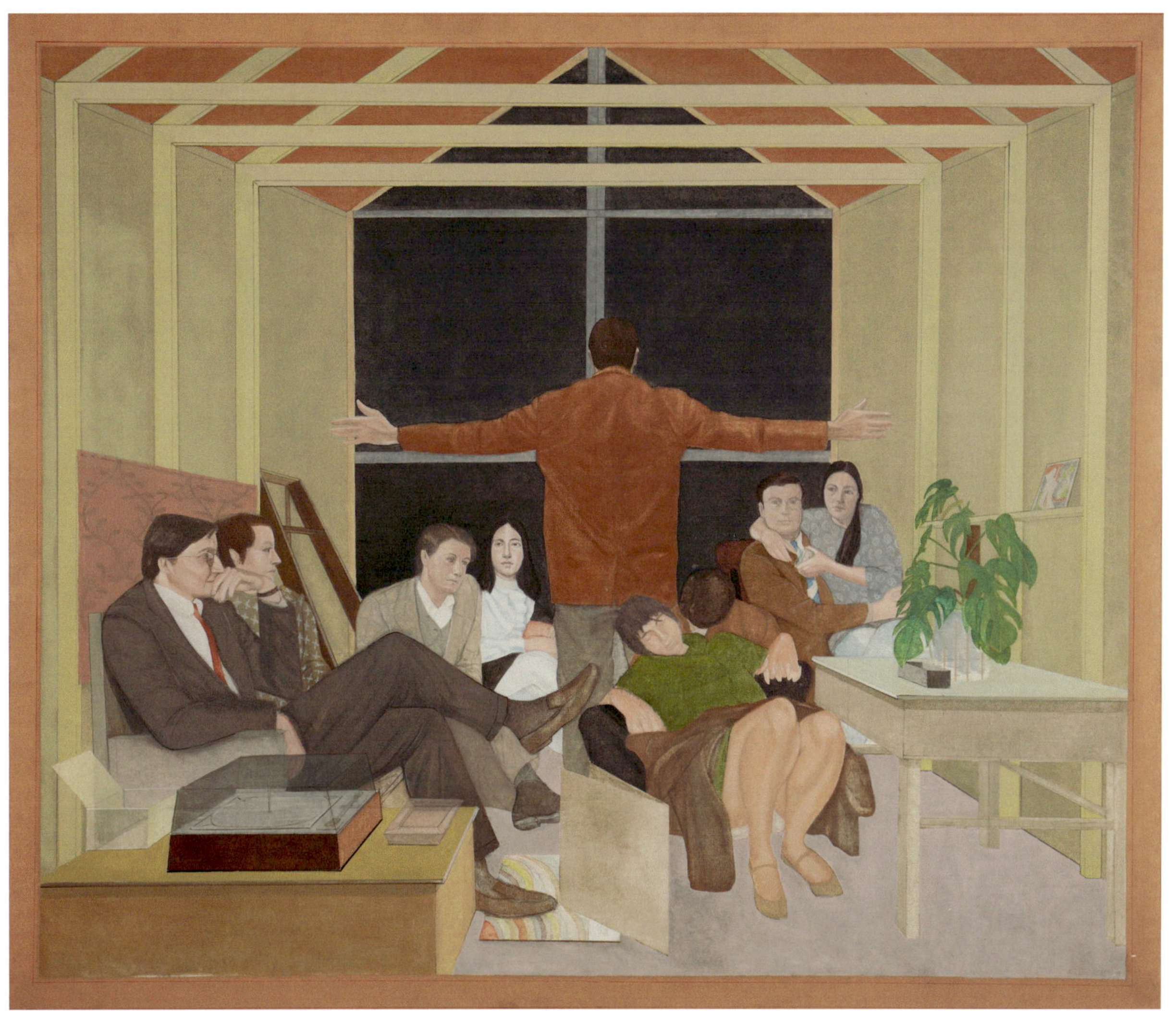

PLATE 98
*A Game of Charades* (aka *Charades*), 1967/1969

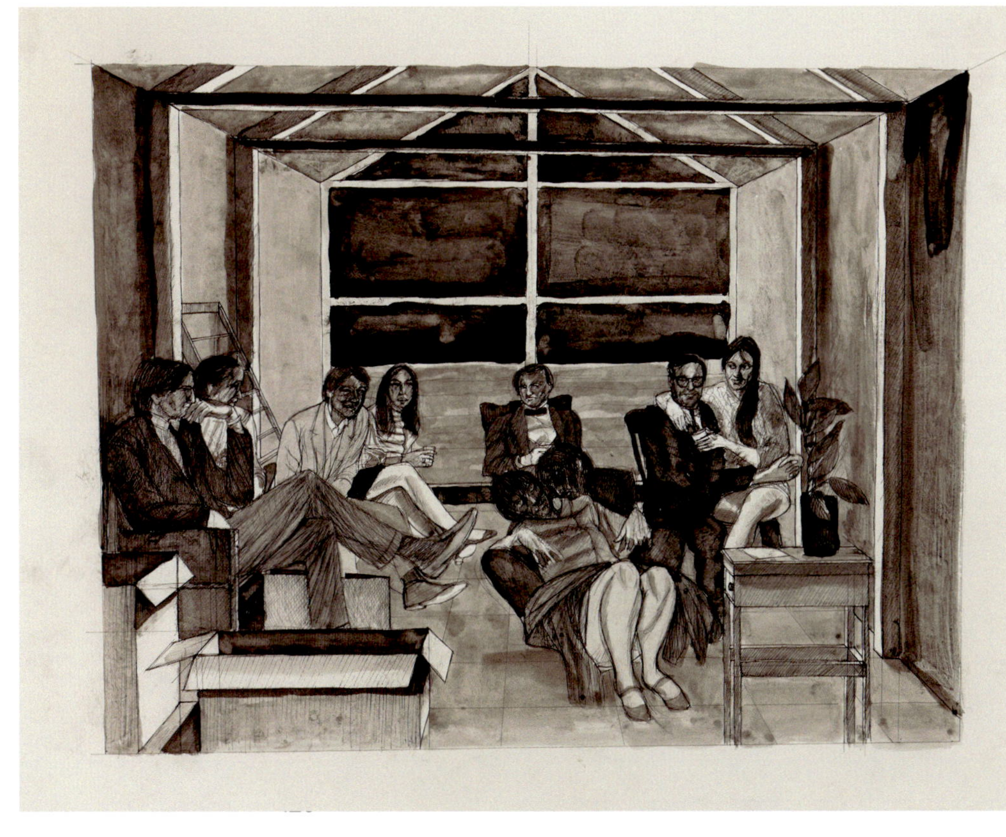

PLATE 99
*Related to "A Game of Charades,"* c. 1969

PLATE 100
*(Curtis Arboretum),*
c. 1970

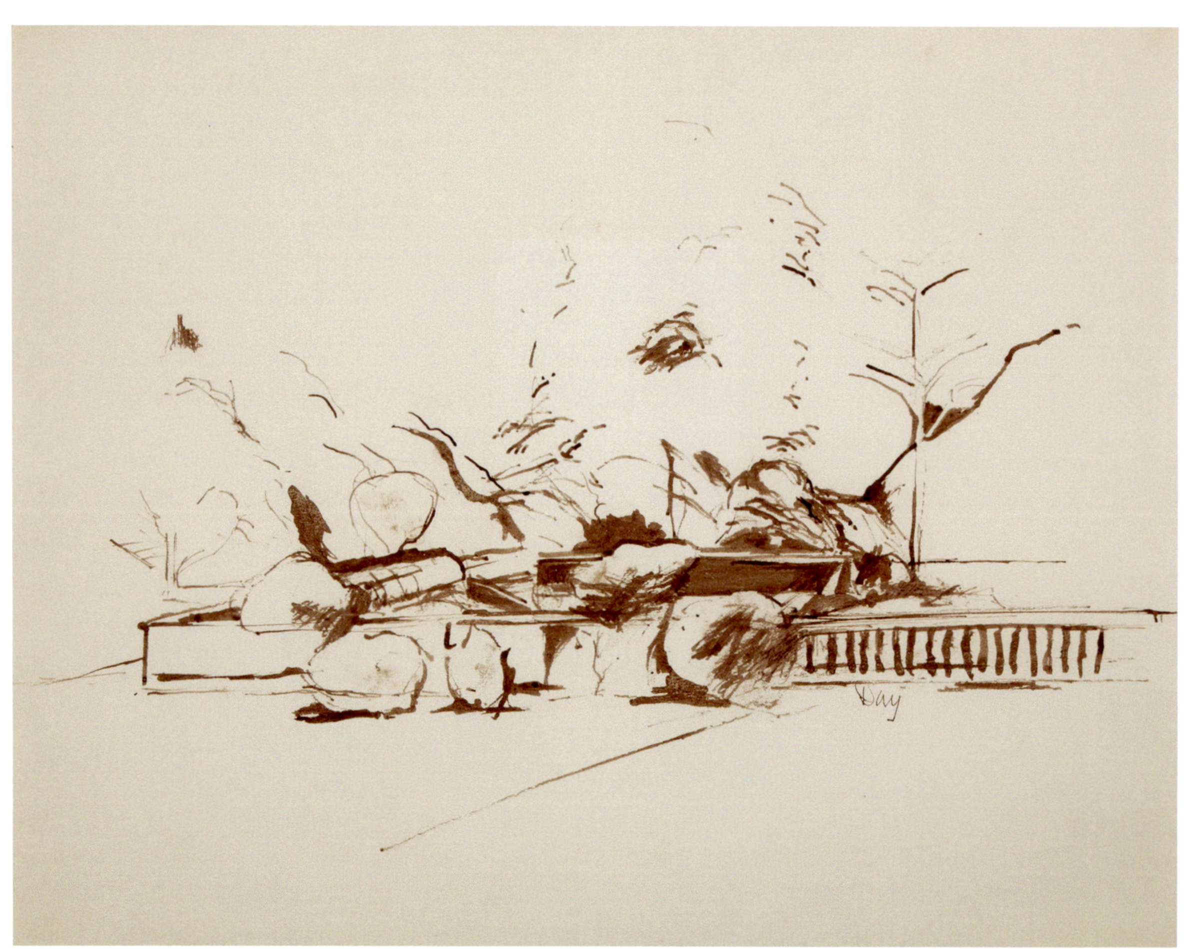

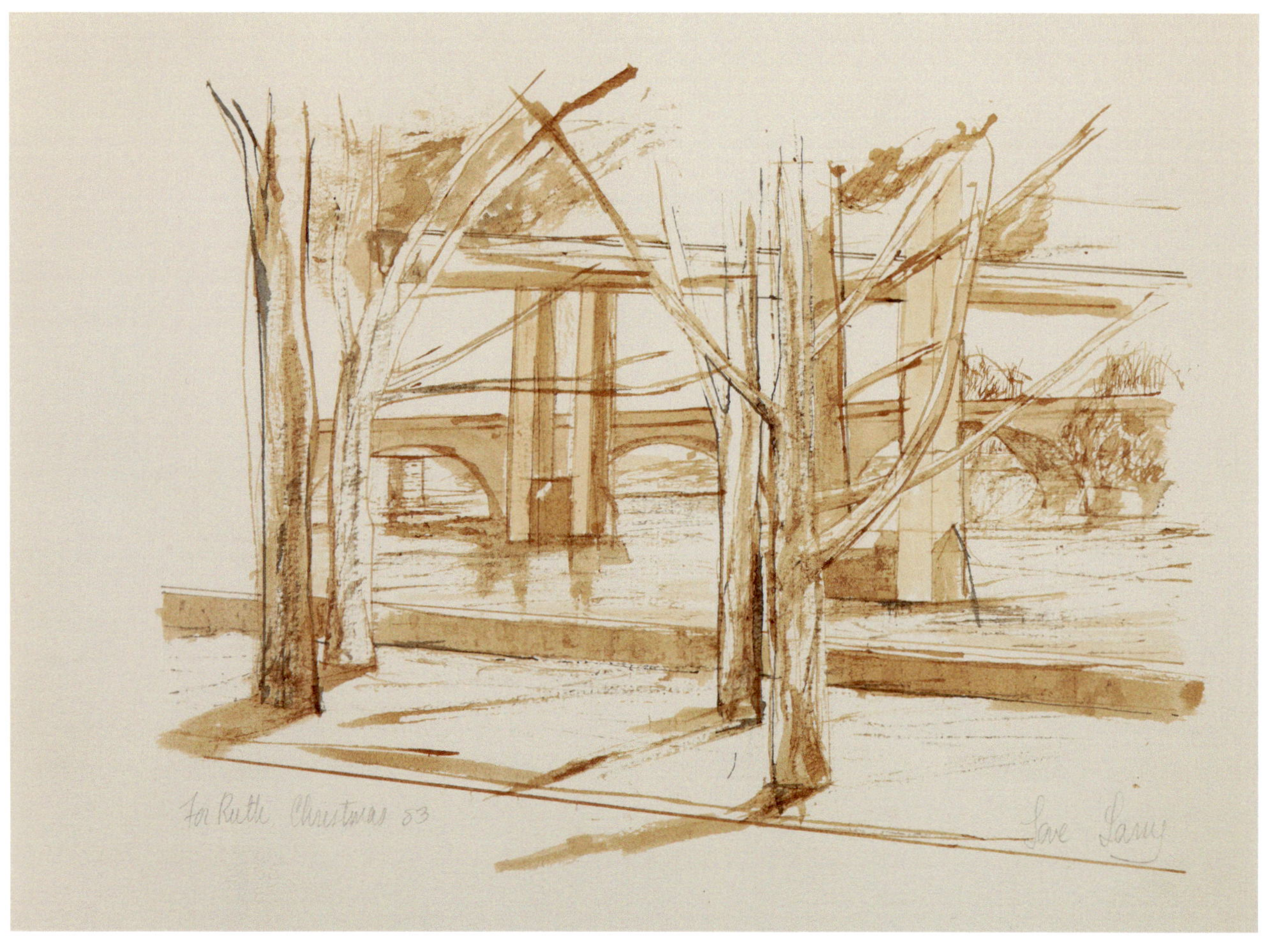

PLATE 101
*East River Drive,*
1983

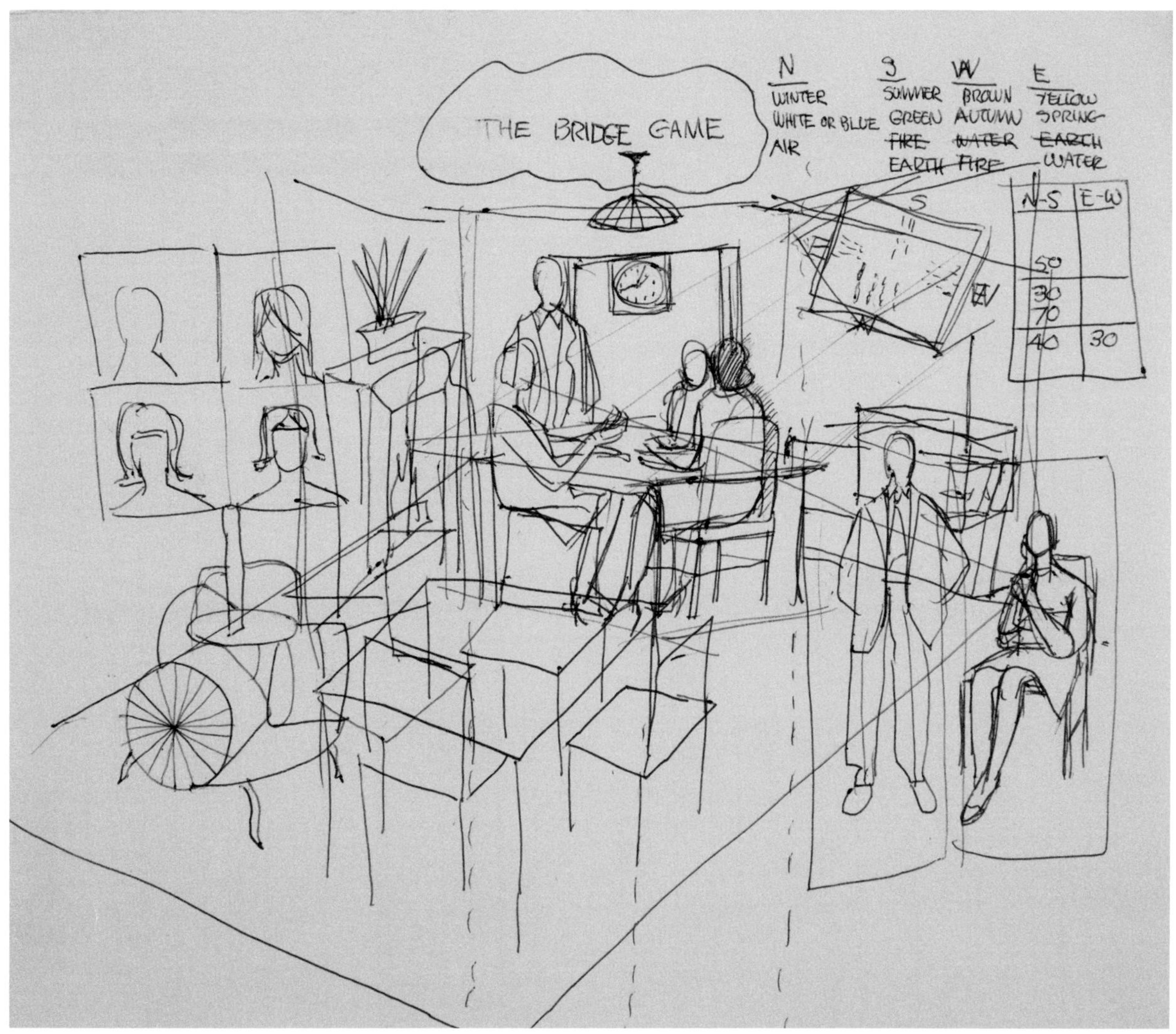



PLATE 102
*The Bridge Game,*
c. 1963

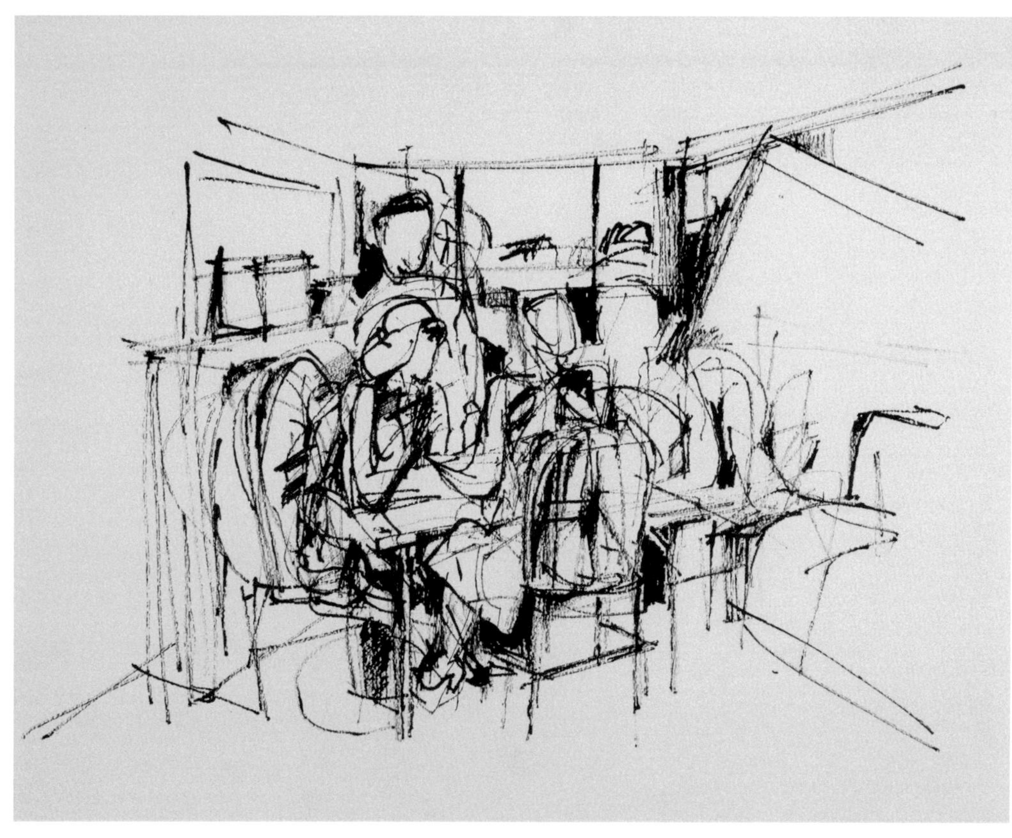

PLATE 103
*The Bridge Game,* c. 1963

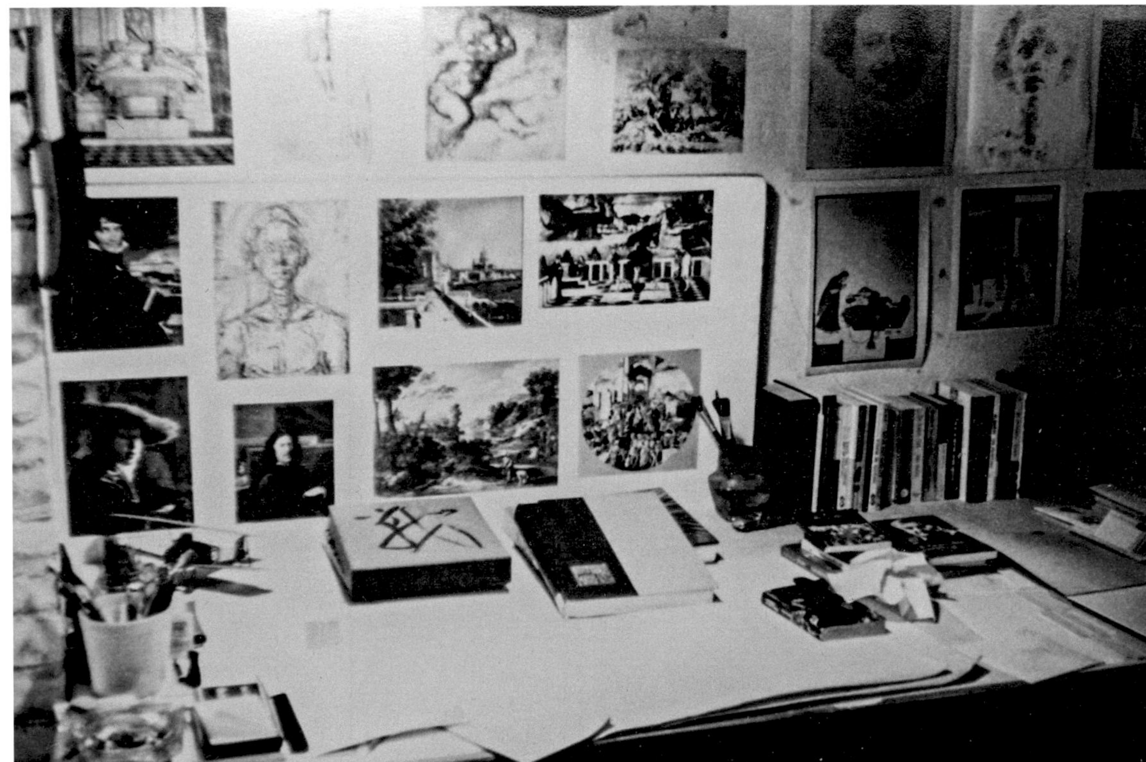

Figure 8.1
Day's studio, c. 1966
(Larry Day Archives)

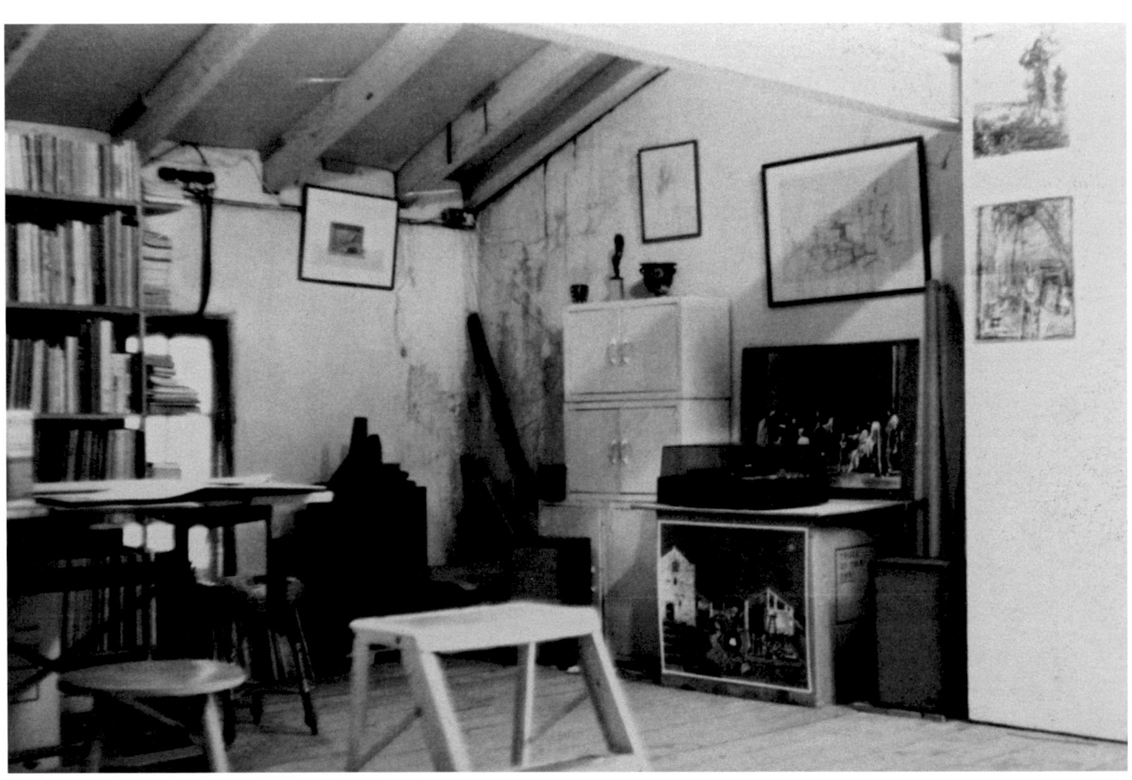

Figure 8.2
Day's studio, c. 1966
(Larry Day Archives)

# The Lion

Published under the name Laurence Day

A young man named George Benton, in the middle of a vacation in Wisconsin, was caught in a violent snow storm. He had been taking a walk through the afternoon when the storm suddenly appeared upon him as if it had been waiting behind a cloud in ambush. The snow came thick and full, around and above him, so that he could see no more than twenty feet in whichever direction he looked. Although at the instant of the first few flakes he welcomed the snow as picturesque, he was soon moved to fear by its surprising fury and started hurriedly back towards the hotel where he was living. Then the snow blotted out the world and he was alone in a small moving space, forty feet long and forty feet wide. He walked swiftly and steadily at first, then ran as fast as he could until he fell over an unseen stone. He got up and continued running until he dropped from exhaustion. He lay still until his breath came back. Then he started walking again. He walked until his fears became overpowering. Then he ran as before. He thought he was going to die.

His eyes hurt and his nostrils ached to suck in breath; his ears burned and his hands and feet blued to the weather. Once he stopped in his tracks and beat at the snow flakes with his hand and kicked with his feet and cursed with his mouth.

In the fourth hour of his attempted escape he came across a large wooden cabin that he had never seen before.

2

George was a good looking man of medium build, about thirty-three years old and engaged to be married to a girl named Jane Gordon. His hair was sandy-colored and his eyes were blue, but not strikingly so. There was in his physical aspect nothing to particularly distinguish him from a crowd and, aside from a missing third finger on his left hand, nothing out of the ordinary about him at all.

He was by occupation a desk clerk in a Boston hotel and had been work-ing at the same place for seven years. He met Jane while she was visiting the hotel and had been going with her for a year and a half. They loved each other but decided to wait until they could find the right sort of place to live in before they married.

## 3

George sat in the room before a large pile of papers. Occasionally he would shift them around into different positions, usually dropping one or two to the floor as he did so. He had been doing this for some time and there were a good many papers scattered about the floor.

It was a small square room, nearly bare, in which the walls were white and without ornament. There was in that room—besides George and the papers—one chair (at which he sat), one table (on which the papers lay), and a large cardboard box. There were two doors and one window. Through the windows could be seen the blizzard. But because the blizzard was at its highest nothing else could be distinguished. At the right of the window (which George faced) stood the first door— that led outside—and on the opposite wall the other door led to another room. This second door had a brilliantly shined knob with a huge keyhole, three inches long and an inch wide. (The keys to both doors, George found, were in the table drawer.)

Every now and then, tiring of the papers, he would go over to the room-door and, pressing his ear closely against it, listen for sounds. He did not listen to find out if the room was empty or not (for he knew it wasn't), but merely to discover whether the occupant was walking or sitting.

He had been in the room three days and was acquainted with its every corner. Exploring the room had been the work of seconds. Nor did it take him much longer to learn there was a lion in the next room.

Luckily, in his first perusal of the room, before he had found the key, he looked through the keyhole to see what was behind the door. The lion was sitting at the far side of the room, a gigantically magnificent male with a great flowing mane that seemed well taken care of. George stared an eternal five minutes, in which time the lion did not move. His first thought was that it was dead or stuffed. Then he saw that it was breathing steadily and twice, while he watched, he saw the animal blink.

"There must be something wrong with the beast's nose," he thought, "otherwise it would certainly have known that I was here—and his ears too, for I made, up until the time that I looked through the keyhole, enough noise to be heard." He had then gone back to the table. "Whatever the case may be, the lion doesn't seem to have the slightest idea that I am present," he said to himself. "How very odd."

He had been very tired then, almost oblivious of facts. In this exhausted state, he idly looked at the pile of papers on the table. They were all of uniform size—about 8 by 11 inches—and all marked with but one figure. There must have been (he thought) a couple thousand sheets (he later counted them and found the number to be 972) and each was a subtle variation of the same figure.

Outside, the blizzard rose in fury, and although the room was warm, if he stared long through the window his teeth chattered and his body shivered with cold.

The first hour he was there he looked through the keyhole twelve times, fingered the papers twice, and looked out the window once.

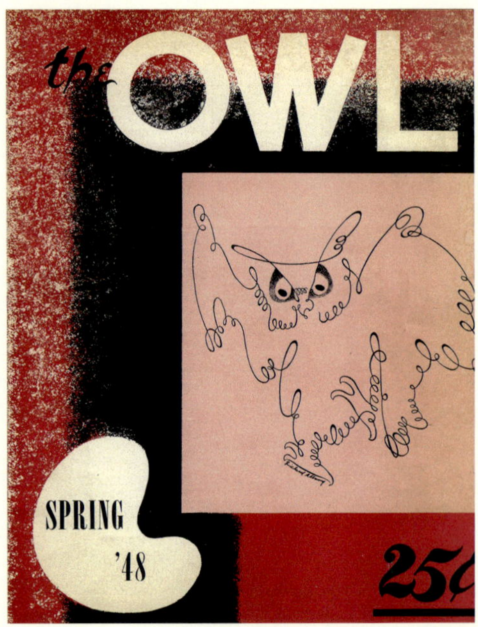

Figure 8.3   Cover of the spring 1948 issue of *The Owl*, in which *The Lion* was originally published

Each time he looked at the lion it was in the same position at the far side of the room.

## 4

He slept soundly for a long time, and he did not dream.

## 5

Getting used to the lion was difficult. He could not stop himself from looking at it no matter what he tried. He would pace the room, play with the papers, exercise, but always in the middle of what he was doing he would stop and go look through the keyhole, and always the lion was in its same position.

Finally towards the end of the second day, he bent down to view the lion as usual, and instead of seeing the beast, saw, as close up against the hole as his own eye, a great moist brown eye staring into his. So big was the eye that only the smallest bit of skin could be seen around it. He shrank back in terror. The shock of meeting with something so unusual completely unnerved him and he fell to the floor almost as one paralyzed.

He could see nothing now but the eye. He imagined it through the window, on each of the papers, painted on the inside of his eyelids.

Gradually his courage returned. There was, after all, no change in his predicament other than that the lion knew of his presence. True, it is more difficult to assume the role of the watched rather than the watcher, but he was, when you came to think of it, in no danger.

Still, when he lay down to sleep that night he did not fall off for some time and then only after he had moved to the section of the wall adjacent to the door.

## 6

The cardboard box had in it a week's supply of food and a pencil. He ate some of the food and with the pencil wrote a letter to his fiancée.

## 7

Dear Jane (he wrote):

I am quite sure that you will never receive this letter, quite sure for two reasons. One is that I shall never send it to you, and the other is that I could not send it if I wanted to. I am, however, going to tell you a few things you did not know before but perhaps some day may learn.

First, you have not understood me. You have not the slightest inkling as to what I am really like, although you needn't be alarmed, for no one else knows either (except, perhaps, the animal in the next room). You know, of course, that I am missing a finger; you know that I hide my hand and never bring attention to it. What you don't know is how I lost the finger—nor do I think you would ever be able to guess. You see, I—George Benton—cut it off myself. Nor have I ever been sorry for having done so.

I remember the night it happened. It was late February and snow still lay on the ground. I was, I suppose, in love with a girl at the time—I say "suppose" to dispel any idea in your mind that it was for her sake that I did it. No, the reason was, in a way, simpler than that. You see, I always considered myself different from other men (I would really have been more different if I considered myself the same) but, and this profoundly disturbed me, I could not say why. I looked average (as you know) and I was very much afraid that my personality or self was average too. What I really needed was something that would make me different—not just physically, that would be secondary—but personally, inwardly; something that I could hold on to, that I could always bring to my mind's eye and say, "See, I am different, here is the proof, absolute, irrevocable truth."

So I cut off my finger. It was a moment of extreme inspiration, the most ecstatic moment that I have ever lived. Every stab of pain brought me bright, delicious pangs of pleasure. I had, in this act, transcended humankind. I became one of the immortals. Not because I had a missing finger. But because *I* cut it off.

It is hard to explain this to you, who are so ordinary, so—shall we say— human. But can't you see that now, no matter what I do, no matter how prosaic an existence I lead, it will be too late—I have won—

## 8

George crumpled the letter into a ball and threw it over to the window. It hit the sill and bounced down to the floor.

## 9

At the end of the third day the blizzard stopped for a half-hour. A great silence fell upon George and the room and he sat, not daring to move a muscle, waiting for the noise of the wind to return. It seemed to him that he had stopped breath- ing. It was like a rest in music, a rest like Beethoven used in his last quartets— loaded with anxiety and anticipation.

The first sound to break in upon the stillness came from an unexpected corner. As George sat there, softly, rhythmically into his brain came the dull pad of the lion's paws on the other-room floor. They came slowly as if the beast were creeping rather than walking. Each pad shook the room like the beat of far-off muffled drums. It kept up until the blizzard started again.

It was the first time he had ever heard the lion, and if the blizzard had not come back he would have sat in the same position until the lion ceased to move—even if it had walked through eternity.

## 10

It snowed for seven days. He occupied his time in odd and fantastic ways— counting the paces of the room, decorating the walls of the room with, at first, murals as accurately as he could draw them, later with lavatory slogans and pictures. It snowed for seven days but it seemed to George like seventy times seven, seventy times seventy-seven. The moments became ugly and deformed and crawled past him with agonizing slowness. He relieved himself in the box and hated himself for his animal necessity. He explored himself with scientific thoroughness.

And there was always the lion. It never occurred to George to question the lion's arrival. The thing that mattered was that the lion was there, sitting in his corner, silently stalking, or even peering through the keyhole. The lion was there, and because the lion was there he was not alone or crazy or, in the usual sense, afraid. The storm lacked its terror because of the knowledge that another shared his fate.

After that first dreadful coming of face to face, George never dared look through the keyhole again; but always at various times during the day and night he would go over and place his ear against the door and listen.

## 11

The day that the snow stopped he could not quite believe it. At first he thought it was another rest period for the snow, and sat quite still for over an hour. The silence smashed at his eardrums. Nor did there come the pad of the lion's foot through the door. He went over and looked through the keyhole—quickly and without thinking. The lion was not to be seen. His heart quickened and his eyes—"The lion has left, surely the lion has left," he thought. And then he heard a slow steady breathing—"No the lion is here, always here."

The fear he felt at the lion's absence crept back on him. He trembled. "Yes the lion was always here," he paused, "and now Jane . . . the papers . . . I shall be a celebrity . . . or was I never missed . . . am I one of the human race . . . that they should weep at my disappearance . . . No—that bond was severed, in silence but with thoroughness, with my finger, with the confession to Jane." He saw the letter where it lay beneath the window. "She doubtless knows now. The letter reached her. I am completely I. She's lovely, but I mustn't see her again. The break is final and irreparable. Good. The cardboard box is all that can be shown of me, the only tie to humanity. I am not yet free, not yet, no, not yet. The lion is the same as me—not human, complete yet not human. Of course I am free. Now, now, forever. The lion I!"

He rushed to the table and pulled open the drawer. The two keys lay side by side. He grabbed the key to the room and ran back and opened it, flinging himself to the lion.

## 12

And yet no man can ever be alone.

The End

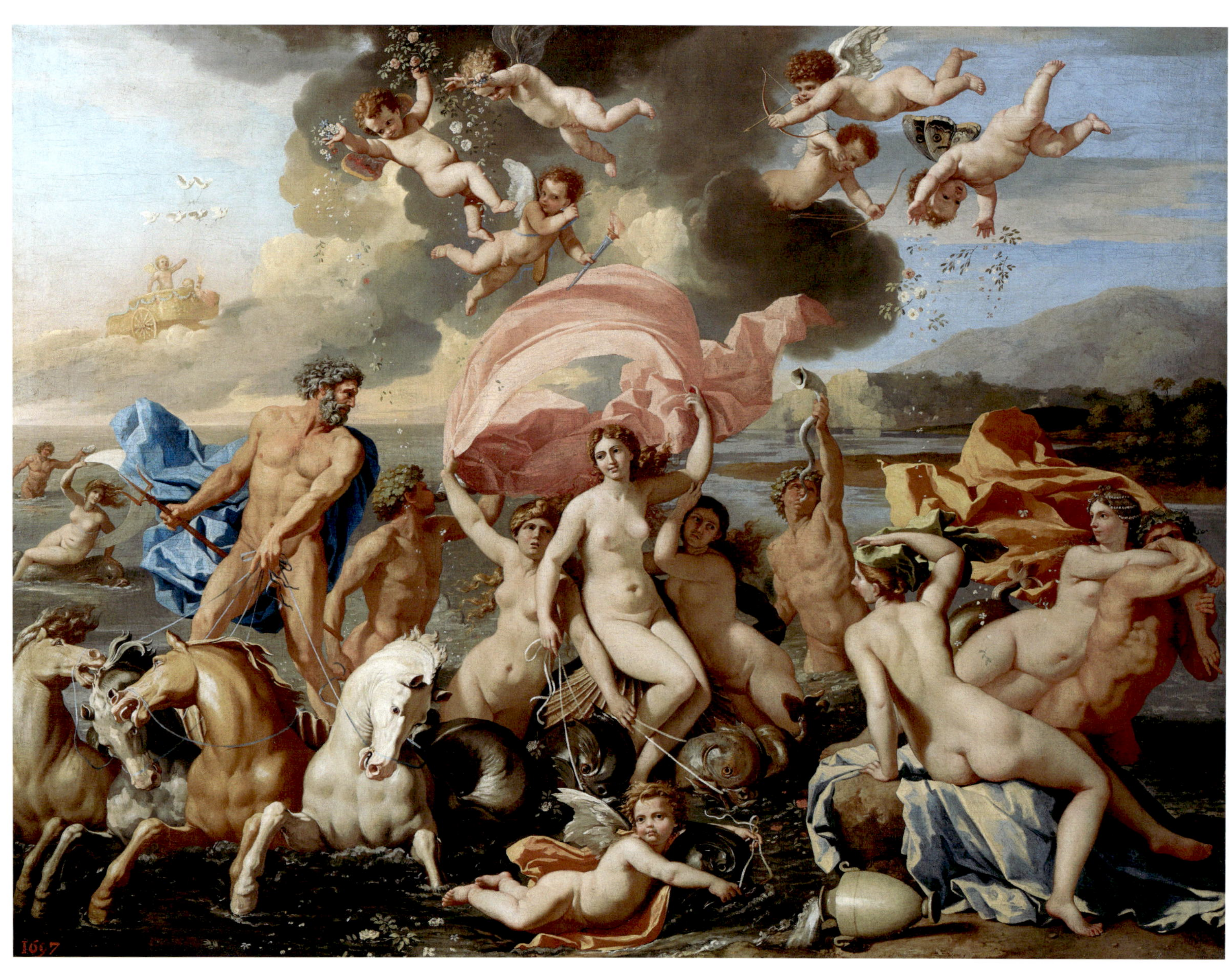

Figure 8.4   Nicolas Poussin, *The Birth of Venus*, 1635 or 1636, oil on canvas, 38¼ × 42½ in. (Philadelphia Museum of Art, The George W. Elkins Collection, 1932)

# Poussin, August 1989

1. Our first art experiences are usually associated with works that we can read literally—a beautiful sunset, a picturesque or touching scene, a handsome man or a beautiful woman—they are what they appear to be, at least at the level that we relate to them.

2. One of the things that we quickly learn is how to distinguish or interpret the literal from the—whatever. Just as we are able to tell the difference between our parents' "Stop that" when they mean it and "Stop that" when we can do what we are doing a little longer, we learn to read all sorts of peripheral signs and become aware that the literal statement is often not the meaning, intended or not, or that a number of different meanings may reside in a general form. (". . . it was left to Freud to discover in a scientific age, we still feel and think in figurative formations." —Lionel Trilling)

3. Poussin as I first knew him in the Philadelphia Museum of Art *(The Triumph of Neptune)* seemed completely artificial; all the figures seemed self-consciously posed and self-consciously generalized. What had this slightly absurd painting to do with the world as I knew it or even the world as Poussin might have known it?

4. What I came to realize was that the painting was a fiction; it was, for some reason or other, distancing itself from the world. More than anything it seemed to be about itself. It was eminently conscious of self. The three large billowing cloths seemed to refer to each other, and one was as it was because of the other two. In fact everything to be as it was because of everything else. It was, for better or worse, a world; and the forms acted out their roles in their appointed places. An elaborate program of abstract thought was being depicted. Not *the* world but *a* world.

5. If the world cannot be defined nor seen whole, it can be imagined by inventing small worlds that have definition which in turn make the world's presence bearable. Not to know, never to know, only to make up stories—this is our lot.

6. Only fiction can breathe in that space between what we know and what we will never know.

7. Poussin brought everything he knew ("I have neglected nothing") to bear on what he was doing. He read, studied, made elaborate models, thought, and felt; and put it all together as a complex, singularly mannered lie. Because in terms of what we know, only a lie tells the truth about what we don't know.

8. The great *Adoration of the Golden Calf*—a scene of instruction, a warning and a celebration—is almost a painting siding with the adorers. Aaron is presented as a sage-like figure; the supplicants are presented in the same way they are presented in Poussin's paintings of events that are approved; the dancers are like the dancers in the bacchanals. Moses is a small figure, not immediately seen, on the left. Are all celebrations the same? Is all belief and adoration a single emotion? By the beauty of the scene, of the painting—the brilliantly colored sky and the many rhythms from Poussin's repertory cast of actors—what does Poussin say to us, what does he show us, how does he instruct us? Only the dead trees framing the golden calf indicate his position and his attitude. Adoration and belief in the false are *moving* experiences. Belief and adoration have to be convincing. False belief and adoration look like belief in the true. What separates the Christian martyrs from the Jonestown martyrs? Everybody is happy as if the golden calf has already delivered. Only Moses and the young man with him are disturbed—and the two figures that look up to them, one showing the accoutrements of surprise. This strange, beautiful, unsettling picture.

9. "Though Poussin believed that nature was the source of all beauty, he did not believe that it should be imitated slavishly: only a vulgar naturalist like Caravaggio would do that, with results which Poussin deplored." —Anthony Blunt

10. "The drawing of objects must be such that the thought they evoke explains their nature." —Poussin

11. In *Narcissus and Echo* the great horizontal line of Narcissus' upper contour shows how superior a form maker and form discoverer Poussin was to his possible model, Paris Bordone in his *Dead Christ Supported by Two Angels.* Poussin's painting is memorable for its great formal authority; it is also memorable as a depiction of art's or the artist's central awarenesses—the ultimate defeat of desire. The work of art starts with the burst of energy that works to destroy the emptiness, the absence that was discovered in the last work and to fulfill that perverse longing to capture and claim art's final meaning. The transformation from energy to the exhaustion of the vehicle of desire (desire itself is never exhausted and only ends in death) is the story of every work—Echo and Narcissus, and the strange, innocent, terribly innocent, half-regretful, half-forgetful, figure of Eros, perhaps art's true, hidden God. It is art's elegy.

12. Strangely, Narcissus and Echo are not presented in the idealized form, that dominates Poussin's work. Narcissus' face is one of Poussin's most naturalistic faces and Echo's, while generalized, is not taken to the point of classical allusion. Only Eros has the features and form that will appear over and over in the paintings. The naturalism of Narcissus makes for a possible homoerotic reading or perhaps an identifying and a self-warning.

13. The sense of containment of the Narcissus image and then the slight falling away of the arm and the leg—inwardness and drawing—seem to describe perfectly Poussin's aforementioned quote of the drawing evoking the thought that explains the nature of the subject. Echo's fitting into the rock's contour furthers her subject and Eros framed by a torch and a lance is analyzed and articulated.

14. The one thing of which I'm relatively certain
Is, that only since this morning
I have met myself as a middle-aged man
Beginning to know what it is to feel old.
That is the worst moment, when you feel you have lost
The desire for all that is most desirable,
And before you are contented with what you can desire
Before you know what is left to be desired;
And you go on wishing that you could desire
What desire has left behind.
—T. S. Eliot, "The Cocktail Party"
Poussin's "Cephalus and Aurora," "Orpheus and Euridice"

15. "*The Golden Calf* is equally bold, in a different way. Here Poussin has attempted something that is very rare in his work—the depiction of figures in violent movement. The result is singular, particularly if we compare it with the treatment of a similar dancing group by a Baroque painter. In Rubens' *Peasant Dance* . . . the movement is continuous and leads from one figure to another, so that the rhythm of the whole dance sweeps across the canvas . . . In Poussin, the effect is the opposite: each figure performs its own separate action, each is in a pose of active movement, but the effect of the whole is static, as if the figures were frozen into marble." (Anthony Blunt)—or into paint.

There comes a time when the focus of desire cannot be maintained, when the focal point becomes diffused into the whole, when only the whole has substance. Whether this is the end of desire or a desire that is different than any that came before it, but still desire and the force that demands responsive action, is not easily answered. Certain work, like Titian's *Flaying of Marsyas,* Poussin's *Apollo and Daphne,* all of the late Cézanne and most of Poussin's drawings, Monet's *Waterlilies* etc., move away from the hierarchical focus, can't be contained in an object or a figure—or a position. There is only the world.

137

16. In Poussin's *Woman Taken in Adultery*, gesture, color, shape, and object are brought together in a way that makes Bernini's statement that Poussin was a great storyteller completely understandable. There are the symmetries: six figures on the side of the woman and child and six figures on the other side; the man seen from the front leaving the scene on the left (possibly the adulterer?) and the man seen from the back leaving on the right. The possibility that the man at the left is the adulterer is suggested by a number of means: the intense red of Christ's robe shifting to the less intense red of the man partly behind the adulteress and back to the intense red of the man leaving. There is the dark wall against the light wall that frames the leaving man. There is the dark pavement block that he stands on, like the one occupied by Christ talking of those without guilt.

17. Guilt and secret complicity affect all but Christ. The city, mostly behind the figures, enters into their configuration by means of lateral direction that undermines recessional space, blank windows and niches that close off rather than open their inner worlds; and the almost empty, almost deserted square and parapets. Even the paved ground comments upon the scene, not only with the aforementioned dark blocks but the line that leads straight back to the woman and child with a rock lying across it. The pavement is like a giant web that catches all in Christ's terrible statements—all of painting's resources are brought to bear on the subject; and the subject, never losing any of its varied meanings, acknowledges and celebrates painting's resources and uncovers its powers.

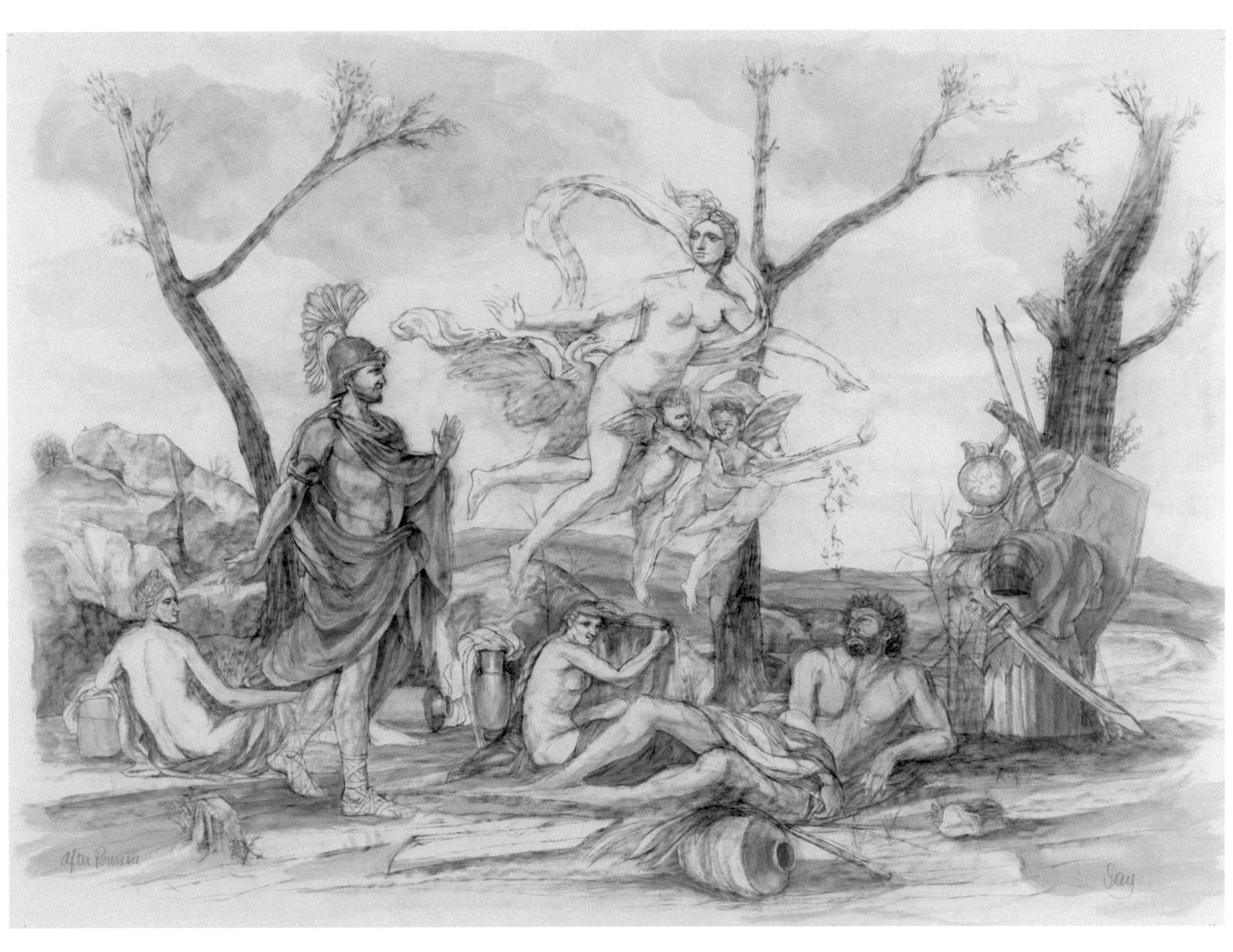

PLATE 104
 *After Poussin*, c. 1983

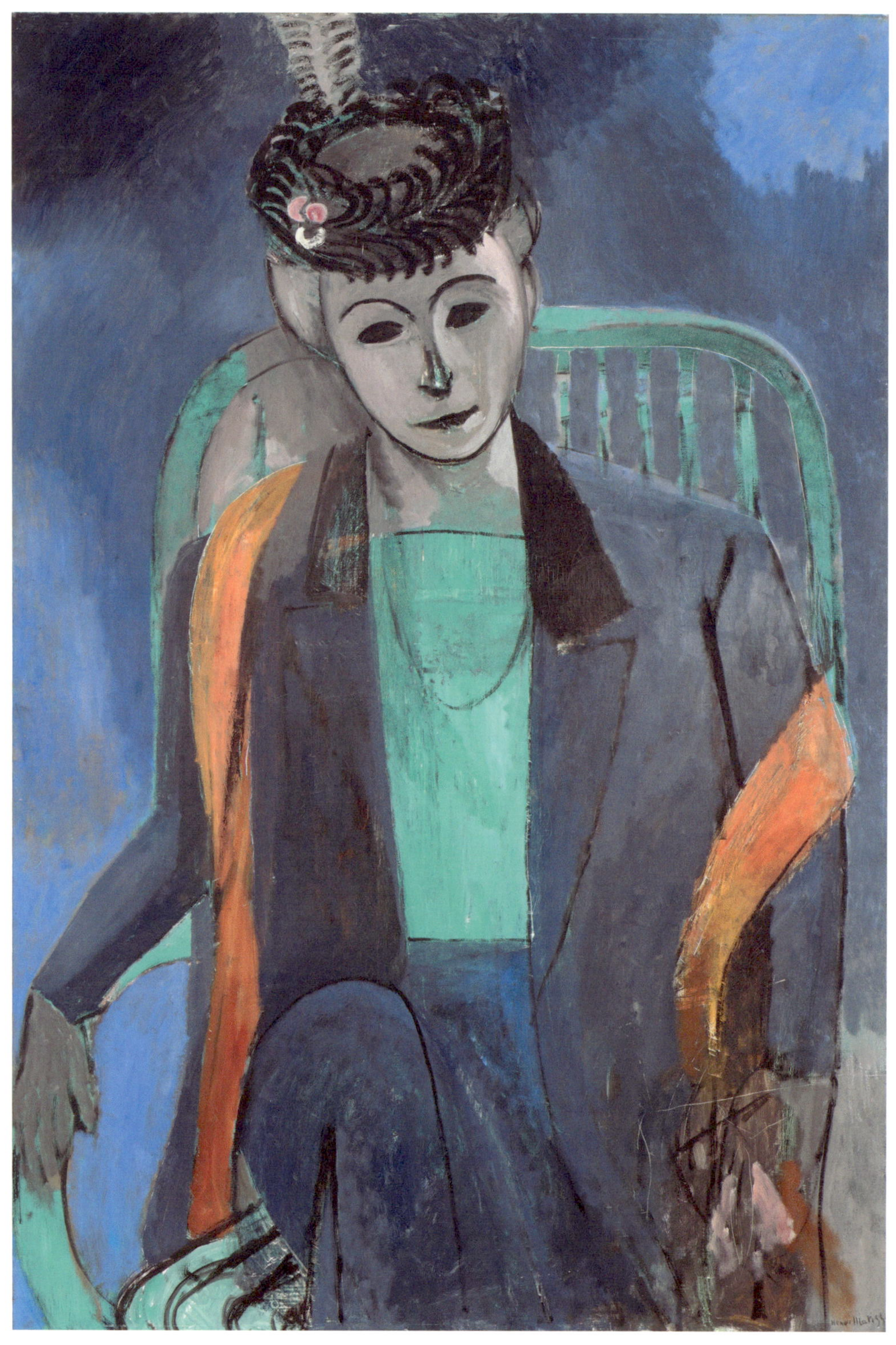

Figure 8.5   Henri Matisse, *Portrait of the Artist's Wife*, 1913, oil on canvas, 57½ × 38½ in. (The State Hermitage Museum, St. Petersburg) © 2021 Succession H. Matisse / Artists Rights Society (ARS), New York. Photograph © The State Hermitage Museum / photograph by Pavel Demidov

# Madame Matisse, undated

What was he looking for? What was he looking at? His wife, the painting, back and forth until both became image, and as image, both became lost, distant, beyond reach. What does any painting look for, or rather, what can any painting find?

At certain times in certain cultures it was believed that the image became the thing itself, that the thing was boundless and could enter the image and invest it with its powers of being without losing any of itself. Icons were sometimes thought to have the power of what they portrayed. Images were magical, waiting merely to be formed in order to become energy. Images were known beforehand, and repeating them was joining in a rite of passage from emptiness to fullness. The image imbedded in the character of painting established itself as the character of painting. Everything was pictorial; the space, the colors, the depicted, the thing outside of painting, was conceived from inside of painting, had its identity as painting or as pure thought, imageless, wordless presence.

For us the icon is still the essence of painting but it has lost the power of the two-in-one, the all-in-one. We see and recognize painting's drive to its center. Painting's aspiration to be fully itself. The problem is that we are now aware of things, others, otherness, in such a way as we cannot deal with ourselves without confronting them. And "confronting" that emanates from what is outside of us. What is our connection? Do we belong here or there? Are we part of this or that—a stone, a pear, a horse, a tree? The so-called material world is our reality, or at least a part of it, that cannot be ignored. The contemporary image, if it represents, represents what in the world we are conscious of—things—and the tricks that consciousness plays on things. The demands of painting must include this consciousness if our beliefs are to be met.

We look at the model, or the pear, or the tree, and we are aware of its presence, dimly, imperfectly. This thing is present as we are present, but how are we present? How much does our being present depend on these other presences and why have we chosen painting and its demands to give us answers—if answers are what we want. We may merely want to experience, and know that we are experiencing, what is going on, what seems always to be going on, even when we are not painting. But painting brings everything into focus, it makes us aware of what is involved when we confront and are confronted by the world outside.

Matisse had his wife pose over a hundred times for a painting 147 cm × 98 cm (almost 58 inches, almost 5 feet high). Over a hundred times! And maybe the painting stopped because she said enough or maybe not; maybe Matisse felt that this was about as far as he could get in transposing her to the demands of painting.

The great flat, frontal torso; the small appendages that bow to the power of flatness and deny their coming-forwardness: in all, there is no attempt to deal with the image through ordinary (outside) consistencies. Madame Matisse's right hand has nothing to do with the essence of hand but only to do with the essence of painting. The pained face is more like a Noh mask than a real face; and the gray of her face is darkened a little and made to serve as a shadow, on the chair and coming down between her lapel and her stole. The green of her blouse is also the green of the chair and there is a trace of it (not painted out) on her nose.

The painting's logic is only understandable as the logic of painting. The many changes that have occurred connect to each other as similar acts, acknowledging that the final image (if ever there could be a final image) is the many-changes and their traces (and so the logic of painting becomes the logic of life).

Because the painting makes no sense as a direct representation of a person, it also lacks the authority of painting's traditional goals. It is arbitrary—a light blue cloud-like shape appears in the upper right-hand corner because Matisse decided he needed (wanted) it there to balance the activity that occurred in the lower left. Even stranger is the linear configuration in the lower right-hand corner that partially holds floating pink shapes and a burnt sienna smudge (possibly a balance to the bit of brightness in the hat). Matisse uses highlights when it suits him, and shadows; he scratches through one layer of paint to another on one of the lapels, and puts a light gray above Mme. Matisse's right shoulder. He does what he wants; but he does not quite know what he wants for over a hundred sittings. His mind is his authority—and his mind's authority is his concept of painting. Painting itself tells him what is possible and what is allowable. No painter has ever been more dictatorial, more ruthless with his forms (whatever painter would ever cut off an entire shoulder as he did in the *Italian Woman* in the Rockefeller Collection), not Picasso, not de Kooning, not Braque. No painter has so clearly dramatized the difference between a concept of painting and a concept of external order.

II

The vast problem in all art is to imply what is not there by what is there—to give off a sense of fullness, of the force, of *the whole world* that affects the particular as the particular affects the whole. (Of course "the whole" is an abstraction too large to be anything else, but its force is undeniable and our awareness of that force—a changing awareness—controls our patterns of thought and belief.)

The point is that a work of art is a whole that is part of a whole.

A portrait is an image that represents all the images that make up that person. It is also the image of an event, the event of a particular seeing of a person, and it is the image of the way the artist makes an image—how memory and allusion and touch and manner co-exist—the personification of what image means to the artist—and it represent what must be and what may be, the necessary and the optional. For a work to be believable it must include in its makeup a sense of the necessary, something that cannot be avoided, an unyielding truth of a sort that seems to lie at the center of the work's origin, and that has but one goal—to be uncovered.

The image has a quality that the thing imaged does not have, and that is intelligibility. Not total intelligibility, for that would wipe it out, render it (after becoming intelligible) superfluous, something the image must never become. All images aspire to immortality. But the thing imaged is known to us only through the changing light and time. It ages as we age, at a faster, slower, or similar rate. And it alters as we alter.

Of course the image is prey to time like everything else, but not as we view it. For us the image is in a different world where time must have a top and it is in that world of the mind that we seek it.

In the painting, time exists and lends support to the painting's truth; but it is always secondary to space, shape and color. Our sense, always conscious of the present, acknowledge the image as a true inhabitant of the present, bringing memory and allusion into its arena. It is the particular magic of the painted image that it is always all there as we confront it.

For an image to be "all there" means that what you see is all that you have to see, all that the artist could possibly want you to see. The essence of painting is in its completeness. A painting never wants to be anything else. "All there" for the eye; but the mind, uninvited, plays upon the image, superimposing ghosts upon it, expanding its aura, at once simplifying and complicating its actuality (simplifying by generalizing what it sees, complicating by imposing on its one's moods, attitudes, and assumptions). To complain (for instance) about the illusion of space in a painting is like complaining about the fictive elements in a novel. A painting is what painting can do, it can create a complete world (and so differing from the experienced world), a world that by standing aside from, as well as inside of, the world engages our attention in its unique expansive way.

III

A painting's power is never exhausted by its esthetic. An esthetic analysis of a painting—a favorable analysis—is possible with a bad painting as well as a good painting. It reveals a painting's physicality and, like the physical analysis of a human, puts aside, except in physical terms, the subject's worth. (If esthetics

accounted for a painting's worth a forgery would be as highly esteemed as
an original.)

Awareness of purposiveness must be taken into account in approaching a
painting. What does Matisse mean for us to grasp with that funny little arm and
funny little leg (funny in the world outside the painting) in his portrait of his wife?

What connections can we make (i.e. arm-stole), what significance can we
attach to those connections, what accumulative build-up (visual harmonies)
presents itself as demand, invitation, challenge and seduction? Although each
painting is "all there" it is obviously helpful to know a group of works by the
painter (especially one as difficult as Matisse), a group of works by the painter's
contemporaries, and a group of works that seem to be in some way related to
the painting in question. In the case of Matisse these might be icons, Japanese
portraits of the Kamakura period, Noh masks, etc. An artist's obsessions, intimate concerns, and singular solutions to nagging problems create clarifying
keys to seemingly perverse encoded works.

Matisse's constant striving for a simpler image, simplicity itself, would
quite often lead to peculiar finalities, as in three other portraits: *The Lady in
Green*, 1909 (Hermitage) with its strange hands, *Greta Prozor*, 1916 (Pompidou),
with such mystifying decisions like the chair, and the *Portrait of a Woman in
White*, 1934 (privately owned), with its representation of the model's right arm.
Indeed as one thinks of the later painting in relation to *Mme. Matisse* one might
well ask was there something about right arms that set him searching—that
form that moves away from the body, horribly coming forward to the agitation
of his eye and hand? Of course it was not right arms or noses or chairs or any
specific thing; all or anything could attach itself to the fauve demon that was
never tamed—that wild restless eye that was always at war with the ordering
mind. Although the years from 1910 to 1920 are usually considered the years of
conflict, of experimentation, in fact that conflict was never settled and remained
the source of power and proficiency throughout his life.

At times the conflict could be clearly stated: the demands of painting ver-
sus the demands of the world. At other times the conflict became more complex
and elusive, making more difficult to pin down what was against what. Can the
lower right-hand corner of *Mme. Matisse* really be understood as answering
to the demands of painting? It does not even seem to be answering to the
demands of Matisse himself. Those forms seem to have just accumulated there,
the residue of an impenetrable desire. Yet they are by no means functionless—
they vibrate like an energy cell and direct the eye into the stole, turning the
whole right side of the image into an upward movement that counters the
downward movement of the other side, giving the still image a sense of vitality
and force.

The conflict is one of will and idea. No artist's will has ever dominated his
painting's world more than the will of Matisse: the cut-off shoulder in *The Italian
Woman,* 1915 (Rockefeller collection), the chair at the bottom of *Interior at Nice,*
1921 (Art Institute of Chicago), the scratched lines on *Mademoiselle Yvonne*

*Landsberg,* 1914 (Philadelphia Museum of Art), the *Large Red Interior,* 1948 (Musée National d'Art Moderne, Paris), etc. etc. "idea" paintings, except that we remember that *Harmony in Red,* 1908 (Hermitage) was originally *Harmony in Blue.*

The will of Matisse—and yet has there ever in the history of painting been more self-effacing images of the artist than *The Painter and His Model,* 1917 (Musée National d'Art Moderne, Paris), *The Artist and His Model,* 1919 (private collection, New York), and above all, *The Painting Lesson,* 1919 (Edinburgh)?

And the idea of painting: a painting as an autonomy, eventually diminishing the painter's role to that of the instigator of meaning, taking its place among the other paintings in the world, from whence it takes on intelligibility and value.

In Matisse's work the conflict can only be resolved when will and the idea of painting are seen as a single force, the idea of painting working through the will of Matisse. A strange distortion of the artist—as medium myth, or is it not a distortion but one of the possibilities that always existed—that the will of the painter might only be the will of painting exerting its pressure in secret consort. That the will of painting is what one becomes part of when one becomes a painter and it is how deeply you become part of that will that makes you matter as a painter. And yet there can be no easy giving in to that will, to the idea that is painting; for the idea that is painting needs the authentication of the artist's purpose. Above all a painting is an event meant to be seen; and it derives all its meaning from its being meant. Without that it is nothing.

*Larry Day*

# The Celebration of Otherness, written by 3 July 1991[1]

First off, you cannot go to a Rauschenberg exhibition without some sort of mindset unless you know nothing of contemporary art. This causes a couple of major problems: 1) you recognize Rauschenberg's modes and methods and there is a tendency to think "more of the same" and see no further; and 2) you remember particular pieces from the past and think "I like those more" and see no further. That this is a problem with any famous living artist is obvious, but when the artist was or is associated with some sort of youthful exuberance and abandon the problem seems greater but for some reason more easily ignored.

At most museum openings or exhibitions there are two easily spotted types: 1) the sophisticated, those who know what they know; and 2) the innocent, those who don't know what they know. Sophistication unless tempered by humility can create pompousness and blindness; and innocence unless tempered by curiosity can create stupidity and blindness. The problems of how to deal with our knowledge and how to deal with our capabilities of alignments and structuring are what keep us going and growing. In a very real sense this is what Rauschenberg's work is about.

As one walks through the ROCI exhibition, quickly at first, just to get an overall look, and then slowly, seeing particulars and details, one can quite easily come to the conclusion that the show is a work having the same general characteristics as the individual units within it. In Rauschenberg's work there are, and always have been, units, clearly defined units that coexist with other clearly defined units—images that have within themselves their definitions and "things" that maintain their thingness. There have always been commitments to co-existence and the belief that co-existence is the only true and meaningful existence.

ROCI stands for Rauschenberg Overseas Culture Interchange, and like the works in which the units maintain identity and cohesion, each word in the title must be taken seriously and fully. It is truly about interchange—encounter, puzzlement, dialogue, and recognition—and it certainly is a response to culture and cultures. In order to have validity the show has to be about the individual as well as the group, however, so the presence throughout of Rauschenberg—witness and guide—makes possible our own individual entries and shapings, our interchanges, public and private, with the exhibition's world.

Public and private: Rauschenberg has always been aware that they are not mutually exclusive. Opposites are just that, and at the same time they belong to each other: Elegance and Vulgarity; Two-dimensionality and Three-dimensionality; Mechanical and Natural; Inside and Outside; Black and White and Color.

As Rauschenberg pulls apart and brings together, it is the bringing together that is always the bottom line. If the show, the whole vast activity called ROCI is about peace, it is because most of the evil in the world today, the brutality and the destruction, grows out of the hatred and fear of otherness. And if there is a center around which the work in the show revolves it is the acknowledging and embracing of the other and the awareness that we grow and are transformed by that embrace.

Each of us coming to the exhibition brings to it our experience, our memories, our connections. After walking through the show the first time and then going into the Early Italian section of the National Gallery I was struck by what seemed to be a similarity of sensibility between Rauschenberg and Agnolo Gaddi. And one thinks of Francis Ponge whose poetry addresses things in a way that makes you and Thing a kind of key: and Herakleitos who pointed out the necessity of opposites to create harmony and who said that nature loves to hide, that if you don't seek you are not going to find anything even if it is right in front of you.

ROCI is both a seeking and a finding. One is always struck, but not always immediately, by the appropriateness of the images Rauschenberg uses. What often looks haphazard at first sight seems in time to be just right. Part of this is the personality of Rauschenberg as expressed in the structure of each piece. For example, in *Guardian Light/ROCI Cuba* the red band going up the entire length of the work seems to stabilize the surface while the light-colored panel, slightly askew, seems active, rising to the right. The dark bands and areas seem to move downward, and this visual activity goes on while the images address the title, and slowly, each other, as one recognizes their connectedness and their positionings.

One could call this a typical work but it is hard to imagine an untypical Rauschenberg. In each piece one can picture the artist's response to the place, the country, and its culture, the seeking and the finding of images and then the seeking and the finding of the format significant to the joining of sensibility's inner and outer forces.

There is in the work the authority of maturity—its self-knowledge and onwardness. There are in the photographs affirmation of vision and process but these examples and evidences in the world have been made available by the mind's formulating lens and point to the inexhaustableness of the artist's central idea. As Matisse said, "You know, you have one idea, you are born with it and all your life you develop your fixed idea, you make it breathe." The onwardness is the pushing of this idea out into the world, encountering the world's great and powerful otherness, acknowledging its nurturing power, its enhancing strength, its transformational illumination. Idea and experience are one.

Embedded in the work, in all the work, is a surprising tirelessness as if each piece energizes the next. The artist's dream, the never-ending making, that makes all true art the celebration of living—and sharing—when it exists. You sense that you become one with the work, part of a somewhat secret society that rejects no applicant.

The earliest pieces in the show, works from 1984 like *Raspberry Crime/ ROCI Japan* with its images of horizontality—ladder rungs, slats, door structures, even cracks—its parts of Japan that are not noticed, and the long multicolored acrylic force that seems to move across the surface one moment and to occupy the surface the next, and *Taki-No-Ko/ROCI Japan*, and others, in their various ways seem to define the complexity and excitement of cultural encounter. So do the last works in the show, dated 1990, like *Malaysian Flower Cave/ROCI Malaysia* with its juxtapositions of natural and mechanical images, natural and mechanical color transitions. Its dominant verticalities within the rectangle, as well as the complexity of the specific encounter, make a kind of celebration of all interchange.

The poet Hölderlin despaired of his inability to make an impression on his contemporaries because he believed that it was the poets, the artists of a culture, who were the ones that had to bring together the disparate experiences, images, things, that if seen with the proper kind of intensity and recognition would give that culture a sense of the wholeness, of the kind of inner belonging that makes up humanity. The poetry that he wrote took longer than he thought to take effect, but for some who have read it the wholeness is felt and the distrust and hatred is dissipated. And for some who have listened to and looked at and read of the world's arts, that sense of being both one and many, of feeling and belonging, is what their lives are all about (as for a number of others it seems strange and naïve to be affected that way).

Rauschenberg seems to be part of that group of artists like Hölderlin and Shelley and Van Gogh and Kollwitz and Mahler and Bernstein and all that thought art mattered, that it could and can alter things, that it could, like Rilke said, make you change your life.

(And if not, what in the hell is it all about?)

## Note

1    Rauschenberg Overseas Culture Interchange was on display in Mexico, Chile, Venezuela, China, Tibet, Japan, Cuba, USSR, Germany, and Malaysia, each a different show, examples from each of which were assembled at the National Gallery of Art, Washington, May 12–September 2, 1991. These ruminations are Day's way of thinking through his responses after seeing the show, the opening of which he probably would have attended.

# Excerpts from a Notebook[1]

It is always the central idea of the painting that is difficult to approach. Anyone can start or do a painting without one (a central idea) as one can do a painting that repeats a former idea—prolific artists have few central ideas, Picasso
perhaps had two that informed work after work after work.

The shift from the art object to the art experience which informed most advanced
art of the sixties has naturally raised to the highest importance the interpreter.
The act of interpretation however eventually is biased toward the interpreter's
experience and understanding and skill and if we come upon the experience from
the outside it is the interpreter who we must identify with and admire.

. . . writers like Blake and Dickens saw the creativity of the artist as continuous
with the general human creativity, that having created the world we live in, keep it.

___ Is this what our involvement with mythology is—an involvement with per-
sistent patterns of behavior; finding meaning in alignment and participation in
felt structures?

To examine an object or an event one, of course, also examines oneself. To examine an event, in a way, puts you in the event. To examine an object it soon becomes
clear that the object has a sphere of influence that extends and transforms.

___ Does an object examined become an event?

Ninety percent of what passes for criticism in the Art journals is the attempted
justification and or celebration of mediocre artists.

To read *ArtForum, Arts, Art in America* for three months would lead one to
assume that we are a nation of geniuses.

Hannah Arendt's "life of the mind"—three/parts: thinking, willing, judging.

A culture is made up on bodies of assumptions. There are interactions, available options such as what we can buy to eat, clothe ourselves with, to amuse

ourselves and so forth. There are sub-cultures within any culture, either by choice or by force (i.e., rock culture, prison culture). There are also sets of common experiences that influence assumptions and options. Uncommon experiences become important to a culture when expressed in one of the ways open in the culture for expression.

The future is individual and collective. Death for the individual is not the future but the end of the future. For the collective, a reluctance to think about the future is a kind of death.

Intense vision usually comes in an everyday situation (if reflection may be considered an everyday situation).

_____ Is reflection a getting outside of *any* situation? Is being "outside" an extreme situation in itself?

> The hermits opting for the extreme in order to find some sort of mystical vision seemed to have to domesticate their extreme position before vision came.

Is there an essential difference between refining and reducing? Considering works I am drawn to I am too often moved by what could be called reductive works or artists: Borges, Webern, La Tour, and so on, to think of myself as unaffected. My own work with its minimum of detail or perhaps its search for the proper or telling detail amongst the host of same indicates that my temperament lies in this direction.

> If something signifies then it cannot be contained. A work, in its particularities, may be the only entry into a body of experience but it is never, exhaustively, that body of experience.

> When signification occurs or is summoned up then it must be considered as affecting the quality of the work. Part of criticism would be the discoveries of how this works (i.e. studies of Milton's God).

The only things we can build our lives on are those things that moved us most when we came in contact with them; those things that seemed as if they were choosing us rather than we choosing them. We confront something, an act, an image, an idea, a sign, and we know that it's for us and then we might have to spend the rest of our lives working out its implications and ramifications.

Some of the things that move us most are the things we take for granted. How we dreamed of the ordinary as ideal when we were in the army.

Cats in their ordinariness seem in complete accord with their essence.

Contemporary art always has the possibility of interesting us merely by being contemporary. Past works may suddenly find themselves attended to because of an alignment of concerns. To be interested in a work of art is no guarantee that we will value the work or the experience of it. It is merely a letter of introduction.

We are defined by our limits. We thrive on limits. We can only live in a certain mixture of air, have to have certain amounts of water and food, can only stand a small range of temptations, have to have certain pressures, cannot stand too much light, too high sounds. The amount of conditions necessary for us to exist are so exact we had to learn how to carry them around with us. Fascinated with what we can't do we invent ways of simulating what is beyond us: airplanes, submarines, gas-masks, asbestos gloves etc.

Lines were never meant to represent something that appeared in nature. Lines are the path the eye or mind takes in making a form intelligible.

The plain *is* hard to see when you focus, concentrate on it. What you start to see is your concentration.

In "magic realism" there is no sense that the visible is a little hard to see, no sense of the "venerable complications" of estrangement, no sense of the awkwardness of self-questioning.

In "literalist" painting there is nothing that can be questioned; everything is as it is. "Ironic realism" uncovers the dilemma of two equally legitimate demands on a single form.

Auden's definition of aesthetics as the rules of the game and as art as the most difficult game.

Is the aesthetic life the most dangerous game?

Trends, fads, cultural pressures, social pressures, rather, are not peripheral to art but the lifeblood of art—the organizing principle.

The ethical imagination seeks (usually without much success) to go beyond the social, possibly beyond the cultural.

Myth—History—Romance: the three modes, separate and interwoven. Art seeks to replenish itself and goes to myth. Myth is the mode for a dying world.

It is always a weakness in the work when something is put in for mere illusionistic purposes. As a work deviates from the structural so it deviates from vision, imagination, and self-meaning.

"Origins" of course, is quite different from the art historian's beloved "sources."

It is possible that the different modes of painting not only make different demands on our knowledge—on the intelligibility of the work—but also make different demands of our understanding as well.

In early writings on art the confusion between sign and substance as proof of the artists skill

> Art as passion (the absence of and longing for an object)
> To make something present (to re-present)

The object as object (sign and substance as one)—Fertility Gods, Fetishes, Icons

In order to work with a sense of authority one must do something about the past. One can demystify it, disparage it, duplicate it (a distancing process), one can do anything but disown it.

The artist making a work—half understood—working through the conventions of the time—often seeing nothing more than praise, success in the field, using the skills and means available to persuade the world to take him or her seriously.

The work—divorced from the artist and receiving alimony but feeling the joys and traumas of independence

## Note

1    Day's writings include brief inquiries and aphoristic commentaries in notebooks of various types and sizes; these excerpts are taken from one such notebook.

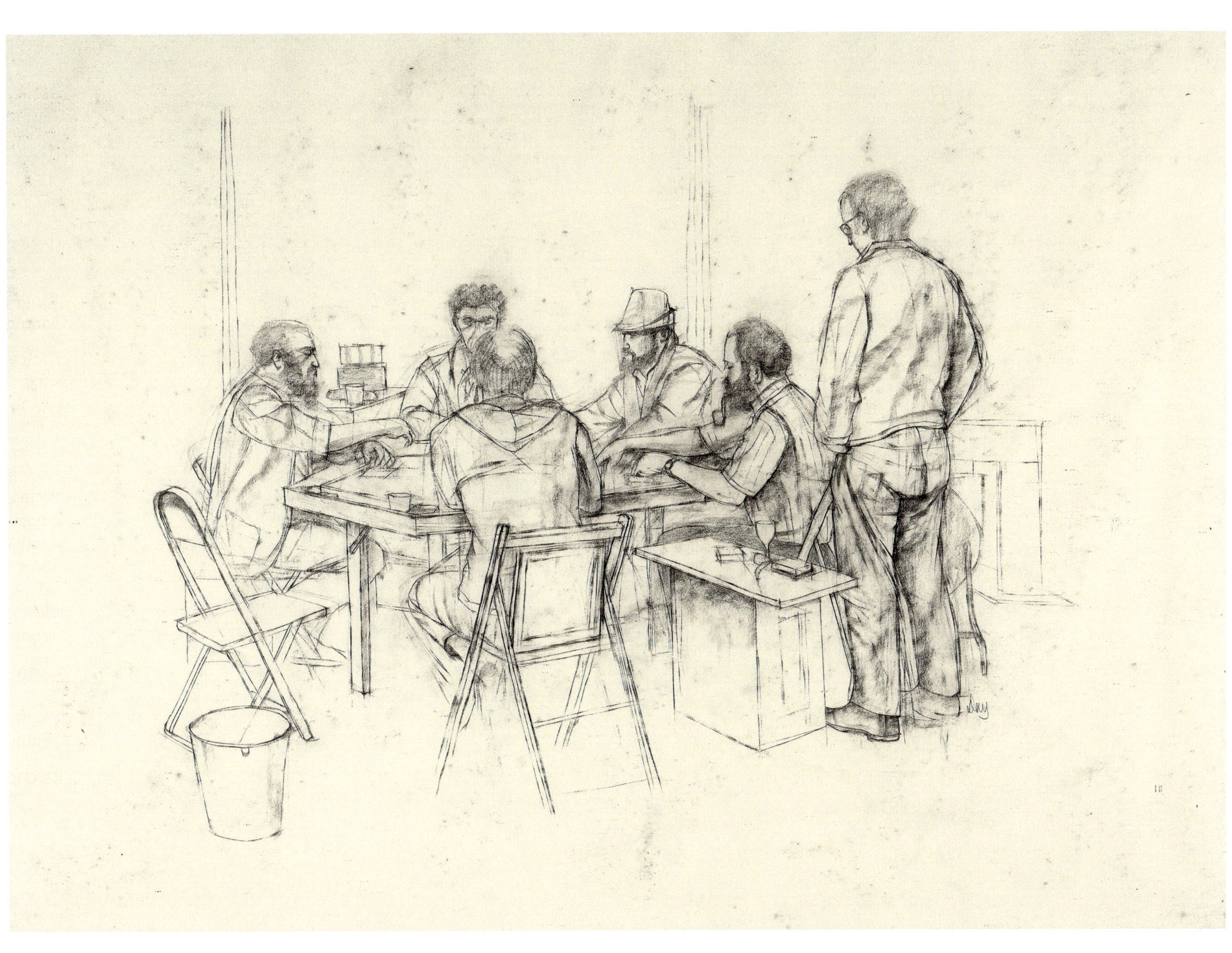

PLATE 105

153

*Poker Game*, c. 1970

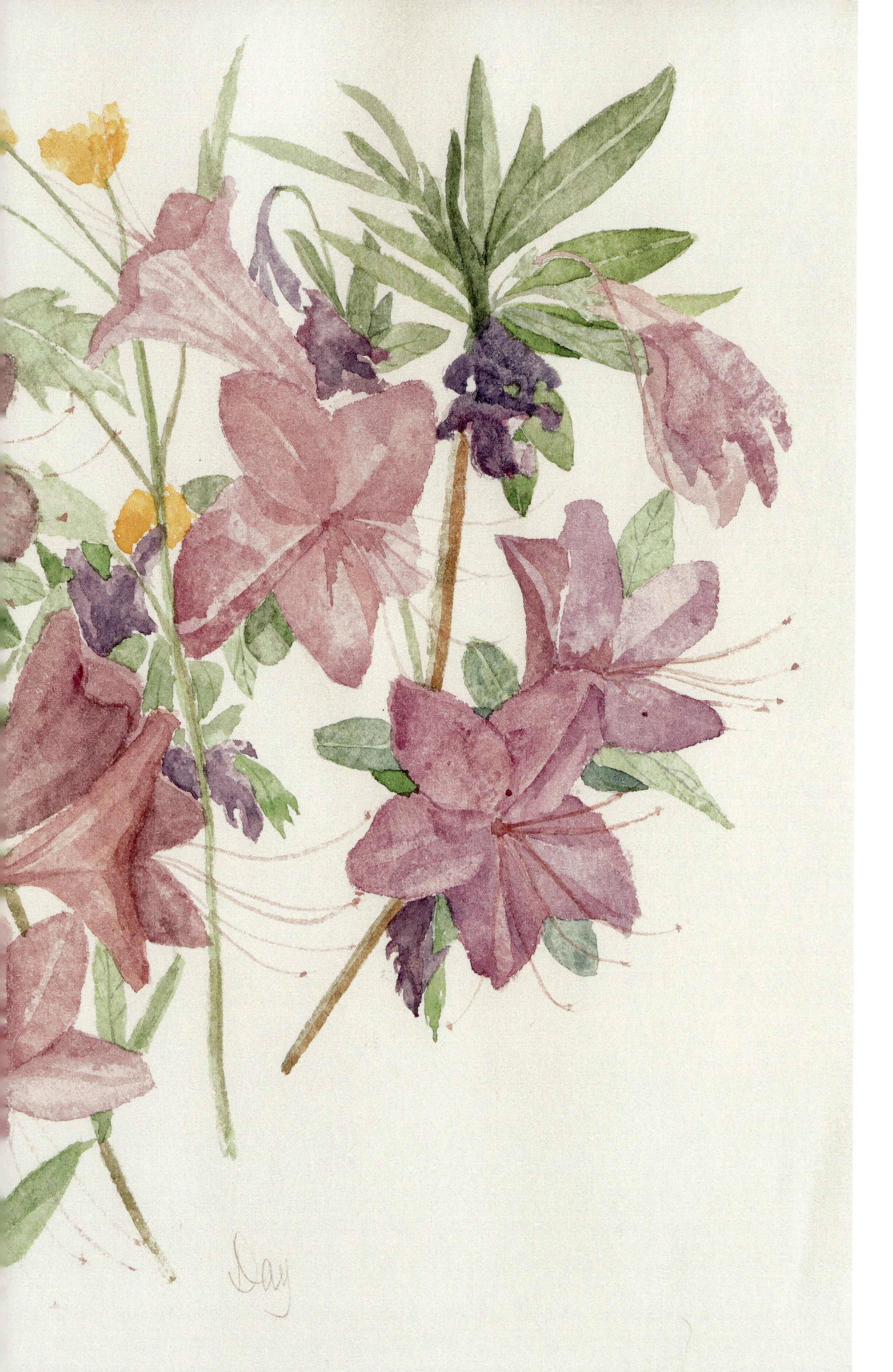
Day

# Selected Chronology

This chronology was compiled during the COVID-19 pandemic of 2020–21. Information provided is as complete as possible with limited library access. Works featured on exhibition announcements are noted only if they, or related works, are included in the exhibition. Entries reflect contemporaneous gallery and institution names; later names are noted only for those that appear under different names in this chronology.

## 1921

**October 29:** Born in Philadelphia to Ethel Day/del Giorno (née Swain, homemaker and seamstress) and Laurence F. Day/del Giorno (American Laundry Machinery Company employee and skilled woodworker). First address is 3924 North Darien Street, but the family moves frequently. Though Day's given name is Lawrence James del Giorno, he is baptized Lawrence James Day on June 4, 1922. He will use both Lawrence and Laurence (as spelled in Army records, college transcript, and other documents at least until the late 1950s), as well as Larry, throughout his life. Legally changes name to Lawrence James Day in 1986.

## 1924

**March 14:** Sister, Ethel, born.

## 1934

Family, including maternal grandmother (Lottie Swain) and an aunt (Lidi Swain), moves to 310 Myrtle Avenue in suburban Cheltenham Township, Pennsylvania. Day enters his last year of elementary school. He will live at 310 Myrtle Avenue through 1985, maintaining studios there and in other Cheltenham locations.

## 1936–40

Attends Cheltenham High School. Serves as humor editor for the school publication *El Delator*. Its 1939 issue describes Day as "one of those jittery Benny Goodman fans. . . . Naturally prefers swing music to classical compositions. . . . Senior representative in Council . . . Played intramural basketball for two years. . . . Music seems to occupy most of his interest. . . . Anxious to become an orchestra leader." The 1940 volume states, "Lawrence is the uncrowned king of humor at Cheltenham. His poetry is a source of interest in the school and is read by all. He worked for the Yearbook and class night program committees in his senior year. Day also shows an interest in music." Day's later recollections of high school include being told that he could not go to college; reading Amy Lowell's two-volume biography of John Keats, which made him want to be an artist (at that time, a poet); taking private painting classes with German immigrant artist Albert Urban, where he copied work by Yasuo Kuniyoshi (stylized rather than realistic); listening to Bix Beiderbecke and jazz; learning to play the coronet; reading Henry Fielding's *Tom Jones*; hearing Igor Stravinsky's *The Rite of Spring*; seeing movies; playing sports; and dancing.

Visits the Philadelphia Museum of Art and the University of Pennsylvania Museum, Philadelphia; Egyptian art (especially Fayum portraiture) is of particular interest.

**June 1940:** Graduates with a diploma in the commercial course; ranks second in a class of 260 students. Finds work as a bookkeeper.

## 1942–45

**September 14, 1942:** Inducted into the United States Army, reporting to the Local Board at Jenkintown Reading Railway Station, Pennsylvania.

**Fall 1942–fall 1945:** First stationed in Chicago, Day visits the Chicago Art Institute whenever possible; a Pierre-Auguste Renoir bather became his pin-up girl. Trains as electrical technician. Later stationed in Georgia, California, and Hawaii. Carries Thomas Mann's *The Magic Mountain* and a book of W. H. Auden poetry in his backpack. During the Pacific Campaign, serves in 506th Antiaircraft Artillery Gun Battalion, Battery B, attached to the Marines. Participates in the invasion of Iwo Jima. Narrowly escapes death twice, once from a kamikaze pilot, once from exploding shrapnel while in a foxhole. Serves as a librarian on Iwo Jima, where he is considered the intellectual of his group and is referred to as "Doc." Draws portraits and writes letters home for bunkmates, noticing the use of metaphor and simile in the language of the Southerners, in contrast to the Northerners' direct, unpoetic language. Writes poems and a novel (the latter of which he will later destroy).

**November 22, 1945:** Receives Readjustment Returnee Travel Orders.

## 1946–50

On GI Bill, attends Temple University's Stella Elkins Tyler School of Fine Arts (later Tyler School of Art, now Tyler School of Art and Architecture), Philadelphia. Had been accepted to Kenyon College, Gambier, Ohio, to study writing with John Crowe Ransom, and considered Tyler a temporary situation, but is immensely happy there, appreciating the school's concern for all the arts, as well as the academic courses. His classes include Painting; Sculpture; Metallurgy and Jewelry; Pottery and Ceramics; Physical Science as Applied to Art; Printmaking; General, Industrial, Advertising, Costume, and Textile Design; Mechanical Drawing; Interior Decoration; Stagecraft; Music Composition; Psychology; Sociology; Criminology; English Composition; Great Writers; Playwriting; and education courses including Methods and Curricula. Important teachers include Dean Boris Blai, Alexander Abels and Emlen Etting

for painting, Raphael Sabatini for sculpture, Fred Becker and Morris Blackburn for printmaking, Rudolf (Rudy) Staffel for ceramics, Alwin Nikolais for dance, and Herman Gundersheimer for art history. Elected junior class representative to the Temple Senate.

Learns fresco techniques and will later attribute his thinly painted surfaces to his interest in fresco and tapestries. Paul Klee, Jules Pascin, and Chaïm Soutine are of particular interest. Is profoundly impressed with the Philadelphia Museum of Art's 1948 Henri Matisse retrospective exhibition, noting especially Matisse's direct, painterly approach—a stark contrast to the layered underpainting and glazing taught at Tyler. Access to Lessing J. Rosenwald's world-renowned collection of prints, drawings, and illustrated books (now at the National Gallery of Art and Library of Congress, Washington, DC) contributes to Day's strong interest in printmaking during these years.

Writes extensively, including translations of poems by Rainer Maria Rilke. In April 1947, serves as features editor for the first issue of *Gargoyles*, a Tyler newspaper that is later issued in a magazine format; is associate editor by late 1948.

Participates in theatrical productions at both Tyler and the Cheltenham Township Art Center (later the Cheltenham Art Center, now Cheltenham Center for the Arts), including playing the lead role in Oscar Wilde's *The Importance of Being Earnest*.

**June 15, 1950:** Graduates with a bachelor of fine arts, a bachelor of science in education, and the Dean's Award, a gold medal "designed and given by the Dean, to the graduating senior student attaining scholarship and achievement in art."

In the summer of 1950, establishes a frame business with former classmates Robert and Barbara Kulicke (Kulicke frames became renowned in the field) and a silk-screen greeting card company with Bertha Hanstein (later known professionally as Bertha Leonard), Iris Cohen, and Phyllis Pitegoff; the name of the company, Hanco-Piday, combines elements of their names. Day's association with Kulicke is brief, and Hanco-Piday lasts only one season.

Private dealer Pearl Fox represents Day's work in her home-based gallery.

**September 1–2:** Possibly attends the Third Woodstock Art Conference, *The Artist and the Museum*, New York.

GROUP EXHIBITIONS

**October 1949:** Title unknown, Graphics Gallery, Dubin Galleries, Philadelphia.

**January 22–February 26, 1950:** *One Hundred and Forty-Fifth Annual Exhibition of Painting and Sculpture*, Pennsylvania Academy of the Fine Arts (PAFA), Philadelphia. Catalogue. Exhibited work: *Paul Revere Coffee Pot* (date and medium unknown).

## 1951

Visits Tyler classmates Billy Richards and George Dunbar in New Orleans.

**Fall:** Teaches art at Abraham Lincoln High School, Philadelphia (through spring 1952), including ceramics.

SOLO EXHIBITION

**Summer:** Title unknown, Dubin Galleries.

## 1951–52

GROUP EXHIBITION

**November 28, 1951–January 4, 1952:** *Xmas Exhibition of Contemporary Paintings, Drawings, Sculpture, Ceramics, Jewelry, and Fabrics*, Dubin Galleries.

## 1952

Member, board of directors, Stella Elkins Tyler School of Fine Arts Alumni Association.

**July 3:** Sails on maiden voyage of the *SS United States* to Southampton, England. Settles in Paris and visits Provence, London, the Netherlands, and Belgium. Spends time in museums and considers the Select café his headquarters. Becomes aware of the art of Balthus (Balthasar Klossowski de Rola). Unable to find an affordable studio, works in a hotel room and draws from models at the Académie de la Grande Chaumière. Is impressed by an exhibition of work by Georges Rouault and buys two lithographs by the artist.

**October 22:** Returns to US.

**GROUP EXHIBITIONS**

**March 22–April 26:** *6th Annual Exhibition by the Alumni of Stella Elkins Tyler School of Fine Arts of Temple University*, Stella Elkins Tyler School of Art, Philadelphia. Catalogue. Exhibited work: *Girl in Green Skirt* (date and medium unknown).

**December:** Title unknown, The Red Door, Philadelphia.

## 1953

Rents an abandoned factory at 236 Harvey Street in the Germantown neighborhood of Philadelphia as a studio (through 1956 or 1957).

**Spring:** Teaches art at Germantown High School.

**Fall:** Invited by Emmanuel M. Benson to join the faculty of the Philadelphia Museum School of Art (later Philadelphia Museum College of Art, then Philadelphia College of Art, now University of the Arts), where he will remain through 1988. Teaches painting, drawing, and art theory, and will serve intermittently over many years as chair of the painting department. Loves teaching and views students as colleagues; integrates literature, music, and philosophy into his courses. Early colleagues include Morris Berd, Paul Froelich, Franz Kline, and Benton Spruance.

**SOLO EXHIBITION**

**September:** *Larry Day: Paintings and Drawings*, Dubin Galleries (inaugural exhibition at new location).

**GROUP EXHIBITION**

**November 7–December 6** [as Laurence Day]: *Regional Exhibition: Oils and Caseins*, Philadelphia Art Alliance. Brochure. Exhibited work: *The Expulsion* (date and medium unknown).

## 1954

**SOLO EXHIBITIONS**

**September:** Title unknown, Dubin Galleries.

**October 25–November 20** (probably 1954): *Nudes and Angels*, Parma Gallery, New York.

**GROUP EXHIBITION**

**May 9–June 11:** *Water Color Drawing Collage: Luman-Dain, Robert Dain, Eugene Feldman, Sam Greenberg, Robert Keyser, Felrath Hines*, Parma Gallery.

## Mid–late 1950s

Frequently visits New York and associates with the Abstract Expressionist circle at the Cedar Tavern. Friends include Kline, Charles Cajori, John Ferren, Philip Guston, and Mercedes Matter.

Plays recorder and writes poetry.

## 1955

President, Cheltenham Township Art Center (through 1958). Organizes and participates in the center's theater group, including productions of Thornton Wilder's *The Merchant of Yonkers* and William Inge's *Picnic*.

**January:** Sees exhibition *Drawings by Lipchitz, De Kooning and Martinelli* at the Philadelphia Museum School of Art; is greatly impressed by Willem de Kooning's drawings.

**SOLO EXHIBITION**

**November 9–28:** *Larry Day: Oils*, Dubin-Lush Gallery, Philadelphia.

**GROUP EXHIBITION**

**April 16–May 15** [as Laurence Day]: *Twentieth Century Drawings: A Loan Exhibition Presented by the Stanford Art Gallery and the Committee for Art at Stanford*, Stanford Art Gallery, Stanford, California. Catalogue. Exhibited work: *Jacob and the Angel (After Delacroix)* (date unknown, graphite).

## 1956

**GROUP EXHIBITION**

**February 3–March 4:** *Regional Exhibition: Prints and Drawings*, Philadelphia Art Alliance. Brochure. Exhibited work: *Landscape* (date unknown, drawing).

## 1957

**June 20–August 12:** Leads a tour in association with the Positano Art Workshop, Italy. Sails round trip on the *SS Castel Felice* from New York to Le Havre; visits Paris, Chartres, Milan, Venice, Ravenna, Florence, Rome, and Naples, ending with two weeks in Positano.

**SOLO EXHIBITION**

**Dates unknown:** Title unknown, Dubin Galleries.

**GROUP EXHIBITIONS**

**January** (probably): Title unknown, The Design Corner, Bala Cynwyd, Pennsylvania.

**October 25–November 30:** *The Third Annual Fall Review of Paintings and Sculpture: 1957 in the United States*, The Pyramid Club, Philadelphia. Catalogue. Exhibited work: *Natalie Charkow* (date and medium unknown). Exhibition honors Henri Marceau, director, Philadelphia Museum of Art.

**December 6–16:** *1st Annual Tyler Fellows Exhibition*, Stella Elkins Tyler School of Fine Arts.

## 1958

Begins showing at Gallery 1015, directed by Gladys Myers in her home at 1015 Greenwood Avenue, Wyncote, Pennsylvania. Myers's stable includes Natalie Charkow (later known as Natalie Charkow Hollander), William Daley, Jerome Kaplan, Paul F. Keene Jr., and Dennis Leon. One exhibition checklist notes that art is displayed throughout the residence—in the "ceramic room," gallery, living room, porch, study, and dining room.

Cofounds the Interlocutors, a discussion group with members from diverse professions that meets monthly at the University of Pennsylvania. Other founders are Walter F. Ballinger II (surgeon), James F. Bodine (bank executive), Samuel Crothers III (architect), Alan G. Kirk II (lawyer), Henry J. Abraham (political scientist), Werner Brandt (physicist), Erasmus H. Kloman (member of Penn's Foreign Policy Research Institute), Joel T. Loeb (business executive), John A. Schneider (television station manager), Harry G. Toland (reporter), and Richard H. Walker (publishing executive). Women are invited to be members beginning in 1977. Many of Day's later figure drawings and a large canvas will be based on the Interlocutors' annual dinner parties with spouses.

Creates large black-and-white drawings and collages with both figurative and nonfigurative elements, reaching up to 8 × 10 feet; none known to survive.

GROUP EXHIBITIONS

**October 5** (opens): *Showing of Painting, Prints, Ceramics, and Sculpture*, Gallery 1015.

**November 21–December 17:** Philadelphia Art Alliance Dining Room. Catalogue. Other exhibitors: Jane S. Eisenstat, Abraham P. Hankins, Ray Spiller, Roswell Weidner, and others.

## 1959

Shares a carriage house studio at 509 Spring Avenue, Elkins Park, Pennsylvania, with Leon (through 1964). Leon will remain a lifelong friend.

SOLO EXHIBITION

**April 8–May 3:** *Larry Day Oils*, Philadelphia Art Alliance, courtesy of Parma Gallery. Catalogue.

GROUP EXHIBITIONS

**Dates unknown** (probably 1959): *Outstanding Philadelphia Artists*, Thalheimer and Weitz Architects, Philadelphia. Sponsored by Gallery 1015. Organized in the hope that more art will be incorporated into Philadelphia buildings.

**January 25–March 1:** *The One Hundred and Fifty-Fourth Annual Exhibition: Water Colors, Prints, Drawings*, PAFA. Catalogue. Exhibited works: *Silent Noon* and *The Table* (both dates unknown, watercolor).

**January 31–March 8:** *2nd Philadelphia Arts Festival: Regional Exhibition*, Philadelphia Museum of Art. Catalogue, with essay by Day, "The Artist as Philadelphian." Exhibited work: *Dark Laughter* (date unknown, gouache).

**May:** Title unknown, Gallery 1015. Other exhibitors: Keene and Itzhak Sankowsky.

## 1960

**June 24–September 1:** Artist-in-residence, Aspen School of Contemporary Art, Colorado (opening season). Ferren is the other artist-in-residence.

SOLO EXHIBITIONS

**April:** Title unknown, Parma Gallery. Nonobjective paintings.

**Summer:** Title unknown, Aspen School of Contemporary Art.

GROUP EXHIBITIONS

**January:** Title unknown, Gallery 1015. Other exhibitors: Keene and Samuel Maitin.

**March 17–April 16** (probably 1960; possibly 1961 or 1962): *A Selection of Drawings by the Fine Arts Faculty of the Philadelphia Museum College of Art*, Offices of the Department of Fine Arts, Philadelphia Museum College of Art.

**May 10–July 27:** *Twelfth National Print Exhibition 1960. Brooklyn Museum*, Catalogue. Exhibited work: *The Venus Worship*, c. 1958, etching.

**October:** Title unknown, Gallery 1015. Other exhibitors: Keene, Maitin, and others.

**November:** Title unknown, Philadelphia Museum College of Art. Other exhibitors: Greenberg and others. Faculty exhibition.

## 1961

**March 21:** Panelist, "Conversations with Artists: Where Do We Go from Here?" Philadelphia Museum College of Art. Moderator: Katharine Kuh, art editor, *Saturday Review of Literature*. Other panelists: Marcel Duchamp, Louise Nevelson, and Theodoros Stamos.

**June 23–September 1:** Artist-in-residence, Aspen School of Contemporary Art. Edward Dugmore is the other artist-in-residence.

SOLO EXHIBITION

**October 25–November 20:** Title unknown, Parma Gallery.

GROUP EXHIBITIONS

**January 20–February 22:** *Philadelphia Italian-American Painters*, Dining Room, Philadelphia Art Alliance. Catalogue. Other exhibitors: John Costanza, Angelo Pinto, Giovanni Martino, and others.

**May 7** (closes): *15th Annual Alumni Exhibition*, Stella Elkins Tyler School of Fine Arts. Receives Second Award for *Untitled* (date unknown, painting).

**November:** Title unknown, Gallery 1015.

## 1962

Shifts from abstraction to representation.

**June 22–September 1:** Artist-in-residence, Aspen School of Contemporary Art. Leland Bell is the other artist-in-residence.

GROUP EXHIBITIONS

**March 29–April 23:** *Five Tyler Fellows*, Stella Elkins Tyler School of Fine Arts, Elkins Park. Other exhibitors: Raymond Gallucci, Mitzi Melnicoff, Robert Ranieri, and Sarai Sherman.

**June 9–24:** *Third Philadelphia Arts Festival: Art Exhibitions*, Philadelphia Museum of Art and PAFA. Catalogue. Exhibited works: at Philadelphia Museum of Art, *Sombre Figuration*; at PAFA, *After Veronese* (plate 60), *Still Life* (date unknown, graphite), and *No Title* (date unknown, watercolor).

## 1963

SOLO EXHIBITION

**Dates unknown:** Title unknown, Elaine Benson Gallery, Bridgehampton, New York.

## 1964

Rents studio at 930 Stratford Avenue, Melrose Park (through the late 1970s).

**June 22–August 24:** Artist-in-residence, Aspen School of Contemporary Art. Perry Hale, Tom Larkin, and Robert Rohm are the other artists-in-residence.

SOLO EXHIBITION

**October 12–November 1:** *Larry Day: Recent Paintings and Drawings*, Gallery 1015.

GROUP EXHIBITIONS

**October 9–November 15:** *Regional Exhibition: Paintings, Sculpture, Prints, and Drawings by Artists of Philadelphia and Vicinity*, PAFA. Catalogue. Exhibited work: *Studio Table* (date unknown, oil). Selection committee: Day (representing Philadelphia College of Art), Joseph Greenberg Jr. (Artists Equity), Benton Spruance (Beaver College), Donald Irving (Moore College of Art), Joseph T. Fraser Jr. (PAFA), Dean Charles LeClair (Stella Elkins Tyler School of Fine Arts), Thomas B.A. Godfrey (University of Pennsylvania School of Fine Arts), Weidner (Fellowship of the Academy), and others.

**October 16–November 6:** Title unknown, Gallery 1015.

## 1964–65

GROUP EXHIBITION

**December 4, 1964–January 2, 1965:** *Faculty Biennial Exhibition*, Philadelphia College of Art.

## 1965

TWO-PERSON AND GROUP EXHIBITIONS

**January 11–February 7:** *Figure Painting*, Philadelphia Art Alliance. Other exhibitors: Sidney Goodman, James McGarrell, and Peter Paone.

**January 22–March 7:** *The One Hundred and Sixtieth Annual Exhibition: Water Colors, Prints, Drawings*, PAFA. Catalogue. Exhibited works: *Bridge Game* (1963, ink) and *The Dart Players* (1963, graphite).

**October 27–November 17:** *Larry Day and Sidney Goodman*, Proctor Art Center, Bard College, Annandale-on-Hudson, New York.

**November 5–20:** *New Works . . . 1965*, Gallery 1015. Checklist. Exhibited works: *Afternoon, Seated Woman, Spools #3* (dates unknown), *Antechamber* (1964–65, oil), and *Afternoon* (date unknown, watercolor). Erwin Weiner joins Myers as co-director and business manager of the gallery.

**Winter:** *Aspen Artists*, Bundy Art Gallery, Waitsfield, Vermont. Catalogue. Exhibited work: *The Dart Players, Still Life with Piece of Plaster*, and *The Tourists* (all 1963, oil). Other exhibitors: Herbert Bayer, Gail Cottingham, David Michael, Mona Michael, Robert Rohn, Louise Stanton, and Yvonne Thomas.

**December 10–24:** *Art for Everyone*, Gallery 1015.

## 1966

SOLO EXHIBITION

**May 22–June 9:** *Larry Day*, Gallery 1015.

TWO-PERSON AND GROUP EXHIBITIONS

**January 21–March 6:** *The One Hundred and Sixty-First Annual Exhibition of American Painting and Sculpture*, PAFA. Catalogue. Exhibited work: *Antechamber* (1964–65, oil).

**July 3–24:** *Larry Day, Drawings and Paintings; Diter Rot, Collage Paintings and Books; Toshiko Takaezu, Ceramics*, Elaine Benson Gallery.

## 1967

SOLO EXHIBITION

**January 6–February 12:** *Larry Day: Watercolors*, Philadelphia Art Alliance. Catalogue.

GROUP EXHIBITION

**Dates unknown** (probably 1967): *10/XII, Exhibition: Contemporary American Drawings*, Indiana University School of Fine Arts Gallery, Bloomington. Catalogue.

## 1968

SOLO EXHIBITION

**March 5–23:** *Larry Day: Paintings*, Terry Dintenfass, New York. Announcement card features *Narrative: To the Memory of Matteo Giovannetti* (plate 96).

GROUP EXHIBITIONS

**January 19–March 3:** *The One Hundred and Sixty-Third Exhibition, American Painting and Sculpture*, PAFA. Catalogue. Exhibited works:

*Group* (1967, oil, plate 13) and *The Game* (date unknown, oil).

**May 8–June 12:** *Realism Now*, Vassar College Art Gallery, Poughkeepsie, New York. Catalogue. Exhibited work: *Summer* (date unknown, oil).

## 1969

SOLO EXHIBITIONS

**February 2–23:** *Larry Day: Paintings*, Fine Arts Center, University of Rhode Island, Kingston.

**February 4–28:** *The Drawings of Larry Day*, Gallery Pane Vino, Philadelphia.

TWO-PERSON EXHIBITION

**December 14–18:** Title unknown, Philadelphia College of Art. Other exhibitor: Berd. One of four exhibitions focused on the painting faculty.

## 1970

SOLO EXHIBITION

**October 28–November 19:** *Larry Day*, Peale House, PAFA. Seventeen paintings, drawings, and watercolors. On view simultaneously with an exhibition of work by Murray Dessner.

## 1971

SOLO EXHIBITION

**Dates unknown:** Title unknown, Brata Gallery, New York

GROUP EXHIBITION

**March 25–April 28:** *Figure Drawing: A Contemporary View*, Westby Art Gallery, Glassboro State College (now Rowan University), New Jersey. Catalogue. Exhibited work: *Nude* (1970, graphite).

## 1972

**January 11:** Lecture, New York Studio School, New York.

SOLO EXHIBITIONS

**January 8–29:** *Larry Day: Thematic Paintings*, Brata Gallery. (Participates in group exhibitions at the New Brata Gallery on April 8–30 and October 23–November 9, years unknown.)

**February 10–March 8:** *Larry Day*, Atwood Gallery of Art, Beaver College (now Arcadia University) Art Gallery, Glenside, Pennsylvania.

GROUP EXHIBITION

**November 12** (opens): Inaugural opening to meet the artists and preview their work, Langman Gallery, Jenkintown, Pennsylvania.

## 1972–73

GROUP EXHIBITION

**September 1972–September 1973:** *The Realist Revival*, American Federation of the Arts, New York. Organized by Scott Burton for the American Federation of Arts. Travels to University of Alabama Art Gallery, Tuscaloosa; Georgia Museum of Art, University of Georgia, Athens; The New York Cultural Center, New York; State University College of Arts and Sciences, Plattsburgh, New York; College of Fine Arts, Ohio University, Athens; J. B. Speed Art Museum, Louisville, Kentucky; and Kutztown State College, Pennsylvania. Catalogue. Exhibited work: *A Game of Charades* (1969, oil, plate 98).

## 1973

SOLO EXHIBITIONS

**February 5–24:** *Larry Day, Seven Views of Philadelphia and Other Works*, Langman Gallery.

**September 30–October 17:** *Paintings and Drawings by Larry Day*, Hiestand Gallery, Miami University, Oxford, Ohio.

GROUP EXHIBITIONS

**Dates unknown** (probably opens 1973): *A Sense of Place: The Artist and the American Land, Part II*, Joslyn Art Museum, Omaha. Exhibition shared with Sheldon Memorial Art Gallery, Lincoln, Nebraska. Catalogue. Exhibited work: *Broad* (date unknown, oil). A smaller exhibition that includes *Broad* is subsequently circulated by the Mid-America Arts Alliance, Kansas City,

Missouri. A version of the exhibition is possibly also presented at Guild Hall, East Hampton, New York.

**June:** *26th Annual Exhibition*, Cheltenham Township Art Center. Exhibited work: *One Chapter from a Floating Life* (1971, oil).

**October 9–30:** *Contemporary American Watercolors*, Proctor Art Center.

## 1974

Visiting artist, Westminster College, New Wilmington, Pennsylvania.

SOLO EXHIBITION

**December 10–21:** *Larry Day: Drawings*, Art Academy of Cincinnati.

GROUP EXHIBITION

**October 1–November 5:** *The Figure in Recent American Painting*, Westminster College Art Gallery. Travels to Philadelphia College of Art; St. John's University, Queens, New York; Westmoreland County Museum of Art, Greensburg, Pennsylvania; and Moravian College, Bethlehem, Pennsylvania. Catalogue, with essay by Day, "Notes on Figurative Art." Exhibited work: *Conversation Piece I* (plate 18). Works by twenty-four artists.

## 1975

SOLO EXHIBITION

**October 18–November 5:** *The Rules of Place, Paintings and Drawings by Larry Day*, Gross McCleaf Gallery, Philadelphia.

TWO-PERSON AND GROUP EXHIBITIONS

**Dates unknown:** *Modern Drawing*, New York Studio School (now New York Studio School of Drawing, Painting and Sculpture), New York.

**March 6–April 12:** *Half a Dozen Philadelphia Artists*, Vick Gallery, Philadelphia. Other exhibitors: Goodman, John Moore, David Pease, Italo Scanga, and Neil Welliver.

**April 20–25:** *Two Artists Look at Philadelphia: Paintings by Larry Day and Humbert Howard*, Peirce Junior College, Philadelphia. Courtesy of

Gross McCleaf Gallery. Eight works by Day, ten by Howard.

## 1976

SOLO EXHIBITION

**October:** *Larry Day*, Art Annex at Hollins College, Virginia.

GROUP EXHIBITIONS

**February 11–March 12:** *Figures in Places*, Westby [Art] Gallery. Announcement card features *A Game of Charades* (plate 98, as *Charades*).

**February 15–March 19:** *American Figure Drawing*, Lehigh University, Bethlehem, Pennsylvania. Travels to the Victorian College of the Arts Gallery, Melbourne, and the Art Gallery of South Australia, Adelaide. Catalogue, with essay by Day, "Notes on Figurative Art." Separate brochure. Exhibited works: *Figure* and *Figure* (both 1975, graphite).

**March:** *In Praise of Space: The Landscape in American Art*, Westminster College Art Gallery. Travels to Gross McCleaf Gallery and Parsons School of Design Gallery, New York. Catalogue. Exhibited work: *Landscape* (date unknown, pen and ink).

**April 11–October 10:** *Philadelphia: Three Centuries of American Art*, Philadelphia Museum of Art. Catalogue. Exhibited work: Untitled (plate 40).

**April 25–May 9:** *New Land, New Covenant*, Bryn Mawr Presbyterian Church, Pennsylvania. Catalogue. Exhibited work: *The Dancing Couple* (date and medium unknown).

**May 6** (closes): *Drawings by William Bailey, Marvin Bileck, Larry Day, and Emily Nelligan*, Westminster College Art Gallery.

**July 28** (closes): *13 Gallery Artists, Drawings*, Gross McCleaf Gallery. Catalogue, with statements by the artists and one work by each.

**July 29–August 8:** *Exhibition of Liturgical Arts*, Philadelphia Civic Center. Organized by the 41st International Eucharistic Congress. Catalogue. Exhibited works: *After Palma Il Vecchio (Raising of Lazarus), Raising of Lazarus No. 2*

(commissioned for the exhibition), and *After Bruegel (Resurrection)* (all 1976, graphite).

**September 8–October 6:** *Artists' Sketchbooks I: Philadelphia*, Philadelphia College of Art. Catalogue.

**September 10–October 10:** *Philadelphia in the Bicentennial Year: Drawings by Philadelphia Artists*, Atwood Gallery of Art. Brochure, with thanks to Day for selecting the exhibition and Grace Hartigan for selecting the awards. Exhibited work: *Bridges and Trees* (date unknown, graphite).

## 1977

**November 9:** Panelist, "Art and Identity: Five Points of View," on building a stronger, more visible art community in Philadelphia. Co-organized by *Arts Exchange* magazine and Philadelphia College of Art. Other participants: Janet Kardon, gallery director, Philadelphia College of Art, and artists Frank Bramblett, Jody Pinto, Phillips Simkin, and Edna Andrade.

SOLO EXHIBITION

**October 1–29:** *Larry Day: Paintings and Drawings, 1976–1977*, Gross McCleaf Gallery. Announcement card features *Partial Portrait* (plate 57).

TWO-PERSON AND GROUP EXHIBITIONS

**Dates unknown:** Title unknown, Wright State University, Dayton, Ohio. Other exhibitor: Gretna Campbell.

**Dates unknown:** *Contemporary Drawing*, State University of New York, Cortland.

**January 16–February 13:** *Contemporary Art of Philadelphia*, Squibb Gallery, Princeton, New Jersey. Brochure. Exhibited works: *Untitled* and *End* (both date unknown, oil).

## 1978

**March:** Fellow, MacDowell Colony, Peterborough, New Hampshire.

**April 17–19:** Presenter, "Painting as Paradigm," *What Is a Painting?* symposium, Philadelphia Museum of Art.

GROUP EXHIBITION

**May 31–July 31** (probably 1978; possibly as late as 1981): *Paintings and Prints by Larry Day, Naomi Limont, Ralph Raunft, Vita Solomon*, Sugarloaf Conference Center, Chestnut Hill, Pennsylvania. Presented by the Tyler School of Art Alumni Association.

## 1978–79

**September 15–November 26, 1978:** *Contemporary Drawings: Philadelphia I*, PAFA.

**March 24–May 20, 1979:** *Contemporary Drawings: Philadelphia II*, Philadelphia Museum of Art. Catalogue. Exhibited works (Part I): *After Hogarth, Backyard, After Adrian Brouwer*, and *Seated Nude Female Figure* (all 1978, graphite).

## 1979

**December 7:** Panelist, "Artists Talk on Art Forum, Figurative Art—A Dialogue with Four Generations," Landmark Gallery, New York. Moderator: Robert Godfrey. Other panelists: John Benton, George Hildrew, and Alice Neel.

SOLO EXHIBITION

**October 6–27:** *Larry Day: Paintings and Drawings, 1978–1979*, Gross McCleaf Gallery. Announcement card features *Construction Site* (plate 68).

## 1980

**March 29:** Receives Temple University General Alumni Association Certificate of Honor for Contributions to His Profession, representing Tyler School of Art.

SOLO EXHIBITION

**October 24–November 9:** *Larry Day: Drawings and Watercolors*, Gross McCleaf Gallery.

GROUP EXHIBITIONS

**July 22–August 4:** *Summer in the City Philadelphia Style: Urban Landscapes and Points of View*, Gross McCleaf Gallery. Works by twelve artists.

**August 5–15:** *Color and Watercolor*, Gross McCleaf Gallery. Works by sixteen artists.

## 1980–89

Senior critic, University of Pennsylvania Graduate School of Fine Arts. Intermittent; specific dates given below when known.

## 1981

**Spring:** Presents University of the Arts's Honorary Doctor of Fine Arts degree to art historian Leo Steinberg.

SOLO EXHIBITION

**October 23–November 9:** *Larry Day: Paintings and Drawings, 1980–1981*, Gross McCleaf Gallery.

GROUP EXHIBITIONS

**March 8–April 19:** *Broad Spectrum: Artists Who Teach at the Philadelphia College of Art*, Allentown Art Museum, Pennsylvania. Travels to the University Art Gallery, University of Pittsburgh; and the William Penn Memorial Museum, Harrisburg (now the State Museum of Pennsylvania). Catalogue. Exhibited work: *Underpass* (1978, oil).

**May 15–June 8:** *Eight Artists: Works on Paper*, Gross McCleaf Gallery. Other exhibitors: Howard, Leonard, Rose Naftulin, Julie Pease, Piper, Doris Staffel, and Seymour Remenick.

## 1982

**June:** Receives the Hazlett Memorial Award for Excellence in the Arts from the Governor's Office, Pennsylvania, and a Citation for Excellence from the Pennsylvania House of Representatives.

**July:** Teaches at the Center for Environmental Teaching and Research, Queens College, Caumsett State Park, Huntington, New York.

SOLO EXHIBITION

**October 20–November 6:** *Larry Day: Paintings and Drawings, 1972–1982*, Gross McCleaf Gallery. Announcement card features *Heidelberg Park* (plate 81).

GROUP EXHIBITIONS

**February 3–23:** *Invitational Exhibition*, Charlotte Crosby Kemper Gallery, Kansas City Art Institute, Missouri. Works on paper by artists selected by Kansas City Art Institute faculty.

**April 1–29:** *Recent Paintings: Larry Day, Eileen Goodman, Humbert Howard, Rose Naftulin, and Doris Staffel*, Hahnemann Medical College (later Hahnemann University), Philadelphia (now closed).

**May 22–June 30:** *The [1982] Hazlett Memorial Awards Exhibition for the Visual Arts*, Southern Alleghenies Museum of Art, Loretto, Pennsylvania. Travels to Westmoreland County Museum of Art and Allentown Art Museum. Catalogue. Nineteen paintings and works on paper.

**July 11** (closes): *18th Juried Exhibition*, Allentown Art Museum. Catalogue. Exhibited work: *Delancey II* (1981, oil).

## 1982–83

**December 17, 1982–February 20, 1983:** *Perspectives on Contemporary American Realism: Works of Art on Paper from the Collection of Jalane and Richard Davidson*, PAFA. Travels to the Art Institute of Chicago. Catalogue. Exhibited work: *Backyard* (1977, graphite and wash).

## c. 1982–86

Advisor, Artists' Choice Museum, New York.

## 1983

**October 1:** Marries Ruth Fine.

SOLO EXHIBITION

**October 26–November 12:** *Larry Day: Paintings and Drawings*, Gross McCleaf Gallery. Catalogue. Seven works.

GROUP EXHIBITIONS

**January 10–February 6:** *Tyler School of Art Painting and Sculpture Alumni Invitational*, Tyler School of Art, Temple University, Elkins Park. Catalogue. Exhibited work: *22nd Street* (1983, oil).

**Summer:** *Director's Choice*, Gross McCleaf Gallery.

**October 22–December 14:** *Affects/Effects 2: Work by the Faculty of Philadelphia College of Art*, Philadelphia College of Art. Catalogue. Exhibited work: *Interior* (1979, oil).

## 1984

**January:** Elected to the 100 Club of distinguished alumni in the centennial year of Cheltenham High School.

**February:** Receives Ingram Merrill Foundation grant.

**Spring:** Diagnosed with bladder cancer, the first of several battles with various cancers over next fourteen years.

**Summer:** Spends a month at Long Beach Island, New Jersey, recuperating from cancer treatment.

SOLO EXHIBITIONS

**March 20–April 6:** *Larry Day, Recent Work*, Hahnemann University Gallery.

**December 5–22:** *Larry Day: Drawings*, Gross McCleaf Gallery.

GROUP EXHIBITIONS

**Dates unknown:** *Annual Exhibition*, National Academy of Arts and Letters, New York.

**March 5–April 1:** *Paintings and Sculpture by Candidates for Art Awards*, American Academy and Institute of Arts and Letters Art Galleries, New York. Catalogue. Works exhibited: *22nd Street* and *Rue* (both 1983, oil).

**July 9–27:** *Director's Choice 1984*, Gross McCleaf Gallery. Works by twenty-one artists.

**September 16–October 28:** *Painter's Choice: New Talent*, Woodmere Art Museum, Philadelphia. Works by twenty-two artists. Day's choice is Signe Sundberg (later known as Signe Sundberg-Hall).

**November 17–December 30:** *Artists' Choice Museum: The First Eight Years*, Artists' Choice Museum. Catalogue. Exhibited work: *Building Reflected* (1982, oil).

## 1985

Moves to Takoma Park, Maryland. Will remain there through 1995.

**August 1:** Critic, Queens College Summer Program, Caumsett State Park.

**[Fall?:]** Critic, University of Pennsylvania Fine Arts Department (intermittently through 1989).

SOLO EXHIBITIONS

**February 17–March 21:** *Larry Day: Paintings and Drawings*, Rider College Art Gallery, Lawrenceville, New Jersey.

**June 12–28:** *Larry Day: Paintings of the 50s and 60s*, Gross McCleaf Gallery. Announcement card features *Sombre Figuration* (1958, oil).

GROUP EXHIBITIONS

**Dates unknown:** *Tyler School of Art Painting and Sculpture Alumni Invitational*, Tyler School of Art.

**April 21–May 19:** *Honorees Exhibit*, Tyler Alumni Gallery (inaugural exhibition), The Diamond Club, Mitten Hall, Temple University, Philadelphia. Works by twelve artists.

**Fall:** *City Views: Panoramas to Particulars, Works from the CIGNA Collection*, CIGNA Corporation Office, Philadelphia. Catalogue. Exhibited work: *Delancey #2* (1981, oil).

## 1985–86

GROUP EXHIBITION

**December 3, 1985–January 4, 1986:** *Survival of the Fittest II: Figurative Works on Paper*, Ingber Gallery, New York.

## 1986

Legally changes name from Lawrence James del Giorno to Lawrence James Day.

**April 17:** Speaker, *Choices: Issues in Representing the Human Face* seminar, held in conjunction with the exhibition *The Human Face*, Rider College Art Gallery (see below).

**July 24:** Critic, Queens College Summer Program, Caumsett State Park.

SOLO EXHIBITION

**May 2–20:** *Larry Day: New Paintings and Drawings*, Gross McCleaf Gallery.

GROUP EXHIBITIONS

**February 3–28:** *Seven Philadelphia Artists Draw: Larry Day, Doris Staffel, Sidney Goodman, Maurie Kerrigan, David Kettner, Keith Ragone, Susan Pasquarelli*, Hicks Art Center Gallery, Bucks County Community College, Newtown, Pennsylvania.

**April 6–25:** *The Human Face*, Rider College Art Gallery. Curated by Boris Putterman. Works by twelve artists.

**September 16–October 11:** *Challenge Exhibitions, 1986–1987, Jurors' Exhibition*, Samuel S. Fleisher Art Memorial, Philadelphia. Other exhibitors: Moe Brooker, Simkin, and Judith Joy Ross.

## 1987

**March–November:** Guest critic, University of Pennsylvania.

**October:** Lends *22nd Street (Buried City)* (1983, oil) to the Art in Embassies Program for exhibition at the American Embassy in Tunis, Tunisia (through February 1991).

SOLO EXHIBITION

**March 24–April 18:** *People and Places: Paintings and Drawings by Larry Day*, Jane Haslem Gallery (later Jane Haslem, then Jane Haslem Salon), Washington, DC.

GROUP EXHIBITIONS

**January 27–February 21:** *Foreshadow: Day, Mentzer, Balance, Hendrick, Stanczak, Johnson, Webb, Friedman*, Jane Haslem Gallery.

**March 2–29:** *Paintings and Sculpture by Candidates for Art Awards*, American Academy and Institute of Arts and Letters Art Galleries.

**October 23–November 29:** *American Drawings: Realism/Idealism*, Boca Raton Museum of Art, Florida. Organized by Jane Haslem. Catalogue. Exhibited works: *Jan Steen Suite #1* (1986, graphite), *Jan Steen Suite #2* (1986, graphite), *Portrait of a Young Woman I* (1985, medium unknown), and *Portrait of a Young Woman II* (1985, medium unknown).

## 1987–88

GROUP EXHIBITIONS

**December 1, 1987–January 14, 1988** (probably; possibly 1988–89): *fan-fare, n.: 1. spectacular display*, Jane Haslem Gallery and Jane Haslem Salon. Works by thirty-seven artists.

**December 11, 1987–February 28, 1988:** *Realism Today: American Drawings from the Rita Rich Collection*, National Academy of Design, New York. Travels to Smith College Museum of Art, Northampton, Massachusetts; the Arkansas Arts Center, Little Rock; and the Butler Institute of American Art, Youngstown, Ohio. Catalogue. Exhibited work: *Backyards* (1976–77, graphite and wash).

## 1988

**May:** Retires from teaching at the University of the Arts. The Larry Day Scholarship Award in Painting is established (continues today). Receives Mayor's Award for Contributions to the Cultural Life of the City of Philadelphia.

**September** (probably): Attends first of several reunions of his World War II 506th Antiaircraft Artillery Gun Battalion, Lancaster, Pennsylvania.

**November:** Receives Penny McCall Foundation Grant, nominated by Rafael Ferrer.

SOLO EXHIBITIONS

**April 27–May 16:** *Larry Day: Recent Drawings*, Gross McCleaf Gallery.

**April 30–May 23:** *Larry Day: Drawings and Watercolors, 1953–1988*, The Hunt Room, University of the Arts. Announcement card features *In the Studio: Self-Portrait with Ruth*.

**May 3–June 4:** *Larry Day, Paintings: 1958–1988*, Jane Haslem Gallery. Catalogue, with text "Larry Day: A Conversation with Ruth Fine." Eleven works.

GROUP EXHIBITION

**September 11–October 22:** *Consonance: Watercolors and Pastels*, Jane Haslem Salon. Catalogue. Exhibited work: *Industrial Area* (1982, watercolor).

## 1989

**Spring:** Visiting critic, University of Pennsylvania Graduate School of Fine Arts.

**September:** Reunion of World War II Battalion, Marietta, Ohio.

**October:** Cancer surgery and monthlong recovery at Johns Hopkins Hospital, Baltimore.

SOLO EXHIBITIONS

**April 5–22:** *Larry Day*, Gross McCleaf Gallery.

**June 7–July 1:** *Larry Day: The Salome Variations*, main ground-floor gallery, Jane Haslem Salon.

**June 7–July 1:** *Larry Day: Paintings and Drawings after Earlier Masters*, second-floor galleries, Jane Haslem Salon.

GROUP EXHIBITIONS

**January 10–February 3:** *Drawing: Points of View*, Belk Art Gallery, Western Carolina University, Cullowhee, North Carolina. Catalogue. Exhibited work: *After Puget* (1987, graphite).

**May 6–27:** *Landscape Is Real Estate: Recent Paintings, Larry Day, William Dunlap, Sarah McCoubrey, Mary Anne Reilly*, Robert Brown Contemporary Art, Washington, DC.

**Summer:** *National Invitational Drawing Exhibition*, Norman R. Eppink Art Gallery, Emporia State University, Kansas. Two-year tour, circulated by ExhibitsUSA, a division of Mid-America Arts Alliance. Travels to State Fair Community College, Sedalia, Missouri; Central Missouri State University, Warrensburg; Kendall School of Design, Grand Rapids, Michigan; Polk County Heritage Gallery, Des Moines; Albrecht Art Museum, St. Joseph, Missouri; Baylor University, Waco, Texas; Indiana State University, Terre Haute; and possibly other venues. Catalogue. Exhibited work: *Group* (1988, graphite). Exhibition includes one artist from each state, plus Washington, DC; Day represents Maryland.

## 1990

**September 6–8:** Reunion of World War II Battalion, Cumberland, Maryland.

**September 10:** Letter from the National Portrait Gallery, Washington, DC, requests slides of his work for their files. Day responds that he does not consider himself a portrait painter and would not be interested in "doing anything in that vein."

**October:** Receives the Oscar Williams and Gene Derwood Award for excellence among poets and artists.

**November 13:** Visiting critic, PAFA.

SOLO EXHIBITION

**Dates unknown:** *Larry Day: Paintings*, The More Gallery, Philadelphia.

GROUP EXHIBITIONS

**February 17–March 24:** *Recent Paintings: Larry Day, Hayes Friedman, Linda Hendrick, Billy Morrow Jackson*, Jane Haslem.

**March 27–May 4:** *Washington Genre Paintings: Davenport Day Fletcher Folsom and Hendrick*, Jane Haslem. Brochure, with texts and illustrations by each artist; Day's work: *Backyard #1* (1991, graphite).

**March 28–April 19:** *Selected Washington Artists Approaching the Figure Part II: Figure Groups and Genre Scenes in Paintings, Drawings, and Prints*, Fine Arts Gallery, Georgetown University, Washington, DC. Catalogue. Exhibited work: *Changes* (plate 19).

**April 19–May 18:** *A View from Baltimore to Washington*, Fine Arts Gallery, Department of Visual Arts, University of Maryland, Baltimore County, Baltimore. Works by twelve artists.

**May 25–July 4:** *Landscape Painting, 1960–1990: The Italian Tradition in American Art*, Gibbes Museum of Art, Charleston, South Carolina. Travels to the Bayly Museum of Art, University of Virginia, Charlottesville. Catalogue. Exhibited works: *Spring Avenue* (1963–64, oil), *Back Street II* (1988, oil), and *City Tree* (plate 77)

## 1991

**September:** Reunion of World War II Battalion, Erie, Pennsylvania.

## 1991–92

TWO-PERSON EXHIBITION

**December 12, 1991–January 8, 1992:** *John Gintoff, Photographs; Larry Day, Drawings*, The More Gallery.

## 1992

**May:** Elected Associate Academician, National Academy of Design.

**Fall:** Visiting scholar, Western Carolina University.

**September 10–12:** Reunion of World War II Battalion, Hagerstown, Maryland.

**October 28:** Meets with students and presents the Daryl Reich Rubenstein Memorial Lecture, Sidwell Friends School, Washington, DC, in conjunction with *Larry Day*, Kogod Arts Center, Sidwell Friends School (see below).

**December 5:** Panelist, "Pluralism: Divergent Modes," PAFA, presented in association with Advanta and *US Artists—Exposition of American Art*.

SOLO EXHIBITIONS

**January 11–February 5:** *Larry Day: Paintings*, The More Gallery. Exhibition announcement features *Lost World* (1990, oil; related).

**February 15–March 24:** *Larry Day, Encounters: Interpretations*, Jane Haslem Gallery. Catalogue, with nine works on paper after earlier masters.

**October 27–November 22:** *Larry Day*, Kogod Arts Center.

GROUP EXHIBITION

**November 2–December 11:** *Urban Spaces: Larry Day, Rudy Burckhardt, Kathryn Wall*, Belk Art Gallery. Catalogue, with five works by Day.

## 1993

Receives grant from the Richard Florsheim Art Fund in support of forthcoming exhibition catalogue *Tempi del Giorno: Eighteen Drawings by Larry Day*.

Represented by Salander-O'Reilly Galleries, New York (through 1998).

**September 9–11:** Reunion of World War II Battalion, Hagerstown.

GROUP EXHIBITIONS

**April 1–May 2:** *168th Annual Exhibition*, National Academy of Design. Catalogue. Exhibited work: *Self-Portraits (A Fable of Identity)* (date and medium unknown).

**July 30–December 5:** *Contemporary Self-Portraits from the James Goode Collection*, National Portrait Gallery. Catalogue. Exhibited work: *Changes* (plate 19).

## 1994

**February 16:** Gallery talk, "An Evening of Art and Music," Rider College Art Gallery. Followed by trio performance of music by Aaron Copland and Ned Rorem.

**May:** Elected Academician, National Academy of Design.

**November 2:** Panelist, "The Self in Contemporary Narrative Painting," National Academy of Design. Moderator: Raoul Middleman. Other panelists: Rosemarie Beck, Louis Finkelstein, Paul Georges, and Gabriel Laderman.

SOLO EXHIBITIONS

**January 27–February 20:** *Larry Day: Paintings and Drawings*, Rider College Art Gallery. Announcement card and exhibition poster feature *Tree in the City* (plate 77).

**January 27–February 20:** *Tempi del Giorno: Eighteen Drawings by Larry Day*, Rider College Art Gallery. Co-organized by Belk Art Gallery. Travels to Belk Art Gallery; Arronson Gallery, Haviland Hall, University of the Arts; Carleton College, Northfield, Minnesota; West Virginia Wesleyan College, Buckhannon; and other venues. Catalogue. Exhibited works: *Tempi del Giorno* series (1992–93, graphite), now in the permanent collection of the Philadelphia Museum of Art,

**October 14–November 18:** *Drawings by Larry Day*, Arronson Gallery.

## 1995

**January 7:** Lecture, in conjunction with the exhibition *Two Approaches to the Figure*, Philadelphia Art Alliance (see below).

**January 14:** Symposium, *The Self in Print and Word*, in conjunction with the exhibition *Tempi del Giorno*, Carleton College; Day is unable to attend but sends a paper to be read in his absence: "What Happens to the Painted World When the Artist's Presence Is Involved (Seen as Opposed to Felt)? What about Narcissus?"

**February 17–19:** Fiftieth anniversary reunion of combat veterans of Iwo Jima, Washington, DC.

**May:** Returns to Elkins Park. He will live at 900 Valley Road for the last three years of his life.

TWO-PERSON EXHIBITIONS

**January 6–February 26:** *Two Approaches to the Figure: Larry Day and Frank Hyder*, Philadelphia Art Alliance.

**January 13–February 26:** *Two Approaches to the Figure: Larry Day and Frank Hyder*, The More Gallery.

## 1996

**April:** Joins Tyler School of Art Alumni Association Board.

**May 8–9:** Visiting critic, Knox College, Galesburg, Illinois.

**July 2:** Lecture, University of the Arts.

GROUP EXHIBITIONS

**January 26–February 18:** *Art in the Area: Members of the Faculty of Philadelphia's University of the Arts Who Live in Our Community*, Cheltenham Center for the Arts.

**February 18–March 16:** *Smith College Invitational Drawing Exhibition*, Hillyer Hall, Smith College. Works by seventy-seven artists.

**April 3–30:** *Contemporary Figurative Works*, The More Gallery. Works by eleven artists.

**June 1–July 14:** *Artist-Select-Artist*, Trenton Artists Workshop Association, Trenton City Museum at Ellarslie Mansion, New Jersey. Invited by Harry Naar. Works by twenty artists.

## 1997

**February:** Completes *Elegies (Homage to Rilke)*, now in the permanent collection of the Rhode Island School of Design Museum, Providence (plates 46–55).

**October 28:** Lecture, "Paintings of My Life," University of the Arts.

## 1998

**April 14:** Dies in Abington Hospital, Pennsylvania.

**June 11:** Memorial service, University of the Arts; *Elegies (Homage to Rilke)* on view in the CBS Auditorium.

GROUP EXHIBITIONS

**January 14–March 6:** *Pennsylvania Treasures I*, Esther Klein Art Gallery, University City Science Center, Philadelphia. Works by twenty-five artists.

**April 2–25:** *About Drawing*, Edward Cain Galleries, Port Townsend, Washington. Works by seven artists.

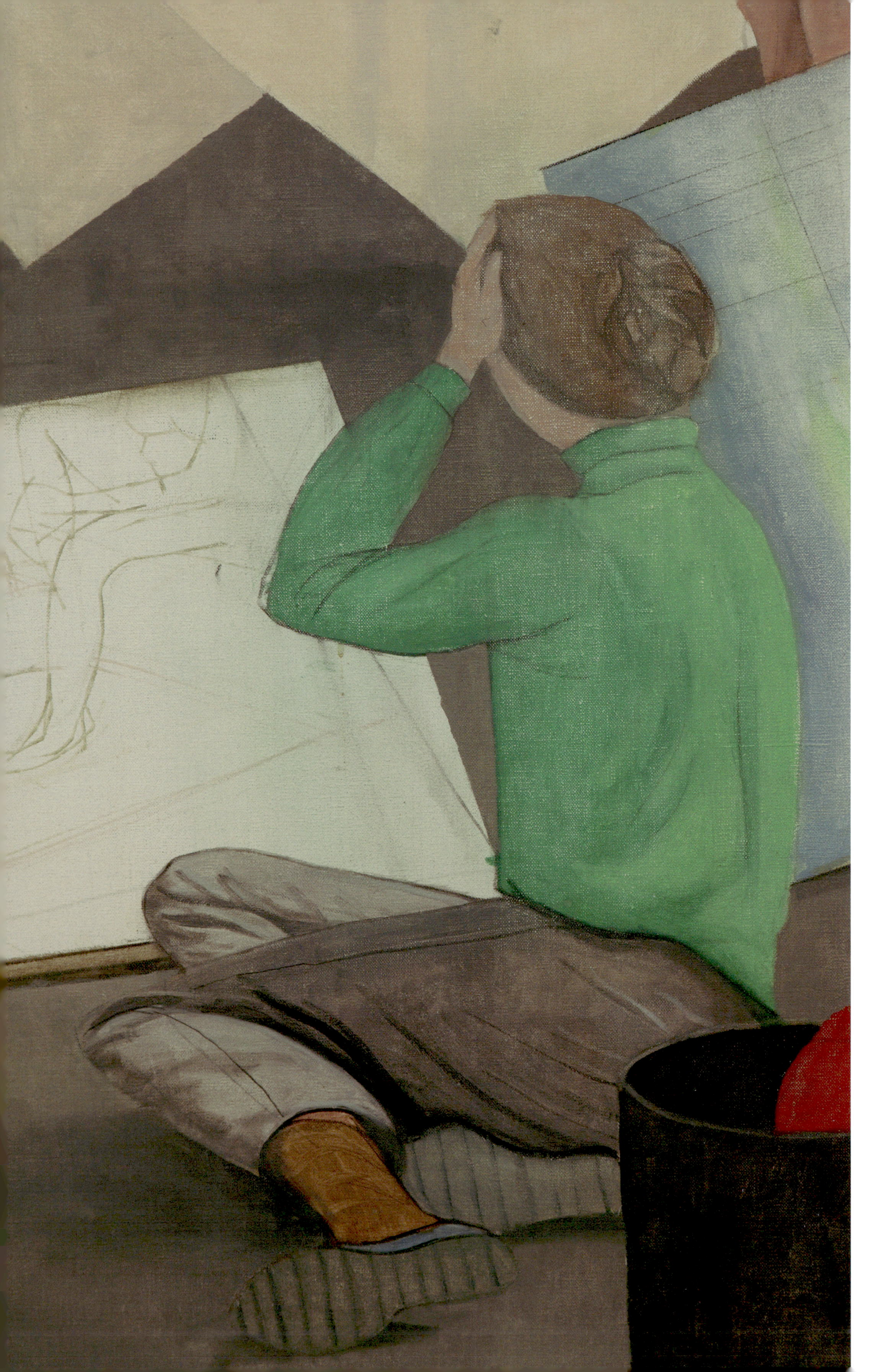

# Checklist of the Exhibition

As of May 13, 2021

This checklist chronologically integrates works on view at the three Philadelphia venues: Woodmere Art Museum, Arcadia University, and the University of the Arts. Works on view at Woodmere are preceded by one asterisk (*), at Arcadia by two asterisks (**), and at UArts by three asterisks (***).

Titles are thought to have been those initially assigned by the artist, followed by "also known as" titles. Titles in parenthesis are posthumously assigned by Ruth Fine, the artist's widow. Works developed over time are listed in the year of completion. Size refers to the full support (canvas or paper) unless otherwise noted; paper types are given when known. If supplied by the artist, edition size is noted for prints. This may be given as a fraction, the numerator of which is the number of the exhibited example, the denominator indicating the intended size of the edition. It is not confirmed that Day printed the full proposed edition.

Not all works in the exhibition are illustrated in this volume; plate references are given for those that are illustrated.

** *(Head 1)*, c. 1950
Lithograph on paper, edition 2/2, 14⅞ × 12¼ in. (irregular)
Lent by Woodmere Art Museum, Promised Gift of the Larry Day Art Trust
Plate 82

** *(Head 2)*, c. 1950
Lithograph on paper, edition of at least 9, 15⅞ × 11⅜ in.
Lent by Woodmere Art Museum, Promised Gift of the Larry Day Art Trust

** *(Head 4)*, c. 1950
Linoleum cut on Atlantic Ledger paper, 11 × 8½ in.
Lent by Woodmere Art Museum, Promised Gift of the Larry Day Art Trust
Plate 83

** *New Orleans*, 1951
Pen and ink on paper, 11 × 8½ in.
Lent by Woodmere Art Museum, Gift of the Larry Day Art Trust in honor of Anne Standish, 2021

** *Head*, 1953
Opaque watercolor and ink on paper, 15¾ × 17 in. (irregular)
Lent by Woodmere Art Museum, Promised Gift of the Larry Day Art Trust in honor of Gretchen Dykstra

** *(Head 5)*, c. 1953
Oil monotype on newsprint paper, sheet 11¼ × 9 in. (irregular)
Lent by Woodmere Art Museum, Promised Gift of the Larry Day Art Trust in honor of Lucy Medrich

*** *(Abstract Figure)*, c. 1955
Opaque watercolor and graphite on paper,
13⅞ × 11¹⁄₁₆ in.
Lent by Woodmere Art Museum, Gift of
the Larry Day Art Trust in honor of Michael
Ciervo, 2020
Plate 3

*** *(Abstract Figure [Natalie Charkow?]),*
c. 1955
Oil on canvas, 48 × 28 in.
Lent by Woodmere Art Museum, Gift of
Natalie Charkow Hollander, 2020
Plate 2

** *Kneeling Angel*, c. 1955
Lithograph on Basingwerk parchment paper,
edition 10/10, 17 × 12¼ in.
Lent by Woodmere Art Museum, Promised
Gift of the Larry Day Art Trust

** *(Kneeling Angel)*, c. 1955
Monotype on paper, 9⅛ × 6¾ in.
Lent by Woodmere Art Museum, Promised
Gift of the Larry Day Art Trust in honor of
Amanda Monroe

*** *Landscape for St. John of the Cross*, 1955
Oil on canvas, 48 × 60 in.
Lent by Woodmere Art Museum, Gift of Anita
and Armand Mednick, 2020
Plate 92

*** *Landscape*, c. 1955
Graphite on paper, 9 × 11 in.
Lent by Woodmere Art Museum, Gift of Peter
Paone, 2011

*** *(Landscape)*, c. 1955
Oil on canvas, 26 × 36 in.
Lent by Woodmere Art Museum, Museum
purchase, 2012

* *(Landscape with Tree)*, c. 1955
Pen and ink and wash on paper, 16 × 20 in.
Woodmere Art Museum, Gift of the Larry Day
Art Trust in honor of Rick Ortwein, 2021

** *Sacred and Profane*, c. 1955
Graphite on paper, 23¼ × 29 in.
Lent by Woodmere Art Museum, Promised
Gift of the Larry Day Art Trust in honor of
Matthew Borgen
Plate 86

** *Sacred and Profane, State 1*, c. 1955
Lithograph on Basingwerk parchment paper,
20 × 26 in.
Lent by Woodmere Art Museum, Promised
Gift of the Larry Day Art Trust in honor of
Larry Brooks
Plate 87

** *Sacred and Profane, State 2*, c. 1955
Lithograph in gray-violet ink on Basingwerk
parchment paper, 20 × 26 in.
Lent by Woodmere Art Museum, Promised
Gift of the Larry Day Art Trust in honor of
Joe Pompilii

** *Standing Angel*, c. 1955
Oil on canvas, 36 × 30 in.
Lent by Woodmere Art Museum, Promised
gift of the Larry Day Art Trust in honor of
Richard Torchia
Plate 88

** *Standing Angel, State 1*, c. 1955
Lithograph on Basingwerk parchment paper,
26 × 20 in.
Lent by Woodmere Art Museum, Promised
Gift of the Larry Day Art Trust

** *Standing Angel, State 2*, c. 1955
Color lithograph on Basingwerk parchment
paper, 26 × 20 in.
Lent by Woodmere Art Museum, Promised
Gift of the Larry Day Art Trust
Plate 89

** *(Abstract Landscape)*, c. 1956
Lithograph on Basingwerk parchment paper,
20 × 26 in.
Lent by Woodmere Art Museum, Promised
Gift of the Larry Day Art Trust
Plate 84

* *Journey*, 1956
Oil on canvas, 38¾ × 44½ in.
Woodmere Art Museum: Promised gift of
Adele Fine
Plate 5

** *(Abstract Landscape with Tree, State 2),*
c. 1956
Etching and aquatint on paper, plate 11⅝ ×
14⅝ in., sheet 16½ × 19¼ in.
Lent by Woodmere Art Museum, Promised
Gift of the Larry Day Art Trust

** *(Abstract Landscape with Tree, State 2),*
c. 1956
Etching and aquatint printed relief on paper,
plate 11⅞ × 15 in., sheet 12 × 18 in.
Lent by Woodmere Art Museum, Promised
Gift of the Larry Day Art Trust
Plate 85

** *(Abstract Landscape with Tree, State 3),*
c. 1956
Etching and aquatint on unbleached Arnold
paper, plate 11½ × 14¾ in., sheet 15¼ × 22½ in.
Lent by Woodmere Art Museum, Promised
Gift of the Larry Day Art Trust

*** *Untitled (with Green and Yellow),*
c. 1956
Opaque watercolor and graphite on paper,
17 × 13⅝ in.
Lent by Woodmere Art Museum, Gift of the
Larry Day Art Trust in honor of Emily Myles,
2020

*** *Untitled (with Green)*, c. 1956
Opaque watercolor, ink, and graphite on
paper, 16⅞ × 14⅛ in.
Lent by Woodmere Art Museum, Gift of the
Larry Day Art Trust in honor of Stephanie
Cehelsky, 2020

*** *Untitled*, c. 1956
Opaque watercolor and graphite on paper,
15⅜ × 14⅛ in.
Lent by Woodmere Art Museum, Gift of the
Larry Day Art Trust in honor of Margo Dolan
and Peter Maxwell, 2020

*** *(Abstraction)*, c. 1958
Oil on canvas, 43 × 38 in.
Lent by Jan Baltzell
Plate 41

*** *Abstraction*, c. 1958
Oil on canvas, 42 × 37¾ in.
Lent by Woodmere Art Museum, Gift of Anita
and Armand Mednick, 2020

* *Abstraction*, c. 1958
Oil on canvas, 51 × 59¼ in.
Woodmere Art Museum, Gift of Natalie Char-
kow Hollander, 2020
Plate 6

** *Rain in Spain (Artist Proof)*, c. 1958
Etching on Fabriano paper, plate 12 ×
14⅞ in., sheet 14 × 19⅛ in.
Printed by Jerome Kaplan
Lent by Woodmere Art Museum, Promised
gift of the Larry Day Art Trust in honor of
Sarah Spencer

*** *Sombre Figuration*, 1958
Oil on canvas, 47 × 41 in.
Lent by Private Collection

** *The Venus Worship, State 2*, c. 1958
Etching on paper, edition of 8, plate 11¾ ×
17⅞ in., sheet 14⅛ × 21 in.
Lent by Woodmere Art Museum, Promised
gift of the Larry Day Art Trust

*** *To Pergamon*, 1958–59
Oil on canvas, 47¾ × 60 in.
Lent by Woodmere Art Museum, Gift of
Natalie Charkow Hollander, 2020
Plate 4

*** *Various Asides*, c. 1958
Oil on canvas, 34 × 27½ in.
Lent by Woodmere Art Museum, Gift of
Gregory and Candace Wilkin, 2017

*** *Wiegenlied*, 1958
Oil on canvas, 60¾ × 54 in.
Lent by the Larry Day Art Trust

*** *After Old Master*, late 1950s
Pen and ink on paper, 27⅞ × 17¼ in.
Lent by Woodmere Art Museum, Gift of
the Larry Day Art Trust in honor of Sally
Larson, 2020
Plate 61

* *Seated Woman*, late 1950s
Opaque watercolor and ink on board,
23⅜ × 17½ in.
Woodmere Art Museum, Gift of Ron
Rumford, 2005

*** *Aspen Variation*, c. 1960
Watercolor on paper from watercolor
block, 18⅛ × 24 in.
Lent by Woodmere Art Museum, Gift of the
Larry Day Trust in honor of Catherine and
William Daley, 2020
Plate 90

*** *Aspen Variation*, c. 1960
Watercolor on paper, 18½ × 24 in.
Lent by Woodmere Art Museum, Gift of
the Larry Day Art Trust in honor of Amanda
Higdon, 2020

*** *(Landscape)*, c. 1960
Watercolor on paper, 18⅛ × 23⅞ in.
Lent by Private Collection
Plate 91

*** *Untitled*, c. 1960
Oil on canvas, 82 × 72 in.
Lent by Woodmere Art Museum, Gift of
Ruth Fine, 2016
Plate 40

* *After Jan Steen*, 1962
Oil on canvas, 58½ × 48 in.
Woodmere Art Museum, Gift of Ruth Fine
in honor of William R. Valerio, 2020
Plate 7

*** *Donatello Variations*, c. 1962
Pen and ink and wash, 60 × 36 in.
(21 mounted works on paper, each 14¼ ×
19⅞ in.)
Lent by Private Collection

*** *After Veronese*, c. 1963
Pen and ink and wash on paper, 16 × 12 in.
Lent by Woodmere Art Museum, Gift of
Ruth Fine in honor of Sid Sachs, 2020
Plate 60

* *The Bridge Game*, c. 1963
Pen and ink on paper mounted to board by
the artist, 7½ × 8 in.
Lent by Private Collection
Plate 102

* *The Bridge Game*, c. 1963
Pen and ink on paper, 12⅛ × 18⅛ in.
Woodmere Art Museum, Gift of the
Larry Day Art Trust in honor of Michael
DeGennaro, 2021

* *The Bridge Game*, c. 1963
Pen and black ink and black and brown
wash on paper, 10⅝ × 13⅜ in.
Woodmere Art Museum, Gift of the Larry
Day Art Trust in honor of Stephen Kerzner,
2021
Plate 103

* *Mrs. Myers*, 1964
Oil on canvas, 46 × 42¼ in.
Woodmere Art Museum, Gift of the Gladys
Myers Estate, 2020
Plate 93

* *Games*, 1967
Oil on canvas, 75½ × 69 in.
Lent by Mark Showell Interiors
Plate 1

* *Group*, 1967
Oil on canvas, 64¼ × 79 in.
Lent by the Pennsylvania Academy of the
Fine Arts, Philadelphia, Bequest of the
artist, 1999.8
Plate 13

* *In the Studio, study for "Group,"*
c. 1967
Graphite on paper, 18 × 23 in.
Lent by the Pennsylvania Academy of the
Fine Arts, Philadelphia, Gift of Ruth Fine,
2019.20.3
Plate 15

* *Untitled, study for "Group,"* c. 1967
Watercolor and graphite on paper, 14⅝ ×
10¾ in.
Lent by the Pennsylvania Academy of the
Fine Arts, Philadelphia, Gift of Ruth Fine,
2019.20.1
Plate 14

* *Miss Charkow and Mrs. Melnicoff*,
c. 1967
Oil on canvas, 39 × 39 in.
Woodmere Art Museum, Gift of Claudia
Raab and Natalie Charkow Hollander, 2013
Plate 16

* *Narrative: To the Memory of Matteo
Giovannetti*, 1967
Oil on canvas, 65½ × 76⅜ in.
Woodmere Art Museum, Gift of Ruth Fine
in honor of Irving and Miriam Brown Fine,
2020
Plate 96

* *Related to "Narrative: To the Memory
of Matteo Giovannetti,"* c. 1967
Watercolor and graphite on paper, 20⅛ ×
26 in.

Woodmere Art Museum, Gift of Ruth Fine in honor of David Bindman, 2021
Plate 97

* *Study for "Narrative: To the Memory of Matteo Giovannetti,"* 1967
Oil on canvas, 13¾ × 20⅛ in.
Woodmere Art Museum, Gift of Ruth Fine in honor of Adele Fine and Dr. Burton Ginsberg, 2021

* *The Venus Society: An Entertainment in Eight Episodes,* c. 1967
*The Foundation*
*The Establishment of Ritual*
*The Discovery of Another Society*
*The Other Society's Base*
*The Struggle for the Uncommitted*
*The Search, Atonement*
*The Merger*
*The Dance*
Watercolor and graphite on paper, each 20¹¹⁄₁₆ × 29¹¹⁄₁₆ in.
Lent by the Rhode Island School of Design Museum, Gift of Ruth Fine in honor of Lora Urbanelli, 2005
Plates 24–31

* *A Game of Charades* (aka *Charades*), 1967/1969
Oil on canvas, 68½ × 78¼ in.
Lent by the Larry Day Art Trust
Plate 98

* *Related to "A Game of Charades,"* c. 1969
Pen and ink and wash on paper, 17⅝ × 20¾ in.
Lent by the Larry Day Art Trust
Plate 99

* *After Poussin,* c. 1970
Pen and ink on paper, 13¾ × 21½ in.
Woodmere Art Museum, Promised gift of Pamela and Joseph Yohlin
Plate 63

* *After Titian,* c. 1970
Pen and ink on paper, 13½ × 16½ in.
Woodmere Art Museum, Promised gift of Pamela and Joseph Yohlin
Plate 62

** *(Center City),* c. 1970
Pen and brown ink and wash on paper, 11 × 11 in.
Lent by Woodmere Art Museum, Gift of the Larry Day Art Trust in honor of Judith Thomas, 2021
Plate 35

** *(Curtis Arboretum),* c. 1970
Pen and wash and brown ink, 16 × 20 in.
Lent by Private Collection
Plate 100

** *(Factory),* c. 1970
Graphite on paper, 20 × 26 in.
Lent by Michael Rossman
Plate 94

** *(Hotel),* c. 1970
Watercolor and graphite on paper, 15 × 21⅜ in.
Lent by Woodmere Art Museum, Gift of the Larry Day Art Trust in honor of Tessa Bachi Haas, 2021

* *Poker Game,* 1970
Oil on canvas, 60½ × 72¼ in.
Woodmere Art Museum, Gift of Ruth Fine, 1999
Plate 11

* *Poker Game,* c. 1970
Graphite on paper, 19¼ × 25 in.
Woodmere Art Museum, Gift of Armand Mednick, 2012
Plate 105

* *(Poker Game),* c. 1970
Pen and ink on paper, 13½ × 17 in.
Woodmere Art Museum, Gift of Ruth Fine in honor of Laura Heemer, 2021

* *(Poker Game),* c. 1970
Pen and ink on paper, 13½ × 17 in.
Woodmere Art Museum, Gift of Ruth Fine in honor of Rachel Hruszkewycz, 2021

* *(Poker Game),* c. 1970
Pen and ink on paper, 13½ × 17 in.
Woodmere Art Museum, Gift of Ruth Fine in honor of Christina Warhola, 2021

* *(Poker Game),* c. 1970
Watercolor on paper, 12 × 16 in.
Lent by Jamie Wyper
Plate 12

** *Related to "Terrace,"* c. 1970
Watercolor and graphite on paper, 8⅝ × 7½ in.
Lent by the Larry Day Art Trust
Plate 76

* *(Couples),* c. 1970
Graphite on paper, 20 × 23 in.
Woodmere Art Museum, Promised gift of Adele Fine
Plate 17

* *Heidelberg Park,* 1972
Oil on canvas, 66 × 78 in.
Lent by Ann Beattie and Lincoln Perry
Plate 81

* *Harry's Class,* 1972–73
Oil on canvas, 60 × 72 in.
Lent by the Larry Day Art Trust
Plate 36

* *Conversation Piece I,* 1973–74
Oil on canvas, 60 × 72½ in.
Lent by Private Collection
Plate 18

* *Picnic (Outing: Homage to Le Nain),* 1970–75
Oil on canvas, 54¼ × 50⅛ in.
Woodmere Art Museum, Museum purchase with funds generously donated by an anonymous donor, 2017
Plate 8

* *Related to "Picnic (Outing: Homage to Le Nain),"* c. 1975
Watercolor and graphite on paper, 14¾ × 20⅝ in.
Woodmere Art Museum, Gift of the Larry Day Art Trust in honor of Pamela Loos, 2021
Plate 9

** *End,* 1975
Oil on canvas, 62 × 56 in.
Lent by Pamela and Joseph Yohlin
Plate 67

** *Industrial Site*, c. 1975
Watercolor on BFK Rives paper, 22 × 30 in.
Lent by Pamela and Joseph Yohlin

** *(Myrtle Avenue)*, c. 1975
Graphite on Basingwerk paper, 20 × 26⅛ in.
Collection of Woodmere Art Museum, Gift of the Larry Day Art Trust in honor of Natalie Charkow Hollander, 2021

** *Yard II*, c. 1975
Graphite on paper, 18½ × 24 in.
Lent by Pamela and Joseph Yohlin
Plate 78

** *Suburban Landscape*, 1976
Oil on canvas, 60½ × 71½ in.
Lent by the Philadelphia Museum of Art, Purchased with funds contributed by Dr. and Mrs. Stephen D. Silberstein, 1977-201-1
Plate 21

** *Zone*, 1976
Oil on canvas, 48 × 54 in.
Lent by Woodmere Art Museum, Museum purchase, with partial funds generously provided by Ruth Fine, 2016
Plate 72

* *Partial Portrait*, 1976–77
Oil on canvas, 54 × 60 in.
Woodmere Art Museum, Museum purchase, 2020
Plate 57

** *Aquarium*, 1977
Oil on canvas, 54 × 65¾ in.
Lent by Woodmere Art Museum, Gift of Natalie Charkow Hollander, 2020
Plate 73

* *Yard II*, 1978
Oil on canvas, 60 × 72 in.
Woodmere Art Museum, Gift of Natalie Charkow Hollander, 2020
Plate 22

* *Nude*, 1978–79
Oil on canvas, 36 × 30 in.
Lent by Penny and Bruce Smith
Plate 58

** *Construction Site*, 1979
Oil on canvas, 54⅛ × 60⁵⁄₁₆ in.
Lent by the Pennsylvania Academy of the Fine Arts, Philadelphia, Gift of Mr. and Mrs. B. Herbert Lee, 1984.18
Plate 68

** *Untitled, study for "Construction Site,"* c. 1979
Pen and wash and brown ink on page from 1971 calendar, 11 × 14 in.
Collection of the Pennsylvania Academy of the Fine Arts, Philadelphia, Gift of Ruth Fine, 2019.20.4
Plate 69

** *Untitled, study for "Construction Site,"* c. 1979
Graphite on September page from 1971 calendar, 11⅜ × 15⅜ in.
Collection of the Pennsylvania Academy of the Fine Arts, Philadelphia, Gift of Ruth Fine, 2019.20.5
Plate 70

** *Study for "Suburban Church,"* 1979
Graphite and sepia wash on paper, 24 × 29½ in.
Lent by Woodmere Art Museum, Gift of the Estate of June and Perry Ottenberg, 2018
Plate 80

* *Picnic*, late 1970s
Graphite on paper, 22 × 29½ in.
Lent by John and Sandra Moore
Plate 95

** *(Deck)*, c. 1980
Graphite and wash on Fabriano paper, 27½ × 39⅛ in.
Lent by Private Collection

* *(Seated Woman in Robe)*, c. 1980
Graphite on Basingwerk paper, 26 × 20⅛ in.
Woodmere Art Museum, Gift of the Larry Day Art Trust, 2021
Plate 56

* *34th Street*, c. 1980
Oil on canvas, 48 × 66 in.
Lent by the Larry Day Art Trust
Plate 23

* *Related to "Break,"* 1981
Pen and ink on paper, 10⅜ × 13⅜ in.
Woodmere Art Museum, Promised gift of Pamela and Joseph Yohlin
Plate 20

** *(Arrow)*, c. 1982
Graphite on verso of 1982 calendar from Zeitlin & Ver Brugge Booksellers, Los Angeles, 9 × 10½ in.
Lent by Woodmere Art Museum, Gift of the Larry Day Art Trust in honor of Bernadine Young, 2021

** *Caumsett*, probably 1982
Graphite and wash on Fabriano paper, 22⅜ × 30 in.
Lent by Woodmere Art Museum, Gift of the Larry Day Art Trust in honor of Anita and Armand Mednick, 2021

** *Caumsett II*, probably 1982
Graphite and wash on Fabriano paper, 22¼ × 29⅞ in.
Lent by Woodmere Art Museum, Gift of Larry Day Art Trust in honor of Diane Pastella, 2021

* *Changes*, 1982
Oil on canvas, 54 × 66 in.
Woodmere Art Museum: Promised gift of Pamela and Joseph Yohlin
Plate 19

** *Lancaster*, c. 1982
Oil on canvas, 60 × 54 in.
Lent by Woodmere Art Museum, Gift of Marinda Schwartz in memory of Harry K. Schwartz, 2020
Plate 74

* *After Poussin*, c. 1983
Graphite and wash on paper, 22½ × 30 in.
Woodmere Art Museum, Gift of Ruth Fine in honor of Jonathan Bober, 2021
Plate 104

** *East River Drive*, 1983
Pen and wash and brown ink, and pen and black ink on paper, 9½ × 12¼ in.
Lent by Ruth Fine
Plate 101

** *(Arboretum)*, c. 1984
Graphite and watercolor on paper, 12¾ ×
15 in.
Lent by Carol Kelley
Plate 79

* *After Pollaiuolo*, c. 1985
Graphite on paper, 22½ × 16⅜ in.
Woodmere Art Museum, Gift of Ruth Fine in
honor of Eileen Neff, 2021
Plate 59

** *Building Reflected* (aka *Reflection*),
probably 1985
Oil on canvas, 60 × 48 in.
Lent by James D. Crawford and Judith M.
Dean
Plate 75

* *Girl with Bow*, 1986
Graphite on paper, 26 × 20 in.
Woodmere Art Museum, Museum purchase,
2019

** *Tree in the City* (aka *City Tree*),
1987–88
Oil on canvas, 54 × 72 in.
Lent by Harold and Jeanne Bloom
Plate 77

* *Salome Variation A*, 1988
Graphite on paper, 23 × 29 in.
Lent by the Larry Day Art Trust
Plate 37

* *Salome Variation B*, 1988
Graphite on paper, 23 × 29 in.
Lent by the Larry Day Art Trust
Plate 38

* *Salome Variation K*, 1988
Graphite on gray paper, 22½ × 26 in.
Lent by Eileen Neff
Plate 39

* *After Steen* (*The Doctor's Visit, 1663–
65*), 1989
Graphite on paper, 29½ × 22 in.
Lent by Natalie Charkow Hollander
Plate 64

** *Three Worlds*, 1989
Oil on canvas, 66 × 48 in.
Lent by Woodmere Art Museum, Museum
purchase, 2017
Plate 10

** *Construction*, c. 1990
Oil on canvas, 48 × 72 in.
Lent by the Larry Day Art Trust
Plate 71

* *Hercules Dressed as a Woman*, c. 1990
Watercolor and graphite on paper, 9 × 14⅜ in.
Woodmere Art Museum, Museum purchase,
2021
Plate 66

** *Related to "Lost World,"* c. 1990
Watercolor and graphite on Arches paper,
14⅞ × 22⅛ in.
Lent by the Larry Day Art Trust

* *After Bosch* (*The Wanderer, 1506–16*),
1991
Graphite on Basingwerk paper, 20 × 26 in.
Woodmere Art Museum, Gift of the Larry
Day Art Trust in honor of Pamela and Joseph
Yohlin, 2021
Plate 65

* *Day by Day*, 1991
Oil on canvas, 49½ × 61¼ in.
Lent by the Philadelphia Museum of Art,
Bequest of the artist, 1999-2-1
Plate 42

* *(Self-Portrait as a Child)*, c. 1991
Watercolor and graphite, 10⅝ × 6¾ in.
Lent by the Larry Day Art Trust
Plate 43

* *Related to "Day by Day,"* c. 1991
Graphite on paper, 22 × 29⅞ in.
Lent by Ruth Fine

** *Related to "Yggdrasil,"* c. 1991
Watercolor and graphite on paper, 13⅜ ×
20¼ in.
Lent by the Larry Day Art Trust

* *Dialogue*, 1992
Oil on canvas, 60¾ × 48¾ in.
Lent by Judith Brodie and Mervin Richard,
Washington, DC
Plate 34

* *Larry and Dennis* (*Related to "Ceres"*),
c. 1992
Graphite on paper, 22½ × 26½ in.
Lent by the Larry Day Art Trust
Plate 44

* *Related to "Ceres,"* c. 1992
Graphite on paper, 22½ × 26½ in.
Lent by the Larry Day Art Trust
Plate 45

* *(Factory)*, c. 1995
Pen and ink on Fabriano paper, 22¼ × 30¼ in.
Woodmere Art Museum, Gift of Ruth Fine,
2021

* *(Masquerade)*, c. 1995
Pen and ink and wash on Arches Aquarelle
paper, 15⅛ × 22½ in.
Woodmere Art Museum, Gift of the Larry Day
Art Trust, 2021
Plate 32

* *(Party)*, c. 1995
Watercolor and ink on Fabriano paper, 22½ ×
29¾ in.
Woodmere Art Museum, Gift of the Larry Day
Art Trust in honor of Hildy Tow, 2021
Plate 33

* *Elegies* (*Homage to Rilke*), 1997
*Elegy I*
*Elegy II*
*Elegy III*
*Elegy IV*
*Elegy V*
*Elegy VI*
*Elegy VII*
*Elegy VIII*
*Elegy IX*
*Elegy X*
Pen and ink on paper, each 22 × 30 in.
Lent by the Rhode Island School of Design
Museum, Gift of Ruth Fine in memory of
Sylvan Cole, 2005
Plates 46–55

# Selected Bibliography

This bibliography was compiled during the COVID-19 pandemic of 2020–21. Information provided below is as complete as possible with limited library access.


## Published Writings by Larry Day

"Alfred Leslie." In *Directions 68.* Introduction by George R. Bunker. Philadelphia: Philadelphia College of Art, 1968. Essay co-written with Morris Berd.

"Art and Identity: Five Points of View." *Arts Exchange* 2, no. 1 (January–February 1978): 24–27.

"The Artist as Philadelphian." In *2nd Philadelphia Arts Festival: Regional Exhibition,* by Henri Marceau et al. Philadelphia: Philadelphia Museum of Art, 1959.

"Artist's Statement." In *Larry Day, Encounters: Interpretations.* Washington, DC: Jane Haslem Gallery, 1992.

"Artist's Statement." In *Tempi del Giorno: Eighteen Drawings by Larry Day,* by Susan J. Barnes and John Hollander. Lawrenceville, NJ: Rider College Art Gallery; Cullowhee, NC: Belk Art Gallery, Western Carolina University, 1994.

"Bread," "Being a Translation from the Russian of Fedyor Alexandrovich Goolsky" (presumably tongue in cheek). *El Delator* (Cheltenham High School) (Spring 1940): 5–6. As Laurence Day.

Colker, Ed, comp. "Present Concerns in Studio Teaching: Artists' Statements." *Art Journal* 42, no. 1 (Spring 1982): 33.

Commentary. In *Broad Spectrum: Artists Who Teach at the Philadelphia College of Art,* by Elsa Weiner. Allentown, PA: Allentown Art Museum; Pittsburgh: University Art Gallery of the University of Pittsburgh; Harrisburg, PA: William Penn Memorial Museum, 1981.

Commentary. In *Cheltenham—60 Years of Art: Anniversary Exhibition,* by Cheltenham Center for the Arts. Cheltenham, PA: Cheltenham Center for the Arts, 2000.

Commentary. In *A Collection of Thoughts about Drawing,* edited by Estelle S. Gross and Burton Van Deusen. Philadelphia: Gross McCleaf Gallery, 1978.

Commentary. In *David Pease: Paintings and Drawings, 1958–1968.* Elkins Park, PA: Tyler School of Art of Temple University, 1968.

Commentary. In *Doris Staffel: Recent Paintings.* Philadelphia: Gross McCleaf Gallery, 1973. Reprinted in *Doris Staffel: Painter, Teacher,* edited by William R. Valerio. Philadelphia: Woodmere Art Museum, 2012.

Commentary. In "Washington Genre Paintings: Davenport Day Fletcher Folsom and Hendrick." *Jane Haslem* [newsletter] (1991).

Commentary. In *Jane Piper: Recent Work.* New York: Bodley Gallery, 1981. Reprinted in *Jane Piper: Selected Paintings, 1976–1990.* New York: New York Studio School, 1991.

Commentary. In *Realism Now,* by Linda Nochlin. Poughkeepsie, NY: Vassar College Art Gallery, 1968.

"Drawing." In *American Figure Drawing,* edited by W. J. Kelly. Bethlehem, PA: Lehigh University; Melbourne: Victorian College of the Arts Gallery, 1976.

"Extracts from Logbook on a Work in Progress." *Art Education Bulletin* (Eastern Arts Association) 15, no. 4 (April 1958): 11–17.

"Faculty Message." *Nous: A Philadelphia College of Art Student Publication,* March 18, 1965, n.p.

"Froth." *El Delator* (Cheltenham High School) (Winter 1940): 33. As Laurence Day. A group of verses.

"Introduction." In *Jane Piper: Recent Paintings.* Philadelphia: Gross McCleaf Gallery, 1981. Excerpt reprinted in *Art Now/Philadelphia Gallery Guide* 2, no. 2 (October 1981): 5.

"Jan Baltzell," "Natalie Charkow," "Ruth Fine," "Eileen Goodman," "Mercedes Matter," "Jane Piper," "Doris Staffel," and "Dorothy Yanik." In

*North American Women Artists of the Twentieth Century: A Biographical Dictionary,* edited by Jules Heller and Nancy G. Heller. New York: Routledge, 1995.

"Jimmy C. Lueders: Rituals of Art and Life." In *Jimmy C. Lueders.* Philadelphia: Woodmere Art Museum, 1998. Essay co-written with Ruth Fine.

"The Lion." *The Owl* (Temple University) (Spring 1948): 9, 32, 33. As Laurence Day.

"Mitzi Melnicoff, 1922–1972." In *Mitzi Melnicoff: A Memorial Exhibition of Paintings, Prints and Drawings.* Philadelphia: Philadelphia College of Art, 1973.

"The Necessities of Representation." *ACM Newsletter* 1, no. 6 (May–June 1981): 1–2.

"Notes on Figurative Art." In *The Figure in Recent American Painting,* by Robert Godfrey. New Wilmington, PA: Art Department, Westminster College, 1974. Reprinted in *ACM Newsletter* 1, no. 1 (April 1980): 2, 9.

"Painting as Paradigm." In *Perception and Pictorial Representation,* edited by Calvin F. Nodine and Dennis F. Fisher. New York: Praeger, 1979.

"Personally Speaking: Reflections on Piero della Francesca." *Croquis: Tyler Alumni Newsletter* 2, no. 1 (1963): 1, 2, 4.

"Realism and Its Discontents." *Crits: Discourses on the Visual Arts* (1993): 36–41. This issue is incorrectly cited as the last; the last issue for which Robert Godfrey and James Thompson were editors dates to 2003.

"Ruth Fine's Landscapes." In *Ruth Fine: California Landscapes.* Lawrenceville, NJ: Rider College Art Gallery, 1991.

"The Seer and the Parodist." *Re-Art* 1 (Autumn 1954): n.p. Subtitled "A reflection of current ideas on the arts," this is the only issue of this Philadelphia-based pamphlet, published by artists Edward Colker and Eugene Feldman; at one dollar each, only ten subscriptions were received.

"Some Part of the World: New Paintings by Rafael Ferrer." *Arts Magazine* 60, no. 3 (November 1985): 26–28.

"Three Days: Palm Sunday, Good Friday, Easter Sunday." *Gargoyles* (Stella Elkins Tyler School of Fine Arts) 4, no. 3 (April 1950): 10–11.

## Archival Materials

Larry Day, Oral history with Marina Pacini, February 21, 1991. Archives of American Art, Smithsonian Institution, Washington, DC.

## Exhibition Catalogues

### SOLO EXHIBITIONS

Barnes, Susan J., and John Hollander. *Tempi del Giorno: Eighteen Drawings by Larry Day.* Lawrenceville, NJ: Rider College Art Gallery; Cullowhee, NC: Belk Art Gallery, Western Carolina University, 1994.

Day, Larry. *Larry Day, Encounters: Interpretations.* Washington, DC: Jane Haslem Gallery, 1992.

Fine, Ruth. "Larry Day, A Conversation with Ruth Fine." In *Larry Day, Paintings: 1958–1998.* Washington, DC: Jane Haslem Gallery, 1988.

Hollander, John. *Larry Day: Paintings and Drawings.* Philadelphia: Gross McCleaf Gallery, 1983.

——. *Larry Day: Series and Variations.* New York: New York Studio School of Drawing, Painting and Sculpture, 2001.

Neff, Eileen. *Larry Day: Paintings and Works on Paper.* New York: Meredith Ward Fine Art, 2007.

White, Bill, ed. *Larry Day: Ironic Realist.* Essay by Scott Noel. Roanoke, VA: Eleanor D. Wilson Museum, Hollins University, 2008.

### TWO-PERSON AND GROUP EXHIBITIONS

Amory, Dita. *168th Annual Exhibition.* New York: National Academy of Design, 1993.

*Aspen Artists.* Waitsfield, VT: Bundy Art Gallery, 1965.

Baur, John I. H., and Elizabeth Carpenter. *Realism Today: American Drawings from the Rita Rich Collection.* New York: National Academy of Design, 1987.

E. M. B. [Emmanuel M. Benson]. *Third Philadelphia Arts Festival: Arts Exhibitions.* Philadelphia: Philadelphia Museum of Art and Pennsylvania Academy of the Fine Arts, 1962.

Burton, Scott. *The Realist Revival.* New York: American Federation of the Arts, 1972.

Cheltenham Center for the Arts, *Cheltenham—60 Years of Art: Anniversary Exhibition.* Cheltenham, PA: Cheltenham Center for the Arts, 2000.

Cocordas, Elaine J. *Affects/Effects 2: Work by the Faculty of Philadelphia College of Art.* Philadelphia: Philadelphia College of Art, 1983.

d'Harnoncourt, Anne. In *Philadelphia: Three Centuries of American Art,* edited by Darrel Sewell. Philadelphia: Philadelphia Museum of Art, 1976.

Donohoe, Victoria. *Exhibition of Liturgical Arts Organized by the 41st International Eucharistic Congress.* Philadelphia: Philadelphia Civic Center, 1976.

Fine, Ruth, Raymond Hernández-Durán, and Mark Pascale. *Contemporary American Realist Drawings: The Jalane and Richard Davidson Collection at the Art Institute of Chicago.* Chicago: Art Institute of Chicago, 1999.

Godfrey, Robert. *The Figure in Recent American Painting.* New Wilmington, PA: Art Department, Westminster College, 1974.

——. *In Praise of Space: The Landscape in American Art.* New Wilmington, PA: Art Department, Westminster College, 1976.

——. *Urban Spaces: Larry Day, Rudy Burckhardt, Kathryn Wall.* Cullowhee, NC: Belk Art Gallery, Western Carolina University, 1992.

Godfrey, Robert et al. *Drawing: Points of View.* Cullowhee, NC: Belk Art Gallery, Western Carolina University, 1989.

*Golden Years: Tyler's Fiftieth Anniversary—A Celebration of Alumni/ae Achievement: Tyler School of Art, 1935–1985* (in three sequential parts: Graphic Arts and Design invitational, October 6–November 2, 1984; Crafts Invitational, November 10–December 9, 1984; Painting, Drawing, and Sculpture Invitational, January 10–February 6, 1985), Tyler School of Art, Temple University.

Goode, James M. *Contemporary Self-Portraits from the James Goode Collection.* Washington, DC: National Portrait Gallery, Smithsonian Institution, 1993.

Goodyear, Frank H., Jr. *Perspectives on Contemporary American Realism: Works of Art on Paper from the Collection of Jalane and Richard Davidson.* Philadelphia: Pennsylvania Academy of the Fine Arts, 1982.

Goodyear, Frank H., Jr., and Ann Percy. *Contemporary Drawings: Philadelphia I.* Philadelphia: Pennsylvania Academy of the Fine Arts, 1978.

Gussow, Alan. *A Sense of Place: The Artist and the American Land Volume II.* Omaha: Joslyn Art Museum; Lincoln, NE: Sheldon Memorial Art Gallery, 1973. A brochure with the same title (lacking *Volume II*) accompanied a smaller traveling exhibition circulated by the Mid-America Arts Alliance in institutions in Missouri, Kansas, Iowa, and South Dakota. An exhibition with this title also was on view in 1973 at Guild Hall, East Hampton, New York.

Harris, George A. *Twentieth Century Drawings: A Loan Exhibition Presented by the Stanford Art Gallery and the Committee for Art at Stanford.* Stanford, CA: Stanford University, 1955.

Hollander, John. *Landscape Painting, 1960–1990: The Italian Tradition in American Art.* Charleston, SC: Gibbes Museum of Art; Charlottesville: Bayly Museum of Art, University of Virginia, 1990.

Jane Haslem Salon. *Consonance: Watercolors and Pastels.* Washington, DC: Jane Haslem Salon, 1988.

Johnson, Una E. *Twelfth National Print Exhibition 1960.* New York: Brooklyn Museum, 1960.

Kelly, W. J., ed. *American Figure Drawing.* Bethlehem, PA: Lehigh University; Melbourne: Victorian College of the Arts Gallery, 1976. A brochure with the same title was also published.

Marceau, Henri et al. *2nd Philadelphia Arts Festival: Regional Exhibition.* Philadelphia: Philadelphia Museum of Art, 1959.

Miley, Mimi C. *18th Juried Exhibition.* Allentown, PA: Allentown Art Museum, 1982.

Munroe, Gerald M. *Figure Drawing: A Contemporary View.* Glassboro, NJ: Westby Art Gallery, Glassboro State College, 1971.

*New Land, New Covenant.* Bryn Mawr, PA: Bryn Mawr Presbyterian Church, 1976.

Nochlin, Linda. *Realism Now.* Poughkeepsie, NY: Vassar College Art Gallery, 1968.

Pagan, Mary Jane. *Approaching the Figure Part II: Figure Groups and Genre Scenes in Paintings, Drawings, and Prints.* Washington, DC: Fine Arts Gallery, Georgetown University, 1990.

Pennsylvania Academy of the Fine Arts. *Catalogue of The One Hundred and Fifty-Fourth Annual Exhibition: Water Colors, Prints, Drawings.* Philadelphia: Pennsylvania Academy of the Fine Arts, 1959.

———. *Catalogue of the One Hundred and Sixtieth Annual Exhibition: Water Colors, Prints, Drawings.* Philadelphia: Pennsylvania Academy of the Fine Arts, 1965.

———. *The One Hundred and Sixty-First Annual Exhibition of American Painting and Sculpture.* Philadelphia: Pennsylvania Academy of the Fine Arts, 1966.

———. *The One Hundred and Sixty-Third Annual Exhibition, American Painting and Sculpture.* Philadelphia: Pennsylvania Academy of the Fine Arts, 1968.

Perry, Donald D. *National Invitational Drawing Exhibition.* Emporia, KS: Norman R. Eppink Art Gallery, Emporia State University, [1989].

Ratcliff, Carter. *Artists' Choice Museum: The First Eight Years.* New York: Artists' Choice Museum, 1984.

*Regional Exhibition, Paintings, Sculpture, Prints, and Drawings by Artists of Philadelphia and Vicinity.* Foreword by Joseph T. Fraser, Jr., 1964.

Scott, Bill. *Jane Piper and Her Circle: Three Generations of Painters in Philadelphia.* Harrisburg: State Museum of Pennsylvania, 2000.

Selby, Roger L. *American Drawings: Realism/Idealism.* Boca Raton, FL: Boca Raton Museum of Art, 1987.

*6th Annual Exhibition by the Alumni of Stella Elkins Tyler School of Fine Arts of Temple University.* Philadelphia: Stella Elkins Tyler School of Fine Arts, 1952.

Stevens, N. Lee, and Nina Purviance. *City Views: Panoramas to Particulars, Works from the CIGNA Collection.* Philadelphia: CIGNA Museum, 1985.

Streuber, Michael M. *The 1982 Hazlett Memorial Awards Exhibition for the Visual Arts.* Loretto, PA: Southern Alleghenies Museum of Art, 1982.

*The Third Annual Fall Review of Paintings and Sculpture: 1957, In the United States.* Preface by Ben Wolf. Philadelphia: Pyramid Club, 1957.

Valerio, William R., ed. *Doris Staffel: Painter, Teacher.* Philadelphia: Woodmere Art Museum, 2012.

———. *The Poker Game and Its Circle.* Philadelphia: Woodmere Art Museum, 2013. Digital catalogue.

Weiner, Elsa. *Broad Spectrum: Artists Who Teach at the Philadelphia College of Art.* Allentown, PA: Allentown Art Museum; Pittsburgh: University Art Gallery of the University of Pittsburgh; Harrisburg, PA: William Penn Memorial Museum, 1981.

## Articles, Notes, Solo Exhibition Reviews, and Obituaries

Allen, Ray. "People in the News: In Memoriam." *CAA News* (College Art Association) 23, no. 6 (November 1988): 15.

"Art Laurels." *Times Chronicle* (Cheltenham), July 8, 1982.

*Art Now: Gallery Guide, Philadelphia Edition* 9, no. 8 (April 1989): PH 5–6. Exhibition listing and illustration.

*Art Now/Philadelphia Gallery Guide* 4, no. 2 (October 1983): PH 4–5. Exhibition listing and illustration.

*Art Now/Philadelphia Gallery Guide* 6, no. 9 (May 1986), PH 5–6. Exhibition listing and illustration.

"Art Students Listen as an Instructor Lectures." *Aspen Flyer,* July 18, 1962, 1.

Benson, Gertrude. "One Man Show." *Philadelphia Inquirer,* November 20, 1955.

———. "Rising Sales Reflect Expanding Art Audiences." *Philadelphia Inquirer,* n.d. Includes review of a Day exhibition about to open at the new Dubin Galleries.

Blackham, Ann. "Artist Larry Day to Hold One Man Show." *Beaver News,* February 8, 1972, 1.

Donohue, Victoria. "Art: An Exhibition by a Steady and Reliable Loner." *Philadelphia Inquirer,* October 12, 1979, 31. Excerpt reprinted as "Art: Larry Day at Gross McCleaf Gallery." *Art Now/Philadelphia Gallery Guide* 2, no. 2 (October 1981): 2.

———. "Art: An Outstanding Phila. Artist Shows His Recent Work." *Philadelphia Inquirer,* November 4, 1983, 39.

———. "Art: A Realist Drawing Exhibition with a Renaissance Touch." *Philadelphia Inquirer,* May 2, 1982.

———. "Art: Galleries." *Philadelphia Inquirer,* November 9, 1980. Donohue calls Day the "Steve Carlton of area art," making reference to the Philadelphia Phillies' left-handed pitcher at the time, and suggests that Day was "arguably the best living painter and draftsman in Philadelphia."

———. "Art: Galleries." *Philadelphia Inquirer,* November 5, 1982.

———. "Art: Galleries." *Philadelphia Inquirer,* June 22, 1985.

———. "Art: Larry Day's New Realist Style Is So Reasonable, Self-Assured." *Philadelphia Inquirer,* September 30, 1977, 24.

———. "The Art Scene: Artist's Subtle Explorations Combine Drawings and Photos." *Philadelphia Inquirer,* January 10, 1975.

———. "The Art Scene: Contrasting Styles Mark Exhibitions by 2 Artists at Peale Galleries." *Philadelphia Inquirer,* November 8, 1970, 8.

———. "The Arts, On Galleries: New Creations from a Painter Turned Sculptor." *Philadelphia Inquirer,* December 15, 1984, 4-D.

———. "Celebrating Philadelphia." *Philadelphia Inquirer,* May 10, 1986.

———. "Landscapes, Figures." *Philadelphia Inquirer,* February 5, 1973.

———. "On Galleries: Gross McCleaf." *Philadelphia Inquirer,* April 15, 1989, 3-C. Includes reproduction of Day's *34th Street* (plate 23).

———. "On Galleries: Two Shows Feature Drawings by Larry Day." *Philadelphia Inquirer,* May 7, 1988, 5-D.

———. "The Subtleties of Larry Day: His Art Demands Attentiveness." *Philadelphia Inquirer*, October 30, 1981, 37.

N. E. "Reviews and Previews: Larry Day (at Brata Gallery)." *Art News* 70 (February 1972): 14.

"Erudite Painter/Teacher Larry Day, the Dean of Philadelphia Painters, to Retire." *The Columns* (University of the Arts) 4, no. 1 (Spring 1988): 3.

"Exhibition Review." *Courier-Post* (Camden), October 20, 1979.

Forman, Nessa. "Around the Galleries, a Builder of Forms—A Stripper of Flesh." *Sunday Bulletin* (Philadelphia), October 2, 1977.

Gilbard, Florence. "Larry Day." *Museum and Arts Washington* 4, no. 3 (May–June 1988): 26, 28.

Grafly, Dorothy. *Art in Focus* 2, no. 9 (Summer 1951). Mention of solo exhibition at Dubin Galleries.

———. "Larry Day at Gross McCleaf." *Art in Focus* 27, no. 2 (November 1975): [7].

Hollander, John. "Review of Exhibitions, Philadelphia: Larry Day at Gross-McCleaf." *Art in America* 6, no. 2 (March–April 1978): 141–42.

"In Memoriam: Larry Day 1921–1998." *Forum: Published for Alumni and Friends of the University of the Arts* 8, no. 2 (Summer 1998): 7.

*Jane Haslem Gallery* [newsletter] (Spring 1987): n.p.

Jarmusch, Ann. "Exhibition Review." *Art News* (March 1978).

———. "If Vermeer Were Alive Today, Would He Be Painting in Philadelphia?" *Art News* 80 (March 1981): 154–59.

Lewis, Jo Ann. "Galleries: Larry Day at Jane Haslem." *Washington Post,* May 14, 1988, C2.

———. "Galleries: Urban Still Lifes." *Washington Post*, April 4, 1987, C2.

"Local Artists Lend Talents to Art Week: '82." *Times Chronicle* (Cheltenham), September 30, 1982.

Medoff, Eve. "Larry Day: The Painting Is All." *American Artist* 44, issue 460 (November 1980): 54–57, 106, 109, 114. (Detail of *Picnic [Outing: Homage to Le Nain]* reproduced on 54)

Neff, Eileen. "Philadelphia, Larry Day: Gross McCleaf Gallery." *Artforum* 28, no. 10 (Summer 1989): 148.

Nemser, Cindy. "In the Galleries, Larry Day." *Arts Magazine* 42 (April 1968): 59.

"New Dubin Gallery." *Philadelphia Inquirer*, September 27, 1953.

"On Galleries: Gross McCleaf." *Philadelphia Inquirer,* April 15, 1989.

Piggott, Janet Purcell. "An Artist Gets into His Paintings." *Times* (city unknown), February 11, 1994.

Preston, Stuart. "Art: Sunshiny Color, Bright Works by Larry Day Exhibited." *New York Times*, April 16, 1960, 35.

"Remembering: Larry Day, Painter." *MacDowell Colony News* 27 (fall 1998): 23.

Schein, David D. "Philadelphia: Day and Dessner Excel." *Daily Pennsylvanian* (University of Pennsylvania), November 1970.

"State Award Conferred on Cheltenham Painter." *Northeast Philadelphia Breeze*, April 22, 1982. Printed on the same date in the *Times Chronicle* (Cheltenham), 25.

Stewart, Patricia. "Reviews, Art: Larry Day." *Arts Exchange* 2, no. 1 (January–February 1978): 41.

Wallace, Andy. "Larry Day, 76, Prominent Phila. Artist, Art Teacher." *Philadelphia Inquirer*, April 17, 1998.

*Washington's Hill Rag*, April 17–30, 1992. Cover illustration: detail of Day's *Heidelberg Park* (painting, 1972).

Wasserman, Burton, "Sensitive Eye." *Courier-Post* (Camden), October 20, 1979.

Weinstein, Ann. "Realist's Works Communicate Complexity of His Emotions." *Roanoke Times and World News*, October 17, 1976.

## General References

### BOOKS AND BROCHURES

Falk, Peter H. *The Annual Exhibition Record of the Pennsylvania Academy of the Fine Arts, 1914–1968*. Philadelphia: Pennsylvania Academy of the Fine Arts, 1989.

Greenwood, Douglas McCreary. *Art in Embassies: Twenty-Five Years at the U.S. Department of State, 1964–1989*. Washington, DC: Friends of Art and Preservation in Embassies.

*Gross McCleaf Gallery*. Philadelphia: Gross McCleaf Gallery, 1988. Brochure celebrating the gallery's upcoming twentieth anniversary.

LeClair, Charles. *The Art of Watercolor: Techniques and New Directions*. Englewood Cliffs, NJ: Prentice Hall, 1985.

Mott, Jacolyn A., ed. *The American Paintings in the Pennsylvania Academy of the Fine Arts: An Illustrated Checklist*. Compiled by Nancy Fresella-Lee. Philadelphia: Pennsylvania Academy of the Fine Arts, 1989.

*Philadelphia Museum of Art Annual Report*. Philadelphia: Philadelphia Museum of Art, 1999. Notes acquisition of Day's *Day by Day* (plate 42).

Scott, Curtis R., Owen Hess Dugan, and John Paschetto, eds. *Paintings from Europe and the Americas in the Philadelphia Museum of Art*. Philadelphia: Philadelphia Museum of Art, 1994.

Simmons, Linda Crocker et al. *American Drawings, Watercolors, Pastels, and Collages in the Collection of the Corcoran Gallery of Art*. Washington, DC: Corcoran Gallery of Art, 1983.

*6th Annual Exhibition by the Alumni of Stella Elkins Tyler School of Fine Arts of Temple University*. Philadelphia: Stella Elkins Tyler School of Fine Arts, 1952.

*Sixty-Fourth Annual Commencement, Temple University*. Philadelphia: Temple University, 1950.

Solomon, Andrew. *The Art in Embassies Program: In Commemoration of the 40th Anniversary of the U.S. Department of State Art in Embassies Program, Washington, D.C.*, 2004.

Strueber, Michael M. *Selections from the Permanent Collection: Southern Alleghenies Museum of Art*. Loretto, PA: Southern Alleghenies Museum of Art, 1996.

### ARTICLES, INTERVIEWS, NOTES, AND GROUP EXHIBITION REVIEWS

Apesos, Anthony. "Reaffirming Western Values through the Depiction of Space." *New Art Examiner* (January 1981): 4–5.

Arneill, Anne. "The Fine Arts: Aspen Contemporary Arts School Opens June 24." *Denver Post*, May 8, 1960.

"Art Gallery Show at Westminster." *The Globe* (New Wilmington), April 29, 1976.

Barkheimer, Harold. "Hazlett Winners to Show Art." *The Tribune-Democrat* (Johnstown, PA), May 23, 1983, TV Entertainment section.

Bell, Susan. "M&AW/Around Town: Urban Landscape." *Museum and Arts Washington* 5, no. 3 (May–June 1989): 44–45.

Benson Gallery. Summer 1966 brochure with exhibition schedule and note of the intended scope of this new gallery in Bridgehampton.

Benson, Gertrude. "New Dubin Gallery." *Philadelphia Inquirer*, September 22, 1953.

———. "Rising Sales Reflect Expanding Art Audience." *Philadelphia Inquirer*, 1953. Discusses Dubin Gallery's impending opening.

Biberman, Jane. "Bertha Leonard's Nostalgia." *Art Matters* (October 2001).

——. "Decorating with a French Connection." *Inside* (Spring 1992): 125.

Bregman, Lillian. "The Art of Living." *Philadelphia Magazine* (September 1986): 223–31. Day's *Building Reflected* can be seen in the background on page 224.

——. "Personal Best," in *Inside* (Spring 1987): 105–113. Article about art collections of several Philadelphians, including Jay and Estelle S. Gross, with reproduction of a large abstract painting by Day.

Burchard, Hank. "From a Plea for Help, a Fix on Art in the 1960s–'70s." *Washington Post,* March 28, 1993.

*CAA News* (College Art Association) 24 (Summer 1989): 13.

Conheim, Maryanne. "Merging Medicine and Art." *Philadelphia Inquirer*, June 9, 1981, 1-B,2-B.

"Currents: Public Invited to Carleton Symposium on 'The Self in Print and Word.'" *Northfield News,* January 11, 1995.

DeShazo, Edith. "Art World: 'Realism' Displayed Cautiously." *Philadelphia Inquirer,* February 29, 1976, 6-NE. Also published as "Art World: 'Realism'—with Apologies—Shown at Glassboro State." *Philadelphia Inquirer* (South Jersey), February 29, 1976. Includes reproduction of Day's *A Game of Charades* (plate 98).

Dobrin, Peter. "An Outpouring of Artwork." *Philadelphia Inquirer*, January 23, 2009.

Donohoe, Victoria. "Academy's Show of Realists Is Big but Sadly Unfocused." *Philadelphia Inquirer*, September 20, 1981, 22-F.

——. "Art: A Comeback for Landscapes." *Philadelphia Inquirer*, March 28, 1975, 23.

——. "Art: An Art Exhibit That Reflects a Gallery's Roots." *Philadelphia Inquirer*, August 19, 1983, E-39.

——. "Art: A Realist Drawing Exhibit with a Renaissance Touch." *Philadelphia Inquirer*, January 8, 1982, 34.

——. "Art: At Last, the Art Museum Finds a Niche for Local Art." *Philadelphia Inquirer*, May 2, 1982, 8. Includes reproduction of Day's *Suburban Landscape* (plate 21).

——. "Art: Back to the Land, the Great Outdoors, as Today's Painters See It." *Philadelphia Inquirer*, August 1, 1980. Includes reproduction of Day's *Outing: Homage to Le Nain* (plate 8, as *Picnic*).

——. "Art: Fine Drawings: A Medium of Intimacy and Realism." *Philadelphia Inquirer*, July 28, 1978.

——. "Art: Is Abstract Painting Regaining Its Popularity?" *Philadelphia Inquirer*, September 14, 1984, 34.

——. "Art: Landscape, Figures." *Philadelphia Inquirer*, February 4, 1973.

——. "Art: New Climate for Heroic Art." *Philadelphia Inquirer*, February 8, 1981.

——. "Art: Return to Nature Is Marked by Exhibitions of Landscapes." *Philadelphia Inquirer*, 1976.

——. "The Arts/Art: Cheltenham Rings in the New." *Philadelphia Inquirer,* June 10, 1973, 9-G.

——. "The Nation, Philadelphia: Maturing toward Modernism." *Art News* 74 (December 1975): 94–95.

——. "Philadelphia Art Scene: Art Alliance Full House." *Philadelphia Inquirer,* February 5, 1967.

——. "Reviews." *Philadelphia Inquirer*, February 9, 1969.

——. "16 Artists Showcase Philadelphia." *Philadelphia Inquirer,* August 12, 1988, 42.

"Drawings Shown at Westminster." *New Castle News* (Pennsylvania), April 28, 1976.

"Feast Your Eyes: Local Artists Lend Talents to Art Week: '82." *Times Chronicle* (Cheltenham), September 30, 1982, 30.

"Figure Painting Show Opens Jan. 11." *Art Alliance Bulletin* (Philadelphia) 43, no. 4 (January 1965).

Forman, Nessa. "Seven Views: Just the Places I Know." *Evening Bulletin* (Philadelphia), 1973.

Gartside, Thomas. "Market Expands in Philadelphia." *New Art Examiner* 13, no. 9 (May 1986): 34–35.

Grafly, Dorothy. *Art in Focus* 1, no. 1 (October 1949). Mention of group exhibition at Dubin Galleries.

——. *Art in Focus* 8, no. 3 (December 1952). Mention of group exhibition at The Red Door.

——. *Art in Focus* 11, no. 4 (January 1960). Mention of group exhibition at Gallery 1015.

——. *Art in Focus* 12, no. 1 (October 1960). Mention of group exhibition at Gallery 1015.

——. *Art in Focus* 12, no. 5 (February 1961). Mention of group exhibition at Philadelphia Museum College of Art.

——. *Art in Focus* 16, no. 1 (October 1964). Mention of group exhibition at Gallery 1015.

——. "At Gallery 1015." *Evening Bulletin* (Philadelphia), October 13, 1963.

Haslem, John A., Jr. *Jane Haslem Gallery Newsletter,* fall 1992.

Kaye, Ellen. "LifeHome: Just Like a Real House." *Philadelphia Inquirer Magazine*, September 6, 1987, 44–45.

Laderman, Gabriel. "Unconventional Realists." *Artforum* 6, no. 3 (November 1967): 42–46.

Leon, Dennis. "Alumni Exhibit at Tyler School." *Philadelphia Inquirer,* April 23, 1961.

Mangravite, Andrew. "Landscapes Alive, Landscapes Dead." *Welcomat*, January 29, 1992, 17.

McFadden, Sarah. "Report from Philadelphia." *Art in America* 67, no. 3 (May–June 1979): 21–31.

Miller, Nancy Bea. "Peter Paone's Secret Flower Paintings." *Fine Art Connoisseur* 10, no. 6 (December 2013): 66–67.

"Philadelphian Honored for Excellence." *Art Matters* 1 (June 1982): 14.

Poley, Rita. "Limited in Space, but Not in Imagination." *Jewish Exponent*, January 22, 1998.

"Practicing What They Teach." *Scene II* (May 1969): 54–56. *Scene II* was published twelve times a year by Discoscene.

Purcell, Janet. "Peer Pleasure: Artist-Select Artist, TAWA at Ellarsie '96." *The Times: Good Times* (Trenton), June 7, 1996, E3, E19.

Ratcliff, Carter. In *The Artists' Choice Museum: The First Eight Years,* edited by Stephanie De Manuelle and Pamela Endacott. New York: Artists' Choice Museum, 1984.

Reyes, Gabriella. "Diverse New RISD Exhibits Feature Nature, Women's Attire." *Brown Daily Herald*, February 4, 2016.

Rice, Robin. "Pennsylvania Treasures I." *Philadelphia City Paper,* January 30–February 5, 1998.

Salisbury, Stephan. "Celebrating a Circle of Art, Poker, and Life." *Philadelphia Inquirer,* July 21, 2013.

Scott, Bill. "Philadelphia: Scott Noel at Gross-McCleaf." *Art in America* 89, no. 5 (May 2001): 182–83.

Sozanski, Edward J. "On Galleries: Work of Jurors Opens Fleisher Challenge Shows." *Philadelphia Inquirer*, October 2, 1986, 5-C.

——. "3 Exhibitions Display Woodmere's Growth." *Philadelphia Inquirer*, February 17, 2013.

Valerio, William R. "Woodmere Ups the Ante with *The Poker Game and Its Circle.*" *Chestnut Hill Local,* July 18, 2013.

Wasserman, Burton. "'Living Treasures' Display Works at Science Center." *Art Matters* (February 1998).

——. "Lueders Retrospective at Woodmere." *Art Matters* (June 1998).

——. "Sensitive Eye: Bright Flashes of Art Brighten an Otherwise Dull Exhibition." *Courier-Post* (Camden), October 20, 1979.

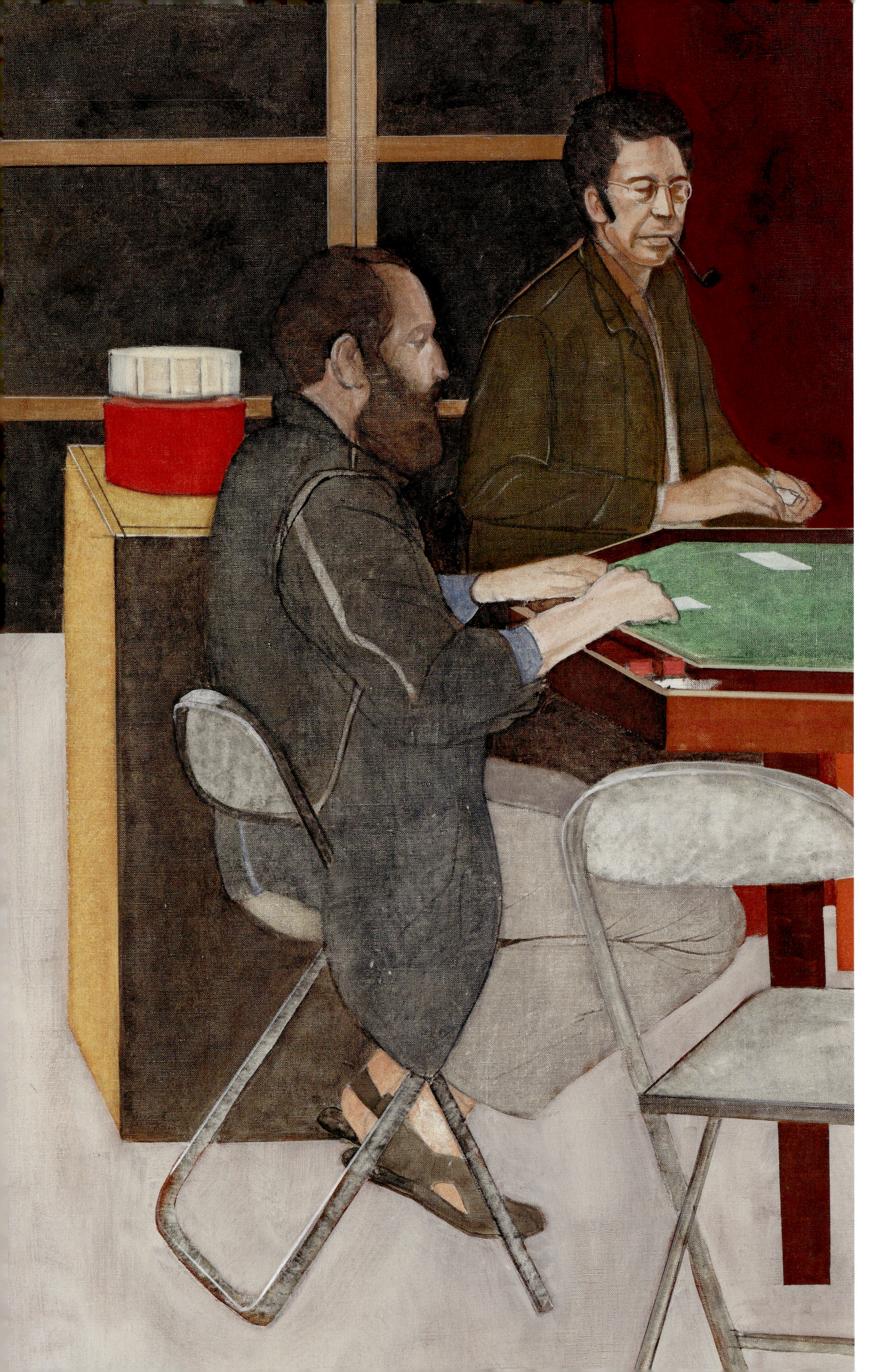

*David Bindman*

# Curator's Acknowledgments

The organization of the exhibition and the catalogue of *Body Language: The Art of Larry Day* has coincided in part with the COVID-19 pandemic of 2020–21. This has kept me on the wrong side of the Atlantic at critical times, so I have been far more dependent than I anticipated on input from Ruth Fine, Larry Day's widow, which she has provided with great good humor. I am grateful to her for bringing me into the project in the first place, and for the images and information she has shared. It has been a wonderful privilege to work with Ruth again, particularly on a subject so close to our hearts. I got to know Larry through her, and I treasure the fondest memories of staying with them in Takoma Park over the years. So it has been a great opportunity for me to share with Ruth in this celebration of Larry's achievements on the centenary of his birth, and to explore aspects of his career that I knew little about beforehand.

We have naturally been more reliant on others than we expected, and we would both like to express our gratitude to those who have helped us. Before COVID-19 set in, private and museum collectors of Larry's work warmly welcomed me to their homes and institutions, where I was able to study the paintings and drawings that they owned. Special thanks are due to those who agreed to share their treasures with visitors to the exhibition's multiple venues. We are most grateful for their thoughtful generosity.

It has been a particular pleasure to work with William Valerio, the Patricia Van Burgh Allison Director and CEO of Woodmere Art Museum, who has put an immense amount of work and enthusiasm into the project. Richard Torchia, Director of Arcadia Exhibitions at Arcadia University, and Sid Sachs, Chief Curator and Director of Exhibitions at the University of the Arts Rosenwald-Wolf Gallery, have also worked tirelessly to keep the project on track at this most turbulent time for all cultural institutions. Likewise, we have been dependent upon their enthusiastic staffs. At Woodmere, we are grateful to Diane Pastella, assistant to the director; Rick Ortwein, deputy director; Rachel Hruszkewycz, assistant curator; and Laura Heemer, registrar, for their attention to the many details of the exhibition organization and catalogue demands, including photography; Hildy Tow, the Robert L. McNeil, Jr. Curator of Education, for organizing provocative programming; and Anne Standish, Pamela Loos, and Christina Warhola for their keen development and communication skills. At Arcadia, we thank Rebecca Kohn, dean of the College of Arts and Sciences, and Matthew Borgen, exhibitions coordinator; and at the University of the Arts, David Yager, president and CEO; Shelton Walker, chief of staff and associate vice president for strategic initiatives; Michael Ciervo, director of exhibition management; Mary Kay Kaminski, program manager, University Galleries; and Caitlin Perkins, director of engagement, University Centers. We also are indebted to exhibition assistant Tessa Bachi Haas for her research assistance and for helping to keep staff at all three institutions on track.

Institutional loans have been made possible by retired director John Smith and curator of prints, drawings, and photographs Jan Howard at the Rhode Island School of Design Museum; Brook Davis Anderson at the Pennsylvania Academy of the Fine Arts; and the staff at the Philadelphia Museum of Art. We extend our appreciation to them, and to the institutional committees who approved the loans from the collections they oversee.

My fellow authors have woven together the story of Larry Day and his art, revealing the density and complexity of this artist's work. To Jonathan Bober, Ruth Fine, Eileen Neff, and Sid Sachs, I offer my great appreciation for their contributions to this book and to their contributions to one another's research.

Joseph Yohlin, a former board member of Woodmere and a member of the Museum's Collections Committee, a dedicated collector of American figurative art including Day's; as well as Robert Godfrey, an artist-educator and former student of Day's, have both been immensely responsive to inquiries, providing information of both a bibliographical and biographical nature, for which we are extremely grateful.

Other former students of Day, artist-educators themselves, who remained in contact with the artist over his lifetime, were critical to affirming our information and suggesting data that aided our work, including Wendy Edwards, Alan Goldstein, Harry I. Naar, Peter Paone, Bill Scott, Burt Van Deusen, and Bill White. Additional colleagues who offered assistance are Sarah Spencer; collector Arnold I. Kalman; Barbara Wolanin; Margo Dolan and Ron Rumford at Dolan Maxwell Gallery; Meredith Ward and Meghan Schwab at Meredith Ward Gallery; at Temple University's Tyler School of Art and Architecture, Hester Stinnett, professor of Printmaking, and David M. Logan, director of academic advising; and Temple's registrar's office, James G. Mundie, associate registrar, and Margery N. Sly, director of Temple Libraries' Special Collections Research Center. For technical advice about photography and video matters, we thank Dan Burns and Gustavo Garcia.

All of us who worked on this project are grateful for the careful and sympathetic editing of Gretchen Dykstra, assisted by Lucy Medrich. Likewise, we were fortunate to collaborate on this catalogue with Ed Marquand and Adrian Lucia and their imaginative staff at Lucia | Marquand in Seattle. Design director Tom Eykemans has created an elegant book that Larry Day would undoubtedly have admired, as do we all. He has been assisted in his work by editorial director Melissa Duffes, editor Kestrel Rundle, and production director Leah Finger, as well as Kim Kent and Jeremy Linden, coordinators of publications and production respectively.

Grateful appreciation is sent across the Atlantic to everyone thanked in the Directors' Foreword who contributed to the *Body Language: The Art of Larry Day* exhibition, catalogue, and educational programming.

# Lenders to the Exhibition

Jan Baltzell
Ann Beattie and Lincoln Perry
Jeanne and Harold Bloom
Judith Brodie and Mervin Richard
James D. Crawford and Judith M. Dean
Adele Fine
Ruth Fine and The Larry Day Art Trust
Natalie Charkow Hollander
Carol Kelley
John and Sandra Moore
Eileen Neff
Pennsylvania Academy of the Fine Arts
Philadelphia Museum of Art
Rhode Island School of Design Museum of Art
Michael Rossman
Penelope and Bruce Smith
Woodmere Art Museum
Jamie Wyper
Pamela and Joseph Yohlin

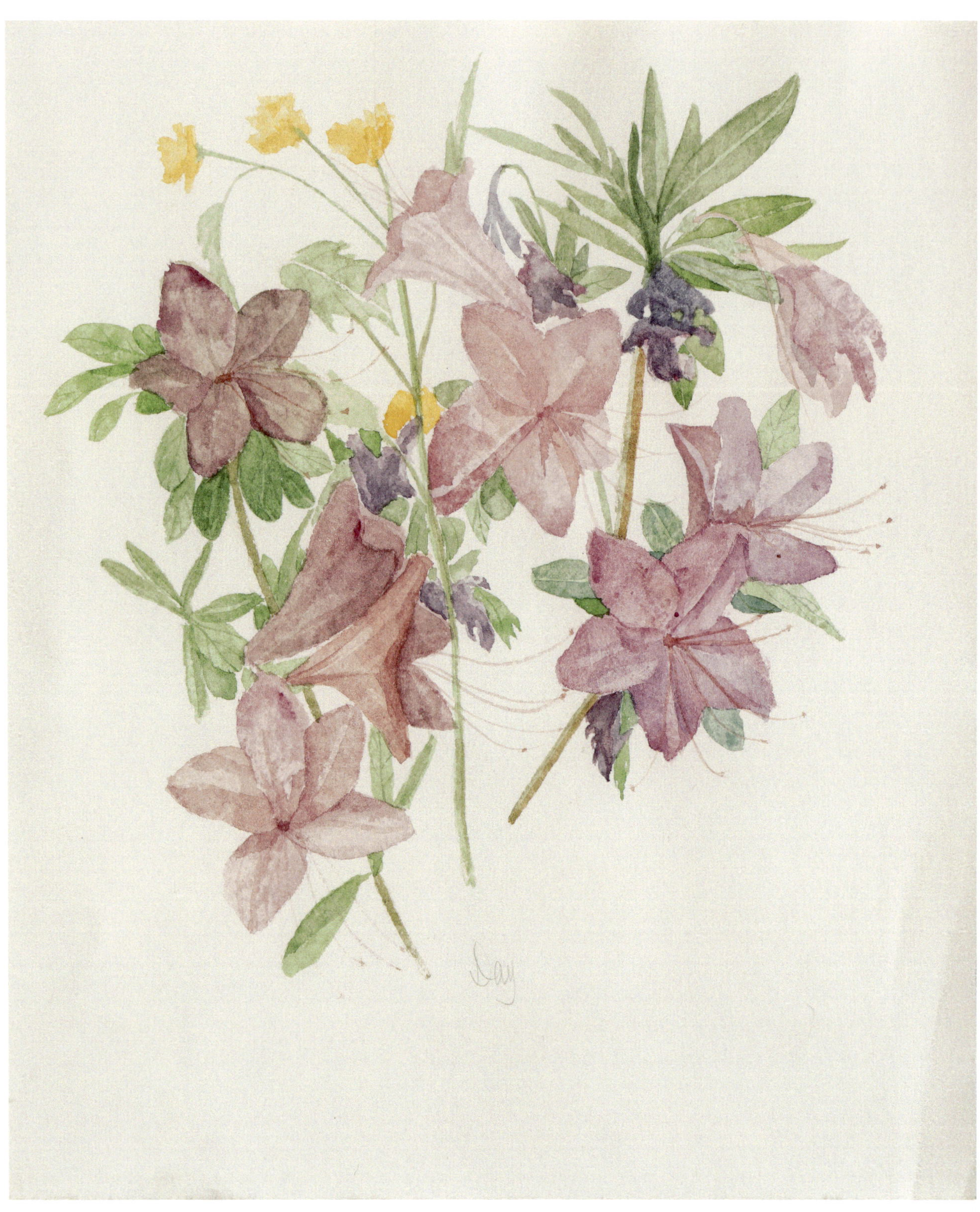

Figure 9.1   *Bouquet*, c. 1980, watercolor on paper, 9⅜ × 8 in. (Collection of Ruth Fine)

# Essayists' Biographies

DAVID BINDMAN is Emeritus Professor of the History of Art, University College, London and Fellow of the Hutchins Center, Harvard University. He has curated exhibitions on William Blake, William Hogarth, and the French Revolution. His recent work has mainly been on ideas of race and art, and he is editor (with Henry Louis Gates, Jr.) of the series *The Image of the Black in Western Art.*

JONATHAN BOBER is Andrew W. Mellon Senior Curator of Prints and Drawings at the National Gallery of Art, Washington, DC, and was previously the Senior Curator of European Art at the Blanton Museum, University of Texas, Austin. In addition to his many exhibition projects and their related publications, Bober has written extensively on Italian drawings of the Renaissance and Baroque.

RUTH FINE, widow of Larry Day, is a painter, printmaker, and independent curator, following her four-decade career with the National Gallery of Art, Washington, DC, lastly as the institution's initial Curator of Special Projects in Modern Art. She has written extensively on modern prints and drawings in the United States and African American art.

JOHN HOLLANDER (1929–2013), poet and literary critic, MacArthur Foundation Fellowship winner, and a member of the American Academy of Arts and Letters, was a close friend of Larry Day and wrote extensively about Day's work during his lifetime. Both men shared a belief in the power of art in all of its forms to transform lives.

EILEEN NEFF is a Guggenheim Foundation Fellow in Photography whose work has been exhibited internationally, including a 2007–2008 retrospective at the Institute of Contemporary Art, Philadelphia, and the Royal Hibernian Academy, Dublin. She wrote reviews for *Artforum* from 1989–2002, and continues to write independently.

SID SACHS is the Director of Exhibitions and Chief Curator at the University of the Arts, Philadelphia. He has written extensively on post-war art in the United States and has organized such ground-breaking exhibitions as *Seductive Subversion: Women Pop Artists, 1958–1968* and *Invisible City: Philadelphia and the Vernacular Avant-garde.*

This book is published in conjunction with the exhibition *Body Language: The Art of Larry Day*, presented in three parts at the following venues: Arcadia Exhibitions, Arcadia University, as *Larry Day: Absent Presence*, August 30–November 21, 2021; Woodmere Art Museum, as *Larry Day: Silent Conversations*, September 25, 2021–January 23, 2022; and Rosenwald-Wolf Gallery, University of the Arts, as *Larry Day: Nature Abstracted*, October 8–December 3, 2021.

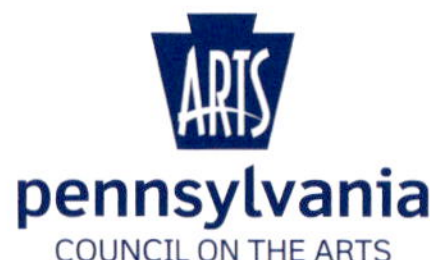

Woodmere Art Museum receives state arts funding support through a grant from the Pennsylvania Council on the Arts, a state agency funded by the Commonwealth of Pennsylvania and the National Endowment for the Arts, a federal agency.

Support provided in part by The Philadelphia Cultural Fund.



Library of Congress Control Number: 2021909455
ISBN 978-1-7354416-7-2

Published by Woodmere Art Museum
woodmereartmuseum.org

Distributed by the University of Pennsylvania Press
upenn.edu/pennpress

Produced by Lucia | Marquand, Seattle
luciamarquand.com

Edited by Gretchen Dykstra and Lucy Medrich
Designed by Thomas Eykemans
Typeset in GT Sectra and Bw Nista by Maggie Lee
Proofread by Ivy Long
Indexed by Enid Zafran
Color management by iocolor, Seattle
Printed and bound in China by Artron Art Printing

Photography by Laszlo Bodo, Matthew Dodd, Jeremy Fogg, Alexander Harding, Kevin Johnson, Jack Ramsdale, and Gregory R. Staley

Details
Front cover: *Narrative: To the Memory of Matteo Giovannetti*, 1967 (Woodmere Art Museum, Gift of Ruth Fine in honor of Irving and Miriam Brown Fine, 2020)
Back cover: *Building Reflected (aka Reflection)*, probably 1985 (Collection of James D. Crawford and Judith M. Dean)
p. 2: *Group*, 1967 (Pennsylvania Academy of the Fine Arts, Philadelphia, Bequest of the artist, 1999.8)
p. 4: *Picnic (Outing: Homage to Le Nain)*, 1970–75 (Woodmere Art Museum, Museum purchase with funds generously donated by an anonymous donor, 2017)
p. 12: *Miss Charkow and Mrs. Melnicoff*, c. 1967 (Woodmere Art Museum, Gift of Claudia Raab and Natalie Charkow Hollander, 2013)
p. 46: *Day by Day*, 1991 (Philadelphia Museum of Art, Bequest of the artist, 1999-2-1)
p. 74: *Hercules Dressed as a Woman*, c. 1990 (Woodmere Art Museum, Museum purchase, 2021)
p. 88: *Aquarium*, 1977 (Woodmere Art Museum, Gift of Natalie Charkow Hollander, 2020)
p. 102: *Landscape for St. John of the Cross*, 1955 (Woodmere Art Museum, Gift of Anita and Armand Mednick, 2020)
p. 118: *A Game of Charades* (aka *Charades*), 1967/1969 (Larry Day Art Trust)
p. 154: *Bouquet*, c. 1980 (Collection of Ruth Fine)
p. 166: *Harry's Class*, 1972–73 (Larry Day Art Trust)
p. 178: *Poker Game*, 1970 (Woodmere Art Museum, Gift of Ruth Fine, 1999)

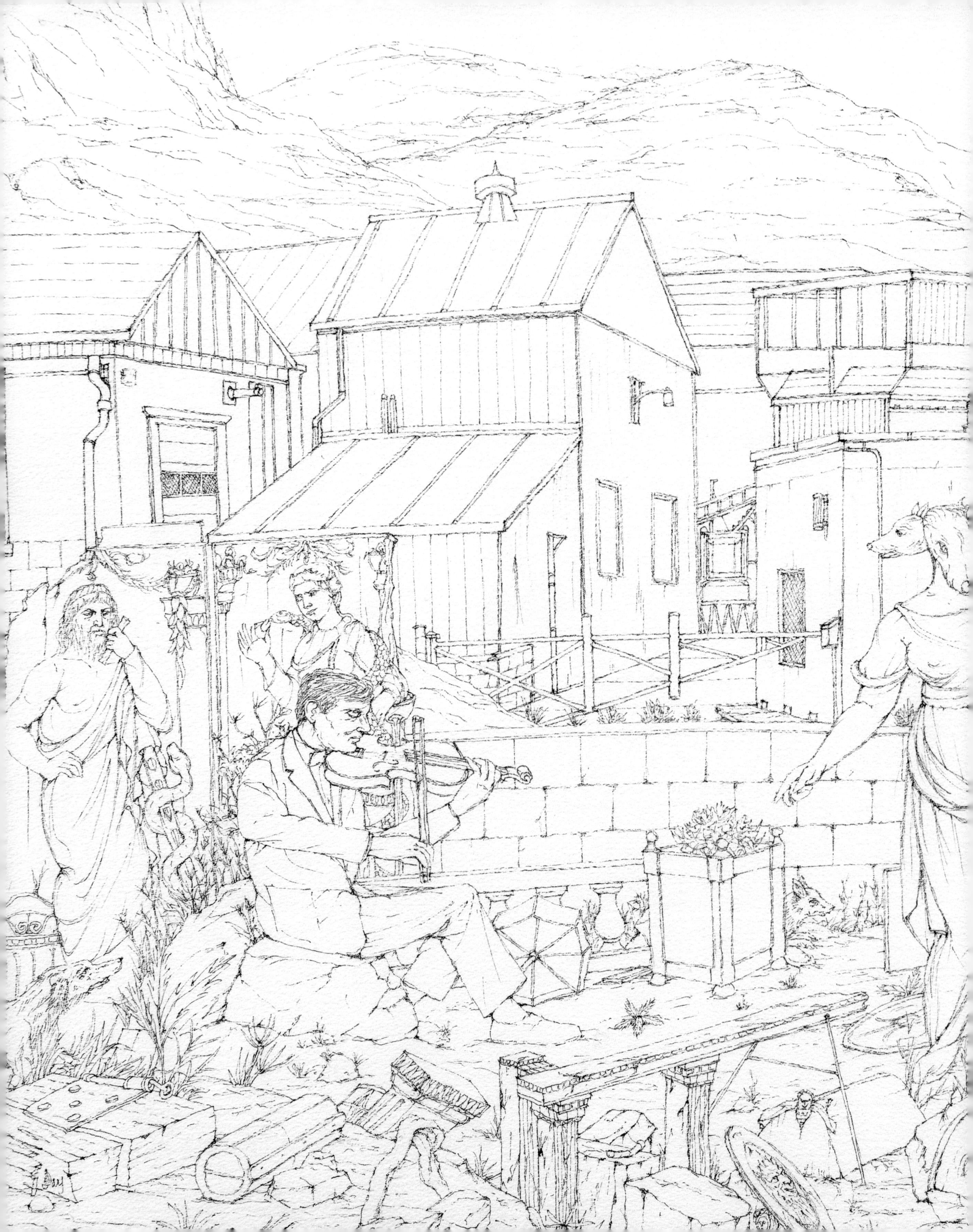